Robert Ball and the Politics of
Social Security

Robert Ball and the Politics of Social Security

Edward D. Berkowitz

THE UNIVERSITY OF WISCONSIN PRESS

The University of Wisconsin Press
1930 Monroe Street
Madison, Wisconsin 53711

www.wisc.edu/wisconsinpress/

3 Henrietta Street
London WC2E 8LU, England

5   4   3   2   1

Printed in the United States of America

Library of Congress Cataloging-in-Publication Data
Berkowitz, Edward D.
    Robert Ball and the politics of Social Security / Edward D. Berkowitz.
    p.   cm.
  Includes bibliographical references and index.
    ISBN 0-299-18950-3 (hardcover : alk. paper)
    1. Ball, Robert M.   2. United States. Social Security Administration—Officials and
employees—Biography.   3. Social security—United States—History.   I. Title.
HD7125.B475   2004
368.4´3´0092—dc21   2003007779

For Peter and Dale

Table of Contents

List of Illustrations

Preface

Robert Ball, the subject of this book, is not an easy man to know. He has an affability that makes him quite approachable, yet his easy manner hides his true emotions from public view. Although he can be charming, an inner reserve prevents him from being warm. He eludes the biographer who wants to understand his character. At the same time, the story of his life illuminates the inner workings of Social Security policy in the last half of the twentieth century. Whatever the difficulties of coming to grips with Ball's personality, it is a story that is well worth telling, particularly when it is buttressed by the use of previously unavailable primary sources.

To aid in the writing of this book, Robert Ball granted me exclusive access to his private papers—now part of the Wisconsin State Historical Society's wonderful Social Security collection—and dictated a three-hundred-page autobiographical memorandum for my benefit. (I have since deposited that memorandum in the historian's office of the Social Security Administration.) For him these generous acts formed part of a lifetime pattern of doing the staff work necessary to get Social Security's story told in an appealing way. Because of all the help I received from Robert Ball, one might say that this book was done with his cooperation, but it is emphatically not an authorized biography. I have felt free to disagree with Ball on points of policy and to present his life from my own point of view.

I have gotten to know Ball not just from this project but also from my previous books and from my own experiences as an observer of Social Security politics. When I published a first book on the role of businessmen and bureaucrats in America's welfare state, I understood so little about the inner bureaucratic world of Social Security that I carelessly described Ball as an actuary.[1] In terms of understanding what people in the agency do, it was a very serious error. Actuaries performed important, yet circumscribed, roles. Using highly specialized training in applied mathematics, they made cost estimates for programs that were designed and guided through the political process by others. As a conceptual thinker and an administrator, Ball had much more to do with this process of design and guidance than did any actuary, including Robert Myers, Ball's fellow employee in the Social Security Administration, who worked with Ball on many projects and fought with him on many others.

As someone with an interest in the history of Social Security, it was inevitable that I would meet Ball in person and that he would become more than a name on a memo in the National Archives. When I was working on a presidential commission late in the Carter era, he took me and a colleague to lunch and explained the current state of Social Security finances. Observing him at close range for the first time, I was struck by how fluid his explanation was and how reasonable he seemed. He described the steps that he felt necessary to shore up Social Security's finances in a tone that was devoid of any hint of panic. He made his suggestions seem like commonsense measures that had nothing to do with partisan politics and everything to do with the pragmatic matter of solving a temporary, easily correctable imbalance in Social Security's current accounts.[2]

After that I discovered that on nearly every aspect of Social Security policy Ball was an authority who needed to be consulted. He indulged my interest in disability policy by recounting his experiences starting the Social Security Disability Insurance in 1956 and his subsequent work administering the program as Social Security commissioner.[3] We spoke at a time during the Reagan administration when people saw the disability insurance program as a microcosm of the American welfare state's faults: it paid benefits that were too generous to people who should have been working. To use a popular image of the era, disability insurance ate up too much of the government's revenues at a time when the government was hard-pressed to meet its obligations. The program was out of control.[4] Ball rejected that line of reasoning. In another bravura performance, he calmly explained that the program aided those who could no longer work because of a physical impairment. He challenged the notion that the program was too generous or somehow out of control, and he worried that the Reagan administration, in its initial zeal to control federal spending, was cutting too many people from the disability rolls.

An interest in Wilbur Cohen took me back to Robert Ball, who once again sat down with me and discussed the relevant aspects of his life. Here was a chance to see a different dimension of Ball as he assessed the life of a man whose career had many points in common with his own. Both Ball and Cohen worked for the Social Security Administration, with Cohen initially closer to the agency's center of power in Washington. When Cohen, a partisan figure, relinquished the congressional brief for the program in the Eisenhower era, Ball picked it up. By the time Cohen decided to leave the agency at the beginning of 1956, Ball had consolidated his position as, in effect, the agency's chief operating officer. Cohen's career then took a different trajectory that brought him first to academia and then to political appointments in the Kennedy and Johnson administrations and ultimately to a post as dean of the School of Education at the University of Michigan. The further his path took him from Social Security, the more his concentration on the legislative details of the program began to waver. Even as secretary of the Department of Health, Education, and Welfare and therefore nominally Ball's superior, Cohen tended to trust the program details to Ball, secure in the knowledge that Ball's views were compatible with his own and that Ball would do a highly competent job putting complex programs, such as Medicare, into operation. Hence, Cohen developed into something of a social policy generalist at a time when Congress passed a bewildering array of Great Society programs, and Ball remained a Social Security specialist.[5]

All of that happened without personal rancor or jealousy. Ball never saw himself in competition with Cohen or envied Cohen his appointment as secretary of Health, Education, and Welfare. Ball seldom emphasized the competitive aspects of his career. He liked to say that he had not sought any of the appointments he received, including his job as commissioner of Social Security. To hear him tell it, the jobs more or less fell into his lap. It was one of the aspects of his character that made him hard to know. Either he was working from a different emotional palette than most people, or he was out of touch with his true feelings.

The historical record showed that Ball did have his share of rivals, yet the rivalries tended to be one-sided. After 1949, Ball received a series of quick promotions in which he leapfrogged over many older men with more seniority in the agency. Some of these men resented Ball's quick rise. Even the person who had recognized Ball's considerable talents, recruited him to a position of influence within the agency, and acted as Ball's friend and mentor felt momentarily disoriented at the notion of Ball as his superior. In a short period, however, he accepted the new arrangement as appropriate and became a key staff support to Ball. Robert Myers, the actuary, developed a real antipathy toward Ball that culminated in an unsuccessful campaign to unseat Ball as Social Security commissioner. Although Ball could discern the occasional fit of animosity or envy in others, he seldom reciprocated. Instead, he kept his distance from emotional conflict. Affable and self-assured, he did not reveal his vulnerabilities.

For all of Ball's cool personality, he inspired loyalty and even affection from his employees and others in the Social Security community. I saw evidence of these feelings on many occasions. During ceremonies to mark the fiftieth anniversary of Social Security in 1985, the large crowd in the Social Security auditorium reserved its loudest applause for Ball. On another celebratory occasion, a Social Security employee timidly approached him and told him that, when he had been commissioner, the agency had reached its apex.[6] My neighbors in Baltimore, some of whom worked for the Social Security Administration in its large headquarters just outside of the city, spoke of Ball in tones of awe. One of my academic friends, with whom I collaborated on a book about Social Security and Medicare, regarded Ball as the epitome of the responsible bureaucrat and looked to him for advice on a wide range of career and personal matters.[7]

Ball's hold over people extended far beyond the Social Security Administration. He had the knack of making himself invaluable to nearly all of the organizations to which he devoted his attention. For example, he left an enduring legacy at the Institute of Medicine (IOM), a part of the National Academy of Sciences that offered him a home just after he left the Social Security Administration in 1973. I came across this legacy when I received the assignment of writing the Institute of Medicine's history and listened to people there speak about Ball.[8] The list of admirers at the IOM included Adam Yarmolinsky, a well-known figure in philanthropic and social policy circles, and David Hamburg, the distinguished psychiatrist and IOM president who later became the head of the Carnegie Corporation.

At the National Academy of Social Insurance, an organization that Ball founded and used as a base of operations in the late 1980s and early 1990s, the staff respected Ball for his courtesy and for the hard work that he did on the organization's behalf. As a part of that staff for a very brief period, I observed how persistent Ball was. He seemed never to forget a particular idea or suggestion. Where others might drop a proposal with the passage of time, Ball would keep raising it again and again, always calmly with no display of impatience, anger, or frustration.[9] In the end, he often achieved his objectives. Indeed, he turned the academy into a viable organization, despite the long odds against its success.

During the 1990s, Robert Ball turned his attention to creating some sort of memoir to reflect on the experiences of his life and, as a subtext to nearly everything he did, to defend the Social Security program. As always, however, current events trumped historical reflection. Remarkably, Ball remained a frontline player in the increasingly heated debate over Social Security financing, and he lacked the time to write his memoirs. The appearance of Robert Myers's autobiography in 1992, which contained what Ball regarded as many inaccuracies, spurred Ball to give some more thought to the matter.[10] He felt that autobiography might be inappropriate. It would be better to have someone else write an account of his life but with Ball as an active participant—an authorized biography.

When Ball's bureaucratic colleague John Trout, who had a deep interest in history and who was a gifted writer, approached Ball about writing his biography, Ball was receptive. Trout produced some chapters, but as a member of the Senior Executive Service working in top management at the Health Care Financing Administration, he found himself with many other responsibilities. Although David Hamburg, as head of the Carnegie Corporation, lent some financial support to the project, it lagged because the two key participants, Robert Ball and John Trout, were so involved in present-day affairs. Eventually Trout gave up, and he and Ball looked for someone else.

That someone else turned out to be me. By this time I was known as someone with a historical interest in Social Security and a knowledge of some of the program administrators. With some reluctance, I agreed to take on the project. I retained a lingering ambivalence about whether someone who kept his emotional distance from people could be the subject of an engaging biography, and at the same time, I knew that it would be difficult to bring an academic sense of detachment to the project. Ball, in his tireless and persistent way, would deluge me with materials, ideas, and suggestions. In a paradoxical way, he would reveal too little and too much about himself, making it difficult for me to narrate the book in my own voice.

My solution was to let the many documents in Robert Ball's papers do the talking. In an abstract sort of way that strategy worked, yet it failed to take into account that one of the documents was the autobiographical memo that Ball had prepared for me. It was impossible not to look at it because it lent a first-person air to what was inevitably a rather dry study of bureaucratic politics and enabled me to fill in some of the gaps left by the other archival materials.

Perhaps not coincidentally my reservations about Ball began to fade. As he drew me into his personal orbit, I became more impressed with him. The same modest self-assurance, sense of reasonableness, and affable good humor that had so affected others began to have its effects on me. As was his custom, Ball did not push his point of view in a strident manner. Instead, as he had in reviewing so many other documents over the course of a long career, he offered suggestions that almost always sounded reasonable. Reading a draft of this book, he seemed to have confidence that history would judge him favorably, and it was only a matter of guiding the historian to the evidence.

Although Robert Ball helped me with this book, it was not a collaboration, and this is not Robert Ball's story as told to me. We see that story in different ways, and this book is my version of it. To use only one of many examples, we disagreed on the quality of his major book, published in 1977.[11] For me it had a dull, inside-baseball quality that characterized many Washington documents. For him it was a successful exercise in persuasion and, I suspect, something in which he took great pride. Still, having argued his case in his autobiographical memo and in his detailed reactions to an earlier draft, he conceded me the point because I was writing an unauthorized biography.

It should nonetheless be said that I share much of Robert Ball's politics. I began and ended the project believing that Social Security represented one of America's greatest social policy achievements and that my historical colleagues, by emphasizing its racist and sexist origins, had not done it justice. What changed in the course of writing this book was my view of Ball. I began to see that his cool personality hid a deep passion for Social Security.

In other words, in common with so many others who started as skeptics and became supporters, I came to see Robert Ball as a reasonable man. Ball, who had used his powers of persuasion and his indefatigable staff work to convert economists, members of Congress, and White House staffers to the Social Security cause, had convinced me that he was the worthy object of a sympathetic biography. I hope that enough of my initial ambivalence and distance remain in the book so as to give it a critical edge and to bolster the credibility of its argument. But I also hope that Ball's substantial contributions to American social policy come through as well.

Acknowledgments

Having detailed my complex debt to Robert Ball, I want also to acknowledge the much more straightforward help of many others who have aided me in this endeavor. Larry DeWitt, the very able historian of the Social Security Administration, generously shared archival materials, pictures, and interview transcripts with me. More importantly, he encouraged me to complete the project and made many constructive comments on the manuscript. He has been an active partner in this project and a good friend. I owe him a great deal. John Trout, my fellow Robert Ball scholar and observer, took time off from an often busy schedule to talk with me about Ball and to offer comments on the draft chapters. Pamela Larson, whose sunny disposition and all-around competence make her a wonderful administrator of the National Academy of Social Insurance, arranged to have Robert Ball's papers transferred to an office in the academy so that I was able to use them. She and Virginia Reno made working at the academy a pleasant experience. Each of these individuals has my thanks.

A number of my fellow academics provided me with opportunities to test out my ideas about Robert Ball before academic audiences. Gareth Davies and Anthony Badger served as my hosts on a trip to England that included papers at Oxford and Cambridge. David Mechanic gave me a chance to talk about Robert Ball at an interdisciplinary seminar at Rutgers, and Ernest May invited me to speak at Harvard's Kennedy School. Through the generosity of Steve Gillon, I presented a chapter of this book at a political history workshop at the Organization of American Historians, and Brian Balogh generously gave me a chance to present another chapter at a workshop on twentieth-century history at the University of Virginia and the Miller Center.

I received financial assistance in completing this book from David Hamburg and the Carnegie Corporation and summer support from Vice President Carol Sigelman's office at George Washington University.

A group of students from an undergraduate research seminar humored me by preparing an inventory of the contents of the great jumble of material in Robert Ball's papers. As always my colleagues in the history department at George Washington University—Muriel Atkin, Bill Becker, Leo Ribuffo, and Andrew Zimmerman, in particular—came to my aid. I also benefited greatly from discussions with Merton Bernstein, Ted Marmor, Jerry Mashaw, Chester Pach, Peter Ochshorn, Roz Kleeman, Kim McQuaid, Eric Kingson, Joel Denker, Howie Baum, Mary Poole, James Patterson, Jennifer Erkulwater, David Farber, Michael Katz, Felicia Kornbluh, Jill Quadagno, Daniel Fox, Colin Gordon, Monroe Berkowitz, Frances Kleeman, and Martha Derthick. Jane Curran edited the manuscript with skill. Sarah Berkowitz raised the intellectual tone of the household throughout the project; Rebecca Berkowitz marveled at how slowly I worked and helped me to keep the project's importance in perspective. Emily Frank, as always, maintained a semblance of sanity in an often insane environment.

I dedicate this book to Peter and Dale Demy, whom I have known for more than forty-five years and who have been loyal friends from childhood to middle age and beyond. They are important members of my extended family who have done more things for me than I can possibly mention. So I offer this book to them and hope that it will compensate in part for the lack of a cello.

Robert Ball and the Politics of
Social Security

Introduction

Robert M. Ball helped to build a Social Security program that in 2001 paid benefits to more than 45 million people, collected $604 billion in revenues, and spent $439 billion on benefits and administrative expenses.[1] The benefits took the form of monthly checks mailed to people who had reached retirement age, become disabled, or lived in a family in which the breadwinner had died, retired, or become disabled. Closely tied to Social Security was another program, called Medicare, that funded a significant part of the hospital bills and doctor fees incurred by people in these groups.[2] As the magnitude of the numbers suggests, Social Security, known more formally as Old-Age, Survivors, Disability and Hospital Insurance, functions as America's largest and most important social program.

Robert Ball, the program's chief administrator from 1953 to 1972 and its chief defender for the rest of the century, crafted this significant and enduring program during the era of its greatest growth and success. To do so, he used the conservative means of contributory social insurance toward the liberal ends of an expanded welfare state.

To understand Ball's contributions to social policy, therefore, one has to get past the often conservative rhetoric that Ball and

3

his colleagues used in order to see the program's liberal results. Although Ball believed that programs for poor people made poor programs, he worked hard on behalf of poor people to make sure that the Social Security program addressed their problems. Even though he advanced the cause of contributory Social Security above that of means-tested welfare, he helped to create a Social Security program that included welfare elements. In other words, Robert Ball took the "social" part of social insurance seriously and interpreted it to mean that the Social Security program should be broad in its coverage and generous in its benefits. That meant he protected and nurtured a benefit formula that in a conservative sense related benefits (the checks that people received) to contributions (the payroll taxes that workers paid) but in a liberal sense allowed poorer people a greater return on their Social Security contributions than richer people. That meant he campaigned not just for benefits payable on the basis of old age to anyone, rich or poor, but also for a disability program of disproportionate benefit to minorities and those with comparatively little education. That meant he devised and Congress passed a special minimum benefit in Social Security to help long-term workers with low wages. That meant he concentrated his political energies in the Ford, Carter, and Reagan years not just on elderly Social Security beneficiaries but also on students between the ages of 18 and 22 and those who wanted to retire before the age of 65.

An Overview of Ball's Career

Robert Ball entered government service in 1939 but did not become an influential figure in Social Security circles until the end of the 1940s. Unlike the program's founders, nearly all of whom had experience in state government, Ball spent almost all of his career in or around the federal government trying to solve problems related to Social Security. Still, he shared an important characteristic with Social Security's pioneers, and that was an interest in labor unions. He studied that subject in college and graduate school at a time when it was a central focus of United States politics. Leaving Wesleyan, a Methodist school as befit the son of a Methodist minister, with a master's degree in labor economics in

1936, Ball actually worked with the labor movement after college and might well have spent his career in the labor movement if circumstances had been slightly different. When he came to the Social Security bureaucracy, Ball brought the same liberal sensibility to the task as others brought to the early days of the National Labor Relations Board. He saw work in one field as a logical extension of work in the other. Social Security, like industrial unionism, represented an improvement in working conditions that was secured through government intervention in the labor market.[3]

Robert Ball's initial Social Security jobs lacked glamour. They were in the field, assisting people who wanted to learn more about the new program and working with employers who needed to create Social Security accounts for their employees. Ball found, as did many in his position, that employers reacted to the program with indifference and disdain, and employees also demonstrated little enthusiasm for the program. The program held little appeal. In 1937 employers and employees had to pay the payroll taxes, even though the first retirement pensions were not scheduled to be paid until 1942. Ball needed to drum up enthusiasm for a program that manifested itself to most people as a tax on their payrolls or a deduction in their paychecks. Ball watched as elderly people in need of government assistance signed up with the noncontributory Old-Age Assistance program, which required only that they demonstrate that they were poor and which had none of the payroll taxes and the complex qualifying conditions of contributory social insurance. Although Congress passed legislation in 1939 that sped up the introduction of retirement pensions to 1940 and allowed the program to pay benefits to the families of deceased workers, Old-Age Assistance, a noncontributory welfare program authorized by the Social Security Act of 1935, enjoyed a substantial lead over old-age insurance, a contributory social insurance program also initiated in 1935. The welfare program reached more people and paid more generous benefits than did the social insurance program.[4]

As Ball worked in Social Security field offices in northern New Jersey during the 1940s, he began to realize that Social Security might never surpass welfare. Despite the existence of large surpluses in the Social Security accounts after 1937—the product of having many more people paying into the program than were receiving benefits—members of Congress were not motivated to expand a program that enjoyed little popular support among their constituents. Congressional actions in both Democratic and Republican regimes (such as the Eightieth Congress elected in 1946) demonstrated that point. Instead of raising future benefit levels, for example, Congress instead cut Social Security taxes (by rescinding scheduled tax increases) and reduced the number of people eligible to participate in the program. If the program hoped to capitalize on its favorable financial position, it needed to broaden its base of political support. As matters stood, the program reached only about half of the labor force because of restrictions imposed by Congress in 1935 that limited the program to industrial and commercial workers. And even if coverage were extended to the self-employed and agricultural workers, it would do little good if the benefits were not set at higher levels than the benefits in the welfare programs.[5]

From the beginning these sorts of strategic problems engaged Robert Ball's attention, even though he was buried inside of a large bureaucracy and largely invisible to the people who ran his agency. Someone thought highly enough of him to bring him in from the cold and install him in a relatively minor post in the Social Security Board's Baltimore, Maryland, headquarters. Early in his Baltimore tenure, he worked on the problem of coverage extension. He surveyed the economic needs of such groups as sharecroppers in the South and tried to solve the administrative problems of providing them with Social Security benefits. As he later noted, "a very high proportion of these sharecroppers were completely illiterate, uneducated, and very poor." Bringing them into the Social Security program meant, according to Ball, "a really big improvement, in their lives, and at the end of their lives. It was important to get them on the rolls."[6] That comment illustrated that from a very early date Social Security employees such as Ball worked to bring the program to groups previously excluded from it.

Ball confronted Social Security's problems more directly when he became the staff director for an advisory council that met in 1947 and 1948. His work in this position earned him acclaim within Social Security policymaking circles and marked his emergence as a frontline figure in the Social Security Administration. Ball controlled the council's agenda and, as much as anyone, composed its recommendations. As part of the council's report, he drafted an eloquent statement about the superiority of social insurance to welfare and made sure that it was adopted by the often quite independent-minded individuals, appointed by the Republican-controlled Senate Committee on Finance, who sat on the council. At his urging, the council recommended coverage extension and large benefit increases for Social Security.[7]

By 1950, Ball had already made a significant contribution to the Social Security program by determining that social insurance was a superior form of income maintenance to welfare. Ball astutely saw the possibility of expanding Social Security far beyond the levels that welfare had reached. That required foresight and imagination, since welfare was so much more generous and better established at the time than social insurance. The result was a much larger welfare state than would otherwise have been achieved.

Ball's work as staff director of the Advisory Council on Social Security earned him a major promotion. He became a division head who reported to the director of the bureau that had major responsibility for Old-Age and Survivors Insurance (more commonly known as Social Security). Ball's division did most of the strategic planning for Social Security policy and worked closely with the Congress on Social Security legislation. It was an important position that required someone with imagination in order to anticipate problems and plan for the future, someone with endurance and tenacity in order to respond to the constant congressional demands for information and help with legislation, and someone with enough tact to be sensitive to the political needs of individual members of Congress. Ball had all of these qualities. He had a broader range of skills than those possessed by other talented Social Security employees. They might be able to turn out a report on a technical matter related to Social Security or handle a managerial problem related to getting checks out to Social Security beneficiaries on deadline. Ball could do those things, but he could also expound on the program's basic philosophy and handle a delicate political situation, all without calling attention to himself. He invariably came across not as a zealot who wanted to push the boundaries of the welfare state or as someone with a deep need for personal recognition but rather as a reasonable man whose job it was to help members of Congress and officials of the executive branch look as good as possible.[8]

As the long period of Democratic rule ended in 1952, Arthur Altmeyer, the longtime head of the Social Security program, designated Robert Ball as his replacement, despite the fact that Ball was still in his thirties and relatively new to the top management ranks of the Social Security Administration. Altmeyer knew that Ball understood Social Security's strategic needs and grasped the importance of expanding coverage and raising benefit levels. Unlike others in Altmeyer's office, Ball accepted the basic tenets of the Social Security faith yet had a supple and flexible mind and projected a nonpartisan image as a helpful civil servant. He was just the sort of person to advise the Republicans as they considered alternatives to Social Security, such as creating a system that paid benefits to everyone and severed the relationship between contributions and benefits. If one threw Ball's basic competence, diligence, and indefatigable work effort into the mix, then the choice was obvious.

Coming to power after four Democratic presidential administrations, the Republicans hoped to turn over the upper ranks of the bureaucracy and replace Democrats with loyal Republicans. The effort reached down to the bureau chief level at the Social Security Administration and meant that the Republicans got to name a new Social Security commissioner and a new director of the Bureau of Old-Age and Survivors Insurance. They dutifully did so, yet Altmeyer's selection of Ball still paid dividends. For a time, as the Eisenhower administration searched for the right people to fill the available jobs at Social Security, Ball served as acting bureau director. Then, after the appointment of a Wisconsin public welfare director as Social Security commissioner and a former Minnesota congressman as bureau chief, Ball became the deputy bureau director. With this inconspicuous title, he ran the program on a daily basis and became, in effect, the program's chief operating officer. He also continued in his role as the liaison between his agency and Congress. Although he needed to coordinate his actions with political appointees in the Department of Health, Education, and Welfare, he retained his role as the program's legislative strategist.[9]

After Congress, following the lead of the advisory council on which Ball had served as staff director, extended Social Security coverage and raised benefit levels in 1950, the great impasse in the program that had inhibited its growth during the 1940s was broken. Social Security, not welfare, became America's largest and most significant social welfare program. By cuing key members of Congress and supervising much of the necessary background work in the preparation of legislation, Ball helped to guide Congress to significant expansions of Social Security in 1952 and 1954. He managed to convince both the Democrats in Congress and the Republicans in the executive branch that the revenues from payroll taxes in an expanding economy should be used to allow Social Security benefits to keep pace with the rate of economic growth. As the benefits of Social Security became more apparent, it became easier to convince previously skeptical congressmen that workers in key occupations, such as farmers, should come under the Social Security umbrella.[10]

Unlike his superiors in the Eisenhower administration, Ball wanted the program to go further and pay disability benefits and provide health insurance. In these endeavors he made his greatest contributions not in the design of the programs or even in selling the programs to Congress but rather in convincing Congress that the Social Security Administration was administratively competent and hence capable of undertaking complex new tasks. In the past, reformers associated with both political parties had doubted the government's basic competence and for that reason often preferred that the private sector, rather than the federal government, undertake important social projects. Ball, as the chief operating officer of the Social Security Administration, helped to put a stop to that perception, at least as it applied to Social Security. He used his position to call attention to the Social Security Administration's business-like administrative methods and its constant efforts to increase its efficiency and lower its operating costs.[11]

Democrats in Congress and Democrats in waiting for the next Democratic administration understood the key role that Ball played in the agency and realized his basic sympathy with liberal legislative goals such as disability insurance, passed in 1956 against the wishes of President Dwight Eisenhower, and health insurance for the elderly.[12] It became a foregone conclusion that when a Democratic administration had a chance to name a Social Security commissioner, Robert Ball would be the choice. When

John F. Kennedy assumed office in 1961, the Democrats in charge of the Department of Health, Education, and Welfare waited a decent interval to establish the notion that the job of commissioner was too important a post with which to play politics and then in 1962, upon the retirement of the longtime civil servant who happened to hold the job at the time, named Ball to the post.

Ball's responsibilities as commissioner remained much the same as they had been as a deputy bureau director. He continued to be the agency's chief operating officer. He streamlined the agency so that it handled only Social Security. Welfare, which had also been administered by the Social Security agency since 1935, became the responsibility of a new operating agency in the Department of Health, Education, and Welfare. Instead of worrying about the continuing scandals in the welfare programs, Ball concentrated much of his energy in getting Congress to pass Medicare, or health insurance for the elderly, and preparing his agency to administer what would be a large and complicated program.[13]

Others made the political bargains that led to the passage of Medicare in 1965, yet Ball shadowed the effort and gave key assistance to the congressmen and to the Kennedy and Johnson administration figures involved in the process. It was his job to determine if a particular plan—and over the course of the period between 1961 and 1965 many such plans appeared—was administratively feasible. Reflecting the political compromises necessary to secure enactment, Congress came up with a law that contained cumbersome features, such as the use of local private intermediaries to handle the basic billing operations and a voluntary program to pay doctor bills, which required a massive registration effort. The politics of passage mattered more to nearly all of the participants than did the logistics of implementation. Politicians in Congress, the labor movement, the health care industry, and the executive branch could add complications to the bill secure in the knowledge that Robert Ball and his agency would know how to handle them in the implementation process.[14]

Relying on a cadre of analysts and managers who had joined the agency in the 1930s, a decade in which fulfilling jobs were in short supply, and on congressional willingness to grant the agency more manpower, Ball made Medicare work effectively.[15]

Some people compared the successful implementation of Medicare to the most complex operations of the Second World War, such as the invasion of Normandy. In both instances, the United States found itself on unfamiliar terrain, and in both instances America achieved what could be perceived as a victory that showed the government off to best advantage and paved the way for future extensions of government power (a cold war and a larger welfare state, respectively).

Ball's high standing as an administrator gave him entrée into discussions about Social Security policy that his agency would otherwise not have had. When Richard Nixon became president, the Republicans found it hard to replace Ball. There was the precedent that the Democrats had set of not changing the Social Security commissioner with the change in administration. There was the perception that Ball's presence was necessary to assure the continued smooth implementation of Medicare and of other extensions of Social Security that were already on the books. There was the feeling that Social Security was one agency and one program that worked and that the new administration should turn its attention to more pressing social problems, such as welfare reform. There was the fact that the Congress remained under Democratic control and Ball had many influential friends in Congress whom the administration would need to pass its own social legislation. There was the fact that Ball already had some contacts in the new administration that dated back to his service in the Eisenhower administration. There was the fact that Ball stood ready to make reasonable suggestions and had none of the reformer's zeal that marked the personnel in other Great Society agencies such as the Office of Economic Opportunity. All of these things worked in Ball's favor and enabled him to keep his job for President Nixon's entire first term.

If anything, Ball's influence increased during the first Nixon administration. In theory the Social Security Administration (SSA) was an agency of the Department of Health, Education, and Welfare, and the commissioner of Social Security reported to the secretary of Health, Education, and Welfare. In practice, SSA enjoyed substantial autonomy, particularly during the early days of the Nixon administration, because few of the Republican appointees at the department level had a detailed knowledge of Social Security. That gave Ball considerable freedom to work with

the Democrats in Congress and fashion Social Security legislation that responded to current economic conditions. In part because of the rising prices that characterized the era and because
of competition between the executive and legislative branches of
government, Congress passed more significant legislation raising the basic Social Security benefit level during Nixon's first
term than at any other time in the program's history.[16]

It was at this point that Robert Ball made his single most important contribution to the development of the Social Security
program. He realized that the Nixon administration favored a
scheme that would take away Congress's discretion in setting
Social Security benefits. Although the president had no strong
feelings about the matter, Republicans in Congress wanted to
create a system of automatic adjustments in the level of Social
Security payments. They proposed linking increases in Social Security benefits with increases in the consumer price index. Unlike many liberal supporters of Social Security, who saw the proposal as a bad political deal for the Democrats that would make
it harder to pass health insurance and other key items on their
agenda, Ball did not reject this idea out of hand. On the contrary,
he saw the merit in having frequent adjustments in Social Security benefits so that they remained current with the price level.
Ball also sympathized with his fellow liberals and shared their
desire to have high Social Security benefits. Using his considerable skills at negotiation, his inside position as an adviser both to
the Nixon administration and the congressional Democrats, and
his thorough understanding of program dynamics, he brokered a
deal. The result was a new "automatic" system for setting benefits accompanied by a large rise in Social Security benefits. Neither President Nixon nor Wilbur Mills, the influential head of the
Ways and Means Committee, got exactly what they wanted from
this deal. The person whom the 1972 legislation satisfied most
was Robert Ball.[17]

The changes engineered in 1972 set the terms of Social Security
politics for the rest of the century. In a system in which benefit increases occurred without the specific intervention of and attendant review by Congress, the state of the program's finances became more dependent on the current state of the economy. No
longer fine-tuned by each Congress, program benefits drifted up-
ward with the consumer price index. By 1974 an economic crisis

had developed that created problems for Social Security. The combination of high prices, high unemployment, and wage growth that lagged behind other prices put a financial squeeze on the program. High prices, under the new system, automatically triggered higher benefits; but high unemployment reduced program revenues, and declining real wages made it that much harder to come up with enough money to fund the benefits that rose with the inflation rate. Because of changes that had been made in 1972, traditional remedies, such as having no benefit increases or small benefit increases, were not available. Also, because of changes in actuarial assumptions endorsed by Ball that accompanied the changeover to automatic benefit increases, the program no longer had as much margin for error as it had in the era between 1950 and 1972.

As one of the program's chief architects, Ball shifted his role to become one of its chief defenders. In the second Nixon administration, he resigned as Social Security commissioner. If he had not done so, the president would have fired him, since Nixon now wanted to fill the entire government with his loyalists.[18] One might have predicted that Ball, 58 years old at the time of his resignation, would have faded from public view and private influence. On the contrary, the changes in the structure of Social Security policymaking worked in his favor.

In the entire period between 1935 and 1972, and particularly after 1950, employees of the Social Security Administration enjoyed advantages over their policy competitors in the White House and in the departments of the executive branch that made social welfare policy.[19] SSA officials had the benefit of longevity over the short-term occupants of the White House, and they spoke the language of Social Security better. Simply put, they knew more about the program than did their nominal superiors in such locations as the Department of Health, Education, and Welfare or the Bureau of the Budget. After 1950 Congress, almost always controlled by the Democratic Party, had little reason to challenge the influence of the bureaucracy since it needed the Social Security Administration to do the staff work necessary to produce Social Security legislation. Well into the 1960s, Congress had little support staff of its own beyond the people who answered mail or made travel arrangements and the odd employee of the Congressional Research Service brought in to help on one project

or the other. If congressmen and their constituents expected Social Security legislation to appear on a regular basis, they had little choice but to collaborate with Ball and his colleagues.

The arrangement seemed to suit both sides. Congress got its
legislation. Ball and the other SSA staffers who worked with
Congress made every effort to be accommodating and unobtrusive. Even as SSA employees drafted legislation and wrote the
committee reports in support of that legislation, they ceded all of
the credit to the congressmen. Robert Ball, with his modest title
of deputy bureau director in the 1950s and only slightly more im-
posing title of commissioner in the 1960s, fit neatly into this
scheme. He sought no public credit and preferred that favorable
publicity reflect on his program, rather than him.

Even in the era of the great Social Security expansion from
1950 to 1972, congressional and bureaucratic interests were compatible but not congruent. Broadening the program to cover
new risks, such as disability and ill health, occasioned a considerable amount of conflict. Ball and his colleagues had a healthier
appetite for this expansion than did influential congressmen
such as Wilbur Mills (D–Arkansas) in the House or Robert Kerr
(D–Oklahoma) in the Senate. In these areas, the relationship between SSA and the tax committees that handled Social Security
legislation was more delicate and more cautious on both sides.
Similarly, the White House and the bureaucracy under its direct
control, such as the Bureau of the Budget and the Council of Economic Advisers, afforded SSA less latitude on these matters than
on others. More cautious about ceding power to Ball and SSA on
disability and health insurance than on old-age insurance, Congress necessarily relied on SSA's ability to design the complicated programs and, after passage of disability insurance in 1956
and Medicare in 1965, to put them in place.

After Ball's departure in 1973, SSA's advantages over other executive agencies and other branches of the government began to
diminish. Benefit increases now came automatically in predetermined amounts at predetermined intervals. SSA required the expertise of computer programmers and others with practical skills
to make sure that checks went out on time and in the proper
amount. That was not something that demanded a commissioner
with tactical political skills or a broad vision of the program's
goals. It made it more legitimate for a presidential administration,

more often as not a Republican administration, to appoint someone as commissioner to fill a particular political need—an African American perhaps, or someone with close ties to a politician
who was owed a favor. As the job of commissioner became more
routine, more like other presidential appointments, it turned
over far more rapidly. Robert Ball, who saw the commissioner's
job as a capstone to a long career at SSA, served for eleven years.
He was the last of the important commissioners; none of his successors came close to matching his length of tenure. Congress
raised few objections because it began to acquire its own sources
of expertise, such as the Congressional Budget Office and expanded committee staffs with specialists on Social Security and
Medicare. The symbiotic relationship between Congress and the
bureaucracy, with SSA staff members sitting in on "mark-up"
sessions of legislation, deteriorated.

Ball's successors did not have as much fun as he did because
they had to manage under conditions of scarcity and disagree-
able crisis. In stringent times and with the reputation of the
agency in decline, Congress no longer authorized new SSA employees so willingly, making the agency that much harder to run.
As managerial problems increased, so did the level of supervision from the Department of Health, Education, and Welfare, thus
further undermining the commissioner's autonomy. The job of
the commissioner became both harder and less important.

The commissioners after Ball did not get to undertake the
same sort of massive, morale-boosting, and expansionary projects that he did. The heroic days of implementing complicated
programs that were the legislative products of program expansion were over. Medicare, which had demanded all of Ball's
managerial and leadership skills to put in place, never led to national health insurance. Even if it had, the task of starting the
program would have been the concern of an agency that had
been carved out of the Medicare operation in 1977 and kept separate from SSA. Ball did leave behind one new program for other
SSA heads to start. This program, unlike Medicare or disability
insurance, experienced so many administrative foul-ups in its
start-up phase that it served to discredit the agency.[20]

As the role of the commissioner diminished and as Social Security became a current budget issue, rather than a matter of
planning future benefit increases, the formation of Social Security

policy tended to be made at the level of the White House and, within Congress, at the level of the congressional leadership, rather than solely at the committee level. Hence, Ball left SSA just as the moment when the commissioner of Social Security was losing influence and when Social Security financing, once handled routinely by the bureaucracy and the congressional tax committees, emerged as a controversial issue.

After leaving SSA in 1973, Ball remained in Washington as an informal consultant on Social Security, working first at the National Academy of Sciences and later at a think tank loosely affiliated with the University of Chicago. That gave him a desk in a Washington location, the secretarial services of a highly competent executive assistant, and little else. At first he thought he had left behind a permanent legacy that would not be challenged and believed it best to devote his time to the next step in the expansion of America's welfare state: the creation and passage of national health insurance. When he encountered the futility of engaging in the politics of health care finance and when he discovered that the basic system of Social Security cash benefits he had put in place was itself under attack, he shifted directions. Somewhat like Dean Acheson, an architect of the nation's basic cold war scheme, was brought back by President John Kennedy to help during the Cuban missile crisis, so Jimmy Carter called Ball into the White House to sit in on Social Security deliberations designed to shore up Social Security financing in 1977. At a time when people rotated through the Social Security commissioner's job and failed to take hold, Ball attended policymaking sessions at the highest levels and, as much as anyone, helped fashion Social Security legislation in 1977. In the Carter years, he had enough contacts with SSA to gather the data necessary to make policy and enough clout to get his views heard where they mattered.

Tensions between liberals such as Ball and neoliberals such as many of Carter's advisers made a continuing relationship between Ball and the Carter administration difficult.[21] Ball, whose departure from government service allowed him to be unabashedly partisan if that served the cause of protecting Social Security, formed bonds with liberal politicians such as the Massachusetts tandem of Edward Kennedy and Tip O'Neill. During the 1970s and continuing through the 1980s, Ball cultivated his relationships with these and other Democrats in Congress—in particular with the congressmen who ran the newly established Social Security subcommittees in both houses and with the House leadership. Contacts with Democrats in the House of Representatives proved valuable after the Democrats lost control of the White House and the Senate in the elections of 1980.

Ball became a point man on Social Security for the Democrats in the complex politics of budget cutting that dominated the Washington scene in 1981. That experience led to his serving as the chief Democratic strategist and negotiator on the Social Security "rescue" commission appointed by President Ronald Reagan at the end of 1981. On the commission Ball held equal rank with such luminaries as the head of the Prudential Insurance Company, the future head of the Federal Reserve Board, and the head of the AFL-CIO, and such politicians as Senators Robert Dole (R–Kansas), John Heinz (R–Pennsylvania), and Daniel Moynihan (D–New York) and Congressman Claude Pepper (D–Florida). The appointment indicated he had advanced in stature since 1972 from the role of staff member to principal player in his own right.[22]

Ball put all of his many skills to use while serving on the commission. He churned out policy proposals, kept his caucus of liberal Democrats together, and used his many Washington contacts to explore possible compromises. As always, he represented himself as someone who wanted to solve a practical problem in the form of a short-range financing deficit rather than as someone with an ideological agenda. As always, he portrayed social insurance as so compatible with America's basic values that Social Security's legitimacy lay beyond dispute. As he represented the situation, Social Security would continue indefinitely into the future, and only incidental tinkering was required to repair it to fiscal health.

Ronald Reagan, who had created the commission, saw the problem differently and held much lower expectations for the commission's success than did Ball. He feared that the Democrats would bring the issue back to Congress and use it as a political club against the Republicans. Predictably, the commission soon degenerated into a round of partisan bickering, and although the civility of the meetings improved as time passed, the commission reached its deadline at the end of 1982 without an agreement. Then, at the last minute, Ball and Reagan administration officials negotiated in secret and came up with a deal. This deal, which preserved Social Security's benefit structure and solved the short-term financing problem by, among other things, delaying a cost-of-living adjustment by six months, became the basis for legislation passed in 1983. The new law reduced the level of controversy surrounding Social Security for another ten years. It represented the most visible of Robert Ball's many accomplishments and cemented his reputation as Washington's leading expert on Social Security. It marked the very pinnacle of his career.

Eventually a new Social Security crisis arrived in which experts decided that, even with the provisions of the 1983 amendments and even with the surpluses in Social Security's current account, the program would not have enough money on hand to pay full benefits to all entitled to them at some point in the twenty-first century. The date kept receding as the great economic boom of the 1990s, with its low rates of inflation and unemployment, rolled on and as new immigrants kept arriving on America's shores. Still, sometime near 2040 the system would not be able to meet all of its obligations. Hence began an epic battle over the retirement of the baby boom generation. On one side stood people who said that, at long last, the magic of contributory social insurance could not save Social Security. To sustain the program, taxes would have to be raised beyond the level of people's willingness to pay them, or benefits would need to be cut below the level of people's expectations. For some the moment seemed right for a system overhaul, in which benefits were cut, but people were allowed to take up the slack by investing part of their Social Security contributions in private securities. In the Washington jargon, this became known as privatizing Social Security.[23]

On the other side stood those who wished to preserve Social Security; remarkably, chief among these was an aging but still vigorous Robert Ball.[24] When President Bill Clinton appointed a new commission to inquire into the matter, he selected Ball as one of the members. Ball came up with a new financing proposal that he took to the very highest levels of the Clinton administration and that influenced Clinton's reform proposals. When George W. Bush proposed his own conservative remedies, Ball stood ready to refute them and to lend advice to the Democrats on how to handle the issue.[25] Even at age 88 and about to move into a retirement community, Robert Ball continued to use the no longer quite so conservative means of social insurance toward the now-liberal goal of the preservation of America's welfare state.

Some Academic Considerations

For some the story of Robert Ball's life makes for a stirring account of how one man helped to build a large social program in an environment often hostile to such efforts. For others this same story illustrates the deceptive means by which the state has been allowed to take over functions best left to private enterprise and individual effort, and by which a program has been expanded beyond the ability to deliver on its promises. Whatever meaning one attaches to the narrative, no one—whatever his or her political orientation—can deny the intricate and intimate connections between the life of Robert Ball and the history of Social Security.

At three central turning points in the development of Social Security, Robert Ball played a role in the program's rescue. In 1950 the program faced a competition with noncontributory welfare programs. Congress revived Social Security by raising benefits and expanding coverage. Robert Ball wrote the key report that motivated congressional action. In that sense, he scripted the 1950 amendments. In 1972 Congress overhauled the system of determining Social Security benefits by linking benefit increases to the rate of inflation. This overhaul enabled the program to expand, even as real growth slowed or stopped in many other social welfare programs during the inflationary 1970s. Social Security became a controversial issue, but Social Security benefits kept right on expanding throughout the controversy. Robert Ball, as much as any single person, orchestrated the developments that produced the 1972 amendments. In 1983 the Social Security program faced a crisis in which its critics warned that it might go bankrupt. Once again, Robert Ball negotiated a settlement of the issue that Congress adopted.

Beyond these three key moments, Robert Ball helped the program to beat back ideological challenges on at least two other occasions. In 1954 he helped steer the Eisenhower administration away from noncontributory pensions and instead got administration backing for a major expansion of contributory Social Security. In 1977, when the Carter administration contemplated what it should do to shore up the system's financing, Ball helped guide it toward a defense of Social Security, rather than some sort of fundamental change.

In a more continuous rather than dramatic sense, Robert Ball put his imprint on the program by leading the Social Security Administration through the two most complex implementation efforts in its history. After the 1956 passage of disability insurance, Ball worked with his chief lieutenants to put into place a program that, among other things, required state agencies to make difficult decisions about whether a particular person was truly unable to work and thus deserved a disability pension. These eligibility decisions needed to be coordinated with a federal operation to send out checks to people who qualified. After the 1965 passage of Medicare, Ball and his associates, among other difficult tasks, selected intermediaries to handle complex billing operations and made sure that hospitals across the nation met the federal government's qualifying standards. Through these actions, Ball set high aspirations not just for the expansion of the program but for the program's administrative capability.

Ball accomplished a great deal in an important venue yet remained relatively unknown to scholars and the general public. That was because the nature of historical commentary on America's welfare state obscured Robert Ball's contributions to American social policy. Although the literature on Social Security was voluminous, much of it had a present-minded, polemical tone as intellectuals in Washington think tanks shouted at each other in an effort to show that the program could not be sustained into the middle of the twenty-first century or that it remained America's best hope for the future.[26] Much of the academic work on the subject came from economists, politicians, and sociologists, with history as something of an afterthought. That meant comparatively little work appeared that used primary evidence to build a narrative on the development of the program over time and that might have highlighted Ball's role in the program. Although Social Security remained a staple of work in historical sociology and in surveys of American social welfare history or of the history of old age in America, no comprehensive history of the program existed that took the story through the 1990s. In the last quarter of the twentieth century, only one historian wrote a book on public policy toward Social Security, and only one biography of a Social Security administrator appeared.[27]

When historians did write on Social Security, they concentrated on topics other than the great expansion of the program in the last half of the twentieth century. Hence, they missed Ball's major contributions to American social policy. Historians, who focused on the creation of the Social Security program in 1935, noted that it covered only about half of the labor force and depended for its financing on a regressive payroll tax. It illustrated not the positive aspects of social reform so much as the racial and sexual divisions that characterized American society. The Social Security Act of 1935, according to a scholar who made a close study of its origins, "was the product of a society that was profoundly invested in the maintenance of white privilege." The act preserved "whiteness" and protected the "'right' of white people to work."[28] It did that by limiting coverage to industrial and commercial workers and excluding such groups as agricultural and domestic workers and thereby excluding the great majority of African Americans from coverage. The fact that a majority of America's agricultural workers were white went unremarked, as did the fact that the program was subsequently expanded to cover nearly every worker in the labor force.[29]

Historians of gender also found fault with the program. In the eyes of one feminist historical sociologist, women were excluded from the old-age insurance program in 1935 because the program based "entitlements on (white) masculine employment categories and patterns—primarily full-time, preferably unionized, continuous, industrial breadwinning work." When women gained mass access to the program in 1939, they did so in their roles as wives and widows and not as social contributors in their own right. As a program that paid family benefits after 1939, Social Security replicated an idealized version of the family in which men worked outside the home and women performed nonwage labor inside the home. Hence, the program encouraged a "gendered basis of social insurance" that "spread gender bias throughout the welfare state."[30] Subsequent efforts of people such as Robert Ball to reduce the gender bias and produce a gender-neutral program went unrecorded, as did the fact that more women received benefits from the program than men.

The result of the historian's analysis was to paint Social Security as a conservative program that failed to respond to America's most pressing social problems. In the broadest sense, the historians demonstrated how a racist and sexist society produced racist and sexist social programs. An important goal of social policy was to ameliorate the inequalities caused by America's racial and sexual divisions. Instead of doing that, Social Security reinforced those inequalities by, for example, paying lower benefits to blacks and women than to whites or men.[31] As one leading historian wrote, American social policy drew "sharp lines between how it would provide for men and women, old and young, white and nonwhite, and especially poor and non-poor, by segregating universalistic, relatively more generous programs from means-tested, ungenerous, stigmatized 'welfare' programs for the poor."[32] Such a view left little room for Robert Ball's contributions. If anything, it made him part of the problem.

Contrary to the expectations of academic historians, Robert Ball played a leading role in expanding America's welfare state in an inclusive direction to embrace the families of nearly everyone in the labor force. He used conservative means toward liberal ends. To clinch that point, one must enter the complicated realm of policymaking for Social Security and observe how Robert Ball's career unfolded.

1

Arriving

If, as Robert Ball claimed, he never sought any of the important jobs that he received, then he enjoyed uncommonly good luck. In the fall of 1947, for example, he had the good fortune to direct the staff of an advisory committee on Social Security. Created by the Senate Committee on Finance, this advisory committee, under Ball's active guidance, produced a report that served as a blueprint for American social policy between 1950 and 1972.

The basic idea that animated the report was that contributory social insurance should be used to defend the nation against the inherent insecurities of the modern economy. Should someone's income falter, the community should aid that person not through old-fashioned relief or welfare—in the simplest sense, payments to people who could prove they were poor—but rather through social insurance. In this manner the problem of poverty among the elderly might be prevented through prudent planning by having people pay for retirement benefits in advance. By tying the payments to working, the incentive for people to work could be preserved, and an American welfare state might be instituted that maintained the efficiency of America's capitalist economy.

When Ball made the case for social insurance in the Senate committee's report, it was neither a new nor a novel argument.

The big three in the development of Social Security in America—from left to right Arthur Altmeyer, Robert Ball, and Wilbur Cohen, along with Labor Secretary Willard Wirtz on far right. The occasion of the photograph was the thirty-third anniversary of Social Security in 1968. Photograph courtesy of SSA History Archives.

Nonetheless, his report had great historical significance. For one thing, it caught Congress's attention at the precise moment that it was prepared to act on the expansion of Social Security. For another thing, it demonstrated Ball's abilities to the leaders of the Social Security Administration and caused them to recruit him to their ranks. By late 1948 Robert Ball, who had entered the federal government nine years before as a low-level field worker at a Social Security office in New Jersey, enjoyed access to the highest ranking and most influential individuals in the Social Security Administration. Within another five years, he would himself be running the agency's largest and most important bureau.

If one wanted to find a link among the three most important people in Social Security's history from 1935 to 2000, it might be their ties to the state of Wisconsin. Arthur Altmeyer, a product of the University of Wisconsin's economics department and of Wisconsin state government, headed the agency from 1936 to 1953. In this capacity, he administered the Social Security, public assistance (or welfare, as it was more commonly called), and unemployment compensation programs. Altmeyer credited his appointment as Social Security commissioner, a post he held under various titles from Roosevelt's second term to the beginning of Eisenhower's first term, to his previous experience as an official "in a state noted for its progressive social legislation."[1]

Some 22 years younger than Altmeyer and only 35 years old in the fall of 1948, when Ball first came to prominence, Wilbur Cohen served as Altmeyer's protégé and his chief congressional liaison; he was the person on whom Altmeyer most relied to carry out his policies. Like Altmeyer, who was born in a small town near Green Bay, Cohen also came from Wisconsin, in his case the urban milieu of Milwaukee, and attended the University of Wisconsin.[2]

Minister's Son

Although born in New York City, on March 28, 1914, in the heart of what became black Harlem, Robert Ball, like the other Social Security leaders, had a connection with the state of Wisconsin. Both of his parents grew up there. His father, Archey Decatur Ball, came from the small town of Newton, where he was born on March 16, 1872, the son of Hiram and Rachel (Arkills). While attending Lawrence College in Appleton, Archey met Laura Elizabeth Crump, whose father owned a farm in the town of Lake Mills, between Madison and Milwaukee. Good students, Laura and Archey both earned Phi Beta Kappa keys at Lawrence. Graduating with the class of 1897, the two began a long courtship that culminated in their marriage in 1903. In the interim Laura taught history in a public school, and Archey went to divinity school at Boston University and spent a year abroad. In 1902 he joined the New York conference of the Methodist Church and served as an assistant at the Madison Avenue Church.[3]

Archey and Laura lived the rest of their lives in the corridor between Boston and New York. Moving often from one congregation to another, Archey held pastoral positions in such locations as Poughkeepsie and Walden, New York, before settling down for a five-year stint at the St. James Methodist Church in New York City. During this interval, Laura gave birth to Robert Myers Ball, her third child. The youngest in the family, Robert was nine years younger than his brother Theodore, known as Ted, and seven years junior to his sister Dorothy. When Robert was still an infant, Archey uprooted the family in the peripatetic manner of a Methodist minister and transferred to Centre Church in Malden, just outside of Boston. Robert, or Bob, as he was called, went to kindergarten in Massachusetts but soon moved to northern New Jersey when his father became affiliated with the Newark Methodist Conference and took a pulpit in Ridgewood, New Jersey, in 1920. Bob spent the remainder of his childhood in Bergen and Essex Counties, places with large numbers of New York City commuters. His father served in the church for the remainder of his career, sometimes as an administrator—he was the district superintendent of the Newark Methodist Conference for the six years of boom and bust between 1926 and 1932—but more often as a pastor. He held the posts of substitute pastor in Leonia and Patterson at the time of his death in 1955.[4]

The formal part of the immersion in religion that went along with being a minister's son never took with Robert Ball. In common with Social Security's other leaders, he tended to downplay his religious heritage. In a curious convergence, Altmeyer, Cohen, and Ball, the trinity of Social Security high priests, to use an expression coined by a policymaker in the era of Jimmy Carter, began life with the usual religious attachments and ended it as Unitarians. Wilbur Cohen, a product of the Milwaukee Jewish community and with a recognizably Jewish name and a conventional Jewish upbringing, turned away from the rituals of the Jewish religion. Ball, the son of a minister, similarly rejected the rituals of Methodism for the less formal structures of the Unitarian religion. He, like Cohen, appeared to have been transformed by the New Deal, away from organized religion and toward a secular faith in the government's benevolence as a force for social uplift.[5]

If Ball moved away from the formal aspects of religion that pervaded his household, he nonetheless assimilated a great deal of his father's teachings and lifestyle. For one thing, he had constantly before him the example of a man whose job was not bounded by the conventional rhythms of daily life. If a member of a congregation took sick at three in the morning, the minister, like the doctor who ministered to the patient's physical needs, had to be available for consultation at the bedside. Similarly, the days of the week had different meanings in a minister's household than they did in the household of someone who took the train to New York on weekdays. The pastoral task demanded that the minister be on call at all times and that he dress up on Sunday for church and Sunday school. When Bob later became the head of the Social Security program, it was natural that he view it as a pastoral assignment and that he, too, would be available for work at all hours.

As a minister, Archey Ball had to balance the tension between being a leader of and a servant to his congregation. As a spiritual leader, a minister held an ambiguous status within the community as a respected, but often relatively impoverished, member. To survive, the minister had to impress his opinions on his followers but at the same time conform to their social norms so as to gain their acceptance. Robert remembered his father as the "head man" of unquestioned authority but also as "a very social person who regardless of the seriousness of his goals, enjoyed almost every day as it went. He was full of laughter and full of humaness." The mixture of solemnity, high purpose, and humor that Ball attributed to his father would be something he would consciously seek to emulate. Theodore Marmor, an academic who spent a great deal of time with Wilbur Cohen and Robert Ball, would later remark on how Ball's "gravity" was "lightened by a readily available twinkle and chuckle" and how his somewhat severe expression and obvious intensity were "frequently softened" by an "easy smile and firm but unaggressive manner." That was the minister's exact stance: firm but unaggressive.[6] Robert Ball would grow up to be a liberal Democrat and an advocate of the expansion of America's welfare state. Still, in the style of Princeton-educated socialist leader Norman Thomas, he appeared always to be a sound and conventional man, unthreatening in manner or appearance.[7]

The link between the religion of Archey and the New Deal activism of Robert was more than a matter of style. As Robert Ball later explained, his father "had always been in the part of the Methodist Church that emphasizes strongly what they call the social gospel; that is, trying to improve the lot of people on earth." As a preacher of the social gospel, Archey came to take a sympathetic position to labor unions and other organizations that sought to improve working conditions. By the time that Franklin Roosevelt emerged as a political leader, years that coincided with Robert's high school and college education, Archey, according to his son, "became quite active in support of all New Deal activities." During the 1930s, as the New Jersey state chairman of the American Civil Liberties Union, Archey took on the battles over free speech for labor union leaders.[8]

The pattern of the social gospel in one generation yielding to governmental activism in another was not without precedent among leaders in the field of social insurance. Perhaps the most prominent example was that of Paul Raushenbush, the son of Baptist minister and leading social gospel figure Walter Rauschenbusch, who came to the University of Wisconsin in 1922 and then met and married Elizabeth Brandeis, the daughter of Supreme Court Justice Louis Brandeis. Together they embarked on a partnership in the style of Sidney and Beatrice Webb in which they theorized about an unemployment compensation program and ran Wisconsin's program from 1932 until 1967.[9]

Some sixteen years younger than Raushenbush, Robert Ball skipped the state-centered phase of the social insurance movement and went directly into government service at the federal level. Nor did Ball take on a partner so directly as did Raushenbush. Still, the pattern was the same, highlighting the transition from a Christian to a more ecumenical motivation for social reform.

As the youngest child, Robert Ball grew up in a more permissive atmosphere than did his brother and sister, and he also enjoyed a more privileged position within the family circle. As the family "pet," he could be secure in his parents' love and still be free to experiment with new ideas. In a broad and overly determined sense, older siblings, particularly oldest sons who were, in effect, the children of record, often experienced a powerful urge to conform to the behavior patterns set by their parents; younger siblings more often demonstrated a freer, intellectually rebellious nature.[10] In Ball's case, this natural tendency was reinforced by the changing social and political environment. Unlike his siblings, Ball came of age during the Great Depression, which began for him at the highly impressionable age of 16. Although the depression did not result in much personal economic deprivation—the Methodists tried to balance the supply of ministers with the demand—it could have not have failed to have made a powerful impression on Ball. He was a product of the age of political purpose and social realism, not the jazz age. The existential dilemmas of prosperity experienced by his siblings yielded to the hard realities of a tough job market for him. Perhaps not surprisingly, he would make a career of a program that emphasized the positive virtues of work and the imperative of saving for the contingencies of old age and unemployment.[11]

Ball recognized his good fortune in having been born last, despite the fact that it meant that he would have a difficult time getting a job. He said that the hard parts of a Methodist upbringing were "pretty much absorbed by my older brother and sister. By the time I came along my parents were much more relaxed." His siblings told him stories about his parents' strictness, but Ball claimed "that just didn't apply to me." Far from foreboding, his parents appeared to him as "inspiring people and very tolerant of me." As time progressed, Archey "relaxed many of the strict teachings of the Methodist Church." His son Robert would, for example, take a drink without feeling the weight of the church's long campaign for temperance. Indeed, Robert came to regard Archey as something of a playmate, someone with whom he could stay up until three in the morning "arguing every question of life and the future of the world and world politics." He conceded that his mother was a little starchy, "somewhat reserved" in public. She had many good works to carry out, running the Sunday School, training the teachers, raising money for foreign missionaries, and leading groups that read the scriptures, not to mention the weekly routine of greeting the congregation after services. Still, within the privacy of her family circle, according to Ball, she shed much of her reserve and became "playful and warm."[12]

Sometimes minister's kids have a hard time in school and are easy targets for bullies who see them as otherworldly, as too soft to face the rough-and-tumble of the playground. Ball seems to have more than held his own. At East Orange High School, located near Newark in New Jersey's heavily urban Essex County, he played football, edited the yearbook, and became involved in student government. He grew to be over six feet tall, always a useful attribute for achieving social status in high school, and appeared to exhibit a natural habit of command.[13]

Robert entered college in the fall of 1931. That fact separated him from the vast majority of motivated, aspiring middle-class high school graduates who lacked the financial means to pay for college and were needed to help out at home. He chose Wesleyan, which was Methodist, however loosely, in orientation and relatively close to home yet not without a certain social cachet.[14] In college he resumed his life as a big man on campus, enjoying both social and academic success. Like his parents he earned a Phi Beta Kappa key and graduated with honors in general scholarship and distinction in his chosen major of English. Although no single professor "particularly changed things" for him, he won a prize awarded by the English department. His choice of English as a major allowed him to read books and novels rather than devote all of his time to a practical curriculum that might prepare him for a career in business or the professions. He apparently felt little urgency to turn his college education into a saleable commodity, perhaps because the depression made the prospect of getting any sort of job seem very remote and perhaps because his father's relative financial security "at a low level of economic well-being" bred in him a "feeling that I could take chances." He also participated in an impressive array of extracurricular activities including serving as a member of a student group that met with the administration on an advisory basis and playing a leadership role in the Delta Kappa Epsilon fraternity.[15]

The fraternity experience showed how Ball managed to conform to college mores at a time when football commanded much more attention than did social activism (although it had much less of a hold over students at Wesleyan than at big state universities) and yet also become involved in New Deal politics. He later remembered that Delta Kappa Epsilon, for which he served as treasurer and later as president, was known primarily for its dances and, significantly for the son of a Methodist minister, its drinking. But as the brothers danced and drank, they also found time to go to Hartford and picket at a strike at the Colt Arms plant. Ball claimed that half of the fraternity participated in that activity, apparently able, like Ball, to maintain a duality of social action and social conformity. Indeed, much of Ball's college career

Robert Ball as an earnest young graduate of East Orange High School in New Jersey circa 1930. Photograph courtesy of Robert Ball.

was typical of that of a college student of his day—right down to his arrest, in the spring of his senior year, that traditional time for high jinks, for disturbing the peace. He paid a five-dollar fine and went about his life.[16]

Ball faced the usual indecision about what to do with his college education. He did not like the idea of studying for its own sake and in this manner preparing for a life in academia. "I'm getting a little sick of this idea of being a professor," he wrote in a revealing letter to his sister. He did not want to fall into an "easy, slippered life and die without knowing whether or not I could really 'take it.'" As his college career ended, Ball came to believe that his life had been too easy. "I've never attempted anything very difficult so I've never failed at anything which mattered to me much," he wrote. "It all amounts to the realization that I am much happier than I deserve to be, and that I'd like to know what kind of a person I am under adversity and whether I'm as selfish as I, at times, appear to myself." The letter, one of the few surviving glimpses into Ball's personal feelings, indicated his desire to make a contribution, not all that well defined, to something that he perceived to be of consequence and, in the manner of a hero in the Hemingway short stories then much in vogue, to test himself in the real world.[17]

Labor Activist

First, however, Ball continued his studies at the postgraduate level. Although he had majored in English as an undergraduate, he did hedge his bets by taking nearly as many hours of economics as he did of English.[18] Norman Ware, an expert in labor relations and a member of the economics faculty, convinced Ball to stay at Wesleyan and obtain a master's degree in the field of labor economics.[19] In the summer of 1935, this subject was a compelling one, with the passage of the Wagner Act and its accompanying guarantees of the workers' rights to organize and bargain collectively. In the following year, the drama of the formation of the Committee on Industrial Organization (CIO) unfolded, and the drive to organize workers in the nation's major industries began in earnest.[20] Intrigued by Ware's offer and stimulated by the subject matter, Ball realized that he could make almost as much money as a Rich Fellow at Wesleyan as he could in the soft labor market, and so he spent academic year 1935–36 taking courses in such subjects as labor problems and labor history. He earned an A in both subjects, but only a B in the more mathematical and theoretically oriented courses, such as economic theory and corporation finance.

Outside the classroom, Ball spent most of his time working on his master's thesis, which he titled "The Industrial–Craft Union Dispute in the American Federation of Labor." He finished the thesis, in which he analyzed past failures of the labor movement in organizing unskilled workers and described the emerging split in the labor movement between craft and industrial unions, in May of 1936, only a few months before the formation of the CIO. The thesis was well received by Ware and the other professors in the economics department, who gave it an A and also gave Ball an A for his oral defense of it.[21]

Although Ball could not have known it, he was already following a route taken by nearly all the early leaders of the Social Security program. Wilbur Cohen, who graduated from the University of Wisconsin in the summer of 1934, wrote an undergraduate honors thesis on the history of the International Association of Machinists. Like Ball's study, Cohen's was institutional in nature, relying on history, rather than econometrics, as the primary mode of analysis. This sort of institutional economics, as it was called, enjoyed considerable prominence in an economics profession that had not yet acquired its exclusively quantitative nature. The professors who taught the subject believed that applied economics—in other words, the sort that could be addressed to contemporary problems—inevitably contained a historical dimension.[22]

During the 1930s, furthermore, applied economists found that their skills were in demand in Washington. Those with a feel for statistics and a knowledge of history came to play prominent roles in the social programs of the New Deal. For example, in the summer of 1934, Wilbur Cohen's professor at the University of Wisconsin received the assignment of directing the staff that wrote the Social Security Act. By that time Arthur Altmeyer was already in Washington, an assistant secretary of labor, and he too became involved in the activities surrounding the creation of the Social Security Act. Like Cohen, he was a student of Wisconsin's famed

John R. Commons, and like Ball he could be described as an institutional economist with a special interest in labor relations.[23]

According to Ball's later recollections, his interest in Social Security stemmed from this period. With his master's degree in hand, he needed to find a job, particularly since he planned to get married right after his graduation in June 1936. It was only natural that he turned for help to Norman Ware, who had colleagues involved in the Social Security program and who told Ball that the program, passed a year earlier in the summer of 1935, was "just starting up. It's going to be a big program. It's an attractive program and an important social program, and it would be good thing if you got in on it in the beginning."[24]

It might well have been a good thing, but there was no obvious way for Ball to get in on it. All he could do was take a civil service examination and hope for the best. It helped in these situations to have some sort of contact in Washington. To cite an example, Wilbur Cohen and Arthur Altmeyer, already in Washington and already on the inside of Social Security politics, simply passed through an invisible door that separated the staff work that preceded the passage of the Social Security Act from the staff work that followed its passage; they were summoned to the Social Security Board on the day it opened its doors and were put to work.[25] Not favored in this manner and with his attention on the Wagner Act, rather than the Social Security Act, Ball had no particular reason to favor working on Social Security over any other New Deal assignment. His first choice, contrary to his later recollections, was the National Labor Relations Board (NLRB). Even in 1941, when he had already put in two years in at the Social Security Board, he told an NLRB recruiter that the NLRB had "perhaps the greatest contribution to make in preserving and extending democracy" and actively sought a job there.[26]

In the summer of 1936, Ball put his problems aside, got married, and went off on a six-week honeymoon. He had met Doris Jacqueline McCord in high school, and the two had maintained their relationship throughout Ball's five years in college and graduate school. For their honeymoon, they pitched a tent along the shores of a lake in the Adirondacks on land that belonged to a friend of Ball's father. According to Ball, in a memory typical of his generation's emphasis on depression austerity, the couple had fifty dollars and got by splendidly for the six weeks. Leaving

Robert Ball, with his wife, Doris, returns to SSA Headquarters in Baltimore on the occasion of the fiftieth anniversary of Social Security in 1985. During the twenty-one years that Ball was more or less running Social Security, Doris did many things to contribute to his success, such as entertaining advisory councils, foreign visitors, executive staff, department staff, and other officials and employees, always, as Ball put it, "in ways that made them feel good about us and Social Security." Doris played a key role in dealing with problems related to race relations at Social Security and in the surrounding community during the 1960s and also worked, in her own right, on problems related to welfare, the recruitment and selection of parole officers, and the creation of the Board of Health in Baltimore County. At the same time, in the manner of wives of prominent public officials during this period, she also ran the household, including taking care of not only their children but also her and her husband's aged mothers, supporting her husband in all endeavors, and, as Ball put it, tolerating his evening hours with "grace and humor." Ball noted, "I could not have had the career I did without her." Photograph courtesy of Robert Ball.

paradise, Ball still had to come up with a job. Stopping off on the way home, he took a civil service examination. It yielded no immediate offers, and Ball began to look in earnest for a job that would support him and his wife. He had little previous experience other than a summer stint on the assembly line at a Ford Motor plant in Edgewater, New Jersey.[27]

If his Wesleyan degrees were not enough to bring him to the head of the civil service list and earn him the sort of secure job

that everyone craved in 1936, they were sufficient to land a position as an internal auditor (more formally, assistant to the assistant comptroller) at the Stern Brothers Department Store in mid-
town Manhattan. Definitely an entry-level job, it paid only a
pittance, $884 a year, and featured the mind-numbing task of bal-
ancing the store's internal checking accounts. Doris took a job as
a receptionist in a doctor's office.[28]

With no intention of remaining at the department store, Robert
Ball soon found a more congenial temporary job as a librarian at
the Junior College of Bergen County, New Jersey. It paid a little
more and gave him a greater sense of autonomy, since at times he
could run the library by himself. Then, in the summer of 1937, he
found a job that played to his strengths and his interests. He became an assistant editor of the *People's Press,* a labor newspaper,
with offices in East Orange. This job involved editing and writing, tasks for which his undergraduate training in English had
prepared him. More importantly, the position allowed him to in-
dulge his interest in and enthusiasm for the labor movement.

In later recollections Ball seldom dwelled on the year and a
half that he spent with the paper, yet the job, unlike the two clerical jobs preceding it, clearly engaged his full attention. It was not
politic for a bureaucrat in the late 1940s and early 1950s to highlight a close association with the labor movement of the late
1930s, because of the perceived association between the labor
movement and the Communist Party. Before he settled into a Social Security career, however, Ball took great pride in his job at
the newspaper and hoped to make it a springboard to a position
with the National Labor Relations Board.

In his 1941 job application to the NLRB, Ball described the
newspaper as the "official organ for the AFL and CIO in northern
New Jersey." Ball's beat consisted of the Patterson, Passaic, and
Jersey City areas, which contained, among other concentrations
of workers, 15,000 dyers and silk workers in Patterson. As one of
the benefits of union membership, these workers as well as
brewery workers, textile workers, bartenders, bakers, teachers,
and laundry workers received the paper in the mail. Ball, for his
part, wrote stories and editorials, sold advertising and subscrip-
tions, spoke at union meetings, and took part "in the organizing
and other activities of the unions."[29]

As the people's journalist, Ball often took to the streets. In June 1937, new to the job, he participated in the efforts of the Textile Workers Organizing Committee of the CIO to organize the workers at the Dun Rite Laundry in Patterson. Not only did he report the news, but he also "helped on the picket line" and tried to mediate some of the disputes over workload. Later that summer he became involved in the general strike of the Patterson silk workers, also under the auspices of the Textile Workers Organizing Committee. He saw his job as building support for the strike within the labor movement, which he did by reading up on the history of Patterson labor unions, maintaining close contact with the silk workers, interviewing employers, attending strike meetings, and going out "with the flying squadrons of pickets on the first two days of the strike." When workers at Hohokus Bleachery struck in September, Ball "went into the workers' homes to investigate living conditions." In the ongoing strike at the Little Falls Laundry, which lasted into the fall of 1937, Ball organized a boycott committee composed of "prominent ministers, lawyers, and outstanding citizens for the northern part of the state."

Aside from taking part in the urgent business of strikes, Ball also played the role of crusading reporter for what he perceived to be the cause of social justice. When he came upon buttons that said "CIO" in large letters and "Civil Insurrection Organization" in smaller letters, he set out to discover who had ordered and distributed them. Posing as someone opposed to union organization, he interviewed the button manufacturer in Newark and obtained the address of the person who had placed the order. Ball confronted the designer and distributor of the buttons in a sympathetic manner and succeeded in persuading the man to give him the rest of the buttons. The obliging man suggested that Ball could make money by taking the buttons to a group of bankers and asking for their support. On other occasions Ball investigated relief and housing conditions in Patterson. In aid of the CIO's organizing drive in Jersey City, Ball wrote about Mayor Frank Hague's efforts to suppress the distribution of union leaflets, and he covered the meeting in the Jersey City Armory to "keep the Reds out of the city."[30]

Robert Ball might well have stayed with the paper or worked as an organizer or analyst with the CIO except that he finally received a summons for a federal job. As it turned out, the job was with the Social Security Board, which, if not Ball's first choice, nonetheless was more than acceptable.

Ball's short tenure with the paper had consequences that carried over into his long career with the Social Security Board. It reinforced his natural sympathies with organized labor, and it caused him to forge intellectual connections between collective bargaining and Social Security. These two benevolent interventions into the private market augmented job security and, as a consequence, contributed to the improvement of working conditions. Both functioned as collaborations between workers and the state. In the Social Security Act, the state collected taxes from the worker and provided a retirement program in return. In collective bargaining, as institutionalized by the Wagner Act, the state acted as a referee that facilitated the process of union representation and paved the way for collective bargaining. Furthermore, the same sorts of institutional labor economists, such as Ball, Altmeyer, and Cohen, who supported the Social Security Act also supported the Wagner Act and worked for the agencies in charge of implementing the two acts: the Social Security Board and the NLRB, respectively. Where others might have seen conflicts between private collective bargaining and public social insurance, these institutional economists saw only continuity. Their emotional attachment to the labor movement strengthened this sense of continuity, as did the fact that the Wagner Act and the Social Security program were both aimed at industrial and commercial workers. Not surprisingly, then, those who ran the Social Security program, such as Altmeyer, Cohen, and later Ball, tended to see organized labor as an important ally, even if some labor leaders maintained their traditional suspicion of the federal government well into the 1940s. As Ball put it, "the position of the Social Security Board . . . was always worked out with the labor movement."[31]

The Social Security Board

Robert Ball's title in his first job with the Social Security Board, which he formally assumed on January 1, 1939, was field assistant in the Newark, New Jersey, field office of the Bureau of

Old-Age and Survivors Insurance (BOASI). Before he greeted the public, he attended a training and orientation program in Washington that was one of the organization's distinctive features, one of the things that gave Social Security Board employees their special sense of purpose. Just as the military required a period of basic training to turn a recruit into a soldier, so the Social Security Board sought to indoctrinate its new recruits in the program's basic mission and functions. Arthur Altmeyer described the pervasive spirit of this training as an "effort to imbue each employee with his affirmative responsibility for carrying out the provisions of the Social Security Act." "We kept the clerks here, as well as the higher-ups, for months before they went out and set up local offices," Altmeyer later recalled. "So they just had religion. They had it complete."[32]

Altmeyer's statements implied that the training served as more than boot camp, an ordeal to be endured. Not only did the recruits learn the technical details of the Social Security program, such as how to determine a benefit level or what constituted proper proof of age, but they also studied the theory of social insurance and the development of social insurance programs at home and abroad. It was meant to be something uplifting, an opportunity for employees doing mundane tasks in ordinary places like Newark, New Jersey, to catch a glimpse of the larger picture and be inspired by what the Social Security program sought to accomplish.

In 1939, as Ball made his way from New Jersey to Washington for training, the Social Security program had more potential than performance to offer its young employees. As originally conceived in 1935, the old-age insurance program, the one that most people came to know as Social Security, was to be given what might be described as a soft launch. Instead of starting all at once, the program would be eased into operation. Beginning in 1937, employers would deduct 1 percent from the first $3,000 of their employee's wages, match that deduction with a similar contribution of their own, and send the proceeds off to the Internal Revenue Service. Employees would receive credit for the contributions in accounts maintained by the Social Security Board. The first benefits were not scheduled to be paid until 1942, or three years from the time that Ball entered federal service. Although the program did make lump-sum payments, which

might be thought of as refunds, if one of the participating workers died, it functioned mainly as a tax rather than a benefit.
Working as a field assistant in 1939 thus required the imagination
to see into the future to the day when the program would become an important force in American life, a little like a home
owner staring at an architect's design.

More readily apparent to the trainees was the fact that the Social Security Board was a large and bureaucratic organization.
Within a year of Ball's arrival the organization would number
about 12,000 people, some concerned with administering the
unemployment compensation and public assistance programs,
some involved in doing research or renting office space, but
most, like Ball, working on some aspect of the old-age insurance
program, whether that meant a job in a central records office or,
like Ball, in some part of the field operation.[33]

Ball participated in the fifty-seventh training class, graduating
on February 18, 1939. By all accounts he acquitted himself well,
catching the favorable attention of Frances J. McDonald, the chief
of the training office. Ball described McDonald as "a very unusual person and very much a maverick in the BOASI." One of
the original employees of what was called at the time the Bureau
of Federal Old-Age Benefits, McDonald came from New Hampshire. He arrived at Social Security under the aegis of John Wi-
nant, the former New Hampshire governor who served as the
first head of the Social Security Board. An experienced bureaucrat with previous service in the Veterans Bureau, McDonald enjoyed a reputation for being able to spot talent among the recruits. Much as a nun might discern in a particularly bright and
pious young student the makings of a future priest, so McDonald
could pick "comers" in the ranks. As Arthur Hess, whose career
closely paralleled Ball's and who ultimately became second in
command when Ball was commissioner and took over as acting
commissioner when Ball left, put it, "Old Francis McDonald had
six-week classes and you were identified in those classes as to
whether or not you were quick on the draw and whether you
were interested and committed." Another prominent Social Security bureaucrat compared McDonald to Johnny Appleseed,
traveling around the country identifying "comers" and spread-
ing the word to officials back at headquarters. The reward for
being quick on the draw was relatively rapid advancement

through the bureaucracy and the possibility of being called in from the field to take on an assignment in the central office.[34]

One can easily imagine that Ball, with his Phi Beta Kappa key and his earnest manner, would be perceived as quick and committed. Throughout his life, when he participated in group activities similar to the Social Security training class, he always avoided the possibility of offending someone by presenting himself as superior or coming across as a smart aleck who held himself aloof from the group. Whatever impression he may have made in his training class, however, he still needed to put in his time in the field. It took him more than three years to make it to the central office, just as it took the Princeton-educated Hess five years.

"I can't stress too much what a lowly job this was," Ball later said of his time first as a field assistant and then, beginning in July 1940, as a senior field assistant in Newark, New Jersey. He spent much of his time outside of the office chasing down missing Social Security numbers. The Internal Revenue Service would report that a particular employer had sent in a tax return with a Social Security contribution but without identifying the employee to whom the contribution should be credited. Ball had the job of asking the employer to identify the employee and of making sure that the employee had a Social Security number. Often he encountered a hostile response from the employer, who regarded the program as a nuisance that generated paperwork and as an intrusion on his freedom to run his business. "Not the whole damned board," responded one employer when told the Social Security Board was calling. Although that part of the job was taxing, it did have its rewards. These consisted mainly of serving as the program's ambassador to unions, Rotary Clubs, and other civic groups.[35]

For all the drudgery involved in fieldwork, Ball, with his congenital optimism, came to see it as invaluable training and as the best sort of introduction to the nitty-gritty details of the program. His colleague Hess agreed that "the field experience was very important," something to look for in a Social Security employee. Those who had worked in the field, Hess said, "knew what it was like, as I did in Wilkes Barre [Pennsylvania], to have to deal with a big foreign element population—Poles, Slovaks—and first generation immigrants and knew what it was like . . . in those days to deal with small business people in the field who detested having to make out Social Security reports and a lot of people who didn't want to have Social Security numbers." Ball concurred in this opinion, even though, as he put it, "I moved up very slowly in [the] field organization and in retrospect I would say that this is certainly all I deserved. There was nothing about my work that was outstanding as compared with other people in this position."[36]

Maybe not, but Ball remained a motivated and ambitious employee with no intention of remaining at a lowly level in the field. "I had decided when I started at Social Security in the training class that this was very likely to be my permanent career and I wanted to have all the formal records look as good as I could make them," he later remarked.[37] He took all assignments seriously, particularly those that came from the central office, such as a request for comments on a revision of what was called the claims manual. After a long year and a half, he received a promotion from field assistant to senior field assistant. He might not have liked too many of the people who supervised him, whom he saw as middle-age men with experience in the insurance business who were grateful to have a job, but he continued to work hard for them. Unlike Ball himself, his supervisors did not regard Social Security as a special calling. They had, after all, already held jobs, already been knocked around by life. Ball was younger, more enthusiastic, more committed. Eventually he got his own field office to run. It was quite small; he had only two employees to supervise. "I consider this appointment an important privilege," he wrote the regional representative who supervised him.[38]

When he arrived in Bayonne, New Jersey, in March 1941 to run the Social Security office there, he quickly realized that there was not enough work to justify having an independent office. His supervisors grasped that fact as well, and eventually the office was consolidated into the Jersey City office. Rather than go to Jersey City, Ball was asked to report to the Elizabeth office. Although he was only an assistant manager there, he received a promotion and had twice as many employees to supervise as he did in Bayonne. It was a chaotic time that coincided with America's entrance into the Second World War.

In fact, the politics of America's involvement in the war figured into the sour relationship that Ball developed with his boss in Elizabeth. Apparently this boss had wanted someone who was already in the office to be his assistant manager and resented Ball's appointment. By this time Ball must have been well able to cope with managers whose energy and zeal for the program did not match his. This situation, however, was something new: a supervisor who flat-out did not like him and refused to be charmed by his ingratiating personality and his willingness to work hard. Political arguments made the situation worse. Ball noticed that his boss, along with the man whom the boss wanted for his assistant, exhibited "a considerable lack of sympathy for England's cause in the war." The situation grew tense enough that Ball decided to get out. He had already updated his paper-work with the National Labor Relations Board. He now began to look more closely at the openings available in Social Security's central office. As the war began, these openings became more frequent as people were called away for military duty. The hostility of his co-workers in Elizabeth, in particular the fact that for the only time in his career he was unable to get along with his super-visor, was "part of the reason why I readily accepted a Central Office position in Baltimore, Maryland."[39]

The regional people in Philadelphia told him not to go to the central office, which was in the process of being moved from Washington, D.C., to Baltimore. The office space specially designed for the Social Security Board in Washington, with floors reinforced to support the weight of the office equipment necessary to maintain Social Security records, was needed for the war effort. The Social Security program transferred its operations to Baltimore, and because it became established there as an important source of employment, it never returned to Washington.[40] Those who worked in Social Security's field and regional offices saw the central office as the home of an alien culture. Central office people were planners and dreamers, divorced from the practical realities of public administration and out of touch with ordinary people. Those who worked in the field offices enjoyed the easy camaraderie of salesmen; the central office was more formal, less congenial.

If Ball stayed in the regional operation, he could expect slow and steady advancement, ending up as a manager of a large local office or perhaps a regional supervisor. Little of that appealed to Ball. His intellect and analytic abilities were not being put to what he perceived as their proper uses in the field. "I was really very much interested in the program itself—the philosophy, the legislative agenda, and where the whole program was going and had gotten more than my fill of the kind of day-to-day work that I had been doing in the district office," he said.[41]

In March 1942, Ball entered the Analysis Division of the Bureau of Old-Age and Survivors Insurance. Of all parts of the bureau, this one was the most cerebral. Unlike the Accounting Operations Division, which had the practical task of maintaining people's Social Security records, the Analysis Division, according to the official manual, had the mission of analyzing the functioning of OASI "in order to provide data necessary for administration, for evaluation of program results, and as a basis for policy decisions." Chief among its purposes was to "draft plans for the extension of coverage to those groups which are now excluded."[42] Hence, Analysis Division personnel tended to be those who could monitor statistical trends, observe the behavior of Congress, write reports on social problems, and formulate legislative proposals. It was work for which Ball's training in economics and his editorial experience suited him far more than did field work.

Although Ball did routine work for the Analysis Division preparing a series of statistics that were published in the *Social Security Bulletin* and undertaking other minor editorial tasks, he felt a sense of exhilaration. Finally he was in an intellectual atmosphere that was not without its own sense of social purpose. In the Analysis Division, people discussed such consequential matters as whether Social Security should be limited to the industrial working classes or whether it should be universal. How much should American social insurance look like European social insurance? What factors made America unique? As Ball listened to his new colleagues debate these questions, he came to the tentative conclusion that American social insurance could do more than serve as an alternative to welfare. It could instead be "a useful program for just about everyone who worked; not just for those in danger of poverty."[43]

Of course, the discussions in the Analysis Division were little more than academic bull sessions. The disparity between the program as it existed and as the analysts envisioned it and the fact that the war limited the immediate prospects for even the most modest reforms gave these conversations a certain whimsical, even playful cast. Ball enjoyed participating in them, and the other analysts came to respect his abilities.

It was at this point that Ball began to make an impression on the organization that he had the right sort of stuff to advance to a high position. Here he first came to know Alvin David, with whom he managed to shed some of his residual reserve and engage in a close friendship. Alvin David, as much as anyone, came to personify the analysis function in the organization. Over the years he would supervise much of the research and writing that went into important policy documents such as the reports of advisory councils and congressional committees.

Like many of the agency leaders, David came to maturity in the depression and found refuge from an inhospitable labor market in the federal government's employ. The 1930s were a particularly auspicious time to start a complex government undertaking such as Social Security, not only because people were receptive to new social programs but also because a large supply of highly motivated and qualified people was available to staff the programs. David was typical of the cohort of people who rose to the top echelons of the Social Security Administration during the 1940s and 1950s. Born in 1906, he studied at the University of Chicago and earned a Phi Beta Kappa key in his junior year. After graduating in 1929, he held a series of jobs as a salesman and accountant in the wobbly economy before landing his first federal position in 1934. That same year he became associated with the National Recovery Administration, the centerpiece of Franklin Roosevelt's first New Deal, and after the Supreme Court put that agency out of business, he found work as an investigator with the Railroad Retirement Board. In October 1936 he joined the Social Security Board, earning $2,600 a year as a junior administrative assistant. He eventually worked his way up to a prominent position in the Analysis Division and its successor organizations.[44]

David and his wife felt comfortable enough with Robert and Doris Ball that, when David went into the army, his wife lived with the Balls for several months. When David was released from the army, he and his wife moved in with Robert and Doris for "quite a few weeks" while they hunted for a house. Beyond these bonds of friendship, Alvin David saw in Ball someone with

superior ability who was destined to be a leader in the organization. He later reported that when Ball first came in from the field
to be interviewed, he realized "here was a world-beater, here was
a ball of fire, and we should grab him as fast as we can. . . . It was
so easy to see. He was head and shoulders above everyone else.
Even though he did not know anything about what was going on
in our neck of the woods, he was just so smart and so good."[45]

Even if not everyone was so enthusiastic in his praise of Ball as
was David, Ball had his share of admirers. Chief among them
was Francis McDonald, who had trained Ball and who had remained interested in his career. In August 1942 he invited Ball to
become the associate training supervisor and do for others what
McDonald had done for him. Ball made the change and almost
immediately became involved in all aspects of the Social Security
Board's training function. Doris had just given birth to a son,
whom they named Robert Jonathan, and the training job seemed
to be a more mature position, closer to something permanent,
than did the editorial work in the Analysis Division.

It proved to be a very good match for Ball's talents. As Francis
McDonald's assistant, he had a chance to attend many top-level
staff meetings and get to know the group of people who ran the
Social Security Board's most important bureau. As an instructor,
he had an opportunity to learn the program in broad philosophical outline and narrow programmatic detail. He could, for example, explain how to compute a Social Security benefit, given a
person's age, contribution record, and marital status. He also
learned what might be described as the official rationale for each
of the many rules that governed Social Security, such as why the
program did not pay benefits to people who reached the age of
65 and remained in the labor force. In so doing, he discovered
one of the talents that he would use throughout his career: the
ability to explain the program and articulate its contributions in a
patient and clear manner.

Robert Ball could discuss even the driest or most controversial
points of Social Security policy in a compelling, non-antagonistic
way, a skill that would later come in handy in such forums as
meetings with politicians at the White House or in formal testimony or closed sessions with congressmen on Capitol Hill. Part
of the trick was repetition. As the years went by, he had been over
the same ground many times. Part of the trick was preparation.

What looked like a casual presentation or remark was often thought out in advance. Robert Ball frequently knew what direction he would like a discussion to take, and in an unobtrusive way he worked to steer it that way, always with deference to his audience and without appearing to dictate the outcome. This extraordinary ability, acquired over the course of many years, was first honed in the lectures and question and answer sessions of the Social Security Board training program.

McDonald gave Ball a great deal of freedom and showed a great deal of confidence in his abilities. As would Ball's other supervisors, McDonald learned to leave Ball alone, with the result that Ball made both of them look good. Ball later said that "he trusted my capacity well beyond what he had any reason to." Indeed, he had immense confidence in Ball. Asked by John Corson, the head of the bureau at the time, where Ball would be in ten years' time, McDonald replied, "in your job." Without hesitation he threw Ball into situations that many people would find difficult to handle, such as asking him to teach a class without warning in front of a large group of people. Rather than have Ball specialize in one type of training, he expected Ball to lead classes in program philosophy, the specifics of the Old-Age and Survivors Insurance program, and in functional topics such as how to interview.[46] McDonald, Ball remembered, "might ask me at 9 o'clock to appear at 10 o'clock before 200 people at the Candler Building [a downtown Baltimore landmark that still exists] in the big Accounting Operations Division to carry on orientation sessions for a brand-new group of employees. Or, with not much more warning we might suddenly take off with a class on interviewing or letter writing for experienced employees. I really did the heavy lifting in this training position and McDonald was a salesman and promoter and we got along just fine, each rather instinctively recognizing our distinctive roles."[47]

Ball said that before he came into the training office he had been a shy person who was afraid to do much public speaking. In the new job he shed that fear and developed into an effective speaker. In front of a class as much as eight hours a day, he found that speaking became second nature. In the training office he learned to use a cigarette as a prop, something to drag on while he contemplated the answer to a trainee's question or composed the next part of his lecture. At the time, of course, smoking was a ubiquitous activity that fouled the air of classrooms and other public spaces. On the days in which class was in session, Ball burned three packs a day.[48]

In the training office Ball made his first contribution to what might be called Social Security's official literature. Late in 1942 he drafted "Notes for Your Guidance," a short statement that enjoyed wide distribution throughout the agency. Attempting to explain how Social Security field personnel should interact with members of the public, it highlighted the program's mission and the need for program officials to be deferential toward those who sought its services. Social welfare agencies, staffed by social workers, often referred to beneficiaries as clients; Ball preferred that his agency treat the public less as clients and more as customers. In language that came naturally to the son of a social gospel minister, Ball noted that field personnel determined the public's opinion of the program. "Yours then is a great responsibility and a great opportunity," he wrote, adding that the Social Security program would survive only as long "as we do the kind of a job that our visitors like and appreciate." He urged that, above all, field personnel be courteous, that they make people "feel at home." He recognized that America was a diverse country composed, in the contemporary cliché, "of immigrants from many lands." Heterogeneity complicated the task of being courteous by making it necessary for field personnel to realize that "each individual is just a little different from any other and some are a whole lot different."[49]

Read today, the statement, although inspiring, has a slightly condescending tone. Presumably someone such as Wilbur Cohen, the son of an immigrant, or others working for the agency whose parents spoke with a thick foreign accent would not need to be reminded that not everyone was alike, particularly by a Yankee like Ball. At the same time, the statement caught the program's aspiration to be a permanent fixture of American life, not a form of emergency relief, that people would approach without a sense of stigma. Benefits that people received as a matter of right, rather than need, were to be delivered by an agency that treated people in a fundamentally courteous way.

Robert Ball spent most of the war years in the training office before returning to the Analysis Division at the very end of the war in February 1945. In his new job, he reported to Alvin David, who was the chief of the Program Planning Section. Ball's specific assignment consisted of analyzing the problems involved in extending Social Security coverage to those excluded from it—farmers, farm workers, the urban self-employed, and household workers. Working with a small staff of four professional and three clerical employees, he prepared reports that detailed how many people fell into the various categories, what sorts of economic problems they faced, how they felt about the Social Security program, and how they might make contributions to and receive benefits from the program.[50]

Despite the apparently academic nature of the work, the job involved Ball in matters that were vital to the Social Security program in the 1940s. The program faced two major problems: it paid low benefits that in many states were smaller than the ones an elderly person could get by going on welfare, and it excluded many people from coverage. Taken together, the problems created a sense of congressional indifference toward the program. In some congressional districts, for example, most of the people worked on farms or ran small stores that sold agricultural supplies and implements. Since such districts contained nearly no one who was on Social Security or who expected to get Social Security, the congressmen who represented them held no stake in the program's improvement. Although they might be persuaded to vote for an increase in federal funds for welfare, it was difficult to get them to accept a rise in Social Security benefits or an expansion of Social Security to cover disability or health insurance. Because enough congressmen shared these views, the Social Security program remained frozen in place throughout the 1940s. Congress created a new set of benefits in 1939, including higher benefits for married couples than for single individuals and benefits for a worker's survivors, and then gave the program little further thought. As prices rose, Social Security benefits became increasingly inadequate, yet congressmen who wanted to help the elderly contemplated increases in welfare, not Social Security. As the disparity between welfare and Social Security grew, so did the indifference toward Social Security. Arthur Altmeyer and the other program leaders realized that breaking through this cycle of indifference meant expanding Social Security coverage and raising benefits. Ball, as the main analyst on the expansion of coverage, thus occupied a key position within the organization.[51]

He was still something of a mole buried within the organization, a technical person, rather than a "face" person who spoke
for the program in Washington. Within the organization, however, he came to be known as the person who had the data on
coverage problems and who could formulate the best arguments
in favor of expanding coverage. Alvin David, Arthur Altmeyer,
and Wilbur Cohen all conferred with Robert Ball frequently, particularly during periods of congressional inquiry into the Social
Security program. The Ways and Means Committee, for example, conducted a full-scale investigation of Social Security in 1945
and 1946, under the direction of Leonard Calhoun, who had once
been a lawyer for the Social Security Board but who had come
to take a conservative position on the program. That meant he
wanted the program to pay only a flat benefit, rather than one
that varied by a person's contributions to the program. His report, however, considered a wide range of issues. On the question of coverage, Calhoun worked closely with David and Ball.
In the final report, issued in 1946, Calhoun called the extension of
coverage "by far the most pressing" issue in Social Security and
suggested that coverage be broadened.[52]

In broad outline, the coverage problem concerned the self-
employed. These included people who farmed the land, ran a
small shop, or performed a professional service. Those on a payroll, whether they worked on the shop floor or in the executive
suite, made contributions to the Social Security program and
could expect to receive benefits from it when they died or retired.
The self-employed, some of whom were very poor, neither contributed to the program nor benefited from it.

When the Social Security Act was passed, Congress cited
administrative difficulties as a reason for excluding the self-
employed. Most of the self-employed paid no income taxes, and
that made it more difficult to collect money from them. Some
people wondered if farmers even had the accounting expertise
necessary to determine their incomes and hence calculate their
Social Security contributions, since the conventional wisdom
held that they kept poor records.

At first, none of that mattered, but the situation soon changed.
Since benefits were not to be paid to anyone until 1942, there was
little clamor on the part of the excluded group to be covered.
Over time, however, coverage exclusions became important to

the politics of Social Security and created administrative anomalies. After the federal government began to collect Social Security taxes in 1937, some people took short-term jobs in covered occupations, and then they returned to the farm and in most cases did not compile enough of a wage record to qualify for Social Security benefits. Others who owned their own businesses collected Social Security taxes from their employees but, because they were not themselves on the payroll, could not participate in the program.

Sorting through the problem of covering the self-employed required Social Security analysts to consider a series of complicated facts and trends. Soon after the Social Security program paid its first benefits in 1940, the war raised incomes and lowered income tax exemptions, with the result that many urban self-employed and some farmers began to pay income tax. Meanwhile, the number of people who owned farms declined, as farms became more mechanized and agricultural productivity increased. Farming, which had engaged 40 percent of the labor force in 1890, occupied only 18 percent of the labor force in 1940. Still, about 1.2 million farm operators under age 65 remained, and they faced difficult economic problems. Only about 5 percent of the farms had a gross value of products above $4,000 in 1940. Although the vast majority of independent farm operators were white, African Americans comprised over half of the nation's sharecroppers, a group in particular economic need. Farm operators and farm laborers, the Social Security Board argued, deserved Social Security protection; the administrative problems, which had delayed coverage, could be overcome.[53]

Ball differed with Cohen and Altmeyer on how to administer a program for household employees and farm workers, two of the key groups that agency officials hoped the Social Security program would reach. Cohen, who had studied European methods for administering social insurance programs, favored the use of a stamp book system in which employers purchased special stamps from the post office and pasted them in an employee's stamp book to reflect quarters worked and taxes paid. Other social insurance advocates, such as Edwin Witte of the University of Wisconsin and J. Douglas Brown of Princeton University, had at one time or another spoken in favor of the stamp book system. Almost alone among these Social Security advocates, Ball disliked the stamp book system. "I was concerned," he said, "about fraud and loss and trading in stamps and didn't really think that approach was going to be feasible in the United States." In time Ball won the argument, and the United States never adopted a stamp book system. Instead, the Social Security Administration, as the agency was called after 1946, developed a simple form that a housewife or someone in a similar situation who hired domestic workers or other "casual" labor could use to use to report Social Security contributions by those workers.[54]

In 1946, as Ball contemplated the demography of domestic and agricultural workers and worked on administrative problems related to their coverage, he was engaged in an academic exercise with little hope of immediate payoff. The argument over the stamp book system nonetheless came to assume a symbolic importance for Ball. It illustrated to him his willingness to disagree with Arthur Altmeyer over an issue, something that he thought made him different from Alvin David and even Wilbur Cohen. David tended to be intimidated by Altmeyer and never could quite get his thoughts together to argue against an Altmeyer position. Cohen was Altmeyer's direct subordinate and seldom disagreed with his boss. By way of contrast, Ball began to see himself not only as a loyal supporter of Social Security but also as an independent operator who had his own slant on social policy problems and who was not afraid to express views contrary to those of top management. For the first time, also, he came to regard himself as a major contributor to Social Security policy, even though he remained, at age 32, buried beneath three layers of bureaucracy—the commissioner's office, the bureau chief's office, and Alvin David's office within the bureau.

Independent Operator

Just as Robert Ball's career at the Social Security Administration was gaining momentum, he decided to leave. At the beginning of 1946, an offer came to be part of a project affiliated with the American Council on Education that evolved into something called the University-Government Center on Social Security. This center offered college professors, as well as state and federal officials, training sessions on Social Security in the hope of improving the way the subject was taught in colleges and the way the program was administered. Ball took on the role he had assumed in the training office, handling substantive Social Security issues and leading discussions on Social Security's place in American social policy. Often top federal officials, such as Arthur Altmeyer, participated in the center's work, such as by answering questions over dinner at a Chinese restaurant in Washington. Although Ball traveled to give seminars, the operation was housed in Washington, D.C., in the offices of the American Council on Education, located across from the White House on Jackson Square. It marked a change in Ball's center of gravity, from the Baltimore headquarters of the Social Security Administration to Washington. The family moved from Baltimore to a Washington suburb in 1946.

The University-Government Center was the handiwork of Karl de Schweinitz and his wife, Beth. Born in 1887, de Schweinitz decided not to follow the family trade of becoming a minister, and like Ball, his first job came as a newspaper reporter. He soon became absorbed in a career as a social worker, working for such private organizations as the Pennsylvania Tuberculosis Society, the Charity Organizing Society in New York, and the Family Service of Philadelphia. Always interested in writing, he published *The Art of Helping People out of Trouble* in 1924 in which he argued, in language that anticipated Ball's "Notes for Your Guidance," that every individual deserved kindness and respect, no matter the nature of his or her personality or behavior. In the 1930s, de Schweinitz served as the executive director of the Community Council of Philadelphia, an effort to bring together the city's social welfare resources at a time of great need. In 1936 he took an executive position with the state of Pennsylvania helping to direct the state's emergency relief efforts and set up its public assistance programs. In 1938 he settled into his role as director of the University of Pennsylvania's School of Social Work. Beth de Schweinitz was a psychiatric social worker who had been a representative in Boston of the Bureau of Public Assistance, the part of the Social Security Board that helped the states administer their welfare programs.

Trained as social workers, Karl and Beth were nonetheless vocal in their support of social insurance. Partly for that reason, Altmeyer asked Karl to survey the Social Security Board's training activities, and de Schweinitz moved to Washington in 1942 as a training consultant for the Social Security Board. There he met Ball. Not only did he and Ball click on a personal level, but the two couples quickly became friends.[55]

When de Schweinitz asked Ball to join him in his new venture, Ball hesitated only for a moment. "It was quite a step for me to leave government to become part of this very small enterprise, entirely dependent on Karl's ability to raise enough funds to keep us going," Ball noted, "but Doris and I didn't hem and haw about it very long because we were so fond of the de Schweinitz.' The idea of working with them was irresistible."[56]

At first glance it would appear out of character for civil servant Ball to chuck his promising Social Security career and go to work for an unproven venture that might well fail, as eventually, it did. It was, however, an era in which many key Social Security officials took a break from the program. Ten months later, Wilbur Cohen accepted a temporary assignment as director of research for the president's Advisory Commission for Universal Training. Arthur Altmeyer took on various postwar tasks that removed him from the Washington scene. The arrival of the Republican-controlled Eightieth Congress in January 1947 and the uncertainty of President Truman's reelection created a sense of pessimism about the program; perhaps it would never break the barriers of coverage and benefit generosity that kept it from surpassing welfare as America's primary response to the insecurities of old age. In such an environment, Ball's decision to take a break from the program fit a more general pattern, yet it also reflected Ball's characteristic optimism not only that the unproven venture would succeed but also that the basic mission of training top staff and professors in the field was worthwhile. It underscored Ball's conviction that the much beleaguered Social Security program had a future.[57]

Although Altmeyer did try to keep Ball at the Social Security Administration, he had little to offer that Ball found tempting. He proposed to put Ball in charge of the Social Security Administration's entire training operation, not just the large one associated with the BOASI. Oscar Pogge, the BOASI bureau chief, suggested that Ball take over the New York Payment Center, a major cog in SSA's operation. Neither prospect appealed to Ball, who had little desire to go back into the field or to take a job removed from the policy action. Instead, he accepted de Schwei-nitz's irresistible offer.

Ball did his new job with his usual enthusiasm. His departure from Social Security proved in the end to be a good thing for his career, enabling him to jump over a long line of people with greater seniority and to emerge as a prominent Social Security bureaucrat. Even at the time, he enjoyed the work at the center, which was more informal and perhaps more rewarding than writing heavily edited and carefully reviewed pieces on cover-age extension for a small audience within the Bureau of Old-Age and Survivors Insurance. The work carried the added bonuses of close proximity to the circle of academics and administrators who shaped America's Social Security policy and the freedom for Ball to write his own scholarly pieces on Social Security for publication in specialized journals.

The most important contact Ball made at the University-Government Center was J. Douglas Brown, an expert in labor-management relations who worked at Princeton. By the time Ball came to know him in 1946, Brown already qualified as one of America's leading academic experts on Social Security. He owed his reputation to his experience. He had served in 1934 as a staff member of the Committee on Economic Security, spending part of each week in Washington working on the problems of old-age security. He devoted the rest of his time, as he had since 1926, to his job as the director of the Industrial Relations Section of Prince-ton University. Brown enjoyed a long career at Princeton, heading the Industrial Relations Section until 1955 and serving as dean of the faculty for a twenty-year term that ended in 1966. In 1937 and 1938, he chaired the Social Security Advisory Council that pro-duced the report providing the model for family benefits in the 1939 amendments. During the war he consulted on manpower issues for such wartime agencies as the Office of Production Management and the War Manpower Commission. Although he studied a wide range of labor-management issues in a manner similar to other academics with an interest in Social Security—most notably Wisconsin's Edwin Witte and Michigan's William Haber—Brown, as much as any academic, kept in touch with de-velopments in Social Security and continued to serve on advis-ory councils through the 1950s and 1960s.[58]

Ball felt a strong intellectual attraction to Brown. He credited

Brown with creating a philosophy for the Social Security program, one that emphasized how the program maintained an individual's freedom and dignity by giving a person benefits that grew out of earned rights. Brown himself made a career of speaking and writing on America's philosophy of social insurance, and Robert Ball became an avid collector of these writings. As often as Ball could, he later invited Brown to Social Security events and to Social Security staff meetings, where Brown was always received with considerable deference and warmth.[59]

In a typical talk, delivered in 1955, Brown called attention to five elements of an American philosophy of social insurance. First and foremost, the American system provided benefits "as a matter of right and not as a benevolence of a government, an institution, or an employer." Second, citizens were eligible for coverage "regardless of class or level of income and that, in principle, exceptions to coverage were to be made only for constitutional or administrative reasons." Third, individual workers established the level of their protection by their "individual contribution to our economy." Fourth, the system provided "protection of the family unit . . . against all the hazards which that unit might face." Fifth and most tentatively, the system relied on "joint contributions by both employer and employee." This element, along with the element of individual contributions, made it possible for social insurance systems to be "within the state but separate from the state."[60] Because of this curious quality and because of the way the system preserved incentives and encouraged self-reliance, social insurance appealed, as Brown put it in another of his essays, "to a wide range of American people left cold by talk of relief. Despite all the talk, few wage-earners like to go on relief, far less rely upon it in advance."[61]

Hence Brown articulated an American philosophy of social insurance that drew a sharp distinction between social insurance and relief. He first did so well before the triumph of Social Security over welfare, during a time in which few members of Congress insisted on this distinction and when relief payments vastly overshadowed social insurance payments in America's social policy. Ball, for his part, accepted Brown's point of view and, like Brown, came to feel that means-tested assistance programs were a much less reliable vehicle for the expansion of America's welfare state than were social insurance programs.[62]

Ball's admiration of Brown went beyond an affinity for Brown's ideas. In Brown, the Princeton-educated economist, Ball, the Wesleyan-educated son of a Methodist minister, found someone of similar pedigree and similar temperament. Ball, a youngest child with an independent streak, had no true mentor; Douglas Brown came as close as anyone to being a mentor. Brown was sixteen years older than Ball, a comfortable distance from which Ball could admire him. He had skills that Ball greatly revered, in particular an ability to maintain cordial relations with nearly everyone with whom he worked. Ball described him as "a master negotiator, as well as an imaginative, principled and solid thinker," a clear picture of Ball's aspiration for himself. He was, in fact, nearly everything that Ball wanted to be; he was, in Ball's words, "completely devoted to the program and its principles" but someone who "never came across as a radical."[63]

In general, Robert Ball, a reserved and diffident man, bonded with J. Douglas Brown. "His basic philosophy became mine, and I tried to carry it a bit further," Ball said. When Brown died, Ball wrote Brown's family that "I have always thought of myself as something of a protégé of his. . . . He, more than anyone else, was responsible for the way my philosophy of the program developed. Both because of his clearly written books and essays and because of his leadership on one advisory council after another, he determined more than anyone else how a whole generation of us reasoned about the program."[64]

In his emulation of Brown, Ball used some of his free time at the center to write an article that articulated and extended Brown's ideas on social policy. He called the piece "Social Insurance and the Right to Assistance," and it became a centerpiece of nearly all his subsequent writings. Again and again, whether in a book about Social Security intended for general audiences or an advisory council report aimed at Social Security insiders, he returned to the social policy formulations of his 1947 article. Ball started with the notion that public assistance, or means-tested welfare, was becoming more of a right in American society. Furthermore, people who received welfare payments increasingly enjoyed the freedom to spend them as they chose. Still, he regarded public assistance as fundamentally flawed. "Public assistance is winning acceptance as a legal right and moral right, but it is not and cannot be thought of an earned right. The basis for eligibility, the fundamental characteristic of the program, is not work or the payment of money contributions derived from work but is the negative fact of being without enough to live on," he wrote. Public assistance, with its means tests, divided the community into those able to support themselves and those dependent on government aid. Such a division led to "feelings of self-doubt and loss of social prestige for the one group and snobbery and prejudice for the other." In contrast to public assistance, social insurance preserved incentives to work and unified, rather than divided, the community. It was easier to administer "in a dignified not demeaning way." Social insurance represented a "contractual obligation"; public assistance came from a history of "repression and punishment." The inevitable conclusion was that, "From the standpoint of freedom, democratic values, and economic incentives, social insurance is greatly to be preferred whenever there is a choice."[65]

Advisory Council

Two months before the appearance of Ball's article in September 1947 the Senate passed a resolution that authorized the Committee on Finance to investigate Old-Age and Survivors Insurance "and all other aspects of the existing social security program" by appointing an advisory council.[66] The politics behind this resolution had to do with the efforts of Senate Republicans, led by Arthur Vandenberg of Michigan, to freeze the Social Security tax rate. As passed in 1935 and amended in 1939, the Social Security law called for scheduled tax increases at regular intervals. As the time for each tax increase approached, however, Congress responded by freezing the tax rate at its present level. In return for supporting this freeze in 1947, the Social Security Administration made a deal with Senator Vandenberg that included the creation of an advisory council. Previous experience with the 1938 advisory council had convinced Arthur Altmeyer and his associates that such an approach represented the best possible way to expand the Social Security program in an unpromising time. "We expect to make some progress through this Council," Wilbur Cohen wrote to Wisconsin professor Edwin Witte in the fall of 1947.[67]

Senator Eugene Millikin, a Republican from Colorado and the head of the Finance Committee during the Eightieth Congress, appointed the members of the advisory council, no doubt with the requisite amount of political consultation with interested groups and advice from the Social Security Administration. "You will, I think, find the Council is broadly representative, and one from which we may confidently expect real assistance," wrote Millikin to Altmeyer at the end of September. In reply, Altmeyer called the group "splendid" and offered "to cooperate in every way with the Advisory Council."[68]

The advisory council's membership reflected the notion, inherited from the Progressive era and from European social insurance programs, that there should be a tripartite division between labor, management, and the general public. In fact, however, the complexity of the American economy made it hard to select truly representative members of each group. Instead the senator chose individuals who had been active in Social Security policy, as well as people who represented groups that were likely to be affected by the council's deliberations. Rather than picking any prominent businessman, or perhaps a businessman from Senator Millikin's home state, the senator chose Marion Folsom of Eastman Kodak. Folsom had worked on Social Security issues within business organizations such as the National Association of Manufacturers and had already served on advisory councils that met in 1934 and 1938. In this sense, Social Security politics trumped conventional electoral politics.

Even the choice of Folsom, who worked for a company that offered many innovative social welfare benefits, needed to be balanced with the appointment of someone from the insurance industry. Unlike manufacturing companies, such as Folsom's, that consumed social welfare services, the insurance industry delivered such services. Decisions about Social Security conditioned the market for insurance. Survivors benefits, for example, were forms of life insurance, a principal product of the insurance industry; public retirement pensions had an important effect on private pensions. It therefore made sense for Millikin to select M. Albert Linton, an actuary and president of the Provident Mutual Insurance Company. Like Folsom, Linton had served on previous advisory councils and acquired a reputation as an expert on Social Security within his industry. In general, he saw his mission as expanding Social Security but at a low benefit level and thus preserving maximum flexibility for the private insurance industry. As a cynical Edwin Witte put it, "With Mr. Linton on the [council] it is a safe guess that nothing will be recommended that even remotely would make social insurance a competitor with private life insurance."[69]

It was a conceit of the Social Security program that companies and workers jointly contributed. Hence even an advisory council picked by a Republican senator and destined to report to a Republican Congress required the active participation of organized labor. Here, as in the case of business, at least two interests needed to be accommodated. When Millikin consulted with James Brownlow of the American Federation of Labor's Social Security Committee, he was told, "Now, we have a man here that we want on and if you don't put him on, I'm going to raise plenty of hell." That man turned out to be Nelson Cruikshank, who directed the Social Security activities of the American Federation of Labor. Cruikshank, who had once been a Methodist minister, combined the fervor of the avid reformer with the competence, discretion, and patience of the Washington staff man. As Robert Ball noted, however, Cruikshank "was more than an ordinary staff person," since he enjoyed the complete confidence of the leaders of the AFL. Even Cruikshank, respected as he was, needed to be balanced by a representative of the CIO. Millikin chose Emil Rieve, the president of the Textile Workers' Union and a CIO vice-president.[70]

Representatives of the general public, an even more amorphous concept than either business or labor, held the balance of power on the advisory council. The largest single group consisted of academics. No fewer than six academics served on the council, including a Cornell dean with a special interest in agricultural administration, chosen because the council was expected to deal with the question of expanding coverage to farmers, and a distinguished woman scientist from Johns Hopkins with an interest in health care finance.

These members, concerned with a particular question, played a secondary role to the two economists who were the council's most influential members. Sumner Slichter, the Lamont University Professor at Harvard, assumed the role of chairman after Edward R. Stettinius, the former secretary of state and nominal chairman, indicated that he would not take a large part in the council's deliberations. J. Douglas Brown, Ball's role model and the second of the influential economists on the council, had chaired the 1938 advisory council and knew more about the Social Security program than any of the other participants. "A number of the other members have not had the close contact with the operation of the program that you have, and I know will look to you for help and guidance," Wilbur Cohen told Brown.[71]

The first stirring of activity took place on October 17, 1947, when Slichter, Brown, Folsom, and Linton met in New York to discuss how to proceed. A key question concerned who to appoint as staff director. Ball later said that Fedele Fauri of the Congressional Research Service (who later became dean of the University of Michigan's School of Social Work) would have liked to have become staff director. His expertise lent itself more readily to the study of public assistance than to Social Security, however, and everyone expected Social Security to dominate the council's deliberations. Slichter, the Harvard economist with a circle of Cambridge friends, thought in terms of hiring Charles Myers, a labor relations expert at MIT. Robert Ball's name surfaced as a possible member of the technical staff, working under Myers.[72]

Possibly because Myers indicated he was not interested or available, Ball became the staff director of the Advisory Council on Social Security. As he later recollected, "I was fairly obvious for the job. There weren't many real experts on [Social Security] that did not currently work for the government." That was key. Millikin wanted someone from outside of the Social Security Administration to direct the council's work. Ball enjoyed the confidence of Brown and Cruikshank, and technically he qualified as someone who did not work for the Social Security Administration. When Slichter, Brown, Cruikshank, and Folsom met again in November to talk about how to organize the council's work, Ball attended as well. The group formally decided to appoint Ball as staff director at that meeting. He took a quick five-month leave of absence from the American Council on Education, although he continued to draw a sixth of his salary from that organization and to lead seminars for it.[73]

If his later recollections are to be believed, Ball approached the job with a great deal of confidence. "I had come to think of myself as knowledgeable an expert on Old Age and Survivors Insurance as there was," he said. In his new job, with offices in the Library of Congress and a staff of five professional and five clerical workers, Ball regarded himself as an independent operator. "Being staff director of this Council was my first job truly on my own. I wasn't anybody's subordinate and I felt that the whole thing pretty much depended on me, as indeed it did," he said.[74]

In thinking about this stage of his career, which marked his emergence as a top-level bureaucrat, Ball stressed his lack of contact with Altmeyer, Cohen, and the others in the Social Security Administration. "I was fully aware of the issues in coverage and had strong positions of my own and really needed help only with the development of the latest factual information," he said. He received most of this information informally through Alvin David rather than going through channels. As David remembered it, Ball and his staff "didn't even ask for it. We offered. I spent many, many hours in the Committee offices working on these issues. There was a long, long period of time in which I commuted nearly every day to Washington." Hence Ball used his contact, Alvin David, to facilitate his own work. Each point that the council discussed featured what Ball tactfully called "differences of opinion" among the often strong-willed council members. To win the arguments, Ball had to be "persuasive on the merits," and no doubt he was.[75]

Without a doubt, the advisory council came at a crucial juncture in Social Security's history. As two recent analysts of the program rather dispassionately put it, "at the end of the 1940s the decade-long failure to adjust benefits was threatening to trivialize the Social Security program." Ball himself captured the dilemma in more dramatic terms. He said that many people complained that the program was doing too little, paying low benefits to too few people, and that perhaps it should be scrapped in favor of a system of flat benefits paid out of general revenues or an expanded public assistance program. "It was the advisory council of 1947–1948 and the amendments of 1950 that I think really settled the issue that we were going in this country in the direction of sticking with contributory social insurance as our major reliance. And we've never faltered from that path since that time."[76]

In essence, Robert Ball, aided by Douglas Brown and Nelson Cruikshank, convinced the advisory council to ratify the arguments that he had made in his article on the right to assistance. Four factors helped him in his efforts. First, the members of the council, whether liberal or conservative, businessman or labor union leader, tended to accept the basic design of the Social Security program and had no strong desire to replace it with a Townsend-style flat benefit (a flat grant for everyone over age 60) or some other social invention. When Townsend asked to appear before the council, the council flatly turned him down.[77] Second, despite Ball's insistence on his independence, the leaders of the Social Security Administration supported his efforts and had already done much of the research in support of the measures he favored. Third, Ball segmented the discussion so that it centered on relatively technical points rather than on the grand design of social policy. "The fact was," he noted, that "agreement was reached on many of the individual parts, and the principles to some extent emerged rather than agreement on principles and then statement of detailed proposals." In other words, Ball did not set off to get the council to ratify such statements as this one that appeared in the final report: "Our goal is, so far as possible, to prevent dependency through social insurance and thus greatly reduce the need for public assistance." Instead he immersed the council in the details of coverage and the benefit formula and only then asked members to accept the basic philosophy of social policy that he had held even before the council's deliberations began. It was a very effective approach that he would use repeatedly in Social Security councils over the course of his career.[78]

Fourth, Ball kept his priorities straight and never altered them. He knew that the main objective was to raise Social Security benefits and extend coverage, rather than, say, to create a general assistance welfare program, federalize unemployment insurance, or start a disability insurance proposal—all undertakings that the Social Security Administration advocated and the advisory council discussed and in two of the three cases recommended. Although his basic approach was pragmatic and flexible, he never lost sight of his basic objectives, and he was always more willing to sacrifice someone else's priorities rather than his own.

Ball's exercise in persuasion began on December 4, 1947, at the first formal meeting of the Advisory Council on Social Security. The group quickly decided that the people who had already met twice would serve as an interim committee (with the addition of labor union official Emil Rieve). In effect the group conceded that Linton, Folsom, Brown, Slichter, and Cruikshank would be the real leaders of the council. This interim committee would meet before each of the advisory council meetings, refine the agenda, and attempt to come to agreement on the major issues. In addition, the group decided to allow Ball and his staff to control the flow of information that it would receive. It discouraged formal testimony from outside groups. The significant exception to this rule concerned Arthur Altmeyer, who appeared at the first meeting, accompanied by no fewer than nine of his colleagues, and gave a presentation that lasted for nearly the entire day.[79]

Like Ball, Altmeyer knew he wanted to expand Social Security benefits and widen coverage. He understood, for example, the priority to cover farm and household employees "because they are relatively poor and need protection." He realized, as well as anyone, that the consumer price index had risen substantially, on the order of 60 to 65 percent, but that the basic Social Security benefit had risen only about 8 percent since 1939 or that average welfare benefits to the elderly had increased five times as much as average Social Security benefits in those same years. He believed strongly that the wage base should be raised. In 1939, when Social Security collected money on the first $3,000 of a worker's income, that wage base covered 97 percent of the workers in the program. By 1945, nearly 13 percent of covered wage earners had income in excess of $3,000. To remain viable, the wage base, Altmeyer believed, should be raised to $4,800.[80]

In his December 4 statement before the council, Altmeyer made the traditional case for Social Security. It began with the common assertion that most people were dependent upon their earnings and therefore "the focal point of our efforts should be to provide reasonable protection against interruption of income due to sickness, accidents, old age, death and unemployment. In other words, we should strive to devise a system which will spread income over periods of non-earning as well as over periods of earning." Altmeyer thought that a Social Security system properly expanded to pay higher benefits, reach more people, and cover more contingencies, such as disability, would be ideal for this purpose. He devoted much of his statement to the ways in which agricultural laborers, domestic servants, employees of nonprofit organizations, public employees, and the self-employed could be brought under Social Security protection as well as to the ways in which the Social Security benefit formula could be modified to raise average benefits. In effect, Altmeyer put on the table the Social Security Administration's wish list that it had been developing since 1939 and hoped for the best.[81]

The reaction was polite but somewhat hesitant. Council members worried that extending Social Security to all employment would be excessive and wondered about the retirement test, which required a person to stop working before receiving benefits. Was it unwise to discourage the elderly from working? The group also expressed somewhat similar reservations about disability insurance for fear it would be difficult to determine who was disabled and who might, with the proper encouragement, be persuaded to work. According to Ball, the Social Security official in charge of making plans for health insurance, I. S. Falk, who worked in the agency's research office (not to be confused with the BOASI's Analysis Division), "was controversial and the Council did not take well to him."[82]

Ball's reaction was to try to keep Altmeyer and the offending Falk out of sight and to limit the council's contact with the Social Security Administration. In fact, however, council members Cruikshank and Brown had their own private conduits to the SSA and continued to correspond with Cohen, who in turn communicated everything to Altmeyer, throughout the council's proceedings. Also, Ball relied on Robert J. Myers, the Social Security actuary, to make estimates of all of the council's proposals, thus creating another link back to the agency.

And even as he cut the council's formal ties to the agency, Ball wasted no time in getting the council to consider Altmeyer's suggestions. As early as December 20, 1947, the interim committee received tentative proposals on coverage and benefits. These were prepared by Ball and his small staff, who quickly made Slichter and the others dependent on their competent staff work. Slichter, who, after all, traveled back and forth to Washington with little time to do background research on the issues, could not be expected to write a position paper on each of the items on the council's agenda. When he did venture an opinion in an off-the-cuff manner, he often inadvertently created conflict. During a meeting of the organizing committee, for example, Slichter suggested that doctors ought to be government employees, similar to teachers, and that the country should have a national health service, rather than national health insurance. Needless to say, Linton and Folsom took offense at that remark, and health insurance never made it to the council's agenda. Slichter quickly learned to leave the presentation of issues to Ball, who could be expected to prepare a rational brief, complete with pros and cons on the issue, and to present that brief in a lucid manner that anticipated possible objections.[83]

Early in 1948, the full council began a formal debate on key matters related to Social Security: coverage of workers in nonprofit institutions, the level of the wage base, the terms of the benefit formula, the appropriate level of minimum and maximum benefits, the amount of money a Social Security beneficiary could earn before he or she lost those benefits, and the appropriate age for women to receive benefits. Already, then, the council was immersed in the details of the Social Security program rather than engaging in a broad-scale philosophical debate on social policy. Few people stopped to think about whether social benefits should be linked to private employment; no one argued that benefits were universal rights that should not be tied to working. No one anticipated the subsequent dilemmas of people who lacked a firm purchase on the labor market, for whom Social Security, whatever the size of its benefits and the universality of its coverage, was irrelevant. Race, as a significant variable, except to the extent that people realized that coverage of farm and domestic workers would affect African Americans, remained outside of the scope of discussion. Gender, another of the concerns that would later influence social policy discussions, did appear on the table but in a way that highlighted differences in the labor force participation patterns of men and women. The basic argument was that women retired earlier than men and that wives tended to be younger than their husbands. Bowing to that trend and not expecting it to change, Ball echoed the recommendation of the Social Security Administration that the retirement age for women, as well as the age at which a woman could qualify for a wife's benefit, be lowered from 65 to 60 years. Special treatment of women, rather than equality for women, was the order of the day.[84]

Although Ball did his best to lead the advisory council without appearing to dictate to it, he soon learned that the council members were indeed strong-willed and often contrary. Major issues related to the expansion of Social Security coverage could pass by without much comment, but then something unanticipated might arise, such as whether extending Social Security coverage to nonprofit organizations, such as the Catholic Church, might challenge their tax-exempt status and weaken the division between church and state. The alliances that formed over this issue were based not on the labor-management-public distinction but on religion. Mary Donlon, who ran New York State's workers' compensation program, joined with Malcolm Bryan, a banker from Georgia, on this matter.

Other divisions were more predictable, such as Albert Linton's objections to raising the wage base above $3,000 for fear of decreasing the size of the private insurance market or his objections to disability insurance on the grounds that the government would find disability to be an uninsurable risk. Disability insurance proved one of the more contentious items on the council's agenda. The final report on this subject contained a brief dissenting statement from Linton and Folsom, identified only as two members. Written mainly by Linton, the statement noted their preference for a public assistance program, rather than a social insurance program, to cover the risk of disability.[85]

Ball realized that, with the exception of the wage base, these were relatively minor matters in the sense that they did not constitute legislative priorities. The important things were to get more people into the Social Security program and to raise benefits above those offered by the public assistance program. Toward this end Ball proposed, on his own motion, a technical change in the benefit formula related to a feature known as "the increment" that had significant consequences. This technical change supplied the glue that held together the council's recommendations and made them viable.

The Social Security benefit formula, stripped of its computational complexity, related people's benefits to their average earnings during their working lifetimes. Ball and Altmeyer favored increasing this benefit level, which meant giving retirees, dependents, and survivors a higher percentage of a worker's average earnings. That necessarily raised costs, however, and led to the prospect of higher tax rates in the future. In looking for a way to raise benefits now and not increase long-range costs or taxes, Ball seized on what was called "the increment." This part of the bene-fit formula called for paying higher benefits to those who had participated longer in the program. For every year a person paid Social Security taxes, his benefit was raised one percent.

The "increment" became an object of discussion in the advisory council. At first the council thought in terms of doing away with the increment for people who started to pay Social Security taxes after 1949. That would include younger workers as well as work-ers in occupations previously not covered by Social Security. At the February 1948 meeting of the interim committee Ball made the case for doing away with the increment altogether. As always, he had a compelling rationale. The present system, he maintained, postponed the full rate of benefits for more than forty years. He wanted to pay what he called "adequate" benefits immediately, even to people in newly covered occupations who would not have much time to make contributions before retirement. By dropping the increment and decreasing long-range costs, the system, he felt, could afford such benefits. After a lengthy discus-sion, his view prevailed. As he later put it, his suggestion "made it possible to get agreement between labor, the public members and business representatives;" it was "really the key proposal in this Council's report and what made the whole thing possible."[86]

Ball did not pluck the idea of dropping the increment from the air. He seldom made things up on the spot. Preparation and a sense of strategy were his long suits. In Altmeyer's briefing pa-pers for the advisory council was the suggestion, perhaps ad-vanced by Alvin David, that "because benefits are so low it might be reasonable to raise the level of benefits to the amount previ-ously anticipated for the mature program" by dropping the in-crement. Altmeyer pointedly objected to the idea, however, and did not propose it to the council. When he read a draft of Ball's re-port, he said that he was satisfied with it but that the suggestion to drop the increment rankled him. In a letter that Cohen helped him prepare, he said that the "recognition given to individual eq-uity through the increment is relatively small in any one year." It was, nonetheless, "of great importance psychologically." A worker expected his benefits to rise as the number of years over which he made contributions rose. Altmeyer conceded that it was "desirable to make considerable concession to the social principle of paying adequate benefits," yet it was also important "to assure those who are regularly employed over many years that their contributions buy more protection as time goes on."[87] In the face of this criticism, Ball remained unflappable. He informed the council in March that the Social Security Administration naturally preferred its own suggestions, but they did "not take strong exception to any of the Council's proposals nor do they regard any of the proposals as unworkable."[88]

Ball's suggestion to eliminate the increment had a galvanizing effect on Social Security policy by dramatically raising benefit levels. In making this suggestion, Ball relied on his political instincts and on his strategic sense of what needed to be done. A less adroit staff director might have allowed the council to degenerate into a fight over basic benefit levels.

As it was, Ball managed to get important recommendations through the council with a minimum of friction. These included suggestions that the self-employed, farm workers, household workers, nonprofit workers (except for clergymen), federal civilian employees, railroad employees, members of the armed forces, employees of state and local governments (on a voluntary basis), and people living in the U.S. island possessions all be brought into the program under amended entry conditions that allowed them to qualify for benefits relatively quickly. Hence, a middle-aged person might qualify for benefits, even though he had not paid Social Security taxes as a youth. The recommendations featured a benefit formula that paid 50 percent of the first $75 of the average monthly wage and nearly doubled the level of average payments. The recommendations also contained what in retrospect was a remarkable statement that eventually the federal government should pay a third of the cost of the program through general revenues, rather than relying exclusively on payroll taxes.[89]

In this manner, Ball cast himself as an outsider whose identity as an advisory council staffer superceded his previous identity as a career SSA employee. In general, despite his own memory of making a misstep when it came time to present the report, he proved exceptionally astute in the report's dissemination. In later years he honed an anecdote, told in a self-deprecating but endearing manner, that centered on his presentation of the report to the Senate Finance Committee. He allowed plenty of time, or so he thought, to get from his office on the top floor of the Library of Congress to that of the Senate Finance Committee. Only it happened that the elevator was out of order, and he had to take the steps. He raced the few blocks to the briefing, and for a brief moment he was out of control, perspiring and breathing hard. Worse, the senators, notoriously late and often absent, were on this occasion comfortably early, and all sat waiting for him. It made a deep impression on Ball, who over the course of his career forged an impeccable set of relationships with members of Congress.[90] Even in this case, his small human error failed to erase the impression he gave of extreme competence.

In presenting the advisory council's report on Old-Age and Survivors Insurance, he did nearly everything else right. First, with the help of Sumner Slichter, he tied together the report's twenty-two recommendations with stirring rhetoric that gave the report an overarching theme. Reports on Social Security, like the law itself, were notoriously detailed, technical, and dull. Ball's report made the point, the same one he had made in his earlier essay, that social insurance was superior to public assistance: "The more progressive the economy, the greater is the need for protection against economic hazards. This protection should be made available on terms which reinforce the interest of the individual in helping himself. A properly designed social security system will reinforce the drive of the individual toward greater production and greater efficiency and will make for an environment conducive to the maximum of economic progress." Contributory social insurance was an earned right that provided a worker with the "best guarantee that he will receive the benefits promised and that they will not be conditioned on his accepting either scrutiny of his personal affairs or restrictions from which others are free." If the recommendations were followed, then public assistance would be necessary only for those aged persons and survivors "with unusual needs and for the few who, for one reason or another, have been unable to earn insurance through work." Expansion of Social Security was necessary, as Ball put it in a nice epigrammatic phrase, because, "the character of one's occupation should not force one to rely for basic protection on public assistance rather than insurance."[91]

Second, Ball worked hard to communicate the basic message of the report and its specific recommendations not only through the text of the report itself but also through special materials distributed to the press that summarized the report and encapsulated its basic lessons. Using a technique that he would later apply in his major book about Social Security, Ball issued a series of questions and answers that explained the reasoning behind the report's recommendations. The presentation showed the subtlety in his thinking. Instead, for example, of asking why the council decided to recommend a rise in the wage base, he asked why the council proposed a rise of only 40 percent, compared with a 60 percent rise in the cost of living since 1939. The answer, perhaps deliberately, was less than convincing, involving an argument that the council members expected the cost of living to fall, just as it had after the inflation of 1919 following World War I. In a similar manner, the recommended level of benefits was called into question not for being much larger than existing benefits but rather for being perceived as "inadequate," leading to the pious response that "social insurance should provide basic protection" but not "relieve individuals of responsibility for providing at least a portion of their own security against old age and death."[92] In this way, Robert Ball proved himself a master of spin.

Third, Ball made astute decisions about which parts of the report to release at which time. The advisory council issued a series of reports rather than one large report. Ball separated the recommendations on expanding Social Security benefits and raising benefits, which he considered essential, from more contentious and less essential recommendations. He sent the "Report on Old-Age and Survivors to the Senate Finance Committee" first and only then followed it with separate reports on disability insurance, public assistance, and unemployment compensation. He did not want to step on his message that the first thing to do was improve Social Security and then, if that were done successfully, create disability insurance. He realized that creating a general assistance category or making federally assisted welfare available to any needy person, which was the council's major recommendation on welfare, would be difficult to accomplish, and he did not want to expend too much political capital on it. As Wilbur Mills and Sam Rayburn (D–Texas), both influential congressmen, told Arthur Altmeyer, they objected to general assistance because its passage would expose them to the charge that they were opening a Pandora's box, in Mills's words, "a vast system of home relief, a WPA for the Truman depression." In unemployment compensation, Ball failed even to get through the advisory council the major liberal recommendation, which was to make unemployment compensation a federal rather than a federal-state program. He knew the area of unemployment compensation was a political snake pit.[93]

Early in 1949, Ball completed the final bit of work for the advisory council, transmitting the report on unemployment compensation. Only then did he issue bound copies that contained each of the advisory council's reports in a single volume. "It has been a most interesting and instructive experience for me to work with the Council," he told Slichter. He was "proud to be associated" with the reports.[94]

The Washington political community picked up on the report almost immediately. Nelson Cruikshank advised his superiors at the American Federation of Labor of his hope that the Senate would "use the recommendations of the Advisory Council as a basis for legislation." Wilbur Cohen agreed that the council's report was the starting point for legislation. More importantly, newly elected president Harry Truman urged Congress to amend the Social Security Act along the lines suggested by the advisory council. Within a few weeks, Congress received Social Security legislation that culminated in the passage of a major new Social Security law in August 1950.[95]

Conclusion

Robert Ball orchestrated the process of consultation and wrote much of the report that supplied the basis for the changes made in Social Security program by the 1950 amendments. In the process he earned considerable praise from the leaders of the Social Security Administration. He performed so well that he was able to leave his job with Karl de Schweinitz and take a job at the top ranks of the Social Security bureaucracy.

What he had done, in effect, was to analyze the problems with the Social Security program, suggest a pragmatic means of overcoming them, and sell his solution to a blue-ribbon advisory council. His suggestions, when legislated by Congress, pointed the way toward a major expansion of the American welfare state by creating conditions that made the expansion of the Social Security program feasible and politically desirable. After 1950, this program enjoyed a degree of acceptance granted to no other social welfare program in America's history. Ball's actions on the advisory council were, therefore, crucial to unlocking Social Security's potential. Having proven his ability, he would go on to become the program's chief administrator in its golden age.

2

Bureau Manager

During the 1950s, Robert Ball became one of the federal government's most successful bureau chiefs. He owed that success to the fact that he ran a popular program. Social Security appeared to many to be a positive force for the improvement of American life, rather than a negative source of aid for people who refused to help themselves. In this regard, it shared the upbeat characteristics of other social welfare programs that Congress held in high regard during this decade, such as the medical research and training programs run by the National Institutes of Health or the vocational rehabilitation program that enabled people with disabilities to lead productive lives.[1] Ball's success also stemmed from the image, widely held by policymakers in the 1950s and 1960s, of Social Security as a well-run program. If many people thought of the federal government as an indifferent substitute for the private sector in the performance of vital services such as delivering the mail, they saw in Social Security a program that was not only well administered but also stood on the cutting edge of technology. Here was a program run by a man who took advantage of the latest data-processing methods and who employed sophisticated management techniques. Ball took pains to make Social Security appear as business-like and efficient as possible.

That meshed nicely with his portrayal of the program as conservative in outlook and ideology: a complement to America's wage economy, rather than a brake upon it. Hence, a rapidly expanding cornerstone of the American welfare state nonetheless conformed to a conservative vision of the government's proper social welfare role in the 1950s.[2]

Both because of Ball's conscious efforts at image-building and the fortuitous economic circumstances of the relatively young Social Security program and a strong economy with rising wage rates, the Social Security program prospered during the decade. Beginning in 1950 and continuing in every election year after that, Congress expanded the program. This expansion took at least three distinct forms. Congress made more workers eligible for Social Security, raised benefit rates, and allowed the program to cover new risks, such as disability. As the responsibilities of the program grew, Congress and the Eisenhower administration allowed the size of the Social Security staff to expand.[3]

Since Ball was, in effect, Social Security's staff director, his prominence among federal bureaucrats increased as the 1950s progressed. In 1954 he received the first of three major awards, the Department of Health, Education, and Welfare's Distinguished Service Award, a form of recognition that gained in significance from the fact that it was a Republican administration that presented it to him. Four years later, Ball was selected as one of ten federal employees to receive the National Civil Service League's annual award. In 1961, at the end of the Republican era, he became a recipient of the Rockefeller Public Service Award from the trustees of Princeton University. The receipt of this award put him in the company of such bureaucrats as the director of the National Institute of Mental Health, the director of the National Park Service, and the deputy director of the National Aeronautics and Space Administration.[4]

In 1962 he gained a more enduring honor: President John Kennedy appointed him as commissioner of Social Security. Once installed in that position, Ball continued as commissioner for the next eleven years.

Throughout this entire period, which stretched from 1950 until 1973, he specialized in the politics, philosophy, and administration of the Old-Age, Survivors, Disability, and Hospital Insurance program. When he worked in the training office and served

as staff director of the advisory council, he had a thorough knowledge of and an interest in all of the programs contained within the
Social Security Act. Those included not only the traditional Social
Security program but also welfare and unemployment insurance
as well. In the 1950s, his concentration narrowed to the program
run by the Bureau of Old-Age and Survivors Insurance: the cash
benefit Social Security program. Unlike some of Washington's
other celebrated managers—Elliot Richardson, who headed three
very different executive departments, comes to mind—Ball dedicated his work in the 1950s to this one program. By the end of the
decade, his association with it was complete.

Returning to the Bureaucracy

When the work of the Advisory Council on Social Security was
finished at the beginning of 1949, Ball headed back to Karl de
Schweinitz's center at the American Council on Education and
resumed his career leading seminars on Social Security and writing on the topic. One of his pieces appeared in 1949 in the official
Social Security journal; this magazine usually published only the
work of Social Security staffers, but the editors apparently still
regarded Ball as the next thing to an SSA employee.

The article reflected on the insecurities that still pervaded the
program. The program's defenders knew that people who were
already old could not pay the full cost of their pensions, yet they
hesitated to raise the tax rates to cover those costs for fear of
alienating younger workers. In the article Ball argued that, rather
than having younger people pay the costs of older people's pensions as well as their own, they only be charged what he called
the "actuarial rate." When the income from this actuarial rate
and interest on the money in the trust fund were no longer sufficient to cover current payments, the government should begin
contributing to the program. At base, then, the article marked a
plea for general revenue financing. As always, Ball paid attention
to the psychological aspects of the funding question. The program needed a definite long-range financing plan because its absence created "a source of confusion and doubt about the program" and undermined public confidence.[5]

Nothing much came of the proposal; Congress never had the

same enthusiasm for general revenue financing as did program administrators, and economic growth in the 1950s lessened the problem's severity. Still, the fact that Ball offered commentary on such an important issue in the official agency journal demonstrated his post–advisory council stature in the field.

Although Ball enjoyed his work at the University-Government Center, he realized that Karl and Beth de Schweinitz faced insurmountable difficulties in keeping it funded. "This activity had kind of wound down," he noted. Ball did his part, helping Agnes Meyer, the wife of *Washington Post* publisher Eugene Meyer and mother of future *Post* publisher Katherine Graham, with an article about Social Security and, shortly thereafter, raising $10,000 from her. That money, according to Ball, allowed the de Schweinitzes, who eventually left for a position teaching social welfare policy at UCLA, to close up the center in an orderly way.[6]

Ball had no difficulty finding alternative work. Early in 1949 a vacancy developed in the Bureau of Old-Age and Survivors Insurance—the position of assistant director in charge of the Division of Program Analysis. This division had been run, indifferently, by Merrill Murray and Jacob Perlman in the 1940s, and now both were gone. The division occupied a place of strategic importance within the Social Security Administration in the sense that it set the philosophical tone for the program and prepared and perfected legislative proposals. In an agency in which much of the grunt work, such as keeping wage records, was done in Baltimore, the division had a definite Washington orientation. Although the position reported to BOASI director Oscar Pogge, Arthur Altmeyer, the Social Security commissioner, made the decision on who would fill it. Without so much as a formal job search, he chose Ball. In Ball's recollection he never even applied for the job; Altmeyer simply told him about it and offered it to him.[7] In November 1949, Ball wrote Karl de Schweinitz that he thought the job presented a "challenging opportunity, particularly in view of the strong and important legislative changes in the area of social security. It therefore involves a kind of responsibility that I have not had before and that I feel impelled to accept."[8]

The new job represented a substantial promotion from Ball's previous position at the Social Security Administration and brought him to real prominence within the agency. The quick promotion for the 32-year-old Ball did not go unnoticed among the others who saw themselves as agency leaders. In particular, Alvin David, Ball's friend and former supervisor in the division that Ball was now being asked to head, objected to Ball's selection over him, and others within the bureau tended to agree. David thought it awkward and demoralizing that he be expected to report to Ball. David's reaction surprised Ball, who realized that the dynamics of their working relationship had already changed. When Ball directed the staff of the advisory council, David, in point of fact, reported to him in the sense that he did the research that Ball used in the council's deliberations. In time a face-saving arrangement was worked out in which David became an assistant to BOASI Director Oscar Pogge. Nonetheless, it was clear that David had been lapped by Ball and that for the rest of his career he would be Ball's subordinate. It happened more or less amicably. Once they had settled into their respective jobs, David gradually came to accept Ball's superior role.[9]

Assistant Director

In 1950 Robert Ball moved his family, which after 1954 would include a daughter, Jacqueline, as well as his son, Jonathan, from Alexandria, Virginia, to a suburb of Baltimore and resumed his SSA career. As an assistant director of the BOASI in charge of the Division of Program Analysis, he supervised about two hundred employees. Most of these workers performed statistical, actuarial, or qualitative research, similar to what Ball had done when he investigated the logistics of coverage expansion in 1945. By the end of 1952, Ball made $10,800 at this job.[10]

When Ball arrived in the Division of Program Analysis, the Committee on Ways and Means had already completed its work on what became the 1950 amendments to the Social Security Act. Before he returned to the agency, Ball accompanied Sumner Slichter, the de facto chair of the Advisory Council on Social Security, during his Ways and Means testimony. Committee chair Robert "Muley" Doughton (D–North Carolina), who saw the proposed amendments as the handiwork of an advisory committee appointed by the Senate, treated Slichter curtly. Although Slichter had a low anger threshold and took exception to Doughton's tone, he proved quite competent in answering the congressman's questions, scoring points when asked if the higher Social Security benefits would undermine the incentive of workers to keep working and to save for their retirements. He pointed out that no one questioned the motivation of top corporate executives to work and save, and they were protected by much larger pension plans.[11]

Ball played no major role in the Senate's deliberations, beyond summarizing the advisory council report in executive sessions, or in the workings of the conference committee that reconciled the House and Senate versions and led to the final passage of the law in August. He arrived at SSA too late for that. But he did become involved in explaining the legislation's significance to the people at SSA who were expected to administer it.

Over the years, this role as the program's interpreter to the people who worked in the field and who were responsible for the program's daily operations became a central one for Ball. Much as his father would have done, he preached to the members of Social Security's workforce, trying to instill in them a sense of mission, hoping to get them to see past their mundane tasks toward the uplifting social goals that lay beyond them. Like the best evangelists, Ball also offered entertainment and emotional uplift. The entertainment took the form of the mild titillation that the audience received from listening to Ball's inside accounts of Washington politics. Although he was in no way flashy or cynical, he nonetheless performed the part of the worldly-wise, shrewd reporter from the cosmopolitan policy center speaking to those who worked in the hinterlands. The emotional uplift came from the way in which he made his audiences feel good about their work, even as he exhorted them to do better.

At the end of 1951, for example, he gave a series of speeches to people who ran Social Security field offices in which he reported on the program's development in the aftermath of the 1950 amendments. For Ball the key aspect of this amendment was Congress's willingness to expand coverage as suggested by the advisory council. He claimed, in fact, that the congressional committees wanted universal coverage under Social Security. The biggest remaining gap in coverage was farm operators, and according to Ball, that development awaited only the assent of the American Farm Bureau.

Although the picture on coverage was rosy, Ball worried about those already retired. Nine out of ten workers were earning retirement protection through Social Security, but fewer than half of those already retired received benefits. In other words, the program might be maturing too slowly, a fact that created pressure to "blanket in" those already old. But if Congress extended benefits to people who had not paid Social Security taxes, that action would undermine "the preservation of a genuine contributory program" and weaken "public understanding of the long-run principles of the program."[12] In this manner, Ball astutely highlighted the problem that would be at the center of Social Security politics for the next four years. Already the fact that older workers paid less for their benefits than did younger workers drew criticism from conservatives such as Senator Robert Taft (R–Ohio) and Congressman Carl Curtis (R–Nebraska), who charged that the program was not really insurance.

Another issue that troubled Ball concerned the need to raise the amount of a worker's salary on which he paid Social Security taxes, something known as the "taxable wage base." If workers paid Social Security taxes on the first $3,000 of their earnings, and most people earned at least $3,000, then most people would pay the same Social Security taxes and receive the same basic benefits (although, to add one layer of complexity, the benefits would differ according to the family structure of the recipients). As Ball explained, the worker who received $3,000 a year in 1939 now made $6,000, and "with such a trend, sooner or later most full-time workers would be getting the maximum amount."[13] If the program were allowed to "drift into one which pays nearly the same to all and that amount a low one in relation to prevailing wages, then the private plans covering organized industrial workers will be very important." Ball viewed such a development as "undesirable" and felt that "it would be much better to provide a major part of the retirement income of all workers from the public program."[14]

It was no wonder, then, that Ball believed that the primary challenge facing the program was one of "program interpretation, of developing public understanding." People needed to understand that a wage-related, contributory social insurance program was superior to other forms of social protection, such as a flat-benefit paid to all the elderly. Americans, according to Ball, "want the sense of paying their own way and the security that comes from this type of program."[15]

As Ball spoke to audiences of Social Security workers, he also undertook his own program of research, another of the interests he would sustain throughout his career. In the 1940s, while at the University-Government Center, Ball had attempted to write a book on Social Security. He soon got swept up in current events and put it aside; he did not yet feel comfortable enough posing as an independent expert to complete such a project, and he labored at writing, going through many drafts trying to get his ideas exactly right.[16] He felt much better about doing quasi-official government reports, which allowed him to use the material he had already studied and reported on for the advisory council. Accordingly, he accepted an assignment from the National Planning Association to write a study of pensions in the United States. It appeared in 1953 as a publication of the Joint Economic Committee.[17]

His report amounted to an update of his earlier advisory council report, with a greater emphasis on the proper relationship between public and private pensions. Where others might have focused on private pensions, obtained through collective bargaining, Ball put Social Security at the center of the analysis. Typically, Ball highlighted areas of agreement, rather than conflict, and these turned out to be the very points he had been making to Social Security workers in his speeches. He cited an emerging pattern in which those who could worked and those who retired received benefits from a "universally available system of publicly administered old-age and survivors insurance, contributory in nature and wage-related, plus supplementary retirement systems which take into account the protection by OASI insurance but give additional benefits." Mean-tested programs were a "less satisfactory" way of providing retired people with income, and Ball believed that there was "considerable agreement on the desirability of relating retirement pay to previous earnings and on the desirability of having the fundamental public program contributory." He added that "the drive to make universal the protection furnished through Government" was very strong.[18]

Not only did Ball make speeches and write reports; he also worked directly with Congress on Social Security legislation.

Here his duties overlapped with those of Wilbur Cohen, who operated directly out of Arthur Altmeyer's office and was regarded as the program's main congressional liaison. "Wilbur was in charge of legislation," Ball noted, "and you were also supposed to have clearance from the Bureau of the Budget."[19]

In the spring of 1952, Ball disregarded these procedural niceties because he realized that rising wage rates made it possible to raise Social Security benefits without a tax increase.[20] Ball knew that this would be irresistible to the members of Congress who were beginning to understand that present and future Social Security beneficiaries constituted an important constituency. On his own initiative, Ball sought out the clerk of the Ways and Means Committee and told him of the opportunity. On the one hand, this action fit his role as the head of the bureau's Division of Policy Analysis. He was simply pointing out an actuarial condition: the official assumption was that wages would remain constant; an increase in the wage level produced a surplus that Congress might wish to spend. On the other hand, his actions shaded into the realm of politics. They paved the way for a benefit increase, thus strengthening the Social Security program in the way that Ball and the other agency leaders desired (the surplus, after all, could have been spent on other projects such as blanketing in those without coverage) and doing so in a way that gave the lion's share of the credit to the Democratic majority during an election year.

At the time, Cohen was out of reach on a trip to South America, and few people expected action on Social Security. Congress was not in the habit of expanding Social Security benefits at regular intervals, having done little, for example, between 1939 and 1950. It fell to Ball to see that the 1950s would be different than the 1940s and to set in motion the events that led to the 12.5 percent benefit increase contained in the Social Security amendments of 1952. Although Cohen and the other agency leaders became involved in the process before it was completed on July 18, 1952, it nonetheless represented Ball's initiation into the congressional foundations of Social Security politics.[21]

In this era, few walls existed between congressional authorizing committees and the operating agencies of the executive branch. As Ball put it, "the committees looked to members of the Executive Branch to more or less staff them on the Social Security issue." Although the chief clerk of the House Committee on Ways and Means knew a great deal about Social Security, he had no staff to back him up. Hence, Social Security Administration personnel helped with such important matters as writing committee reports or explaining technical issues to conference committees. Ball became so intimately involved with the work of the congressional committees that at one point during a closed session of the Ways and Means Committee, Wilbur Mills asked who agreed on a point, and Ball joined the rest in raising his hand. "Not you. Committee members," said the somewhat irritated chairman.[22]

Acting Director

The election of 1952 threatened to interrupt a promising pattern of bureaucratic and congressional collaboration to expand the Social Security program. For the first time in Ball's career, Republicans won both the presidential and congressional elections. This victory produced a significant turnover among those who administered the program and those who made Social Security policy in Congress. Despite these threats to the established Social Security leadership and perhaps because of them, Robert Ball prospered in the Eisenhower era. By the time Eisenhower assumed the presidency, Ball had become the acting director of the Bureau of Old-Age and Survivors Insurance. Within a year he made himself indispensable to his new bosses in Baltimore and Washington.

Arthur Altmeyer chose Ball to head the bureau. He did so by adding a half sentence to Ball's job description, indicating that Ball should serve as the bureau's deputy director. Up until that time, there had been no deputy directory, and by selecting Ball, Altmeyer effectively moved him in front of the other assistant directors, all of whom outranked Ball in terms of seniority and experience. When Oscar Pogge retired as bureau chief at the end of 1952, Ball suddenly found himself the bureau's acting director.[23]

Although Oscar Pogge enjoyed civil service protection, he expected to be replaced by an Eisenhower appointee. At this point in his career, Pogge disliked confrontations and had no desire to be involved in a dispute with the new administration. None of the assistant directors, who regarded themselves as civil servants performing nonpolitical administrative functions, saw a reason to resign. Some of these individuals believed themselves better qualified to run the Bureau than Ball. Hugh McKenna, a Republican by political preference who had worked for Social Security since August 1936, served as a regional representative in New York, and headed Social Security's field operations since 1942, felt particularly aggrieved. "I was the youngest and certainly the least experienced in terms of running big organizations and my assumption of the top job was upsetting to these older, more experienced men," Ball recalled. Altmeyer, he believed, wanted "to have someone in this key job knowledgeable about and interested in the philosophy of the program and its legislative expansion, and none of the older, more experienced administrators in the Bureau fit that description."[24]

Oveta Culp Hobby, Nelson Rockefeller, and Roswell Perkins, Eisenhower administration appointees who ran the department that oversaw the Social Security Administration, replaced most of the program's topline administrators within a year of taking office. Arthur Altmeyer resigned as commissioner of Social Security. "I realized, of course, that with the change of administration my continuance as an official in a policy-making position was quite impossible," he later wrote. He submitted his resignation without hesitation, yet he resented the "natural suspicion and unwillingness of the incoming administration to rely upon the advice and judgment of any official identified with the New Deal, the Fair Deal and the 'welfare state.'" He found it particularly hard to work with Hobby, whom Eisenhower chose as federal security administrator and then, with the April 1953 creation of the Department of Health, Education, and Welfare (HEW), as that department's first secretary. Altmeyer believed that on the surface Hobby, a member of a Houston publishing family and the former head of the Women's Army Auxiliary Corps, possessed "glacial calmness, . . . objectivity, and decisiveness." Beneath this confident exterior, she was in fact "sensitive, shy, and uncertain."[25]

If Altmeyer left without a fight, others, such as Jane Hoey, who ran the public assistance programs, put up considerable resistance about losing their jobs. Hoey, a trained social worker, said that she did not regard being fired as a personal matter so much as an assault on the professionalism of the position itself. She worried that her job would be stripped of its professional and technical components and that she would be replaced by someone unfit to perform the necessary specialized tasks. In other words, Hoey feared that the Republicans might not respect the expertise, which she regarded as inherently apolitical, that sustained America's welfare state.[26] The Republicans, quite correctly, realized that an expansion of the welfare state was, by its very nature, political. It therefore seemed both logical and politically expedient to replace people such as Hoey or I. S. Falk, who had spent more than fifteen years crafting disability and health insurance plans for Congress to consider.

In the process of scraping away the political surfaces of Social Security, the Republicans needed to be careful not to rub out the agency's operating capacity. Gaining control of Social Security's future could not interrupt the process of sending checks to those already qualified to receive them. To run the program, therefore, the Republicans needed operational people such as Hugh McKenna. Robert Ball fell into a more tenuous position. He was necessary, perhaps, to maintain continuity with the old regime, but whether the Republicans wanted to keep him for the long term in such a visible position remained an open question.

In the short run, Robert Ball, more than any other Social Security official, gained from the change in administration. Wilbur Cohen, for example, survived the transition but only barely. Although he took over Falk's job as head of the Bureau of Research and Statistics, the administration never gave him much responsibility for the formulation of policy. His influence came from his behind-the-scenes manipulation of the Democrats in Congress and his work with an apparatus of Social Security supporters that had developed in the 1940s. Well before the end of Eisenhower's first term, Cohen made plans to leave Social Security and take a job as a professor at the University of Michigan.[27] For Ball, the Eisenhower administration represented a different sort of trial. In 1953, Hobby and the other department leaders auditioned Ball for the part of Social Security's chief operating officer, although, even after he passed the test, his formal title never matched his responsibilities. In particular, they dispatched him to testify before Congress as the administration's chief witness at an important hearing, and they put him in charge of a key group advising Secretary Hobby on Social Security.

The "Hobby lobby," as the group advising her came to be known, reflected the secretary's uncertain attitude toward Social Security. The secretary felt she needed to choose from a number of conflicting approaches, and she appointed a group of consultants to advise her. The members of this group did not reflect the customary assortment of people representing labor, management, and the general public, such as in the 1938 and 1948 advisory councils that had been selected by congressional committees and the Social Security Administration. Hobby preferred an informal bunch of consultants over a formal advisory committee. Her list included three businessmen, a pension expert and Republican national committeeman from New Hampshire who had visited Eisenhower in Europe and urged him to enter New Hampshire's primary, and only one person whom Ball, Altmeyer, and Cohen considered sympathetic to their cause.

Even though this group contained M. Albert Linton, the actuary who had served on Ball's advisory council and who knew a great deal about the subject, Hobby realized that the effort required someone to serve as staff director. Altmeyer, who had not yet left the government when the Hobby lobby first met in March, suggested Ball.[28] The choice of Ball reflected Altmeyer's confidence in him. It was also, to some extent, a matter of necessity since Altmeyer realized that Cohen, the other logical choice, was too partisan a figure to work comfortably with Hobby's appointees or with others who might drop in on the proceedings, such as Congressman Curtis. Ball had experience staffing an advisory group picked by Republicans. He also enjoyed a comfortable working relationship with Marion Folsom, the Eastman Kodak executive and Social Security expert whom Eisenhower had named as undersecretary of the Treasury and who was expected to influence the administration's Social Security policy. "I suppose I seemed to Mrs. Hobby a logical selection for the staff director of this group of consultants she had gotten together," Ball said.[29]

The issue that the consultants faced involved economic, social, and political components. Conservatives, such as M. Albert Linton of the Provident Mutual Insurance Company, wanted to limit the size of Social Security benefits so as to create a broader market for private insurance. They realized that with so many people paying into the program and so few getting benefits the program was likely to generate surplus revenues from year to year. They feared that Congress would use these revenues to expand benefits without making proper arrangements to fund those benefits in the future. Hence, they believed that the program, as it was constituted, contained a built-in bias toward expansion and long-run insolvency that could only be remedied through higher payroll taxes or infusions of general revenue. The social cost of such a program was that many people remained without Social Security coverage because they had not had an opportunity, either because of their age or their occupation, to contribute to the program. Conservatives therefore proposed schemes with universal benefits financed in such a manner so as not to create a surplus in the trust fund. The most famous of these plans in 1953 was one approved by Linton and endorsed in a special referendum in November 1952 by the U.S. Chamber of Commerce. Liberals, meanwhile, objected to the way in which plans such as the Chamber of Commerce proposal awarded benefits to people who had not paid for them, severing the link between contributions and benefits and encouraging flat benefits. They worried that flat benefits would also be small benefits and that Social Security would become irrelevant to the nation's retirement policy.[30]

The Republicans looked with suspicion on the liberals, even though the liberals appeared to be making the conservative point that people should pay for their benefits. Ball blamed this feeling on the fact that they had been out of office so long "that they came in with a great feeling of suspicion about existing programs . . . and also a great suspicion of the bureaucracy . . . that most of the people at the higher levels of the civil service at least were probably loyal to the previous administrations as individuals."[31] The liberals doubted the sincerity of the conservatives, even though the conservatives appeared to favor the liberal objective of expanding the program so that it reached more people. Boiled down to its political, rather than ideological, essence, the conflict involved the Republican feeling that Democrats used conservative means to obtain the liberal end of larger benefits and the Democratic sentiment that Republicans employed liberal means toward the conservative end of smaller benefits.

It was, at the very least, a confusing situation, and it was not surprising that Oveta Culp Hobby felt she needed someone to guide her through it. Ball worked hard to win her confidence, although he admitted that this confidence "did not come easily at first."[32] It did not help matters that Cohen and his allies outside of the government worked hard to subvert the Hobby lobby by calling attention to its conservative majority. Ball noted that the selection of the Hobby lobby generated a "quick, negative reaction" because it contained no representatives of labor unions or farmers. Cued by Cohen, the labor unions and other liberal groups objected and succeeded in forcing Hobby to expand the group to include representatives of the American Federation of Labor and the Congress of Industrial Organizations, as well as others sympathetic to the existing program, such as the director of the American Public Welfare Association.[33]

If this move exacerbated tensions between the Democratic holdovers and Hobby, it nonetheless made Ball's job easier as the staff director of the Hobby lobby, known formally as the "consultants on social security." The augmented group that met in April 1953 resembled the advisory council that had assembled late in 1947, although without a Douglas Brown or Sumner Slichter "public figure" to moderate debates. Ball followed his usual procedure of focusing on agreements, rather than disagreements, and came up with the fact that both the insurance executives such as Linton and the labor officials such as Nelson Cruikshank wanted to expand Social Security coverage. To be sure, they disagreed on what they meant by Social Security, but Ball chose not to emphasize that.

At the end of its deliberations, the group agreed to a report that fit nearly seamlessly into Ball's plans for the expansion of Social Security. In a plainly packaged document that lacked the rhetorical grace of Ball's earlier reports and made no mention of his participation, the consultants recommended that state and local government employees, self-employed professionals such as doctors, farm operators, and farm workers still excluded from coverage all be brought into the Social Security system.[34] The consultants endorsed the objectives of the program, which they understood to be the inclusion of all workers, the payment of benefits related to prior earnings as a matter of right, and contributory financing. To be sure, the report said nothing about the appropriate size of the benefits or payroll taxes or the wage base on which workers should pay taxes or whether to pay benefits to those already retired. "Most of the ideas that would have caused dissension were turned off and not taken up by the group," Ball noted. He added that by endorsing an extension of coverage, the group, "in effect, endorsed the principles and ideas of the Social Security program itself." All in all, it was an effective exercise in damage control.[35]

Ball's performance certainly impressed Eveline Burns, a Columbia University expert on Social Security and a Hobby lobby member. She described Ball's performance as "absolutely remarkable." She marveled at the way in which Ball got his points across but "never intruded himself" into the discussions. "Where Bob is so skillful is that, quietly and gently, and in connection with something else, he will bring out, without in any way involving a confrontation, what the true facts are—gently, sweetly, with his great depth of knowledge." Nor did the committee "resent what he did." Burns believed that, on the contrary, all the members of the Hobby lobby were impressed with Ball's "integrity, his knowledge of the act, his helpfulness, and his self-restraint."[36]

At the same time that Ball led the Hobby lobby through the logistics of Social Security expansion, he also prepared to deal with Congressman Curtis's investigation of the program, which culminated in formal hearings that took place in November 1953. Rather than send someone closely identified with the administration to the hearings, Secretary Hobby chose to send Ball. "Instead of supporting me," Ball noted, "she in effect told me to go on up and testify and she would sort of make up her mind about me depending on how I made out."[37]

The hearings led by Curtis differed in many respects from the usual proceedings of the Ways and Means Committee. For one thing, they marked the Republicans' debut as the congressional proprietors of Social Security. For another thing, they were the product of a subcommittee rather than the full committee at a time when the Ways and Means Committee had no permanent subcommittees. In addition, the subcommittee relied on a special staff recruited for the investigation, rather than on Social Security Administration or Library of Congress personnel. Karl Schlotterbeck, the staff director, was a noted critic of the Social Security program who favored a plan similar to the Chamber of Commerce proposal.[38] A chief counsel asked questions of witnesses, and the staff also included a group of conservative economists. In the hearings, Curtis sought to expose the inconsistencies and other flaws in the Social Security program in order to demonstrate that it was not a true insurance program and that its costs outweighed its benefits. Rather than mount a defense of the program, the administration chose to view the hearings as an inquiry into a program created by the Democrats. Departmental officials wanted to see what Curtis could dig up.

Ball testified for six days that stretched between November 12 and November 25. The occasion marked his first appearance as a principal congressional witness, another featured role he would play throughout his career. The same conciliatory, patient, helpful yet directive approach that served him so well in advisory councils also worked to his advantage during congressional testimony. During the Curtis hearings, Ball's objective was to keep the investigation as low-key and nonconfrontational as possible. "The strategy," he later noted, "was . . . to not escalate the hearing, . . . to keep it at a technical level, and to bore everybody to death." He tried to answer all questions, no matter how hostile, calmly and without a hint of flamboyance. "We made, I think, as good a defense of where the program stood as could be made without stirring up a big philosophical division and helping them get attention," he said.[39]

On his first day of testimony Robert Winn, the chief counsel, grilled him about people who received Social Security benefits even though they lived in foreign countries. He answered that the fact that people lived abroad would not prevent them from receiving benefits. At his next appearance, Winn made a concerted effort to make Ball look ridiculous:

MR. WINN: With respect to Section 210 (a) (15), which with certain
    exceptions within itself excludes from OASI coverage commercial
    fishermen and others of related occupations, is it a fact that when
    an employed officer or member of a crew engaged in commercial
    fishing on a vessel of less than 10 net tons in size is fishing for
    salmon and halibut, he is covered by the OASI program, whereas,
    under the same set of circumstances, if fishing for some other kind
    of fish he is not covered by the program?
MR. BALL: Yes; that is true Mr. Winn.[40]

During Ball's next appearance, Curtis read letters into the record that showed the arbitrary and seemingly cruel nature of Social Security benefits. One told the story of a woman who lived with her brother until he died. Although she had kept house for him for fourteen years and depended on his income, all she received upon his death was a lump sum death benefit in the amount of $255 that did not even cover funeral expenses. Asked to comment, Ball replied blandly, "That is correct, Mr. Chairman. There are no monthly benefits payable to brothers and sisters."[41]

Ball had a good ear for when he should say little and when he should give long, expansive answers. In contrast to his terse comment about benefits for brothers and sisters, he chose to answer at considerable length the counsel's question about whether the 1939 amendments cut benefits to single people:

> MR. BALL: As I suggested earlier, Mr. Winn, it really seems to me that it is more accurate to say that in place of one type of benefit there has been substituted another and that for the cutting down of benefits for a single retired worker, we have had substituted protection on a family basis for survivors and dependents. It is true that if you look at the group of single workers at the end of their lifetime, you can say that something has been taken away from a group. But I really think that the more realistic way to look at this is to look at individuals as they start out under the program. They do not know at that time whether what they need is survivorship protection or dependent's protection and they are paying for the risks of survivorship and dependent's protection as well as the retirement side. So I think it is a shift in the kind of protection that is provided, really, more than it is a cutting down of benefits for a group as it starts under the program.[42]

Ball described his experience with the Curtis committee as "exhausting," yet he thought his efforts were worthwhile because "the situation was pretty delicate."[43] Curtis proved not to be much of a threat to the program. Although he scored a publicity coup with his exposé of benefits paid to foreigners at the expense of American taxpayers, the press soon lost interest in the hearings. Through his undramatic, labored answers to questions, Ball gave the press little reason to attend. The proceedings soon degenerated into detailed explorations of the inner workings of the Social Security law.[44]

Even by the time Ball testified, it was apparent that Hobby and the other administration leaders, including newly appointed Social Security commissioner John Tramburg, would endorse the existing program.[45] Ball had won Hobby's confidence.

"We gradually got to know each other," he said, "and she began to get to know the organization."[46] The consultants' report, the fact that Curtis turned up nothing damning, and Ball's insistent argument that "social security was a very sensible program and a conservative way of going about the problem" all combined to make Hobby favorable toward the program.[47] By the end of the year, Hobby "was quite committed to the program and to me, although it was quite clear that she was not going to lead any crusade to expand its substance beyond the extension of coverage."[48]

By December 1953, the Republicans had not only endorsed the program but they had selected a new director of the Bureau of Old-Age and Survivors Insurance. During his year as acting director, Ball had not hesitated to "exercise the full authority of the Bureau Director," as he put it. Indeed, Ball tried hard to get the divisional directors to work with one another rather than to regard their divisions as "separate baronies," as they had become under the lax rule of Oscar Pogge. As one of Ball's friends in the organization wrote him, "you gave the impression of both knowing the job and liking it." "You are right about my enjoying the period as Acting Director," Ball replied.[49]

Deputy Director

Nothing much changed when Victor Christgau, a former Republican congressman from Minnesota, took over as BOASI director. Although he had the proper political credentials for the job, he also had a background as a manager of social programs. When he left Congress in 1933, he served as the Minnesota administrator for the programs created by the Agricultural Adjustment Act and later the Works Progress Administration. In 1939 he became the director of the state's unemployment compensation program. Ball and Cohen had helped to select him for the job, and they no doubt approved of the way in which Christgau began his tenure by noting his pleasure that the organization was "already staffed," and an "organizational pattern has been established." Even before he took the job, Christgau deferred to that staff and that pattern. He insisted, for example, that Ball remain at SSA as his deputy.[50]

Ball never made much of a secret that he, rather than Christgau, ran the bureau. Christgau deferred to Ball on administrative and program matters and seemed content to be a front man. "It's hard to convey, without seeming to denigrate Vic Christgau, the degree to which he was willing to delegate to me," Ball told an interviewer many years after the fact. "He used to just say, 'Well, I think whoever can do it best, ought to do it.' Then almost always it would be me that he thought could do it best."[51] "I think it was quite widely known throughout the Department and the Committees in Congress, as well as within the BOASI itself," Ball said on another occasion, "that I was actually, in most important respects, running the Bureau, although I was always careful to keep him out in front." In an unguarded moment, Ball wrote one of his correspondents during the 1980s that, after 1953, "I was the top administrator as well as frequently the top policymaker pretty much regardless of title."[52]

For their first legislative production, the new Republican team produced comprehensive Social Security legislation that passed in August 1954 and extended the pattern of election year amendments to the program. Ball participated in nearly all phases of this legislation, from the initial fall 1953 departmental meetings in what was called the chart room, established by the dyslexic Nelson Rockefeller, who preferred charts to long text documents, to the final summer 1954 deliberations of the conference committee. The aspect of the legislation on which Ball made the most difference was the extension of coverage to farm operators.

When Ball and Hobby first broached the matter of extending coverage to farmers and farm workers with Senator Eugene Millikin (R–Colorado), Millikin was very skeptical. He asked Elizabeth Springer, the chief clerk of the Finance Committee, how many letters the committee had received advocating the extension of coverage to farmers, and she produced only about seven letters. Ball realized that the American Farm Bureau, the largest and best funded of the farm organizations, opposed the measure. Although the Farmers Union favored the measure, it operated in only a few western states. Ball, who had studied coverage issues since 1945, saw the possibility of persuading the Grange to support Social Security coverage. When he had worked for Karl de Schweinitz, he had taken advantage of the proximity of his office to the Grange headquarters and talked a few times with the president of the Grange, whom he found to be mildly supportive. This contact proved helpful in 1954. The Senate, as Ball had thought it would, had passed the Social Security bill without including farmers; the House included a provision covering farmers in its bill. At a crucial moment during the meetings of the conference committee, Ball produced a telegram from the president of the Grange indicating he was in favor of the House version of the bill and presented it to Representative Wilbur Mills (D–Arkansas). Ball realized that "there was certainly no real ground-swell for coverage among farmers—at best there was indifference and on the part of the larger farmers, hostility."[53] Nonetheless, the measure passed. "It really is a miracle to get farm coverage. I am still amazed," wrote Arthur Altmeyer from his new home in Madison, Wisconsin.[54] On this issue, Ball made the key difference.

After the passage of the 1954 amendments, Ball made a series of speeches explaining their significance to Social Security officials. He was careful in these speeches to praise all of the people who had worked on the amendments, beginning with newly appointed Social Security commissioner Charles Schottland and BOASI bureau chief Christgau and including nearly all the divisions in the bureau. He also called attention to the fact that an expanding program meant an increase in the Social Security workforce. To implement the 1954 amendments, the bureau staff would expand by 3,900 people to reach a total of 17,900. As for the amendments themselves, Ball, with some exaggeration, called them the most significant changes in the program since 1939 and the introduction of family and survivors benefits. The amendments made coverage nearly universal, indirectly introduced the concept of disability to the program, increased benefit levels, made the relationship between contributions and benefits more direct, and raised the future tax rate from 6 to 8 percent. Most important of all, according to Ball, the amendments "were sponsored and enacted by the opposite political party than the one in power when the system was established."[55]

To be sure, the Republicans emphasized different features than the Democrats. For one thing, they pushed what Social Security officials called equity (making sure that people who paid more into the system received more for their money) rather than adequacy (guaranteeing a decent benefit to all participants regardless of their contributions). Although a strong advocate of the adequacy features, Ball understood the importance of relating benefits to contributions. As he told one of his audiences, "A contributory wage-related system can endure only if the contributors get treated fairly in relation to their contributions. The continual pushing up of the minimum and the first step in the formula is to transform the nature of the system and to try and make it do the work of public assistance."[56] For another thing, the Republicans gave higher priority to rehabilitating individuals and getting them back in the labor force rather than paying them retirement benefits. Roswell Perkins, the assistant secretary of HEW in charge of legislation, emerged as a particularly strong champion of this cause. It was he who acceded to the idea of allowing people with disabilities to receive retirement benefits at age 65, even if they had stopped paying Social Security taxes, because he thought that the act of certifying people with disabilities would provide a way of identifying candidates for rehabilitation.[57]

Neither of these Republican predilections differed in broad outline from the Democratic objectives of expanding the Social Security program, at least not in 1954. Robert Ball, as always, sought areas of agreement and lauded the 1954 amendments with real enthusiasm.

Despite his relative contentment over the development of the program, he nonetheless was attentive to other opportunities that came his way. At the end of September 1954, he learned that he had been suggested as a candidate for the director of social welfare in the state of California. He replied, "I am very much interested in the work that I am doing and am rather doubtful that I would want to leave it for this position. On the other hand, I have long had great interest in the total field of social welfare and am attracted by the possibility of broadening my experience." Submitting a detailed application, he learned in October that he was a finalist for the position. He then wrote to a wide range of his colleagues and supervisors inside and outside of government letting them know that the California authorities might contact them for a reference. "California would be very lucky to get you, but the nation would certainly suffer a heavy loss if you left your position," Loula Dunn, the director of the American Public Welfare Association, replied. After writing a letter of recommendation,

Douglas Brown told Ball that he did not want him to leave the federal government but, if he did, the California job was an attractive one. Brown believed, however, that the federal government would remain "the greater positive force in total welfare progress over against even the leading states." As he headed off for a November interview in California, Ball told Nelson Cruikshank that "the pros and cons of the job are very close in my mind at this time and I really don't know what I would do if it were finally offered to me."[58]

The interview apparently went well, and Ball received a call from a California representative asking if he would take the job if it were offered to him. Ball answered that he had decided to withdraw his name from consideration and to remain at his present job. He told Beth and Karl de Schweinitz, with whom he had stayed in Los Angeles, that the job "seemed much more attractive to me than it did to Beth—particularly the extra money—so that it was a harder choice than you might think." "There were many things about the job that were attractive," Ball wrote to Nelson Cruikshank in a candid letter, "definitely more salary, a new State to get acquainted with, perhaps a little more freedom in running one's own show and possibility of experience in a part of social security that I never worked in." In the end, he decided to stay because "there is so much going on and because I think this program is of such growing significance."[59]

Ball's decision not to pursue the California job meant that, unlike Wilbur Cohen and Arthur Altmeyer, he would remain at Social Security through the Eisenhower administration. Brown, for one, thought that Ball had made the right decision, "in the long run, conducive to your own basic satisfaction and of a most valuable career well fulfilled." Secretary Hobby, who had served as a reference, expressed her relief over Ball's decision, calling it her "good news for the day," a sentiment echoed by Under Secretary Nelson Rockefeller.[60]

By the time Hobby left the department in the summer of 1955, the result in part of the inept way in which she handled the distribution of the polio vaccine, she had become one of Ball's strong supporters. She made a point of writing him a thank-you note before she left Washington in which she mentioned her "increasing appreciation" of Ball's contributions to the Social Security program. Ball continued to correspond with her after she returned to

Houston and resumed her work at the *Houston Post*, although the relationship remained somewhat formal on both sides. They never addressed each other by their first names—it was always Mrs. Hobby and Mr. Ball.[61]

Things got even better and easier for Ball when Marion Folsom, his friend from the Advisory Council on Social Security, replaced Oveta Culp Hobby as secretary of HEW. From the start, Ball enjoyed a close working relationship with Folsom. Even before Folsom started the job, Ball offered to be of assistance. "Those of us who have had the opportunity of working with you in the past are looking forward particularly to working under your leadership here in the department," he wrote.[62] When Folsom became secretary, Ball noted his position was "pretty secure, although I am sure there were people at the White House level who would have been glad to get rid of me."[63]

The Folsom Era

Folsom's tenure at HEW coincided with a particularly difficult period in the relationship between the department and its largest operating agency. The issue was disability insurance. The Republicans, even those with big business connections who were generally sympathetic to the expansion of Social Security, opposed the payment of Social Security benefits to people forced to leave the labor force because of a physical or mental impairment that made it impossible for them to continue working. The holdover Democrats in the Social Security Administration, which is to say the people who ran the agency, favored disability insurance. In the 1954 amendments, administration officials believed they had made concessions to the Democrats and gone as far toward a disability insurance program as they wished to go. The Democrats, once again in control of Congress after the 1954 elections, saw disability insurance as a good issue to serve as a wedge between them and the Republicans. They believed that forcing the Republicans to vote against the measure would help the party in the 1956 presidential elections.[64]

In the long and convoluted fight that culminated in the passage of disability insurance late in July 1956, Ball attempted to get a reluctant Marion Folsom to support the measure. Never one to move too far ahead of business opinion, Folsom resisted. Ball believed, however, that Folsom favored a "modest type of disability program" and that Folsom tried without success to get the administration to support it. Ball also thought that Folsom was looking for a way in which he could leave room in his public pronouncements to support the measure in the future. As for Congress, the House supported the measure, and the Senate, or at least the Senate Finance Committee, opposed it. The House passed a version of the measure in 1955. When the Senate Committee on Finance took up Social Security legislation in 1956, it failed to include disability insurance in the bill it sent to the Senate. During the Senate hearings, Folsom testified against the bill, although Ball made every effort to soften the tone of the testimony and believed that Folsom wanted him to participate in the process for that very reason. "It was a matter of degree of opposition," Ball said. "I accepted the idea that the administration had decided to oppose it but I wanted to make the opposition more reasonable, I thought, and flexible." Ball and Assistant Secretary Roswell Perkins fought over every word of Folsom's testimony, "I arguing for the softer word and he for the harsher word each time."[65]

Having failed to get the administration to support disability insurance, Ball turned to the congressional Democrats and worked with them. He realized that Senator Robert Kerr (D–Oklahoma), a member of the Senate Committee of Finance and an important power broker within the Senate, held a key position in the debate. When Kerr asked for Ball's help to draft a disability insurance plan for Kerr, Folsom acquiesced. According to Ball, Folsom agreed to this request "on the theory that it was best for the country and for the program to have the best possible form of legislation, even if it was legislation that the administration opposed."[66] To help Kerr support the legislation, Ball came up with the idea that disability insurance should have its own separate trust fund. That way, if disability insurance turned out to be more expensive than anticipated—an argument that M. Albert Linton and other opponents of the measure stressed—its financial distress could not spread to the rest of the Social Security system and undermine the entire program. Kerr accepted Ball's proposal and worked closely with him on "the technical work of getting a program set up."[67]

Disability insurance passed as the result of an amendment to the bill offered by Senator Walter George (D–Georgia) on the floor of the Senate. On July 17, 1956, the Senate voted on this amendment and approved it by the extremely narrow vote of 47–45. One reason that the measure carried by what was in reality a one-vote margin (a tie would have meant that Vice President Nixon would have cast the decisive negative vote) was that six Republicans voted in favor of it. These included ultraconservative senators such as Joseph McCarthy (R–Wisconsin) and George Malone (R–Nevada), who wanted to force Nixon to vote on the measure as a way of weakening him in the 1956 election and embarrassing the administration.[68]

As a civil servant, Ball needed to act in as restrained a manner as possible throughout the debate over disability insurance. The fact that he assisted Kerr strained the bounds of his civil service position. Unlike Wilbur Cohen, who flew in from his job as a professor at the University of Michigan for the Senate vote, or Nelson Cruikshank of the AFL-CIO, who worked the corridors even as the final vote was proceeding, Ball could not lobby. Everything he did had to fit within the limits of technical assistance rather than political advice. He could offer advice on the best design of a disability insurance program but not on how best to frame the legislation so that a particular senator favored it, although the line between nonpartisan expertise and partisan politics was a very fine one. Ball had probably crossed the line when he changed the disability legislation to suit the predilections of Senator Kerr—that was pure politics with only the thinnest veneer of nonpartisan public administration. In the end, when the measure passed, Ball abandoned any pretense of neutrality. According to Nelson Cruikshank, "Ball and some of the others were literally dancing in the aisles and it didn't seem to bother them that Rod Perkins was looking down at them down the full length of his nose."[69]

In the period just before and after the passage of disability insurance, Ball moved with even more than his customary caution so as not to offend Folsom or the other administration officials. Just after the passage of disability insurance, he told the program's district managers that disability insurance was "born of controversy," and the bureau's administration of it "will be watched in a way that nothing else we have ever done has been watched." The legislation offered the Social Security Administration an easy out. Because of political pressures to make the measure as conservative as possible, it allowed the individual states, acting under contract to the federal government, to determine who qualified for disability benefits. No one in the Social Security Administration, and certainly not Ball, was a fan of this administrative feature, which SSA officials believed would lead to inconsistencies from place to place, errors in making decisions, and backlogs in processing cases. It was tempting to let the states try and fail at this complex administrative task. Ball warned agency workers not to think that way. "Even though we will contract out with State agencies for making the determination of disability, there is no way we can contract out the responsibility of being satisfied with the job that is done. The successes and failures of this part of the program, as in all parts of OASI, will be *our* successes and *our* failures," he said.[70]

Even though the agency and not the administration had won on disability insurance, Ball felt it very important that the agency do nothing to show up the administration. In this period, Ball went out of his way to emphasize the compatibility of the program with basic Republican precepts. He told the district managers that a job was better than a disability benefit, even an earned benefit. Ball implied that Social Security was not the answer to every social problem. "For the million or so children receiving assistance because of the absence of the father social insurance is not the answer," he said. Nor was Social Security to be regarded as a substitute for private pensions and individual savings, even though Ball had strongly favored the expansion of Social Security over private pensions and had expressed that view in his 1953 report. Different circumstances required different emphases. Now Ball echoed the official line that Social Security should "serve as the base on which the individual builds for himself an income which can be used to support the good life." Ball even hinted that maybe the Congress (read as the Democrats) should not have so much power over the program. Perhaps benefits should not rise by congressional fiat, but instead "the concept of a variable annuity" should be built into law itself.[71]

Ball assured his Republican supervisors that the program was entering a new era of stability. Between 1950 and 1958, the Bureau of Old-Age and Survivors Insurance had more than doubled in size, going from 11,000 to 22,500 employees. Its budget had tripled. Ball expected this rate of growth to slow down. The only thing that lay ahead was a benefit increase, which Ball regarded as a routine part of the program's development, and the bureau would use labor-saving technology, such as relying on magnetic tape rather than punch cards, to implement the increase. In the relatively calm years that lay ahead, Ball pledged that the bureau would carefully examine how the program was administered. Ball realized that the bureau's Division of Accounting Operations, which kept the Social Security records of America's workers, faced the "biggest single work job in the field." This division, along with the Division of Claims Control, which awarded and disallowed benefits, would be exhorted to employ the latest techniques in data processing.[72]

Statement of Bureau Objectives

During the second Eisenhower administration, Ball turned his attention to formulating a set of bureau objectives, which he completed in 1958 and circulated widely to Eisenhower administration officials. On the one hand, the existence of these objectives was a way of underscoring the bureau's commitment to the sorts of efficiency goals that both Ball and the Republicans favored. President Eisenhower, for example, had spoken of the need for "efficiency and economy" in social welfare policy.[73] On the other hand, the objectives helped to lend coherence to the bureau's work and raise the morale of bureau workers. Ball believed that the objectives gave "unity to Bureau effort" and provided a means for the various parts of the bureau "to organize their work toward accomplishing what should be accomplished." As the organization measured its progress toward meeting the objectives, it would be able to point out to its employees and those who evaluated it in Congress and the White House that the bureau was doing a "tremendous job."[74]

Ball did most of the work on the *Statement of Bureau Objectives* himself, writing the first draft over the course of a summer vacation in New Hampshire. Although part of the inspiration came from management guru Peter Drucker's idea that the most successful organizations were the ones with clear ideas about their central purposes, the statement reflected Ball's intuitive grasp of the techniques of management.[75] It anticipated by many years the vogue for mission statements that would become a clichéd aspect of life in any large organization, the need to orient a government organization toward the service of its customers, rather than the mere fulfillment of inner bureaucratic needs, and the goal of making employees feel like valued members of the organization. When the head of the Health Care Financing Administration issued a strategic plan in 1994 that talked of the agency's mission—"we assure health care for beneficiaries"—and noted that "HCFA is dedicated to serving its customers," the rhetoric had a tired feel.[76]

Writing some thirty-six years earlier, Ball used similar rhetoric to impart a fresh sense of purpose to his agency's efforts. The way in which the agency completed its tasks created "a personality and character for the organization appropriate to a program based on the concept of right." Ball concluded with a peroration that he also used as an applause line in his speeches: "The business of the United States is the most important, challenging, and exciting business in the world, and we must be able to attract the best minds and skills of the next generation." People who did the government's business should feel good about their work. That meant they should be given "interesting, challenging" tasks in an environment that nurtured their development.[77]

In articulating the bureau's objectives, Ball accepted the Republican principle that private companies provided the appropriate models for well-run enterprises. "We who are in government owe it to the country to set an example of Government business that will compare favorably with the very best in industry," he wrote. Beyond the routine daily tasks, "we have the same sort of long-range responsibility which the management of a private corporation has to its investors." That meant that the bureau needed to perform its administrative operations at the lowest possible cost through "the latest money-saving machinery, improved methods, simplified procedures and all ways in which an economical and efficient job can be done without lowering quality." The most important objective of all was "to process initial claims with all practicable speed and pay continuing benefits on time." Rather than being coldly efficient, the agency should be warmly efficient, striving to adopt policies and procedures "that are as little burdensome on the public as possible" and maintaining an attitude of "friendly and dependable service."[78]

Although Ball's desires for the program's and the agency's expansion were covered by a blanket of business-like prose, they were present just below the surface. For example, Ball announced it as one of the bureau's basic objectives that coverage under Social Security be universal. The Republicans were not opposed to this goal, yet they wanted to approach it more slowly than did Ball. Ball also advocated a program of research that would enable the bureau to approach "with foresight" the issues that would arise as the program matured. Ball cast this objective in terms of improving the program's effectiveness, yet it could also be read as a desire to explore such topics as health insurance—something viewed much more sympathetically within the agency than outside of it.[79]

Another slightly jarring aspect of the bureau's objectives was that they applied only to the Bureau of Old-Age and Survivors Insurance, rather than to the entire Social Security Administration. That no one found that odd reflected the way in which the contributory social insurance program had come to dominate the SSA's work. Public assistance and such other activities as those of the Children's Bureau, a part of the Social Security Administration since 1946, occupied much less of the agency's and the public's attention.

Ball won almost universal praise for creating the *Statement of Bureau Objectives*. One measure of success was that the bureau integrated the objectives into its basic operations. The objectives were used in orientation, as a basis for work planning, and as a means of bringing "everybody together in a common approach to things." Another measure of success was that people outside the agency regarded the objectives as further proof of the bureau's commitment to its social mission and of the bureau's competence.[80]

Fedele Fauri, who had worked on the Social Security program as part of the Library of Congress staff that served the congressional committees before he left the federal government to become the dean of the University of Michigan's School of Social Work, noted, with tongue in cheek, that "we in the hinterlands are always glad to receive documents that are put out by our national planners who reside near the Potomac." He quickly went on to praise the booklet as a "nice job," and, in the manner of one adept at handicapping people's relative positions in the bureaucracy, added that he was glad to see that Victor Christgau gave Ball so much credit for the idea. Beth de Schweinitz, a friend who could be expected to react sympathetically, pointed to the document's "clarity and succinctness, combined with a practical idealism" that she said typified Ball's approach to government. When Arthur Flemming, the veteran educator and public administrator, took over as HEW secretary in the summer of 1958, he hastened to add his note of praise. Flemming, given to bouts of enthusiasm for the causes in which he believed, called the document "the finest statement of its kind by a Government agency that it has been my privilege to read." It demonstrated why the bureau enjoyed such a "high reputation ... in the field of management."[81]

Report of the Business Consultants

Not content with the *Statement of Bureau Objectives,* Ball went further and encouraged a process in which a group of business consultants appointed by Marion Folsom reviewed the bureau's operations. Early in 1957 Marion Folsom asked Reinhard Hohaus, a vice president and chief actuary of the Metropolitan Life Insurance Company, to chair the group. Instead of looking at the Social Security program, as Hobby's consultants had done, this group would focus on the technological and procedural aspects of the bureau's operations. They wanted to ascertain how well the program was managed, not whether the program constituted good social policy. In keeping with the Republican notion that managerial guidance should come from the private, rather than the public, sector, the group contained executives from such well-regarded companies as Sears Roebuck, General Electric, Eastern Airlines, Prudential Insurance, and American Telephone and Telegraph. Only one of the consultants, a former congressman with experience on the Civil Service Commission, knew much about government programs. The group met for the first time in July 1957 and, after visiting district offices and observing the program's Baltimore operations, issued its report in the summer of 1958.[82]

Robert Ball in SSA's computer center in the mid-1960s. Always proud of his reputation as an effective manager, Ball spent as much time on administration of the Social Security system as he did on legislative development of the program. Photograph courtesy of SSA History Archives.

Ball and Jack Futterman, the bureau's resident expert on administration, assisted the consultants to the point of influencing and even writing their report. Futterman, a Social Security veteran who started with the agency in 1936 and would serve as one of Ball's principal deputies before his retirement in 1972, took the lead in staffing the project.

Another of the talented depression-generation SSA employees, Futterman was a product of the City College of New York. When he graduated in 1933, he thought he might teach in New York City schools and gain a secure job. Too many other people had the same idea, however, and Futterman realized that the waiting list was just too long for him ever to work in the city schools. He looked elsewhere, taking a federal civil service examination. In time he received a call from Social Security, and in November 1936 he reported for work in one of the Social Security Board's downtown Baltimore offices. Like Robert Ball, Futterman was discovered by Francis McDonald, who ran training sessions for new Social Security employees. Spotted by McDonald and identified as a comer, Futterman entered the fast track for Social Security career employees. Along the way he served as an assistant to Alvin David, and in the summer of 1957, at a particularly hectic moment in Ball's office, he took on a similar job with Ball. That summer, while Ball recuperated in New Hampshire, Futterman cleared off his desk.[83]

Although Futterman and Ball never achieved the same level of intimacy as did Ball and Alvin David, they nonetheless developed an effective working relationship, based in large part on Futterman's admiration for Ball. Futterman considered Ball "the most able person that I had experience dealing with in government activities." Ball returned the compliment in the form of glowing performance evaluations. In 1959, for example, Ball told Futterman that he was doing a "terrific job." He praised Futterman's knowledge of important bureau operations, his program sense, his native intelligence, and his devotion to hard work.[84]

With Futterman's assistance, Ball remained close to the work of the business consultants, particularly when it came time to write up their report and present their findings. In March 1958 he sent a confidential draft to Hohaus and his assistants. "I have just gone ahead and written it up the way I would do it," he told them. "I hope I have kept the ideas and spirit intact. I realize I have taken a lot of liberties in the presentation but of course have no pride of authorship. . . . This version, you will appreciate, is a personal job on my part and represents only an attempt to be helpful to the group as an individual." Ball later admitted that he and his staff were "deeply involved" in everything the consultants took up and "really wrote the report for them." Although Ball would strenuously object to charges by academic observers that he co-opted advisory groups, he confessed that in this case the charge "may have had some merit."[85]

When it came time to present the report, Ball also played an active part. He tried to persuade Hohaus, whom he knew from the Hobby lobby, that the consultants, rather than the Social Security Administration, should release the report. Hohaus, the author of an essay on how the program combined the goals of adequacy and equity that the agency had circulated widely, had a reputation not unlike Marion Folsom's. Regarded as a business statesman with a tolerant attitude toward the program, he might well have agreed to release the report. "If he would agree to it, I think it would be good to have him issue a press release. Items in the press would have a little more punch if they were attributed to outside business consultants," Ball advised Social Security Commissioner Charles Schottland. Hohaus demurred. Although he had a favorable reaction to the materials that Ball prepared, he did not feel that the consultants should issue a press release on their own. Nonetheless, if anyone asked, he would make a strong statement in favor of the program.[86]

The report lauded the Bureau of Old-Age and Survivors Insurance in emphatic terms. It led with the notion that the bureau was carrying out its job "in a sound and vigorous manner." The consultants highlighted the way in which the bureau "pioneered in the very difficult manner of introducing automatic machinery in the area of paperwork, with substantial savings to the Trust Fund." Further, the quality of the bureau's staff compared favorably with the staffs of insurance companies doing similar work. The courtesy and efficiency of the people who worked in the district offices matched that of the people who sold washing machines for Sears Roebuck, and apart from wishing that the offices were more centrally located, the consultants could offer no suggestions for improvement of these offices. In general, the consultants' recommendations were few, except to encourage the bureau to expand what it was already doing, particularly when it came to using automated data-processing equipment.[87]

Early in 1959, the program received another glowing report card, this one from an advisory council that conducted a yearlong study of Social Security financing. Chaired by SSA Commissioner Charles Schottland, the group included such regulars as Douglas Brown, Nelson Cruikshank, and Reinhard Hohaus and such newcomers as Arthur Burns, the Columbia University economics professor and adviser to President Eisenhower, and Elliott V. Bell, a publishing executive associated with former New York governor Thomas Dewey. The group reported that the program was financially sound and that the law made adequate provision for meeting costs, both in the short and long term.

Looking to the future, the group believed that it would probably not be necessary to raise payroll taxes to 9 percent in 1966 as contemplated by the current law. In keeping with Ball's vision of the program, the council did not foreclose making changes in the program as changes occurred in the labor force and wage levels, nor did the council necessarily feel that the taxable wage base should remain forever at $4,800. The earnings base, the council noted in language that reflected Ball's influence over the report, determined how much money was available to the program and the extent to which benefits were related to earnings. All in all, however, Ball did not seek to use this advisory report as a vehicle to expand the program, so much as a reassuring communication, endorsed by Arthur Burns and other conservatives, that no changes in Social Security financing were "required or desirable."[88]

The End of the Eisenhower Era

In this same period, Ball maintained his role as an active liaison between the SSA and the Congress. Late in 1959, the Ways and Means Committee appointed another subcommittee, known as the Harrison Committee after Representative Burr Harrison (D–Virginia), to investigate the program. The subcommittee held hearings that focused on the agency's administration of the disability insurance program, with the objective of making it easier for applicants to receive disability benefits. Just as he had in 1953, Ball testified before the committee at length and gave an impressive chart presentation that illustrated how the SSA handled disability claims. The hearing resulted in an agreement that the disability program could be expanded to cover people under the age of 50, a result that the agency, if not the administration, found congenial. All agreed that Ball had done a good job defending the program and saving the administration from embarrassing questions about why the congressmen's constituents were finding it so difficult to qualify for disability benefits.[89]

As usual, Ball tried to deflect some of the praise that came his way. He gave the credit for the agency's good performance before the Harrison Committee to his associate Arthur Hess, who was responsible for running the disability insurance program. He believed that, because of Hess's leadership and the "hard and intelligent work" of Hess's staff in the Division of Disability Operations, the bureau "had a good story" to tell Congress.[90]

Of course, it also helped that Ball was good at using charts to illustrate his points. He admitted that chart talks, a technique he learned from Nelson Rockefeller, became "something of a specialty for me." Cultivating the art of designing charts and creating a special workshop to produce them, the agency became known for making the Department of Health, Education, and Welfare's best presentations. In time Ball and his colleagues became experts in the strategic use of what generations of teachers called audiovisual aids. They learned to exploit the situations in which charts would further the agency's objectives but also to be sensitive to the occasions when charts would make the agency look too slick or extravagant. When Ball appeared before appropriations committees, for example, he never brought charts that might give the impression that the agency had spent too much money on them.[91]

During the second Eisenhower administration, Ball learned how to attract attention but also how to direct it elsewhere. He continued to win awards, which he insisted be affirmations of the program, rather than purely personal accomplishments. When, for example, he was named as one of ten outstanding federal career employees by the National Civil Service League in 1958, the newsletter that went to BOASI employees invited them "to feel the warmth of reflected glory."[92]

Even as he won this award, Ball faced an embarrassing incident with his superiors who feared he had overstepped his administrative role and engaged in partisan politics. At the time, the administration hesitated to recommend a benefit increase in the recessionary economy, and members of the outside Social Security apparatus, such as nongovernmental employee Wilbur Cohen, pushed Wilbur Mills, newly installed as the chairman of the Ways and Means Committee, to initiate one on his own. In talking with Folsom, Mills made the mistake of substituting Ball's name for Cohen's, so that Folsom believed that Ball had been secretly lobbying Congress to do something that the administration opposed. Ball, despite his favored status and storied performance, needed to assure Folsom that he was innocent of any wrongdoing. He wrote the secretary that he had not had any personal or written contact with Mills for the last two years other than to send him a pro forma congratulatory note when he became committee chairman. "I do not understand what [Mills] could possibly have meant," Ball said. "It was just one of those substitution of names that occurs," Ball later remembered. "We got that straightened out."[93]

A conversation that Ball had with Folsom a year earlier illustrated just how delicate the relationship between dedicated program careerists like Ball and temporary political overseers like Folsom could be. Folsom telephoned Ball, an interesting fact in itself, since it meant that the secretary reached back two layers into the bureaucracy to gain information. He knew, however, that if he wanted to know about a politically sensitive matter that involved a technical aspect of Social Security he should talk with Ball rather than with Social Security Commissioner Schottland or BOASI Director Christgau.

In this instance, Folsom asked about some work that people in Ball's office had done for the AFL-CIO. Was it customary for Social Security to supply the labor union with cost estimates for a proposal that the administration did not favor? "Yes, I think it is," replied Ball. Would Social Security supply such services to any organization? "I think we do it—certainly we would do it for a congressman." Some people, Folsom said, thought that SSA had written the AFL-CIO bill, and Folsom preferred to tell such people that SSA offered only technical advice. "We gave them special technical advice," Ball said. The AFL-CIO presented the SSA with a proposal and the SSA supplied technical help that, Ball emphasized, the SSA would do whether it agreed with the proposal or not. "Then there is no difference than what we have done before?" asked Folsom. "No—we take the position that if we don't help any individual or organization, within reason, they then will get some Congressman to ask for it and we have to do it anyway." The object was to get proposals that were workable, and if the SSA supplied help for proposals it favored "we almost had to . . . do this for other proposals."

Folsom, although eager to be convinced on this point, still had his doubts. Would the SSA help such organizations as the Chamber of Commerce and the National Association of Manufacturers? Yes, it would. But wouldn't it make a difference who worked with the organization—might the organization be talked out of a proposal? "By the time they got to us, they had a firm position," replied Ball. For example, the AFL-CIO wanted a 10 percent increase in benefits and asked the SSA to suggest an appropriate formula to effect this increase. Folsom appeared relieved. "Well then they had already decided on the basic proposal before they came to you and what you did was to help them work it out technically?" "Yes," said Ball.[94]

As that conversation indicated, it took considerable effort for Ball to persuade an often skeptical Folsom that the SSA operated in the best interests of the Eisenhower administration. Folsom and others were all too willing to believe that, like Wilbur Cohen, who openly advocated such things as health insurance benefits for Social Security beneficiaries, Ball also favored the expansion of the program. Ball, for his part, continued to lobby hard for program expansion in private but to sound reassuring in public. In a private conversation at the Bureau of Budget, for example, Ball made a forceful presentation advocating the expansion of disability benefits to cover people of all ages. According to one account of the meeting, when the budget officials questioned Ball, he "snowed them under with lengthy answers to short questions."[95] In public, at this same time, Ball made speeches in which he said, "The impact of social insurance has been revolutionary but it is based on conservative notions. Social insurance relies on the tradition of self-help and like staff retirement systems and private insurance is connected in people's minds with the responsible and prudent management of their own affairs."[96]

As the Republican era ended in 1961, Ball won considerable plaudits for his cautious yet effective style of administration. At the end of his tenure as HEW secretary, Arthur Flemming wrote Ball that it had been a real privilege to observe his "outstanding work in the Bureau. You are a career civil servant of whom this country can well afford to be proud."[97]

Toward Kennedy

Beyond these pro forma expressions of praise, Ball won much more tangible prizes. At the end of the 1950s, his program prepared to move into a brand new headquarters, a status symbol afforded few executive agencies. The prevailing outlook was that government buildings should be threadbare in their appointments and utilitarian in their design. People did not want to see their tax dollars spent on luxurious accommodations. Nor did the public much favor permanent buildings for government agencies except for the most durable of government functions. That the Capitol, Supreme Court, and White House should be places of permanence and architectural distinction seemed appropriate to the American style of government. In the cold war era, Americans could tolerate the presence of the Pentagon, although many believed it right for this building to be situated across the river from Washington rather than centrally located. Social agencies remained more ephemeral endeavors, less worthy of monumental architecture. In the 1950s, few in Washington, for example, could have pointed out where the headquarters of the Works Projects Administration (WPA) had been. The Social Security Administration was not atypical in this regard. It had started out in Washington and then moved to Baltimore, with the bulk of its operations occurring in nondescript warehouse-type buildings on Baltimore's dilapidated inner harbor.

In the late 1950s that began to change. The General Services Administration acquired a parcel of farmland for a new SSA headquarters. It was located in a rural, soon to be suburban, part of the county that surrounded Baltimore. As the agency's de facto chief operating officer, Ball played a large part in the headquarters project. He helped to select the site, which was near the intersection of the beltway that was to be built around the city and the major east-west artery from the city into the hinterlands of western Maryland. Although the beltway had not yet been constructed, one could already imagine it as suburbia's main street. Ball also made many decisions on specific architectural details, such as the color of the auditorium curtains—the auditorium and a large cafeteria, complete with its own retail bakery, were two of the complex's dominant features, features that had been lacking in the makeshift downtown headquarters—the type of tiles in the operational building, and the appropriate composition for the cobblestones in the parking lot. He picked out the glazed brick for the building's facade and the furniture that graced the commissioner's suite.

As befit a technologically advanced organization, the commissioner's office featured a dedicated phone line over which one could transmit documents from Baltimore to the agency's Washington offices at the Department of Health, Education, and Welfare. With conscious irony, SSA officials called the contraption, a prototype for the modern fax machine, "the monster." Another

A happy Robert Ball in front of SSA's headquarters in suburban Baltimore. At the time, SSA's campus was the second-largest federal office building—second in size only to the Pentagon. Photograph courtesy of SSA History Archives.

labor-saving device was a dumb waiter that ran from the commissioner's office on the top floor to the offices occupied by the heads of the agency's operating divisions on the floors below. Using this dumb waiter, executives, or at least the secretaries who carried out their wishes, could pass notes back and forth without the time-consuming necessity of sending them through the central mail room.[98] (Over the years, the mail room for this organization that received so much mail became a sort of organizational gulag inhabited by workers without much connection to the organization. At one point Ball, with the aid of local law authorities, had to break up a numbers ring that was being run from the mail room. As the years passed and the mail service declined, SSA employees routinely advised their correspondents to write them at home.)

By 1960 the headquarters was ready for occupancy, just as the country was giving serious consideration to replacing Eisenhower with John F. Kennedy. As the campaign progressed and Kennedy's election became a real possibility, Ball became a little more unbuttoned about his plans for the program's expansion.

In notes that he prepared for an October 1960 talk to SSA regional managers, he called the fact that so many people lived in poverty "a national disgrace." He also included a twelve-point wish list for the program's improvement that began with a change in the way that benefits were computed, ran through the liberalization of survivors and disability benefits, and concluded with the medical care and hospital care for beneficiaries.[99]

When Kennedy did win the election, Ball, with little hesitation, prepared for the transition. He sent Nelson Cruikshank a plan for the expansion of the program that provided for a large benefit increase on the order of 20 percent. "I am sure you appreciate that these materials have not had any discussion in the Government," he added.[100] He simply assumed, even before Wilbur Cohen was named as an assistant secretary of HEW, that Cohen would get a post in the new administration and began to meet with him.

Cohen, in turn, received an assignment from Kennedy's assistant Ted Sorensen to head a transition task force concerned with health and Social Security. Meeting in December, the task force prepared a report that signaled a major change in the intended direction of Social Security. In place of an emphasis on the cash benefit part of the program, the new administration expected to make medical care for the aged, a proposal known as Medicare, a focus of its legislative efforts. Even Ball said that he "was somewhat surprised at how little Wilbur's report recommended for the cash benefit program. But this was to be the story until Medicare passed—hold off on cash benefits and save any money for Medicare."[101]

The situation illustrated how the Democratic victory, although welcome, was a mixed blessing for Ball. On the one hand, a Democrat in the White House meant approval for projects, such as Medicare, that the Republicans had been reluctant to grant. On the other hand, Democrats in the executive agencies shifted the locus of responsibility for policy formulation from Ball's level inside the BOASI to the upper levels of the Department of Health, Education, and Welfare. In particular, Cohen reemerged as an important influence over Social Security policy with his appointment to the post that Roswell Perkins and Elliot Richardson had held in the Eisenhower administration. Unlike these individuals, Cohen needed little education on Social Security, and

White House staffers, such as Sorensen, and HEW Secretary Abraham Ribicoff looked to Cohen for leadership on the issue.

The question remained as to what position Ball would occupy in the Kennedy administration. Cohen resisted suggestions that either he or Ball be named as Social Security commissioner since William Mitchell, the incumbent, was Cohen's friend and had been with the program in the previous Democratic administrations and served as commissioner in a Republican administration. Cohen believed that Mitchell provided a perfect symbol of the nonpartisan nature of Social Security. To maintain that sense of nonpartisanship Cohen wanted Mitchell to stay, thus making the point that the commissioner's job need not necessarily be changed with every change in administration (a point that would serve Ball well in 1968). So Mitchell remained as commissioner even though Cohen greatly admired Ball and felt little sense of rivalry with him. As things had worked out in their respective careers, they had never stood in one another's way. In later years, Cohen liked to take people aside and tell them how his skills and the skills of Ball and actuary Robert Myers all complemented one another. Ball believed that Cohen "would have liked to have me in the job at some point." Mitchell, according to Ball, "was quite a pedestrian caretaker and pretty much left the . . . program . . . up to me and I went on much I had been under the Republicans."[102]

Not everything remained the same in terms of the work that Ball did. Where in the 1950s he gave speeches on good management, he now made speeches on such topics as "health insurance and government." A general talk on social welfare policy that might have mentioned the Social Security program's progress in the 1950s now included passages about the program's inadequacy in the absence of Medicare. Using a line that became standard in the agency's rhetoric, Ball argued that "The cash benefits of social security, even when supplemented by private pensions as increasingly they are, cannot meet the costs of major illness."[103] Where in the 1950s Ball and his agency prepared memoranda on such cold war topics as how the agency might distribute benefits after ninety-two cities had been simultaneously bombed and the nation sustained 50 million or more casualties, he now began to receive more memos on the topic of civil rights. When black Social Security employees in downtown Baltimore worked overtime, for example, they found there was no place to eat that would serve them. Just as President Kennedy worried that African diplomats would be refused service at restaurants on the route from Washington to New York, so Ball wanted to make sure that "our employees, Negro and white, are not confronted with degrading or distasteful experiences while in Baltimore to take their basic training."[104]

As political circumstances changed, so did Ball's image. In the 1950s he projected an image of competence, as befit someone with a fiduciary obligation to the American people. The image was enhanced by his tall stature, his eyeglasses, and the gray sheen to his hair. As one perceptive academic wrote, he could have posed for a picture of a Fortune 500 executive. In the early 1960s, journalists described him, in terms consistent with the public image of the New Frontier, as earnest but fun-loving, a "vigorous, youthful, business-like man." His credentials for a job in the Kennedy administration included the facts that he was Phi Beta Kappa, had won national awards, and climbed mountains.[105]

The awards continued to come Ball's way. In March 1961 officials at Princeton named him as one of six individuals selected to receive the Rockefeller Public Service Award. Unlike the other honors that he had received, this one came with a cash gift and a grant to further his education, should he want to do so. Learning of this honor, Ball made his customary show of modesty. "I was very much surprised at being selected," he said. "It's a signal honor and should reflect the earnest work done by the thousands of people who make up the Social Security program."[106]

Almost a year later, William L. Mitchell, who had been a Social Security bureaucrat since 1935 and a prominent official in Georgia before that, announced his retirement as the commissioner of Social Security. Reporting the news, the *New York Times* wrote that Mitchell "may be succeeded by Robert M. Ball of Baltimore."[107] The appointment made sense. A decent interval had passed since the change in administration, enough to satisfy Cohen that the job was nonpartisan in nature. On the basis of his internal reputation and his external recognition as a gifted administrator, Ball headed the list of possible appointees. His appointment would reinforce the notion that the commissioner of Social Security should be an expert in that area, rather than a political appointee to whom the administration owed a favor.

Mitchell was glad to leave. "He had never liked the strain of possible major and minor disasters and read the morning papers with apprehension," Ball noted. "I doubt if anyone other than myself was considered for the job after Mitchell. I was the logical choice."[108]

After President Kennedy made "the logical choice" in the middle of March 1962, Washington insiders expected Ball to be on the job by early April. The press, to the extent that it took note of Ball's appointment, underscored the fact that he was the first head of Social Security to have spent his entire career with the agency and to have risen in the ranks—a bureaucrat made good. Little opposition was expected from the Senate, which confirmed him on April 3. Although Ball might have to implement Medicare, he told reporters that that task would be no harder than starting disability insurance. Despite this bravado, signs indicated that Medicare's passage was no sure thing. At the same staff meeting at which the heads of BOASI's divisions discussed Ball's appointment as commissioner, they also heard a report that editorial opinion in the nation's newspapers ran two to one against the administration's health insurance proposals.[109]

Conclusion

On April 17, 1962, Robert Ball became the new commissioner of Social Security. Wilbur Cohen read the oath of office. "I feel honored to pass on the torch to Robert M. Ball," Cohen said. When Cohen stated that Ball would have the responsibility for administering the new health insurance for the aged, the audience laughed, aware of the glib way in which Cohen glossed over the political difficulties that lay ahead. Cohen praised Ball's "great ability, great sense of social responsibility and great dignity" and emphasized how important it was to promote someone from the career civil service to the job. Outgoing commissioner Mitchell referred to Ball's "intellectual capacity, integrity, industry, and resourcefulness" as well as his "developmental work on the hill." Ball, for his part, promised to "contribute to the sound program planning for the long-range future and effective administration, step-by-step as we go."[110]

Robert Ball taking the oath of office as commissioner of SSA from Wilbur Cohen, the assistant secretary for legislation in the Department of HEW and a long-time friend of Ball's, in April 1962. Photograph courtesy of Robert Ball.

Ball's appointment made formal what had merely been understood for nearly a decade. Whatever his title, he ran the Social Security program. In many ways the Eisenhower era was the most successful for Ball and for the program. The steady passage of significant legislation, a streak that ended only in 1960, the tremendous growth of the agency and of the program, all testified to the respect accorded Social Security during the 1950s by Congress and the White House. In this period, Ball facilitated the process of growth by offering carefully designed plans to raise the level of Social Security benefits and the level of the taxable wage base and to expand the program into new areas such as disability. He also furthered the agency's goals by reassuring his political superiors that the program was well managed and by reinforcing the point that the program was conservative in its methods and outlook. He did these things from a position that allowed him to influence events behind the scenes rather than as a highly visible administration official.

In many ways, this situation was a congenial one. It offered power without the requisite responsibility at a time when the program was ripe for expansion and when one could, with the right amount of subtlety and skill, play one political party off against the other. As commissioner, Ball would continue to demonstrate his competence as an administrator, and the program would enjoy many triumphs, yet as the program expanded, it began to face problems that were not quite as tractable as those it had encountered in the 1950s. And Ball, rather than John Tramburg, Charles Schottland, or William Mitchell, would be in charge.

3

Medicare

As much as any single extended activity of Robert Ball's career, the passage and implementation of Medicare showcased his administrative strengths. Aiding Congress in passing Medicare and putting the program into operation, the Social Security Administration's major preoccupations between 1961 and 1967, required Ball to demonstrate his meticulous attention to detail. The process forced him to be persistent, particularly during the long period of frustration between 1961 and 1964 when SSA came close to persuading Congress to pass Medicare but could not quite close the deal. After passage of Medicare in 1965 Ball utilized his evangelistic talents to exhort SSA employees to perform the almost impossibly difficult task of moving from the passage of legislation to the actual beginning of the program in 1966.

Throughout the long process, Ball relied heavily on his Baltimore deputies to run the agency while he was off in Washington, testifying before Congress or meeting with one of the many groups that expected to be consulted about the operation of the law. Putting Medicare in place, therefore, drew upon the talents not just of Ball but also of the cohort of gifted bureaucrats who had been recruited to the Social Security program in the 1930s. Alvin David, Jack Futterman, Arthur Hess, and Ida Merriam, a skilled analyst in charge of long-range research, all played important roles.

In the end the implementation of Medicare was a success in the sense that a larger number of elderly people began to receive quality care than ever before. Hospitals met the immediate challenges of treating an unprecedented number of elderly patients. The complicated paperwork that these visits generated, was, for the most part, competently processed by intermediaries, acting on the federal government's behalf in offices across the nation. Despite this initial success, the program eventually became the subject of considerable acrimonious criticism. Costs that exceeded projections were themselves objects of heated debate. As costs continued to mount, it became clear that the process of national health insurance had stopped with Medicare. Ball had initially thought of Medicare as a transitional program on the road to national health insurance for people of all ages. Instead, the program, although expanded and modified in many respects, nonetheless lingered on into the next century without major change.

Reorganization

Before Ball could turn his full attention to Medicare, he sought to put his distinctive stamp on SSA's administrative structure. In particular, he orchestrated a reorganization in which his agency, which ran the Old-Age, Survivors, and Disability Insurance program (OASDI) and supervised the nation's major public assistance or welfare programs (aid to the blind, the permanently and totally disabled, the elderly, and dependent children), gave up responsibility for administering the public assistance programs. The result of the reorganization was to make the entire Social Security Administration look like the old Bureau of Old-Age and Survivors Insurance in which Ball had worked since the mid-1940s.

The rationale for the reorganization could be put in quite flattering terms. "I think it was somewhat unique probably in the history of federal bureaucracy to have a person with two jobs to recommend that he be relieved of half of them," Ball told an interviewer who asked him about the subject.[1] His friends, such as Karl de Schweinitz, wrote that the move illustrated the "essence of your genius. . . . Not one in a thousand executives would give up present territory for the sake of a surer founded, subsequent development."[2]

In fact, the move reflected not Ball's selflessness so much as his desire to create an environment in which he would enjoy the most success and his understanding that the move would be easy to accomplish. He realized that those interested in welfare would welcome the creation of a new agency dedicated to the administration of the program, "just as the education people welcomed the idea in later years of having a Secretary of Education."[3]

When Robert Ball became commissioner, he joked with his fellow employees in the BOASI that he was not really leaving the bureau to take on such hard tasks as dealing with Cuban refugees or running the Aid to Dependent Children (ADC) program, both of which fell into SSA's domain. He soon saw that the ADC program, America's chief welfare program, would prove to be a considerable administrative headache. He began to complain to his administrative aide Jack Futterman that he was spending an inordinate amount of time before Senator Robert C. Byrd (D–West Virginia) defending the welfare program. As Futterman later noted, "he was having a rough time defending welfare. . . . His interest was Social Security and indeed all his basic talent went in that direction." Futterman, among others, encouraged Ball to "give up part of his empire."[4] Ball soon agreed that welfare, if he continued to administer it, would, as he put it, take up "most of my time to the neglect of what I was more interested in."[5]

Things might have been different if welfare had not proved to be so controversial. As matters stood, however, Senator Byrd, who headed the District of Columbia Committee in the Senate, mounted constant attacks on the way the Aid to Dependent Children program was administered in the nation's capital. At the time, Byrd, who had been a member of the Ku Klux Klan, was, in Ball's words, "quite anti-black."[6] As a means of showcasing black promiscuity, his staff person on this issue organized night raids to demonstrate, in the jargon of the field, that there was a man in the house. The presence of a man helping to raise the children and contributing to the upkeep of the house violated the terms under which the District of Columbia, and all of the states at the time, awarded welfare grants, or so it could be argued.[7] To receive welfare, the law required that the father be disabled or absent from the home. But if another man had taken his place, what then?[8]

As the man responsible for welfare programs on a nationwide basis, Ball had to answer Byrd's charges that the welfare program was being run inefficiently and, in its inefficiency, was also contributing to immorality. It made for lurid headlines. It also consumed time and tarnished the image of all SSA programs by association. Ball noted that, for the first time, the "demands of the welfare side of the job . . . were much greater than the demands of the insurance side." Rather than constantly switching from one job to another, it seemed prudent to drop one of the jobs.[9]

It worried Ball that the welfare authorities who worked for him in the Social Security Administration did not have very good information on such sensitive matters as how many welfare households contained a man.[10] He disliked his lack of control over welfare and felt much less comfortable with it than he did with social insurance. He later insisted that he was neither antiwelfare nor disinterested in the welfare program. He argued instead that he decided that both programs would be better off under separate administrators, and as a consequence he engineered the creation of what became known as the Welfare Administration.[11] As it turned out, the change proved to be advantageous for Social Security and disadvantageous for welfare, but Ball had no way of knowing that in 1962, nor could he be sure that keeping welfare and Social Security in the same agency would have improved welfare's image during the 1960s. The Welfare Administration met with frustration after frustration until it was quietly abandoned in 1967 in favor of a welfare agency with a slightly different emphasis. The Social Security Administration, by way of contrast, glided from triumph to triumph during this period.[12]

Ball's year running the welfare program left a strong impression on him. He remembered in particular the vindictiveness of Senator Byrd, with whom he later worked in quite an amiable fashion on Social Security and whom he came to regard as a statesman. During this period, however, Ball found Byrd to be sadistic, "riding the ambulances on Saturday night with the

District Police as they picked up victims from the bloody fights."
In an uncharacteristically egocentric fashion, Ball dwelled upon
his few triumphs over Byrd. On one occasion, for example, he
was called into Byrd's office for what he thought would be a private discussion. When he arrived, he discovered stenographers
present and without any warning found himself in the middle of
an on-the-record session with Byrd. As Byrd grilled Ball in what
the senator expected to be an ambush interview, Ball, to Byrd's
surprise, gave fluid answers to Byrd's questions. Not getting
anywhere in embarrassing Ball and exposing corruption in the
welfare program, Byrd dismissed the stenographers and abandoned the session. "You're quite a guy," he told Ball.[13]

Although Ball's efforts to reorganize the SSA along congenial
lines reflected his preferences, they also meshed with the desires
of Wilbur Cohen. Neither Abraham Ribicoff nor Anthony Cele-
breze, the two secretaries of Health, Education, and Welfare who
served President Kennedy, cared much about the matter. They
found running the department to be an overwhelming experience, and the organization of the Social Security Administration
was just one of many details that they were glad to leave to others. By way of contrast, Wilbur Cohen, at the time an assistant
secretary in the department, wanted the Kennedy administration
to pass a major welfare reform package. Working largely on his
own initiative, Cohen helped shepherd new welfare legislation
through Congress in 1962. Cohen thought the creation of the
Welfare Administration would be a good way to implement that
legislation he had done so much to create, and he recognized, as
he put it, that "Mr. Ball wanted to get rid of welfare."[14]

As Ball confided to Karl de Schweinitz at the time, "the process
looks different to different people and for the next several years I
am very happy to have it look different to different people."[15]

The reorganization amounted to more than shifting a few lines
on the HEW organizational chart. It also contributed to the sep-
aration between public assistance and social insurance that became such a distinctive feature of America's welfare state. Academics who denigrated the "bifurcated welfare state," divided
between generous social insurance programs and stingy welfare
programs, often failed to appreciate the historical development
of social welfare policy in the United States. Until the creation of

the Welfare Administration in 1963, public assistance and social insurance had moved in lockstep, the former paving the way for the latter. Until the later part of the 1950s, welfare had meant Old-Age Assistance, and the fact that Old-Age Assistance was so widespread and so generous helped to motivate the Social Security Administration to persuade Congress to expand Social Security. Little stigma was attached to the receipt of welfare, since elderly individuals, most of whom had either worked in the labor force or been married to someone in the labor force, were presumed to have "earned" their welfare. In the 1950s, even as Congress passed the legislation that permitted Social Security to triumph over Old-Age Assistance, it did not hesitate to create a new welfare program, Aid to the Permanently and Totally Disabled, as an alternative to passing Social Security Disability Insurance. Once again, a welfare program preceded a social insurance program in an important area of social policy and aided in the expansion of Social Security. Only toward the end of the 1950s did welfare come to mean Aid to Dependent Children. Although the existence of predecessors to ADC, such as Progressive-era widows pension laws, helped to legitimize the notion of survivors benefits in Social Security, ADC, the only welfare program intended primarily for children, failed to produce any improvements in Social Security. Unlike the other welfare categories, this one developed separately from Social Security. The creation of the Welfare Administration only reinforced the bureaucratic isolation of what came to be called Aid to Families with Dependent Children, and this isolation in turn contributed to stigmatizing the program's recipients. After 1962, welfare and social insurance tended to move along separate trajectories, with Social Security being viewed as a legitimate form of self-help and Aid to Families with Dependent Children being regarded as a source of moral degradation and economic inefficiency. In his zeal to run Social Security better, Ball might have contributed to that unfortunate distinction, although whether he and his agency could have rescued Aid to Dependent Children from the "welfare mess" of the 1960s and 1970s remained unclear. And, without a doubt, the expansion of Social Security that Ball helped to engineer in the 1960s and the 1970s marked a definite improvement in America's welfare state.[16]

Passing Medicare

If reorganization came easily, the passage of Medicare, the prime form of social insurance under discussion at the time, proved much harder. The idea was a simple one. Just as workers and their employers paid payroll taxes that financed Social Security retirement pensions, so the same system of tax collection could be used to finance medical care for retirees. Thus, when an elderly person went into the hospital, he would not need to worry about paying the bulk of his bill because the government would, in effect, do it for him. Although the concept was simple, the politics was difficult. Powerful congressmen, such as Senator Robert Kerr (D–Oklahoma), an influential figure on the Senate Finance Committee that had considerable control over Social Security legislation, and Wilbur Mills (D–Arkansas), the congressman who controlled the Committee on Ways and Means, opposed the idea. Essentially, their opposition ended the discussion. Unless the measure could get past the Ways and Means Committee, for example, it stood no chance of passage in the House of Representatives.[17]

Robert Ball downplayed his role in the passage of Medicare, choosing to highlight the role of others. During the Eisenhower administration, he could not take a frontline position on the issue and was forced to work behind the scenes. "I was a civil servant . . . So a lot of these things that were going on to promote legislation I just wasn't in on. I was just brought in for technical and planning advice," he said of activities undertaken by HEW Secretary Arthur Flemming to begin a medical care program in the Eisenhower administration.[18] During the Kennedy administration, Wilbur Cohen took the lead, with Ball as his chief lieutenant.

Not as visible as others on the issue, Ball nonetheless played a major role in Medicare's creation. In 1957 he helped to prepare a bill for Congressman Aime Forand (D–Rhode Island) that was the forerunner of the Medicare legislation passed in 1965. The AFL-CIO took the lead in publicizing and releasing the bill that, if passed, would have provided sixty days of hospitalization for Social Security beneficiaries.[19] Later Ball helped his New Hampshire neighbor Robert Burroughs write up a memo with a health insurance plan for the elderly that Burroughs presented to President Eisenhower. "Nobody knows about my involvement, it is

Burroughs to the President. I don't know whether [HEW Secretary Arthur] Flemming ever did know about my involvement, which was stretching my role as a civil servant a little, but I did it on my own time during my summer vacation," Ball recalled. Although Eisenhower reacted favorably, Bureau of the Budget Director Maurice Stans pointed out to him that he had campaigned against health insurance for the elderly.[20] The initiative died, but when the Democrats came back into power in 1961, Ball was fully prepared to work on it. It quickly became his major preoccupation.

Ball's ability to work effectively on Medicare with Congress stemmed in part from the fact that he had able people to assist him in doing the necessary background research and political analysis. In the realm of legislative proposals, for example, he trusted Alvin David, the person in the bureaucracy with whom he had the tightest relationship. By the time of the Kennedy administration and the battle to pass Medicare, David headed the Division of Program Analysis, the nerve center for legislative proposals, and the division that Ball himself had once headed.[21]

Whatever David's title, his real job consisted of being staff to Robert Ball, a position he had held ever since the work of the 1948 advisory council. By the 1960s, the two of them spoke to one another in almost telegraphic terms. Ball had only to suggest a problem, and David would do all he could to solve it. Often David could anticipate a problem and work on it before it surfaced, with the result that he could hand Ball a memo on the problem just as soon as it arose. Ball had an almost insatiable appetite for information, particularly at crucial moments of testifying before Congress or marking up a bill in closed committee sessions or working through a bill in a conference committee. In a competent and sensitive way, David fed Ball's habit.[22]

Despite Ball's desire for complete control of his office, he realized that he could leave the daily operations of the agency in other people's hands while he concentrated on events in Washington. For running the Baltimore store when Ball was often off in Washington on a congressional or political errand, he relied on Jack Futterman. For his part, Futterman saw his job as relieving Ball of some of the responsibility for managing SSA's internal operations, so that Ball could operate, in Futterman's words, as the "program's Washington ambassador." "Well, he was always working at the department level. Always working legislatively, at the behest of anything that any of his superiors wanted or anything that a Congressman expressed a desire to know or to have done," Futterman said. Occasionally their paths would cross at the end of a long day in Baltimore, with Futterman still at his desk and Ball getting ready to go home so that he could get some sleep before heading off the next morning from his suburban Baltimore home to Washington. It was then, at an hour that tended to diminish formality, that Futterman and Ball engaged in "man to man exchanges" that, in their spontaneity, helped to relax Ball.[23]

Above all else, Ball trusted Futterman's loyalty and his competence. That meant, during moments such as those when Medicare was under consideration, Ball could focus on that and "almost totally ignore the matter of running the SSA organizational show." According to Futterman, "RMB had a lot of different loops and the administration and operational one was the furthest removed from his then laser-like focus."[24]

Medicare went through countless iterations in the period between 1961 and 1965. The only idea that remained constant throughout the long process was that health insurance for the elderly would be financed through the Social Security program. Nearly all the other details changed, such as whether the SSA should administer the program itself or whether it should permit other organizations, such as the regional Blue Cross hospital insurance plans, to act as intermediaries on SSA's behalf. Other details that became the object of political bargaining included just which benefits the program should contain—how many days of hospitalization per year, for example—and how much an elderly person should pay out of his or her own pocket and how much the program should pay.[25]

As SSA's Washington ambassador, Robert Ball worked with Wilbur Cohen and other HEW officials in making deals with influential politicians and health care providers in order to get the measure passed. In June 1961, for example, he conducted confidential telephone conversations with Harry Becker, a Blue Cross official, to see if Blue Cross might be recruited as a legislative ally. Eventually, Blue Cross and its parent organization, the American Hospital Association, became sympathetic to the legislation and won the right to have member hospitals conduct their Medicare business through local Blue Cross plans.[26]

In 1962 Ball expended considerable energy trying to persuade members of the Ways and Means Committee to support the legislation. He realized that the administration was one vote short of gaining a majority in the committee. He thought that a plan that SSA was developing for Representative Burr Harrison (D–Virginia) might serve as a vehicle to attract the vote of Representative John Watts (D–Kentucky) and provide the necessary margin that would then persuade Wilbur Mills to report out a Medicare bill to the House of Representatives. Harrison, Ball believed, wanted a "self-financed, social security approach to health insurance" as a way of lessening the burden on general revenues posed by paying medical bills through public assistance. Still, to get Harrison's approval for a specific proposal, Ball and his staff had to tinker with many of the details in the Kennedy administration's Medicare bill. The bill specially designed for Harrison paid a larger portion of the expenses for catastrophic illnesses and a smaller portion of the expenses for less serious illnesses than did the administration measure. It did not include patient diagnostic services because Harrison felt that such services, offered by hospitals, would provide too much competition for local doctors. The Harrison bill also limited benefits to those who had already paid for them through Social Security taxes, although present Social Security beneficiaries would receive a benefit increase that would be earmarked for Medicare and, in that manner, be allowed to receive Medicare.[27]

Ball knew that Representative Watts shared Harrison's concerns and, in addition, worried that the Medicare program, targeted for the elderly, would eventually be expanded to the entire population and become a very costly program as it matured. As Ball noted, Watts "indicated sympathy with the point of view that social security, because of its self financing and ear-marked contributions," had clear advantages over a public assistance plan. Try as he might, however, Ball could not persuade Watts to support the proposal designed for Harrison, and there the matter died for 1962. In 1964 Watts once again refused to support the measure.[28]

It became increasingly clear to Ball and his associates that the road to Medicare ran through Wilbur Mills. If the administration could get Mills's support, he would bring along Watts, Harrison, and the other recalcitrants. The Arkansas congressman did not oppose Medicare outright. As Ball put it, "he never quite locked the door; he always acted as if well maybe it would be conceivable that we could whip out something. So we'd try another plan. Some of the plans got pretty thin. Compromised an awful lot to see if we could get his vote."[29] A particularly crucial moment came in 1964 when the measure finally passed the Senate. At the time Ball believed that there was a chance that some compromise could be worked out in conference that Mills might accept. In the end nothing worked, and the measure failed, just as it had in the previous Congress. In retrospect, Ball admitted that there was no real chance of passing the measure in 1964. "But since you don't know when it's taking place, you have to bet, even if there were the smallest odds, to make every effort—even if they are a hundred to one against you."[30] In pursuit of this impossible dream, Ball, hoping to come up with the right combination to unlock Wilbur Mills, worked with SSA staff members late into the night.

This behavior was typical of Ball, who believed, as one of his close associates put it, in "running out every hit that didn't have a chance in hell." He thought nothing of having Bureau of Program Analysis staff work around the clock, "even if there was only one chance in a hundred." His associates tolerated this behavior because they knew that Ball would match them in effort and intensity. "Bob Ball had a way of throwing himself utterly, without limit, into things. . . . The tighter a situation got, the more important it got, the more he wanted to be in full control of every aspect of it," his associate noted.[31]

During the courtship of Wilbur Mills, Ball used his public pronouncements on Medicare to reinforce his private negotiations with the congressmen. He repeatedly stressed that Medicare, once passed, would not become the basis for a national health insurance program that covered people of all ages. "The problem of the aged is a unique problem and . . . I can think of no practical way to meet this problem than through the Social Security approach. The younger members of the population do not have the same problem," he said. He noted that even Medicare would not meet all of the medical needs of the elderly since it would not cover physician and surgeon fees. Would Medicare lead to the government's control of medicine? "Emphatically not," replied Ball. As always, Ball pushed the conservative aspects of Social

Security, in particular that it was "soundly and responsibly financed" and that it complemented private insurance and pension plans.[32]

Thirty years after the passage of Medicare, Ball admitted that he, like most of the Medicare proponents, had been an advocate of national health insurance. Medicare was a fallback position that Ball favored because it seemed to have the best chance of gaining political acceptance. Medicare's design, he noted, was based "entirely on a strategy of acceptability—what sort of program would be difficult for opponents to attack and what kind of program would be most likely to pick up supporters." "Although the record contains some explicit denials to the contrary, we confidently expected it to be a first step toward national health insurance," he said.[33]

In the end Ball nearly lost control of Medicare. On December 2, 1964, after the death of President John Kennedy in 1963 and Lyndon Johnson's landslide victory in 1964, Wilbur Mills sent a signal that he was willing to accept Medicare. "I can support a payroll tax for financing health benefits just as I have supported a payroll tax for cash benefits," he told the Little Rock Lions Club.[34] Hearings began in earnest in 1965, as Mills carefully worked his way through a comprehensive bill that would contain Medicare. He completed his first review of the bill on March 2 and then improvised a variation on the proposal that left a permanent mark on American social welfare policy. Instead of simply adopting the administration's much-amended Medicare proposal, Mills chose instead to combine three different approaches in one bill. He proposed, and everyone soon accepted, the notion of using the administration's approach to hospital insurance, adding a voluntary program to cover doctor bills, and including also an expanded public assistance program to pay the doctor and hospital bills of the medically indigent or those on welfare.[35]

It was the voluntary program to cover doctor bills that was the stunner. Ball believed that Mills did not think of this idea ahead of time but rather came up with it on the spot: "The combination of the fact that the AMA was pushing improvements in assistance, that the Republicans had pushed a voluntary plan with government subsidy for the doctors' bills and that the Administration

Robert Ball proudly displays the new Medicare cards he is about to present to Representative Cecil King (D–California), left, and Senator Clinton Anderson (D–New Mexico), right. Photograph courtesy of Robert Ball.

was pushing hospital bills: I think everything kind of came together and he said, 'why not do them all?'" Ball admitted that everyone in the room was "flabbergasted." Still, after consultation with Cohen and the administration's political allies, Ball set his staff to work on designing the specifications for what became known as Medicare Part B. Viewed from Ball's perspective, Medicare Part B contained many objectionable features, such as voluntary coverage and financing that combined general revenues and contributions from the elderly themselves (through expenses that they would pay out-of-pocket when they visited the doctor and through deductions that would come from their Social Security checks). Although it was not something Ball would have proposed, it nonetheless met his immediate needs. It was acceptable. It provided a way "to get the program we had been fighting for for such a long time."[36]

Robert Ball's press conference on the implementation plans for Medicare. The successful implementation of Medicare was one of Ball's proudest administrative accomplishments. CBS newsman Daniel Schorr sits two places to Ball's left. Photograph courtesy of SSA History Archives.

Sweating the Details

Ball might have taken a back seat to Wilbur Cohen, Wilbur Mills, and President Johnson on Medicare's passage, but he assumed primary responsibility for its implementation. The complex process began with a document that Ball described as a "big master plan of tasks and assignments."[37] In formulating this list of assignments and in keeping track of them, Ball relied on Jack Futterman, yet much depended on Ball's own sense of detail. Ball used his spare moments to query SSA staff members on the details of their operations. Riding in his government car from Washington to Baltimore or sitting in his Washington or Baltimore offices, Ball dictated memoranda that his secretarial staff transcribed and distributed to key members of the organization. These were often short queries about the status of a particular project, or ideas for Social Security legislation, or comments on a draft of an article or memo or speech, or simply free-floating thoughts about something that had caught Ball's attention.

The memoranda showed how Ball worried about the details. Unlike other administrators for whom only the big picture mattered, Ball dabbled in the small stuff. Typical of the often obsessional way he approached things were his thoughts on a visit by the secretary of Health, Education, and Welfare to SSA to attend an awards ceremony. Ball wanted everything to be perfect. Toward that end, he asked what songs the SSA chorus would sing, what arrangements had been made for pictures, whether the secretary's remarks would be recorded, what press arrangements had been made, whether hostesses would be stationed in strategic places to show people to their seats, whether the loudspeaker would be checked immediately before the ceremony, and whether there would be water on the podium placed in a location where the secretary would be able to find it but not spill a drop. Transferring his attention to the outside of the building, Ball asked about the parking arrangements and the condition of the flower beds. "How have we chosen people to be in the auditorium from SSA?" he wondered. "I want to be sure the union has representatives and, of course, a mixture of grades, races, sexes etc. I want to be positive that no one leaves and that it is completely full. I would rather have a few people standing in the back than not completely full." Not content to end there, Ball dictated instructions on the importance of having someone waiting in the wings of the stage to whom Ball could signal should a problem develop during the ceremony and on the need for key members of the SSA staff to stand near the secretary at the reception. Each of these things mattered, he stressed, because the "opportunity to act as host is, of course, part of creating a picture of efficiency and consideration. I want to be sure everything has been thought out and goes exactly right."[38]

Despite this slavish attention to particulars, Ball also managed to create a sense of mission within the agency that transcended petty detail. Before, during, and after the implementation of Medicare, he gave talks to the headquarters staff and to the regional managers in which he convinced the members of his audience that they were participating in something important. Because Ball talked so glibly and convincingly of the philosophy behind Social Security and Medicare, he motivated SSA employees to work hard; listening to him, they came to believe that their work made a difference in people's lives, that it mattered.[39]

The deadlines imposed by Congress in implementing Medicare added to the sense of urgency and heightened employee morale. Because of the "general aura of emergency," people "stretched themselves," Ball said.[40] Reflecting on the matter many years later, Ball talked about "a supportive atmosphere created by something very big." It was simply not true, Ball claimed, that people shied away from working hard. On the contrary, "they are stimulated by a big challenge," and as a consequence, "morale was never better at Social Security while working overtime at these almost impossible tasks."[41]

Even those in midlevel positions within the agency noticed the high morale that prevailed during this period. There had been benefit increases, but no major policy departures since the passage of disability insurance in 1956. After this period of relative calm, SSA employees faced the beginning of Medicare with enthusiasm and the confidence that they could accomplish the job. One of the people responsible for drafting the regulations that accompanied Medicare described the prevailing mood as one of euphoria, anxiety, terror, and confidence, all present in equal measure. He summed it up as a "unique and heady experience, never again to be duplicated, of a free floating organizational atmosphere."[42] In fact, the situation resembled nothing so much as the earliest days of the Social Security program itself, when, according to one official who was there at the time, people worked "ten to twelve hours a day, some days sixteen hours, and then four hours on Saturday and sometimes on Sunday to repair the damage resulting from the depression."[43]

Accommodating Organized Medicine

In 1965 the organizational atmosphere may have appeared "free floating," yet SSA was definitely a hierarchical organization, with Ball in charge. His principal deputy in implementing Medicare and the first director of Medicare's operations was Arthur Hess, a graduate of Princeton who took a civil service job with the Social Security Board in 1939. Like Ball, he had started out in the field, in his case in offices located near Wilkes-Barre in the anthracite coal region of Pennsylvania, and then received the call to come in from the cold to the central office in Baltimore. Eventually, he found his way to the Division of Program Analysis, where Ball and Alvin David also worked. Within this division, Hess became a specialist in disability insurance, part of a "shadow planning organization" that tried to anticipate problems in implementing the measure before it became law. Despite this head start, Congress threw the SSA a curve, just as it would later do on Medicare, and put the states, rather than the Social Security Administration, in charge of making disability determinations. Assigned to run the new disability insurance program, Hess adapted quickly, learning how to negotiate with the states.

Hess came to believe that his disability experience was invaluable for his later assignment running Medicare. For one thing he figured out how to work cooperatively with doctors. For example, he set up a medical advisory committee for disability insurance, and as he noted, "We said to them, 'Let's forget about all this socialized medicine stuff. We've got a professional job to do. How do you do it? How can we work with the medical societies and the medical profession?'" By the time Medicare came along, Hess "knew on a first name basis some of the biggest guys in the AMA and in the state medical societies." For another thing, he learned to work through intermediaries.[44] In the case of disability, these intermediaries were state-run rehabilitation offices that were supposed to certify applicants for disability benefits. In the case of Medicare, these intermediaries were Blue Cross and private insurance companies that were given the responsibility for the day-to-day operations of the program.

Arthur Hess, who became acting commissioner when Ball left the agency in 1973, spent almost his entire career in Ball's shadow but claimed not to resent it. He never considered himself Ball's equal as a Social Security executive. "He was running rings around me," Hess remarked. Instead of competing with Ball, Hess, like Futterman and David, prided himself on the effective way that he worked with Ball. "I was agile enough and smart enough that I could pick up and follow through for him," he said. When Ball gave him assignments, he knew that Hess would carry them out "with a minimum of checking back with him." On the occasions when Hess ran into problems, he realized that Ball had a "broader imagination and more authoritative views" because, Hess believed, of Ball's extraordinary range of Washington contacts: "He was on a close, first-name basis with an awful lot of people whom I just barely knew."[45]

Just as he had with disability insurance, Arthur Hess, like his boss Robert Ball, worked hard to implement Medicare in a non-adversarial manner, deferring to doctors on questions related to the quality of care, to the hospitals on how to calculate costs, and to the insurance companies on administrative details. One of Hess's colleagues described Hess's facility at "sitting down with a bunch of doctors who hated him when he walked in the door and wound up saying, 'This guy—if that's what our government is going to be like, it might not be so bad.'"[46] Ball said that Medicare began smoothly because "we brought people into the process," with twenty working groups, under the general direction of Arthur Hess, meeting on technical and policy issues.[47] Hess recalled "a whole year of consultation with literally hundred and hundreds of people in identified areas of concern."[48]

At the center of the process of consultation was the Health Insurance Benefits Advisory Council (HIBAC), a part of the administrative machinery that had been created by the statute itself. In a bow to the council' s importance, both Ball and Hess attended each of its meetings. These featured the interested parties, including the labor unions, the American Medical Association, and the American Hospital Association, meeting across a table and hammering out their differences in discussions moderated by Brookings economist Kermit Gordon, the council's chair. According to Ball, HIBAC represented a highly successful exercise in American pluralism: people holding diverse views "really did come together and work cooperatively to put the medicare program into effect."[49]

It helped in creating this consensus that all the parties took their cues from the Social Security Administration and that the SSA, in the person of the conciliatory Hess, did little to antagonize them. It was SSA that could lay the best claim to interpreting congressional intent in creating the legislation since Ball, David, and Hess had been in the room throughout the process. And the same people within the federal bureaucracy who did much to write the law also helped to implement the law. During the long legislative process, the bureaucracy was in a sense writing shorthand notes to itself about what Congress intended and how the

SSA might turn those intentions into administrative realities. Working within stable committee structures, sitting next to career bureaucrats from the executive branch with considerable longevity and expertise, congressmen felt little need to tie the bureaucracy's hands with explicit directions, as they would in a later era when the executive and legislative branches were controlled by different parties. One might even say that the largely permanent Congress that made Social Security legislation (Mills and the members of the Ways and Means Committee in particular) trusted the largely permanent Social Security bureaucracy (Ball and Hess and their subordinates) to implement the law in a responsible manner. Congress, never anxious to court controversy, relied on the bureaucracy to interpret such concepts as what constituted "reasonable costs" that were to be paid to hospitals or "reasonable charges" that were to be paid to doctors.[50] That gave SSA a great edge in the HIBAC meetings and in other aspects of the implementation process.

Even below the level of Ball, Hess, and David, Social Security contained a talented group of bureaucrats who staffed nearly all aspects of Medicare's implementation. As staff director of HIBAC, for example, Ball chose William Fullerton. Like Hess and Ball, Fullerton started out in Social Security field operations, working in field offices in Rochester, New York, and Reading, Pennsylvania. Brought into central administration, he, in common with others whom the agency considered its best and brightest, ended up in the Division of Program Analysis.

Fullerton's career illustrated another point of continuity between the bureaucracy and the people who wrote and carried out Medicare. After launching and staffing HIBAC, Fullerton left SSA early in 1967 and accepted a job with the Congressional Research Service. Specializing in Social Security and Medicare, he brought the SSA viewpoint directly to the inner circles of Congress. That was because he was not some passive researcher but rather an intimate adviser to the Congress that legislated Social Security and Medicare bills. As he explained, "In those days Ways and Means and the Senate Finance Committee didn't have their own staff working on those subject areas, so whenever they took up that kind of legislation we would go over there to the committees in their executive sessions and act as staff to the committees." In January 1970, Fullerton joined the permanent staff of the Ways and Means Committee. Through Fullerton and others like him, Ball's influence and that of SSA spread from the agency to the Congress.[51]

SSA dominated the implementation of Medicare, yet it did not seek to make waves. Part of the reason that things went so smoothly in the initial stages of Medicare was that none of the principal players in the Social Security Administration, and certainly not Ball, saw their job as challenging hospitals or the medical profession. Ball put it succinctly when he said, "by and large our posture at the beginning was one of paying full costs but not intervening very much in the way hospitals, or at least the better ones, conducted their business."[52] Hess emphasized the fact that the entire program was voluntary on the part of hospitals and doctors. In the Part B program, for example, neither the patients nor the doctors had to participate, and the doctors could bill participating patients as much as they pleased, leaving it up to the patients to secure a portion of the costs from the local carrier, most often a private insurance company, that was administering the program on behalf of the government. The doctors, in the program jargon, did not have to accept assignment and take what they could get from the program.[53] As Ball noted, Medicare simply "accepted the going system of the delivery of care and the program structure was molded on previous private insurance arrangements. Reimbursement of institutions followed the principle of cost reimbursement that had been worked out with the American Hospital Association and the majority of Blue Cross plans. Physician reimbursement followed the direction of private commercial insurance, making payments based, by and large, on what physicians charged their other patients."[54] Few doctors or hospitals could object to that, and that was why HIBAC meetings went to smoothly.

It was not a bad deal that SSA offered to the medical profession, and Ball worked with his usual intensity and devotion to get them to take it. He gave the same sorts of inspirational talks that he delivered to his employees to the parties that would profit from Medicare. In speeches to groups such as the American Hospital Association, Ball solicited their support by offering them money on very easy terms. He assured them that it was the government's intention to "meet actual costs" of providing services, however widely those costs might vary from one hospital to another and however much they increased over time. Because Medicare's budget would grow with the nation's expanding payrolls, there would be adequate financing to cope with the rising costs of hospital care. As hospitals acquired new equipment, adopted new techniques, and made other improvements, Ball emphasized that the "additional operating costs will be reimbursed," thus providing "the proper financial underpinning to improvements in care." In moments like these, Ball appeared almost to be inviting inflation.[55] "In most fields, you get only what you pay for," he wrote in an internal agency article describing the implementation effort, and he promised that the federal government would not skimp on its payments for the medical care of the elderly.[56]

Senator Paul Douglas (D–Illinois) captured the tone of Medicare implementation when he said that it was necessary to get the cooperation of hospitals, and "the wheels won't turn unless the axle has a little grease." In this spirit, the government made concessions to the hospitals that even went beyond paying the actual costs of the services rendered. For example, hospitals received an extra 2 percent of their allowable costs to cover expenses that could not otherwise be specified. The result was similar to the cushy cost-plus financing common to defense contracts, without the hospitals having to do the hard work of getting the contract in the first place. Instead of concentrating on the marginal costs of serving Medicare patients, Social Security allowed hospitals to capture a portion of their fixed costs.[57]

Social Security officials went along with these suggestions in part because they wanted to secure the cooperation of all the hospitals and most of the doctors in the country. Participation of doctors and hospitals was a prime measure of Medicare's success. But from the beginning of the program, such an accommodating policy invited criticism. Even before Medicare began operations in July 1966, the policymaking system for Medicare was not totally unified, even after the hospitals and many of the doctors came to see what a large bonanza Medicare would bestow upon them.

One critic was Jay Constantine. He came to Congress not from the Social Security Administration but from the national Blue Cross office and consequently never gained the deep sense of loyalty to Social Security that was ingrained in nearly all of the other Medicare pioneers. In 1962, he went to work for the staff of the Senate Committee on Aging, headed by Senator Pat McNamara (D–Michigan), who was a critic of HEW administrator and SSA alumnus Wilbur Cohen and of the Kennedy administration's strategy on Medicare. Staff director Bill Reidy, Constantine's boss, criticized the administration for being too willing to compromise with the doctors, hospitals, and other Medicare opponents. In December 1965, Constantine moved to the Finance Committee, working for Russell Long (D–Louisiana), another very independent minded legislator, as a self-professed watchdog over the Medicare and Medicaid programs. Under Long, the committee staff was expanding slightly; no longer did it rely on one staff member and one phone line.

By April of 1966, Constantine served as the principal staff member for closed committee hearings on the reimbursement policies to be used in Medicare. These took a very critical tone on such practices as the cost-plus form of reimbursement for hospitals. As Constantine recalled, HEW Undersecretary and Ball confidante Wilbur Cohen attended the hearings, "glaring at me and pissed." Only the crush of the deadline to implement Medicare by July 1, 1966, and some nimble bureaucratic maneuvering by Ball saved the Social Security Administration from having to renegotiate its reimbursement procedures.[58]

Ball knew that the hostility generated by Jay Constantine had an institutional basis. Senator Long and the Senate Committee on Finance felt frozen out of the policy negotiations concerning Medicare and believed that, in writing the law, Congress had shown too much deference to Wilbur Mills and the Committee on Ways and Means. "I think the Senate Finance Committee wanted a real role after passage and since they hadn't had too much to do in the shaping of the legislation, they could take a very aggressive stand in critiquing what went on," Ball said. [59] When it came time to issue regulations implementing Medicare, therefore, Long's committee decided to exercise its muscle and to show that the SSA had exceeded its authority. Ball astutely picked up on this maneuver and outflanked the committee. He went to see Elmer Staats, who headed the General Accounting Office (GAO), and asked for a legal opinion as to whether the SSA had exceeded its authority. The GAO agreed that everything SSA had done was within the legal limits. When the Senate Finance Committee

Robert Ball looks on as President Lyndon Johnson talks to HEW Secretary John Gardner at left. Photograph courtesy of Robert Ball.

asked the GAO for a formal opinion on the matter, it received the same reply. The regulations stood as written.[60]

Signing Up for Part B

Writing regulations formed just one part of the complicated implementation effort. A few days after President Johnson signed Medicare into law on July 30, 1965, Ball issued a report to his superiors in HEW in which he noted that "work of staggering proportions lies ahead." SSA's assignments included signing people up for Part B of Medicare, issuing identification cards to Medicare recipients, certifying hospitals, extended care facilities, and home health agencies for participation in the program, choosing and then meeting with the carriers and intermediaries to develop the routines for administering the program, and coping with the many other changes in the 1965 law, such as paying Social Security beneficiaries a retroactive benefit increase in September 1965 that would cover the months between January and August.[61]

Of all of these administrative problems, Ball cared the most about the implementation of Medicare Part B, for both logistical and ideological reasons. The logistical problems stemmed in part from the improvised way in which Mills had created Part B. Since it came from nowhere, it left SSA with no opportunity for the "shadow planning" that it had used to fine-tune the implementation of other important legislation. Where the agency had spent years thinking about how to put hospital insurance in place, it had given no thought to how to launch Mills's voluntary program.

The voluntary nature of Part B posed considerable ideological problems for SSA. At its base social insurance depended on its compulsory nature, which permitted a broad pooling of risk and eliminated problems common to private insurance. The lingering fear about health insurance and the standard argument against private coverage were that only sick people would elect coverage, driving up costs until it became impossible to offer it at a price where people could afford to buy it. Covering everyone— the sick and the well—took care of that problem. Part B, however, allowed people the luxury of choice. Someone who did not want to pay for it could decide not to get it. If too many people decided not to get it, then the possibility existed that the whole program would sink under its growing costs. Even beyond this problem, because Part B was voluntary, it would necessarily involve a tremendous outreach effort to convince people to sign up for it. The enrollment period started almost immediately, beginning on September 1, 1965, and was scheduled to last only a short period, ending in March 1966 (although Congress later extended it).[62]

For Ball and the SSA, Part B represented the latest in a series of odd congressional creations that SSA simply had to accept and make work. For the most part, SSA benefited tremendously from its working partnership with Congress. That was the source of all the benefit increases and program liberalizations, and Congress permitted SSA an almost collaborative role in the legislative process. On controversial matters, however, Congress had much less discretion, and in recompense for the largesse and in aid of the continuing working relationship, SSA had to take what Congress gave it. The general strategy was to persuade Congress to start

small but to create a program that could be expanded in an incremental manner into something much larger—slices of salami
that, piled on top of one another, soon made a satisfying sand-
wich, to use Wilbur Cohen's famous image. Sometimes, however, Congress gave SSA something fundamentally different from
what it wanted—not salami at all but something else—and
forced SSA to work with it. Examples included a disability insurance program administered by the states and, in this instance, a
voluntary health insurance program to cover doctor bills. SSA
could try to sabotage such a program by implementing it in such
a way as to show it was unworkable, but that was never Ball's
style. Instead, he did something more subtle. He ran Medicare
Part B as though it were not a voluntary program at all but rather
a regular, compulsory, social insurance program that took a
slightly different form.[63]

Ball led his agency in a promotional campaign to sell Part B to
the 19 million elderly people who were eligible. Newspapers,
radio, and television all contained reminders of the need to sign
up. Post office trucks carried Medicare messages, and the post office set out piles of applications in each of its 34,000 offices as
well as cooperating in special projects in which, for example, the
return address for forms was specified simply as "social security
office," without a specific address. Those already on the Social
Security rolls received special punch-card application forms, and
by the middle of November 1965, 8 million of the 15 million on
the rolls had responded. During one memorable week, a million
returned forms flooded the SSA mailroom. Eighty-eight percent
of those who responded indicated that they wanted to sign on
for Part B, which, because it would be subsidized by general revenues, presented its beneficiaries with an extremely attractive
deal. In that sense, Congress, with SSA's consent, had stacked the
deck by making Medicare Part B cheaper than it could have been
had similar coverage been offered by an insurance company.

Nor was the agency content to stop there. As new people came
to apply for Social Security benefits, they learned about Medicare
Part B. Welfare recipients and civil service pensioners received
special pleas to sign up for Part B. SSA secured the addresses of
still more people through the Internal Revenue Service, because
of a new feature that required tax filers to put their Social Security number on the return. Hence, someone over age 65 who had a

Social Security number and had not yet filed an application for Social Security benefits, but who had filed income tax returns in the past two or three years, could be identified by comparing the SSA computer tapes and the IRS computer tapes—an early example of how computers could be put to practical use.[64] In other aspects of the campaign, special mailings went out to nursing homes, urging the administrators to tell their patients about Part B. The agency even entered into a special project with the Office of Economic Opportunity, the organization that ran the War on Poverty, to hire people who could go out and talk with hard-to-reach groups, such as those in the inner cities and those shut in at home.[65] The rural counterpart of this project was a joint effort with the Department of Agriculture's Rural Community Development Service to get to people in country backwaters that might otherwise be ignored. Church groups, trade unions, and councils on the aged also played key roles.[66]

By May of 1966, after Congress extended the deadline to sign up by two months, 90 percent of Americans aged 65 or older had signed up for Part B.[67] The SSA had turned out the voters and won the election in a landslide. The potential disadvantages of a voluntary program had largely been overcome because of the high participation rate. Soon after the July 1, 1966, start-up for Medicare, Ball spoke with pride of his agency's efforts. "I truly believe," he told the employees in the Baltimore headquarters—some assembled in the auditorium and others listening to loud-speakers that pumped the talk throughout the entire facility—"that the preparation for the administration of the medicare program is absolutely unique in the history of public administration in terms of its being a great cooperative effort involving such a large number of governmental and private organizations working together in a very cooperative spirit."[68]

The cooperative nature of the effort extended to the process of certifying hospitals and other health care providers for Medicare participation. Most of this responsibility, a delicate task because it hinted at the possibility that the federal government might regulate the hospitals, fell to the states. First, hospitals, nursing homes, and home health agencies asked to participate in the program. Then agencies designated by the states, usually state health departments, investigated to see if a health care provider met the program's quality standard. That put the Social Security

Administration at some remove from the process. So did the fact that the program accepted the accreditation standards of the Joint Commission on Accreditation of Hospitals. If a hospital met those standards and agreed to form a utilization review committee, it automatically gained the right to receive reimbursement from Medicare. Most of the nation's more than 7,000 hospitals fell readily in line.[69]

Civil Rights

If there was a problem in accrediting hospitals, it came in the area of civil rights. Title VI of the Civil Rights Act of 1964 required that activities receiving support from the federal government be integrated.[70] Any hospital that expected to receive federal money from the Medicare program, therefore, would have to be integrated. Although the Medicare law did not say that directly, Congress had made it clear that Title VI applied to Medicare.

For Ball and the SSA, civil rights compliance presented a problem of many dimensions. The first aspect of the problem was overtly political. Although Congress might have passed the Civil Rights Act of 1964 and the Voting Rights Act of 1965, the Congress with which the SSA dealt contained more than its share of southerners with seniority on the Ways and Means and Finance Committees—someone such as Herman Talmadge (D–Georgia), who occupied an important place on the Senate Finance Committee yet remained an ardent opponent of civil rights initiatives. The second aspect of the problem reflected the trade-off between the success of Medicare and other social policy goals of the Johnson administration. Hospitals remained highly segregated institutions in the sections of the country in which Jim Crow social arrangements lingered, because hospital activities involved intimate body functions in which racial taboos were strongest.[71] Yet if all the hospitals in a particular area were not authorized to provide Medicare services, that would mean significant gaps in Medicare coverage. Above all else, Ball and his staff wanted Medicare to succeed, and civil rights posed a significant obstacle to that goal. At the same time, Ball and most of his staff were unambiguously in favor of civil rights initiatives, as were many others in the SSA.

Prompted by Ball, SSA staff members tried to resolve these tensions by steering a cautious course, attempting to get the hospitals in the South to change their practices without, at the same time, seeking to alienate southern congressmen. Wherever possible, officials tried to use the federal government as, in effect, an excuse for integration, enabling local authorities to argue that they had no choice.

SSA operated at some remove from the process because the Public Health Service, rather than SSA, received lead responsibility for the civil rights aspects of Medicare implementation. In March 1966, the Public Health Service, which had a long tradition of cooperation with local health officials, mailed a questionnaire to the participating hospitals concerning civil rights. In May 1966, HEW Secretary Gardner told Lyndon Johnson that about 6,900 hospitals had assured the federal government that they were in compliance with Title VI. The government cleared 5,500 of these hospitals, but that left 1,400 that required further investigation. Gardner estimated that 15 percent of the hospital beds in the country were in areas in which there might be a compliance problem. On the eve of Medicare's start-up on July 1, 1966, Ball had information that in Louisiana, Mississippi, Alabama, and South Carolina less than three-quarters of the general hospital beds had been cleared for Title VI.[72] Indeed, in Mississippi only 34 percent of the hospital beds were in compliance when Medicare started.[73]

Of course, the law contained escape hatches that worked in SSA's favor and made it possible to start the program without complete compliance. As late as the end of 1968, Ball told an interviewer that SSA "took the position from the very beginning that hospitals would have to be desegregated before they could start the program," but he admitted that even then there were a "handful of hospitals, largely in the Delta area of Mississippi and Alabama" that held out and refused to integrate.[74] As it turned out, however, Alvin David, acting with his usual prescience, had anticipated the problem. He told Ball as early as April 1966 that it was reasonable to assume that some southern hospitals would not take steps to comply with Title VI by July 1. In life-threatening situations, however, the law allowed beneficiaries to receive services from a hospital, even if it was not integrated. Emergency medical services could also be provided by hospitals that failed to meet the Medicare standards. These escape hatches mattered because neither Ball nor David wanted there to be a shortage of participating hospitals at the start of Medicare.[75]

The bulk of the work getting hospitals to comply with Title VI fell on a special detail of Public Health Service and 165 Social Security Administration personnel assembled in April 1966, given a quick orientation at the Center for Disease Control, and then sent out in the field to inspect, negotiate, and cajole. Although most of the SSA personnel were white southerners, presumably with southern sensibilities, they understood that Ball and Hugh McKenna, in charge of field operations, wanted integration to happen. Already these people had worked to eliminate segregation from SSA field offices. One of the people assigned to the special detail noted, for example, how the office in Flagler, Florida, contained rest rooms and water fountains for whites and blacks in the early 1960s, but that agency pressure had brought about change.

The members of the special detail discovered that segregation was intertwined with the health care system. One Social Security employee told the story of a visit to a hospital in Louisiana. When the members of the visiting group got to the laboratory, they were dismayed to see that the blood was labeled "black" or "white." Continuing their tour, they arrived in the nursery and were encouraged to notice black babies alongside white babies. Something about the scene in the nursery nagged at them, however. That night they made an unscheduled visit to one of the employees who worked in the nursery. She told them that someone had come into the nursery with the warning that feds were visiting. Hospital employees hastily put the black and white babies together.[76]

As Ball and Hess suspected, some of the resistance to integration was more symbolic than real. Arthur Hess described a visit to a southern hospital in which the administrator and the board members were "ranting and raving but as we were leaving, one board member came up to me and quietly said, 'keep the heat on.'"[77] Some southerners, in other words, used Medicare as an excuse for integrating their hospitals on the pretext that if they failed to do so, they would lose a substantial source of money. They realized that it was expensive and inefficient to maintain separate facilities for whites and blacks.

Still, such things as assigning rooms without regard to race or color or inviting black doctors to serve on the staffs of white hospitals took years to achieve, even though Ball routinely lauded the program on its civil rights performance. On the sixth day after the formal start of the Medicare hospital insurance program, for example, he called civil rights compliance "by hospitals throughout the country and particularly the hundreds and hundreds and hundreds of hospitals who have changed their fundamental practices throughout the South" one "of the most encouraging aspects of administration in the whole medicare program."[78] Within a few years, Ball came to believe that the agency had not compromised at all on the civil rights aspects of Medicare. "No plans or pledges for later desegregation were taken," he said.[79] Maybe not, but the federal government allowed the local hospitals considerable leeway in meeting their obligations.[80]

Part B Carriers

Acting on behalf of the federal government, the Social Security Administration negotiated with parties interested in Medicare, rather than dictating the terms of policy to them. "I'll never cease to be so impressed with how people of such diverse views (who had been fighting so hard with each other about whether to have Medicare) really did come together and work cooperatively to put the medicare program into effect," Ball later said.[81] For Ball, then, the story of accommodation was a great success, yet it could also be read differently. For one thing, the story showed that opposition to Medicare really paid off because it meant that those who had expressed strong contrary views, such as the American Medical Association, earned the right to be consulted in the implementation process. For another thing, the lack of opposition to key aspects of Medicare's implementation reflected a process of political negotiation that might have weakened the program's performance. The selection of the companies and organizations that would administer the voluntary Part B of Medicare—the part that covered doctor bills—might serve as a case in point.

Picking these carriers was an act of consummate political skill. Congress, working closely as always with the SSA, expected the

carriers to be efficient and effective, yet it also hoped that the selection of carriers would produce a "configuration that would be
broadly representative of the various types of health organizations qualified to perform the necessary functions." That would,
in theory, provide a natural experiment to see what type of organization could perform the necessary functions best—a quasi-
public organization such as Blue Shield or a private insurance
carrier or perhaps a prepaid group health plan.[82] SSA, working
with the Health Insurance Benefits Advisory Council, issued
qualification criteria in November 1965. In general, the criteria
favored large, established health insurance organizations that
could demonstrate "unquestionable capability to administer effectively and efficiently. . . . for a beneficiary group of significant
size." As if to underscore that fact, SSA required that the interme-
diary should have experience in making "prompt and proper
payment under the concept of 'reasonable charges.'" This requirement necessitated that the carrier know about "customary
and prevailing charges for physicians services" as well as having
"a wide range of ongoing professional relationships in the field
of medical and health care" in the area for which it would administer the Part B, supplementary medical insurance program.[83]

All in all, 136 organizations submitted proposals to SSA to be
Part B carriers. Nearly all of the large commercial insurance companies competed, and nearly all were given some territory to administer. Of the fourteen largest health insurance companies, for
example, all fourteen were chosen to play at least some role in
the program. In general, SSA awarded contracts to Blue Shield
in the areas with "strong" Blue Shield plans and to commercial
insurance companies in their home bases or where they had a
large market share.[84]

Politics played a large role in the final selection process. In the
state of Alabama, for example, Senator John Sparkman, a congressional stalwart who had run for vice president on the 1952
Democratic ticket, recommended to Ball that the Life Insurance
Company of Alabama be selected. The Alabama Medical Association, the organization representing the doctors in private practice who would have to work with the carrier selected, had no
objections to the Life Insurance Company of Alabama but also
recommended the Equitable Life Assurance Society of America.
The association preferred commercial insurance over a Blue

Shield plan. When SSA investigated, it found the Equitable to be preferable to the Life Insurance Company of Alabama, but Ball felt that Senator Lister Hill, Sparkman's colleague who wielded large influence over the federal health care policy, favored an Alabama organization over an outside company like the Equitable. Complicating the situation, SSA believed that the "factual situation" dictated the choice of Blue Cross–Blue Shield of Alabama over both of the commercial carriers. As a result of these conflicting forces, SSA had to postpone a decision on Alabama.[85]

In the state of Arkansas, the choice was clearer. Congressman Wilbur Mills wrote a letter in December 1965 indicating that the Arkansas Blue Shield would be an "ideal organization" to serve as the Part B carrier for that state. SSA had little choice but to go along with its primary patron. Ball told Cohen that Arkansas Blue Shield was "not a particularly strong plan but it is adequate and has the support of both the medical society and Mr. Mills." Since all of the interest groups were neatly aligned in that relatively small state, SSA put aside any scruples it might have had about efficiency and effectiveness and went with Mills's choice.

All across the nation, selection of a Part B carrier was a matter of political negotiation. Hence, Ball and Cohen conscientiously consulted members of the congressional delegations with interests in the selection of a Part B carrier in particular states. Before selecting the Aetna Company for Alaska, for example, Ball and Cohen checked with Senator Ernest Gruening (D–Alaska), and before picking Equitable for Idaho they talked with Senator Frank Church (D–Idaho). In states with larger populations and more divided congressional delegations, multiple consultations were necessary, as was the case in Illinois, which was split in its support between the Chicago Blue Shield and the Continental Insurance Company. Before a decision could be made, both Senator Paul Douglas and Representative Dan Rostenkowski (D–Illinois) were consulted.[86]

Ball and SSA accommodated not only the predilections of individual members of Congress but also the often related concerns of the large commercial insurance companies, such as Prudential in New Jersey or the Mutual of Omaha in Nebraska. As Ball told Cohen, Prudential was "clearly the right selection" in New Jersey, although there would be objections from representatives of a "fairly good but not outstanding" Blue Shield plan in that state.

In fact, Ball knew from his staff's contacts with Herman Somers, a politics professor at Princeton and a personal friend of both Ball and Cohen, that the New Jersey Blue Shield had good physician relations but processed claims slowly.[87] In Nebraska, Ball expected "possible objection from a medium level Blue Shield plan," yet stuck with Mutual of Omaha.[88]

Although Ball tried hard to diversify the selection of Part B carriers and to include group health plans that operated on a prepaid basis and emphasized preventive care, he always stopped short of confrontation and knew when to yield to political realities. For example, he indicated his preference to give the borough of Brooklyn to Group Health Insurance, Incorporated, because it was "a unique organization with considerable strength in the area and probably deserves special recognition."[89] Started as a health cooperative, the nonprofit company had a strong consumer orientation and enjoyed significant support from labor. To cite just one example, the Newspaper Guild of New York, an important union in the New York City area, covered its members through Group Health Insurance. The state of New York was large enough and diverse enough that SSA felt comfortable dividing it into three areas and awarding part to Blue Shield, part to the Metropolitan Life Insurance Company, and part (Brooklyn) to GHI. In an effort to garner support for Group Health Insurance in Brooklyn, Ball was even willing to spend some of his congressional good-will capital and talk with Congressman Eugene Keogh (D–New York) about the matter.[90] For the state of Virginia, however, Ball thought it best to yield to pragmatic politics. "On the basis of Congressman Jennings' reaction," he told Wilbur Cohen, "we might as well give Virginia to an insurance company and we really need more work for Travelers than we have previously given it on the basis of its general position in the industry."[91]

In the end, Ball had a large map of the United States printed on a piece of durable white paper with all of the state boundaries carefully drawn. He then got a sharp pencil and in his nearly illegible handwriting wrote the name of the carrier on the state for which it had been selected. The result was a map dominated by Blue Shield organizations but with room for large private carriers like Aetna in Iowa, Connecticut General in Connecticut, and the Equitable in New Mexico. In this way, the federal government began its program of public health insurance by awarding large contracts to private insurance companies and to organizations that represented the interests of private physicians. To get the program off to a strong start, political accommodation held sway.

A Successful Launch

Ball later claimed that it was computers that made possible the implementation of Medicare.[92] If so, the process also contained more than its share of very low-tech features, such as the big map of the United States on which Ball scribbled in the names of the Part B carriers. Pencil and eraser took precedence over typewriter and whatever rudimentary form of word processor existed, and calculations were as often made by adding machines as by computers. Ball's notes were a mass of scribbled pages with cross-outs and recalculations, as he sought the smoothest way to put the program into operation.

What greased the wheels was Ball's ability to expand the bureaucracy to take on new and complex tasks. Even before the formal passage of Medicare, Ball submitted a supplemental budget request that would increase the size of the staff from 38,500 to 44,000 people. Much of the growth would take place at the agency's Woodlawn headquarters. Already housing some 10,000 employees, the complex in suburban Baltimore would now be expanded by an extra 170,000 square feet of office space in order to hold some 2,000 more employees.[93] A few months after Medicare's passage, Ball upped his requests for extra personnel to some 8,000 new employees who would work at headquarters and in 80 new Social Security offices across the country. By the spring of 1966, he talked about opening 100 new offices and hiring 9,000 new staff members. That did not include the 3,000 temporary employees, necessary to get Part B applications processed, who were on board by May.[94] All these people and offices aided an effort that involved processing 8 million new applications for benefits, enrolling 17.2 million in Part B, distributing 19 million health insurance cards, and printing 100 million booklets that explained the program.[95]

Such a huge operation, imposed on an already large program, changed the shape of the SSA bureaucracy. Ever since 1937, the core of the agency's operations had taken place inside the Bureau of Old-Age and Survivors Insurance (and even earlier in the Bureau of Federal Old-Age Benefits). This bureau contained much of the agency's operational capacity, calculating benefits and sending out checks, and much of its capacity for analysis and planning as well. When disability insurance was passed in 1956, the new program, although substantially different from the rest of the SSA's operations, remained within the older bureau. Ball found that such a pattern could no longer be sustained with the passage of Medicare. Instead, he thought it necessary to create the Bureau of Health Insurance that ultimately became the foundation for a new agency, known as the Health Care Financing Administration that Jimmy Carter created in 1977.[96] In a short time, each of the major programs run by SSA had its own bureau, including the Bureau of Disability Insurance and the Bureau of Retirement and Survivors Insurance.[97] Creation of these new bureaus meant the establishment of a new power centers within SSA that would compete with each other for such things as computer resources and executive talent.

Whatever the bureaucratic ripples the process created, the implementation of Medicare became a celebrated administrative success. "As I look back at it," Ball later recalled, "I don't see how in the hell we did it."[98] A sense of euphoria enveloped the agency. All the many moving pieces—the hasty efforts to name Part B carriers, the intense negotiations over civil rights compliance, the massive effort to get people to sign up for Part B, the creation of the requisite forms and bureaucratic procedures—fit together well enough to allow the elderly to receive care from hospitals and doctors with a minimum of bureaucratic snafu. That fact alone amounted to a considerable triumph.

The agency had worried in particular about a shortage of hospital beds as the elderly rushed to take advantage of Medicare on the July 1, 1966, start date. In the first few days of Medicare, however, no special problems turned up. A check of ninety potential trouble spots where people feared that pent-up demand would overwhelm local hospitals revealed nothing amiss. In this regard the decision to begin the program in July, a time of relatively low hospital utilization, helped smooth Medicare's launch. As Ball reported to the SSA employees in Baltimore only six days after Medicare's start, "the program has come into being smoothly with a minimum of disruption and is going to become a regular part of American life without the great problems and difficulties that some people were forecasting."[99]

For his work on the implementation of Medicare, Ball earned the ultimate bureaucratic accolade. President Lyndon Johnson made a special trip to Baltimore on October 12, 1966, and in front of SSA's employees personally thanked Ball for the job he had done. "I want to pay a very special tribute to Commissioner Ball," Johnson said. "And when I commend him, I commend the thousands of dedicated, tireless social security employees who have served him diligently, capably, and well." It was the first time a president of the United States had ever visited the agency, and according to Ball, the visit left SSA employees "walking on air." Thanking the president for his visit, Ball claimed that Johnson's "personal expression of appreciation for the successful launching of medicare will spur us all toward greater achievement."[100] Indeed, the visit set off a new round of Social Security expansion, with Johnson deciding on the helicopter ride from the White House to Woodlawn to recommend to Congress a 15 percent increase in the level of basic old-age benefits.[101]

By the time of Johnson's visit, Ball had already learned that the president's sense of gratitude and largesse had limits. When Ball gave an interview on Medicare's successful implementation that landed on page one of the *New York Times*, the president made one of his celebrated phone calls. Just which office was Ball running for, the president wanted to know. He proceeded to instruct Ball that when the news was good, he wanted to release it.[102] Getting the point, Ball returned to his usual low-key media presence. Soon after the start of Medicare, for example, he got in touch with his old friend Douglas Brown and urged him to use his Princeton connections to the Oakes (Ochs) family to lobby the *Times* to run an editorial on Medicare. "In addition to saying something good about the program," Ball reasoned, "it would be helpful for the future to have the *Times* recognize the magnitude and success of the administrative effort with all the various elements and organizations involved."[103] With Ball, it was almost never about personal aggrandizement and almost always about advancing the program. Put another way, one could say that the program's success was Ball's form of personal aggrandizement.

Reconsiderations

For the most part, the news was good in Medicare's early years, but not even Ball could sustain the mood of euphoria. Although he put his initial energy into making the program work, he refused to accept the program as it was given to him by Congress. At first he wanted to expand it so that it covered more people. Within a few years, however, he lobbied to change it. No longer wishing merely to accommodate the health care industry, Ball began to think in terms of regulating it. This desire to change the program rather than merely to make it larger signaled a change in Ball's political strategy. Between 1950 and 1965, SSA worked on an incremental model, either pushing for higher old-age benefits that covered more people or widening the program to cover new risks. Even when presented with a program that the agency considered administratively awkward, such as disability insurance, it tried hard to make it work and then to make it larger. Medicare did not fit that established mold.

At first Ball defended Medicare. In an expansive interview with the trade journal *Hospitals* that appeared at the beginning of 1967, Ball, described as a "dead-serious practitioner of the administrator's art," said he "couldn't be anything but pleased that by the middle of November [1966] some two million persons had received inpatient hospital services and that by and large the hospitals had received their reimbursements." He also underscored the accommodating way in which the hospital insurance part of the program was financed. At the very heart of the program, he noted, was the federal government's willingness "to pay the full cost of care, whether or not that gets more expensive by reason of innovation and improvement." Even in this contented recitation of Medicare's achievements and potential, however, some problems appeared. One was the actuarial integrity of the program in the face of rising hospital costs. Ball dismissed cost as a serious problem because Medicare's revenue base, the nation's payrolls, was a constantly expanding resource. Should problems develop, Congress could always raise the wage base on which employers and employees contributed toward Medicare. Ball also believed that doctors would be able to reduce the length of hospital stays, and thus reduce program costs, through such measures as doing more procedures on an outpatient basis.

The second problem was that Ball obviously felt that Medicare did not go far enough in its coverage. He mentioned, in particular, expanding the program to cover people receiving disability benefits and to pay for prescription drugs.[104]

Only two and a half years later, *U.S. News and World Report* headed a similar interview with Ball, "Is Medicare Worth the Price?" To be sure, he still lauded the program. He believed it meant that, for the first time, many of the nation's elderly had gained access to the nation's best hospitals and that minorities had access to the same care as anyone else. Because Medicare certified hospitals for participation on certain quality standards, it meant, as Ball noted, better hospitals for everyone, not just the elderly. Ball admitted, however, that the cost of the program had become a real concern that he could no longer glibly dismiss. Simply put, the program was spending more money, more quickly, than the actuaries had anticipated. Hospital costs had gone up, and so had the rate at which the elderly used the hospitals. In a similar manner, physician fees had taken what Ball described as "quite a spurt" in the program's first three years As a result, SSA had been forced to increase the monthly premium that it charged beneficiaries for Part B coverage from $3 to $4 a month, not a large dollar amount but nonetheless a 25 percent increase that provided a portent of potential problems. In groping for the causes of these increases, Ball believed that physicians knew that Medicare's fees would be based on customary charges and therefore did all they could to raise their rates before Medicare went into effect.

And there were real abuses of the system, too, as in doctors seeing large numbers of patients in congregate settings such as nursing homes and barely taking the time to stop and say hello. Such "gang visits" violated the spirit of the program, as did seeing patients more times than were necessary in order to wring out the most money from Medicare. Indeed, more than five hundred doctors managed to collect more than $50,000 each from the program. "I find it disturbing to have this many with such large payments," Ball said.[105]

Ball's cautious yet open criticism of the program reflected his reading of the political situation. By 1969, with the start of the Nixon administration, influential critics of Medicare were easier to find than they had been in 1965. In Congress, Jay Constantine of the Senate Finance Committee staff, who had never liked the way that Ball had handled the program, stepped up his attack. In 1969, he obtained permission to conduct a staff investigation of the program, the results of which were published in 1970. The report took a harsh tone. It commented on how the Medicare program had consistently cost more than the actuaries had predicted because of "soaring costs resulting from price increases and greater than anticipated utilization of covered services." It discussed how Medicare paid more to physicians than did other Blue Shield contracts. It described the performance of the private carriers as "erratic, inefficient, costly and inconsistent with congressional intent." All in all, the report had a muckraking tone in its effort to uncover inefficiency and inept administration at all levels of the program.[106]

Although Jay Constantine later claimed that Ball had tried to kill the report by going over Constantine's head and lobbying senators, Ball had a different version. Constantine remembered receiving a call from Nelson Cruikshank, the veteran lobbyist from the AFL-CIO who was tightly affiliated with Ball, saying, "You guys are trying to kill Medicare." In typically combative language, Constantine replied, "Nelson, you're full of crap. Ball called you. You haven't even read the damn thing. You guys just want blank checks."[107] Ball believed that if he tried to soften the impact of the report, it was because he always worked hard on congressional relations. "Our theory," he said, "was to leave no attack unanswered and to make public and Congressional relations as well as competent administration high priorities." In the case of the Senate Finance Committee report, Ball even managed to use it to advance his own careful agenda to change the program. "We took the criticism of the Senate Finance Committee as a point at which to step up the pressure on the contractors, and I believe the hearings did contribute to improvements in this way," he remembered.[108]

Another prominent critic of Medicare lived in the White House. Richard Nixon's arrival in 1969 changed the political atmosphere in which Medicare policy was conducted. Acutely aware of Medicare's rising costs, Nixon did not have Johnson's pride of paternity in the program. The new president tended to see both Social Security and Medicare as strategic traps in which the Democrats tried to maneuver the Republicans into untenable

and unpopular positions. "I am becoming increasingly concerned with the sharply rising costs of both the Medicaid and
Medicare program," Nixon told his appointee as secretary of
Heath, Education, and Welfare in the first days of his administration. According to analysis performed for Nixon by economist
Arthur Burns, rising costs created pressures to change the program, possibly by adding general revenues to the hospital part of
the program. Nixon and Burns feared that bringing in general
revenues would make it "increasingly difficult to resist proposals
for progressively liberalizing the program."[109]

Ball had sensitive antennae that allowed him to detect changes
in the external political environment. By 1969 he realized that he
no longer needed to accept the program uncritically. As always,
however, he remained quite circumspect about the changes that
were necessary. Asked to predict the future of the program in the
1969 *U.S. News and World Report* interview, he mentioned that
disabled people might be brought into the program and prescription drugs might someday be a possibility, and the program
could at some point cover the costs of dentures and eyeglasses.
He said that there was little chance for full-blown national health
insurance as long as "employees can obtain good comprehensive
coverage at reasonable rates."[110]

Whatever he may have said, the truth was that full-blown
national health insurance was exactly what Ball wanted. In the
Nixon era, however, he couched his proposals not as expansions
of the government's power so much as steps toward prudent
management of the nation's health care expenditures. At times
he portrayed his agency as recovering from the binges of the
Johnson era and taking steps toward sobriety. "The more we got
into the administration of the program," he later said, "the more
we saw the need for change." In particular, he saw as flawed the
notion of reimbursing hospitals for their expenses after the fact,
rather than setting up-front limits.[111] The Social Security Administration, in other words, had been too accommodating, too accepting of the existing system.

In a long report that he wrote in 1972 at the very end of his service as Social Security commissioner, Ball elaborated on these
themes. Medicare had simply accepted "the going system of the
delivery of care" by modeling its reimbursement patterns on
Blue Cross plans for hospitals and private insurance policies for

doctors. Hobbled with this costly structure, which, of course, the agency had cheerfully accepted in 1965, Medicare nonetheless had become a major success: "Millions of older people have received more and better care that they otherwise would have and they have received the care under conditions which protected both their dignity and their pocketbooks."[112]

Ball believed that seven years after Medicare's passage the atmosphere, as he put it in one of his speeches at the time, was not just different, but "completely different." The public now favored changes in the basic system of health care financing and looked to Medicare "to help provide the leverage to bring about change."[113] According to Ball, the program no longer received criticism for interfering too much in the health care system but rather for interfering too little. The program, in other words, had to take on responsibility for seeing to it that the health care system was managed better in an effort to control costs and improve the quality of care. "What the change adds up to," Ball concluded, "is that as a community we are now willing to say that Medicare is a *health care program* with responsibility for preventing the risk and pain of unnecessary and poor quality care and with the responsibility to see over time that good care is provided." No longer was Medicare a simple social insurance program directed "solely at an economic risk" of the elderly being unable to afford health care.[114]

By the terms of Ball's analysis, more parts of the health care system, rather than less, needed to be brought under the government's control so as to increase the system's efficiency. Although Ball remained a believer in the need to expand the federal government's presence in the health insurance program, his position had shifted between 1965 and 1972. In particular, Ball realized that it would take more than an incremental expansion of Medicare to bring about national health insurance. Something more like fundamental reform, one that moved the federal government's posture from accommodation to regulation, would be necessary.

The fight for national health insurance would not go the same way as the fight to expand retirement benefits through Social Security.[115] Reading the history of old-age insurance into Medicare, one might have taken an expansive view in 1965. One could have predicted that coverage would expand—perhaps to encompass different age groups in incremental strides toward national health insurance—in an analogous way to which coverage had been extended to more and more occupational groups under Social Security. One could foresee the triumph of Medicare over Medicaid just as old-age insurance had triumphed over Old-Age Assistance and social insurance always triumphed over welfare. One might also have anticipated that the benefits would become more adequate, perhaps encompassing long-term care as well as hospital stays, in a manner similar to the way in which disability insurance had been added to old-age insurance. In the case of Medicare, however, those developments failed to materialize.

From Ball's point of view, things started out in an encouraging manner. Those close to him in the Johnson administration took a first step toward Medicare's incremental expansion early in 1968. Led by Wilbur Cohen, who had risen to the rank of HEW secretary, they proposed "kiddycare" to pay for prenatal and postnatal care of all mothers, as well as the costs of delivering the baby and the baby's care during the first year of life. Using the reasoning he had learned over the course of his professional career, Cohen advised that kiddycare should not be limited to the poor and that the plan's benefits should be funded through the payroll taxes to create a "contributory, earned right." It was important, he said, to give people the "psychological feeling that they have helped to pay for their protection."[116] Philip Lee, a prominent health care official in the Johnson and later the Clinton administrations, commented that he and many others believed that kiddycare would become the vehicle to move national health insurance forward. "We thought by 1975 there would be national health insurance," he said.[117] Ball tended to agree. Kiddycare, he thought, would be "the next step on the way to universal coverage."[118]

In this instance the future failed to arrive on schedule, a portent of things to come in the 1970s. To a certain extent, Medicare did expand in a predictable manner between 1965 and 1972, so that by the time of President Richard Nixon's second term it covered the recipients of Social Security Disability Insurance. Still, the same legislation that contained this expansion also contained rudimentary steps toward health care planning so as to avoid unnecessary capital expansion and support for experiments on how best to implement the idea of prospective reimbursements rather than paying hospitals their "reasonable costs." In other words, the same legislation that expanded the program also contained measures to constrain its future growth. Within a few years, the goal of containing health care costs crowded out the goal of passing national health insurance from the policy agenda. Despite repeated attempts by Ball and others, notably President Bill Clinton, to link the two goals, the cause of national health insurance foundered. On the road to national health insurance, America stopped at Medicare, which never developed into the comprehensive program that Ball desired.[119]

Medicare nevertheless assumed great important in Ball's career. It became a potent symbol of the federal government's administrative competence. "With all the difficulties," Ball later instructed a noted program critic, it was "possible for an agency like Social Security to implement a brand new program of a completely different character than the one they were familiar with and to do it in a short space of time with the enthusiastic support of the staff throughout the country and government as a whole." Ball noted that Kermit Gordon, who had headed the Health Insurance Benefits Advisory Council, told him jokingly that SSA should have been in charge of implementing all new programs.

Ball even thought he knew why SSA had done such a good job on Medicare. One reason was that the political superiors in the Department of Health, Education, and Welfare and the White House did not interfere. According to Ball, the people in these places wanted the program to succeed and knew that the way for that to happen "was to let the Social Security Administration move quickly on policy, administration, and implementation without a lot of second guessing and clearances." Another reason for Medicare's great success was that Congress, like the White House, also left SSA alone and did not try to change the legislation before it went into effect. They also trusted Ball to make them look good.[120]

Medicare, then, was an administrative success in the sense that Ball, Hess, David, Futterman, Fullerton, and many others made it work. It provided reimbursements to hospitals and doctors for medical care of the same quality that the other paying customers received. Such success was not something automatic; Congress did not create some sort of self-perpetuating machine that ran on its own. Instead, the process required someone to think through the details and to use considerable imagination in anticipating and solving problems. In demonstrating that sort of imagination, Ball revealed himself to be an extremely gifted administrator.

At the same time, Ball also helped to fashion a trap for American health care policy. Once an accommodating system of health care finance was in place, it proved difficult to retain the benefits of that system and simultaneously to transform it into a regulatory system that reached people of all age groups and kept costs within politically acceptable limits. In that sense, Medicare inhibited the progression from a locally oriented, publicly and privately regulated health care system of the type found in America between the 1940s and the 1960s to a nationally oriented, federally regulated system of national health insurance.[121] In Medicare, then, Ball got a little more than he had bargained for, a system that he wanted to change but could never disavow.

4

Expanding Social Security

If Robert Ball shaped the Medicare program through his administrative actions, he played an even more central role in raising the level of Social Security benefits in the years between 1965 and 1972. If anything, the arrival of the Nixon administration in 1969 increased, rather than decreased, his influence over Social Security policy. Unlike the Democrats, who fielded their own team of Social Security experts in the Department of Health, Education, and Welfare, the Republicans came to the issue with much less ready expertise and a feeling of vulnerability that they could always be outspent on the issue by the Democrats. It helped to have a reliable expert like Ball running the program, even though Nixon's White House staff believed, as Martha Derthick put it, that "he worked for the Democrats or they for him."[1]

Once Ball knew that the Nixon administration would allow him to remain as Social Security commissioner, he orchestrated a complex process that led to a rise in real value of benefits by some 23 percent and that preserved those high benefits against the risk of inflation. The process involved negotiations among three sets of actors with agendas that were both distinctive and complementary toward one another. The Nixon administration favored cost-of-living adjustments that would automatically set benefit levels according to the inflation rate but opposed high benefit levels. Representative Wilbur Mills favored high benefit levels but opposed automatic cost-of-living adjustments. Robert Ball and the Social Security Administration favored high benefit levels and automatic cost-of-living adjustments.

To add to the complexity, each of the actors did not have complete control over its policy recommendations. The Nixon administration faced internal dissension over the desirability of cost-of-living adjustments from conservatives in its ranks and over the goal of keeping benefits low from the liberals in its ranks. Wilbur Mills needed to reach consensus within the Committee on Ways and Means, and neither Republicans nor liberal Democrats on the committee shared his goals. Robert Ball and the Social Security Administration could not permit much distance to develop between their policy positions and those of the Nixon administration. Within the Social Security Administration, particularly in the actuarial ranks, criticism was developing of the methodology that Ball used to reach his policy recommendations.

Despite these constraints, Ball came out the winner in this complicated contest that unfolded over the course of the first Nixon administration. In so doing he displayed his mastery of Social Security policymaking. His talents produced a major expansion of the Social Security program in a Republican era, just as he had helped to create similar expansions in the Eisenhower administration. As a result, Congress took the one action that was most responsible for the expansion of Social Security, and by extension the growth of America's welfare state, in 1972.[2] The Nixon-era legislation set in motion the events that would lead to the modern debates over the program's long-term solvency.

Social Security Benefits in the Johnson Years

Ball maintained a strong sense of discipline in pursuing expanded Social Security benefits and in advocating changes to the ways in which Congress set the level of Social Security benefits. In the modern political parlance, he stayed on message. When Medicare was under active consideration, he did little to distract the public's attention from that goal. In a 1964 interview in *U.S. News and World Report*, for example, he dismissed the problem of keeping cash benefits up-to-date with the cost of living, noting that the Social Security system was "largely inflation proof." As wages rose, payroll taxes, or contributions as they were called in the jargon of Social Security, yielded more money. Someone paying, say, 5 percent on his wages of $10,000 would pay $100 more to Social Security if his wages were to go up to $12,000. The surplus income that was generated by rising wages provided a "certain amount of leeway for Congress to raise benefits without raising the payroll tax." In this way, the system protected its current and future beneficiaries against inflation, "particularly when you recall that wages in this country have, on average, risen much more than prices."[3] Hence, Ball advocated no major changes in the old-age benefits; passage of Medicare mattered most.

Indeed, in the period leading up to Medicare, Ball made the public case that the Social Security program needed little improvement, other than to add Medicare to it. He continued to assert the virtues of social insurance in order to prove that health care should be financed through Social Security. He routinely cited the fundamental values and features of Social Security that caused it to mesh with what he asserted to be core American values. In the winter of 1965, for example, he published an article in a law review that explained how Social Security benefits grew out of a person's work and how these benefits therefore constituted an earned right. Compulsory coverage and benefits clearly defined by law, combined with a conservative financing mechanism, made it likely that the program would be able to meet its commitments "into the indefinite future." The advisory council report of that year contained an introduction, written by Ball and often cited with approval by him to the effect that Social Security operated "through the individual efforts of the worker and his employer and thus is in total harmony with general economic incentives to work and save."[4]

For all that Ball appeared satisfied with Social Security, he still wanted to expand it. Even in the 1965 law review article, he cited the most important future problem for Social Security as maintaining the adequacy of the cash benefits. Although the 1965 Medicare legislation contained a benefit increase, it would do little other than restore the purchasing power of existing benefits. Ball thought still more was required, and he mentioned that his agency had been studying techniques to adjust benefit levels automatically in response to changing economic conditions. As the price level rose, benefits could also rise through some sort of automatic formula that would not require the specific intervention of Congress. Ball believed that rising wages would make this change feasible, just as they supplied the engine for Social Security's expansion in the traditional system. Because wages rose faster than other prices, the additional income generated would more than pay for the increased benefits, just so long as the taxable wage base—the amount of wages on which wages were payable—was increased as earning levels rose.[5]

In 1965 he floated this idea of what insiders called the "automatics" as little more than a trial balloon and in 1967 noted that the agency had not yet resolved the question of whether to recommend such a proposal publicly. "We have not endorsed that proposal," Ball told a reporter in 1968. On the one hand, there were good arguments for it. On the other hand, Congress felt it was better to take a periodic look at the whole program—not just to increase benefits, as the automatic adjustments would do, but also to examine the relationship among the various types of benefits. Should, for example, a widow get 75 percent of the basic benefit, as had been the case since 1939, or should widows be paid 100 percent of the basic benefit?[6]

Although Ball did not formally embrace the idea of automatically adjusting benefits to the cost of living, the idea clearly attracted him. In a confidential memo to his chief legislative lieutenant Alvin David in March 30, 1965, he spoke of the need to think ahead to the legislative program that lay beyond Medicare. He included five items on his future agenda, all of which were subsequently enacted. One had to do with disability; the remaining four concerned ways to raise benefit levels, whether through an increase in the wage base or a general benefit increase. Ball also mentioned what he described as "the beginning of some automatic features such as keeping the benefits up to date with the cost of living index and keeping the wage base up to date with the wage index." Finally, he toyed with the idea of changing the actuarial assumptions that underpinned the program, in particular the "limited use of a rising wage assumption." Rather than planning on wages remaining static and then spending the unexpected surplus when wages rose, Ball thought it might be better to assume "a modest 3% rise in wages" that would make it possible to increase benefits but not payroll taxes.[7]

The idea of tying benefit increases to changes in prices appeared to be a logical way of planning for the expansion of the Social Security, yet during the program's first thirty years the idea had not been seriously proposed, much less adopted by Congress. Enacted during a severe deflationary depression, the program had no initial need to take inflation into account. Indeed, much of America's reform tradition, whether of the populist or New Deal variety, stemmed from an era when falling, not rising, prices constituted the major policy problem. Things like the free coinage of silver in the populist era or minimum wages during the New Deal were efforts to induce inflation in the face of severe deflation. Only during the Progressive era had reformers worried about maintaining the real value of benefit levels in such programs as workers' compensation, which specified a maximum amount of money an injured worker could receive.[8]

Such worries faded by the time Social Security came along. When raising benefit levels became a real possibility in the postwar era, policymakers thought they had hit upon a politically effective system to accomplish this result. Wilbur Cohen had called it a "miracle" that rising wages made it possible for Congress to raise the benefit level without raising the tax rate.[9] The major stakeholders in the system, such as organized labor and the Democratic congressmen on the Ways and Means Committee, had come to appreciate the uses of what the actuaries at Social Security called the "level wage hypothesis."[10] It enabled Congress periodically to perform its miracle and regularly raise benefit levels to the growing support of an appreciative public. It also made it possible to tie politically contentious items, such as disability insurance and Medicare, to the politically popular item of raising basic benefit levels.

Congressional predilections for the old-fashioned, discretionary, non-automatic system of raising benefits meshed with the opinions of many economists. As the magnitude of the money that flowed through the Social Security program in the form of taxes collected and benefits paid out increased after 1965, economists, attentive to the nuances of fiscal policy, realized that Social Security was itself an important form of fiscal policy. The way the program operated could therefore exert an important influence over the economy. Although conflicts between economists and program administrators stemmed from the very beginning of the program, when Social Security taxes in 1937 started to pull money out of the economy, the conflict became more overt as the size of Social Security and the importance of economists in the policy process increased during the 1960s. Simply put, Social Security did not always operate in an appropriately counter-cyclical manner. That was true when the Social Security taxes started and took money out of circulation in 1937. It would be equally true if benefits were tied to increases in the cost of living. As an inflationary cycle started, Social Security benefits would expand and, in effect, amplify that cycle.[11]

Ball understood all that, but he pursued the idea of automatic, rather than ad hoc, cost-of-living adjustments anyway. During the Johnson administration, he bided his time because he realized that Wilbur Cohen and the representatives of organized labor opposed the idea. According to Ball, Cohen and many other Democrats believed that "benefits getting out of date" caught Congress's attention and allowed for new legislation that not only dealt with inflation but, significantly, made other improvements in the program.[12] In this view, to open up the program to legislative changes was, in effect, to expand it.

Wilbur Mills, for his part, wanted Congress to get credit for voting on what were called benefit increases, even though, as Ball noted, "they only restored previous purchasing power." Ball, who pointed out that there had been no general benefit increase between 1958 and 1965 when Congress had been distracted by Medicare, thought that there was "too much of a delay between benefits falling out of date because of inflation and when changes could be made by legislation. I favored the automatics and assumed that it would be possible to get Congress's attention for liberalizations without this stimulus."[13] As he explained, "if you take three or four years to catch up—or even two—with the cost of living, a lot of people had the experience of not being able to buy what they had previously been able to buy." Many of these people died without ever seeing their purchasing power restored.[14]

At least superficially, Social Security politics proceeded as usual in the period after the passage of Medicare. After negotiating with Wilbur Mills and with Senate Committee on Finance chairman Russell Long, the Johnson administration succeeded in obtaining a 13 percent increase in the basic Social Security benefit level at the beginning of 1968. This benefit increase was funded in the traditional manner, and no plans were made to shift over to a system of automatic benefit increases in the future. Behind the scenes, however, two significant developments occurred as Congress considered what were called the Social Security Amendments of 1967 (passed by Congress in 1967 but not signed by President Johnson until 1968). The first was that Social Security legislation became embroiled in fiscal policy considerations to a greater extent than ever before. The second was that disputes over welfare reform, once a benign subject that generated no controversy, threatened to derail the passage of the bill.[15]

Staying On in the Nixon Administration

The election of Richard Nixon in 1968 changed the range of possibilities in Social Security legislation. Unlike the Johnson administration, the new administration appeared to favor the adoption of automatic adjustments in benefit levels to reflect the cost of living. The Republicans had included the measure in their 1968 platform. Ball called it "their main proposal" in the Social Security area, their means of differentiating themselves from the Democrats and still appearing compassionate on social policy. If one assumed, as appeared reasonable in 1968, that the Republicans were destined to remain the minority party in Congress, then their position made sense. Instead of being outbid by the Democrats each time Congress considered Social Security, the Republicans could instead put the question of Social Security benefits on an automatic basis—a political move designed to put the program out of the reach of politics and hence one likely to appeal to nonpartisan advocates of good government. Representative John Byrnes (R–Wisconsin), the ranking Republican on the Ways and Means Committee, had watched over the course of many years as Wilbur Mills had outmaneuvered the Republicans on Social Security legislation. It was not surprising, therefore, that Byrnes became a chief proponent of the automatic adjustment idea, as did Melvin Laird (R–Wisconsin), the ranking Republican on the House Appropriations subcommittee that dealt

President Richard Nixon being introduced to Robert Ball in February 1969 while visiting HEW headquarters. Also shown, left to right: Alanson Wilcox, Charles Johnson, James Kelly, Bernard Sisco, and HEW Secretary Robert Finch. Photograph courtesy of Robert Ball.

with Social Security. Byrnes and Laird hoped to end the biennial rush to pass expensive Social Security legislation.[16]

Since Ball was confident that Byrnes and Laird were wrong and that the adoption of automatic cost-of-living adjustments would not slow down the growth of Social Security or delay the program from reaching such other goals as national health insurance, he continued to support automatic cost-of-living adjustments in the Nixon years. The only difference that the change of administration made was that he could do so more openly. In 1970, for example, he told an interviewer that he was "very enthusiastic" about the "automatic provisions," which he called "sound and desirable" measures that could not easily be categorized as conservative or liberal.[17] As that statement implied, Ball worked hard to temper his rhetoric in the Nixon years and to portray changes in Social Security in conservative terms. For example, he could agree with Representative Byrnes on the need for automatic adjustments in benefits without highlighting his agenda for other forms of expansion.

The fact remained, however, that he was a liberal Democrat who wanted to expand the program more than did Richard Nixon. Since many within the administration knew that, they gave serious consideration to replacing Ball with a more loyal Republican. Remarkably, Ball managed to stay, despite the presence of a serious rival for the job who had at least as much experience with the program as Ball did.

Ball remained as commissioner of Social Security because he fought hard to do so. He used his Republican contacts to persuade Robert Finch, Nixon's choice as secretary of Health, Education, and Welfare and Ball's nominal superior, to keep him in the job. One such contact was pension expert Robert Burroughs, a New Hampshire resident with whom Ball had been friendly ever since the Hobby lobby in 1953. Ball told Burroughs in February 1969 that Finch had indicated that he could stay but that no final decision had been made. Burroughs proceeded to use his California connections to lobby Californian Finch. "There is still no public announcement about my staying on here but all indications are that I will," Ball wrote his brother at the end of March. A month later Ball assured Burroughs that, "nothing has changed as far as a public announcement is concerned, but there seems to be a general assumption that I will be staying."[18]

More than lobbying on Ball's part enabled him to keep the job. People within the administration, at least those in the Department of Health, Education, and Welfare, wanted him to stay. Finch and HEW Under Secretary John Veneman convinced the administration officials in charge of personnel to keep Ball. He later noted that they supported him because the "reputation of Social Security as a well-run organization had been firmly established and that's what they cared about. They were suddenly in charge of a lot of other programs that were having difficulty and they were glad to leave SSA alone." Perhaps naively, Finch and Veneman, who saw the department as a bastion of the Republican Party's liberal wing, believed they would be able to make the policy decisions themselves at the departmental level and rely on Ball, considered the supreme administrator after his triumph with Medicare, to implement them at the agency level. Then again, as Ball admitted, they faced considerable disarray as they

tried to take over control of the department from the career bureaucrats, nearly all of whom were Democrats, who ran it. "They
weren't really clear on who they were to get rid of and who they
had to keep," Ball recalled. "For example, they talked with me as
if I were a civil servant when, in fact, I was serving at the pleasure of the President."[19] By the time they got matters straightened out, Ball had already won their trust.

Although Ball received some support from Wilbur Mills, a
powerful figure with whom the new administration would have
to deal on economic and social policy, he faced the opposition of
John Byrnes. In June of Nixon's first year in office, Ball decided to
call on Byrnes and perhaps win his support to remain on the job.
Affable as always, Ball eased into the subject at hand. He had
heard rumors that Byrnes had some reservations about his remaining on the job and wanted to know if they were true. Byrnes
responded in an equally politic manner. He had no reservations
about Ball as a person and respected him for his integrity and
competence. Nonetheless, he had advised the administration that
it would be a good thing to change the top leadership at Social
Security in order to have someone who reflected the Republican
point of view in charge. Byrnes said that he had significant philosophical differences with liberals such as Wilbur Cohen and assumed that Ball would not have worked so happily in the Johnson administration if he did not share Cohen's views. Byrnes
feared the introduction of general revenues into the program and
worried that the minimum benefit would be raised so high as to
turn Social Security into a welfare program. Ball reassured Byrnes
that he shared the congressman's concerns. Although the two
parted amiably, Ball failed to convince Byrnes that he should
keep his job.[20]

The Battle with Robert J. Myers

Not only did Ball face problems with Byrnes, he also had to contain dissension within his own ranks. For more than a year, he
conducted a battle with Robert J. Myers, the program's respected
chief actuary, whose experience with Social Security went back to
the staff of the Committee on Economic Security in the summer
of 1934. Myers, who made the cost estimates for Social Security

legislation, enjoyed a close working relationship with both the House Committee on Ways and Means and the Senate Committee on Finance. As he summed up the situation, "there were few people who knew the program better than I did. There were fewer still who had worked there longer than I had, and even fewer who were Republican."[21]

Not as sophisticated a political operator as Ball, Myers tended to see things in well-defined actuarial terms; he had little of Ball's tactical subtlety, although he had considerable interpersonal skills and could be authoritative in congressional testimony and persuasive and cogent as a writer. He had gotten along reasonably well with Ball over the years, although as he put it, "I can't say we were pals." Still, as Martha Derthick noted, "the system tends to reject its actuaries," and Myers proved to be no exception.[22]

Myers claimed that his dissatisfaction with Ball began in the Eisenhower years when Ball, among others, "engaged in an underhanded and undercover campaign to thwart the administration's goals." The result was a larger Social Security program than the Eisenhower administration wanted to have and governmental encroachment on what some Republicans believed to be the turf of private pensions. Myers seethed as he watched Ball operate. "Once I figured out what was going on, I was offended," he later wrote. "This was just wrong, and it was dirty." Despite these feelings, Myers conceded Ball, whom he identified as "the foremost expansionist," his prerogatives as commissioner during the liberal Kennedy and Johnson era.

When Nixon became president, Myers entertained the thought that it would be his turn to run the agency. As the weeks passed and Ball stayed in the job, Myers was "stunned." He watched the way in which Ball ran the agency during a Republican administration with "growing anger" and finally decided to take his complaints, along with voluminous documentation in support of those complaints, to top management. If Myers could not have the job as his own, he figured he could at least let the Republican office holders know of Ball's disloyalty and possibly get Ball fired.[23]

Myers found it difficult to raise concerns in the administration over Ball. Secretary Robert Finch refused to see him and referred him to Under Secretary John Veneman, who told him that the administration knew of Ball's activities but chose to do nothing about them until after the 1972 election. Recognizing the futility of talking with department officials, Myers took his case to the White House, where he met with Clark Mollenhoff, an investigative journalist and special counsel to the president. Although sympathetic, Mollenhoff could do little to help Myers, who also pressed his case with his colleagues in the actuarial profession.[24]

Myers next decided to take his case public and to make speeches attacking Ball. Appearing before the American Pension Conference at the end of October 1969, Myers charged that expansionists in the Social Security Administration believed that the "government should provide a level of income replacement that is virtually as high as income before retirement." The Social Security staff, according to Myers, "have had the philosophy—carried out with almost a religious zeal—that what counts above all else is the expansion of the Social Security program." Some were dedicated to the expansion of the program "so that it takes over virtually all economic security needs."[25]

Myers did not name names, at least not in public, yet he made it clear that he had Ball in mind. He expanded on his feelings in an interview with the *Washington Star,* which ran a story with a provocative lead: "The chief actuary of the Social Security Administration charges that Democratic holdovers and career employes [*sic*] are sabotaging the Nixon administration's 'moderate' philosophies and substituting their own 'expansionist' policies." Asked to comment on the story by a congressional committee, Myers said, "an injustice is being done by the top Social Security Administration staff in continuing their research and planning activities along expansionist lines, contrary to the Nixon administration's policies."[26]

Ball handled Myers's charges with relative calm and considerable political savvy. He realized that, in attacking Ball, Myers was also criticizing the Nixon administration for allowing itself to be misled. The story in the *Star,* for example, mentioned that Myers placed the blame on Secretary Finch for trying too hard to please the Democrats. Ball prepared a statement in which he said he was "puzzled" by Myers's comments. "Mr. Myers does actuarial work," Ball said, and noted he was surprised that a career employee would make public statements implying criticism of the administration.[27] Myers quickly disavowed any intention of criticizing Finch, yet the damage had been done. Increasingly, Myers looked to be a disgruntled employee who put his personal vendettas above policy considerations. The more he protested and claimed to be acting in the public interest, the more intemperate he appeared.

To be sure, though, Myers attracted Ball's attention, particularly when Myers decided to publish a popular version of the speeches he had been giving as an article in the *Reader's Digest*. The piece appeared in the April 1970 edition under the title "Social Security at the Crossroads." It contained a personal and unflattering reference to Robert Ball, quoting a remark that Ball had made about introducing general revenues into the program. In language certain to resonate with the magazine's readers, Myers wrote that, "This means that after you pay as high a Social Security tax as can be directly squeezed out of you, you'll have to hand over ever bigger federal income and other taxes so as to provide a Social Security subsidy—a subsidy that will be as difficult to control as any other that finds its way into the federal bureaucracy." With this article, Myers had, as he put it, "nailed my theses to the church door," and he realized that it was time for him to leave the mother church.[28]

Ball awaited the appearance of the article with considerable apprehension. He tried to get an advance copy and to anticipate just how widely the article would be advertised. It promised, as Ball told Veneman, to "create quite a flurry of publicity."[29]

Ball expected Myers to resign simultaneously with the appearance of the article and had only another two weeks to wait before Myers submitted a formal letter of resignation to Secretary Finch. Myers used the letter as a public vehicle—he sent it to 150 people and kept several copies handy to give to others as the occasion arose—to dramatize his case and express frustration over the way in which his grievances had been treated. "Evidently no credence is placed in what I have related to you personally or in other evidence I have furnished to you," he wrote. He submitted his resignation with a sense of dismay because he had hoped to serve the Nixon administration "with great enthusiasm, since I strongly believe in its philosophy and goals."[30]

Even after the appearance of this letter, Ball chose to do nothing. Consulting with his superiors, he hoped to be able to fire Myers with cause, rather than over a broad philosophical disagreement. After submitting the letter, Myers remained at the

Social Security Administration and continued to make his speeches. Ball waited for an appropriate moment to accept Myers's offer to resign. "I finally ordered him to stay in Washington one time when he had a speech scheduled," Ball remembered. Choosing to ignore Ball's order and Ball's offer to send someone else from SSA to make the speech, Myers flew off to Miami Beach, rather than attending an advisory council meeting as Ball had wanted him to do. Shortly afterward, John Veneman wrote Myers and fired him for insubordination, even though Veneman's formulaically polite but short letter indicated otherwise.[31]

Extending the conflict, Myers, no longer with the government, charged that Robert Ball had attempted to "muzzle and intimidate me with regard to three speeches that I was making in support of the Nixon Administration's position on Social Security legislation."[32]

By this time, however, Ball had consolidated his position at HEW. Robert Finch, Nixon's first secretary of Health, Education, and Welfare suffered health problems related to the frustration and exhaustion of running the department. He resigned in favor of Elliot Richardson. The late June 1970 appointment of Richardson increased Ball's sense of security within the Nixon administration.

Ball had history with Richardson, who had served at HEW as an assistant secretary in the late 1950s, worked closely with Ball, and regarded him as an exemplary public servant. Then and later, Richardson made many testimonials on Ball's behalf, telling one person who interviewed him in 1977 that Ball "was the greatest bureaucrat I ever worked with. . . . He had all the moves and was extremely well plugged in on the Hill." In a book published toward the end of his life, Richardson said that he kept a list of "All-Time All-American Bureaucrats" in his head, and he put Robert Ball, along with vocational rehabilitation administrator Mary Switzer, at the very top of the list.[33]

Richardson was perfectly willing to defend Ball against Myers. On the same day that Richardson arrived on the job, a letter went out from Under Secretary Veneman offering to set the record straight on Myers's resignation. Written by Tom Joe, one of Ball's close friends in the department and a principal architect of the Nixon welfare reform proposals, the letter stated that "Commissioner Ball took no action which, in fairness, could be construed as an attempt to 'muzzle and intimidate' [Myers]."[34]

A relieved Ball wrote to his former boss Victor Christgau that the SSA was looking for a new chief actuary. "It was quite a long struggle," he added.[35] Nor did the struggle end with Myers's departure. Instead, Ball continued to shadow Myers's activities, reading his articles and asking SSA staff members to comment on them. He worried particularly about Myers's work as a consultant to the Social Security committees in Congress. Because so much of Social Security politics in the period between 1969 and 1972 was about actuarial assumptions, Ball was concerned about Myers's ability to undermine the Social Security Administration's legislative agenda. He warned an associate in 1972, for example, to be "very careful about dealings with Bob Myers in Bob Myers' role as working for the Senate Finance Committee" and told Alvin David to check out some statements that Myers made to the committee "since we'll certainly be asked" about them.[36]

If Ball showed a special sensitivity to Myers, he had much too cool a personality to maintain any permanent grudge. To be sure, relations between the two, both of whom remained active participants in Social Security affairs for the rest of the century, continued to be somewhat distant. Within a few years, however, Ball began to reestablish a working relationship with Myers that persisted through the 1980s and into the 1990s. The 1992 publication of Myers's autobiography, which reopened the question of his departure from SSA, caught Ball uncharacteristically off guard, unsure about how to respond to what he considered the personal attacks in the book. He decided to write Myers a careful memo, which ran to some forty-eight pages, raising questions about the book. In it Ball said that he was "genuinely surprised" by Myers's comments coming so many years after the fact. "I wouldn't have been at all surprised in 1970 or perhaps for several years after that," but Ball could not fathom how Myers could remain so angry for so long. He failed to appreciate the depth of Myers feelings, since, having won the battle, Ball had moved on to other things.[37]

The Policy Debate in the Nixon Administration

Even as Ball fought to keep his position and dueled with Robert Myers, he plunged into the inner social policy debates of the

Nixon administration. The point of departure was a report by Arthur Burns, the Columbia economist and former economic adviser to President Eisenhower, that looked into Nixon's campaign promises and made some initial recommendations to the president. Burns opposed the idea of automatic adjustments in Social Security benefits to compensate for rises in prices, even though Nixon had proposed such a measure during the campaign.

Burns gave two main arguments. The first was that benefits would go up as prices rose but not down when prices fell. The second was that the measure would, as Burns put it, "institutionalize inflation." The elderly, many of whom lived on fixed incomes, constituted an important constituency against inflation because it affected them more adversely than it did other groups. If their pensions were guaranteed against price rises, they would then drop their "powerful resistance to inflationary policies" and lose interest in the problem altogether.

So Burns fell back on the traditional policymaking system for Social Security. He recommended that Nixon propose Social Security legislation to compensate people for the recent increase in prices but not include automatic increases for the future. Burns's position coincided with that of Wilbur Mills, who, everyone assumed, held a lock over Social Security policy. Burns hoped that Nixon would send Congress a special message on Social Security later in the year.[38]

Within a few weeks of becoming president, Nixon read Burns's brief report and asked his other economic advisers, his Treasury secretary, his domestic policy counselors, and his HEW secretary for their reactions. Preparing Finch's reply to the president, Ball played things cautiously. Despite his own predilections in favor of automatic adjustments, he advised Finch and Veneman not to push for immediate adoption of the measure. At the same time, he recommended that they not reject the measure, as Burns had, but rather wait until a Social Security advisory council had had a chance to study it.[39]

The Social Security Administration presented Secretary Finch with a balanced brief on the subject of automatic cost-of-living adjustments. It began by noting Nixon's endorsement of the idea during the campaign and then mentioned that Gerald Ford (R–Michigan), John Byrnes, and Melvin Laird—all influential Republicans—had introduced bills on the subject. With so much already invested in the measure by the Republicans, it would not be prudent simply to dismiss the measure as Burns wanted to do. On the contrary, it had much to recommend it. Since benefits would rise with or without the automatic adjustments, then it made sense to "recognize this fact in the law and give the beneficiaries and potential beneficiaries the additional sense of security that would result." Such a system would reduce the lag between benefit adjustments and might have the effect of taking Social Security out of politics, enabling proposals to be studied by an advisory council rather than in the partisan atmosphere of Congress, where Republicans suffered a permanent disadvantage.

At the same time, the Social Security Administration conceded that some of Burns's arguments had merit. If benefit increases occurred automatically "in ways that cannot be fully anticipated, there may be no opportunity to offset the inflationary impact." Then there was the practical matter, recognized by all, that Wilbur Mills opposed the measure, which meant it would very likely fail to get past Congress, at least for the moment. Putting these things together, the Social Security Administration concluded that the issue was too close to call and that a final decision on it should be postponed. In the meantime, the administration should propose a traditional benefit increase, perhaps on the order of 7 percent, payable from the surplus generated by rising wages and raising the taxable wage base from $7,800 to $8,400.[40]

In the spring and summer of 1969, the Nixon administration debated three important Social Security questions. The first was how large a benefit increase to recommend to Congress. The second was how to finance the increase and in particular how to mesh the benefit increase with other aspects of fiscal policy. For example, the Bureau of the Budget went along with the idea of a 7 percent increase that was being discussed early in the year but hoped to finance it with higher tax rates, which would yield higher budgetary surpluses in 1970, than the Social Security Administration advocated. In addition, the bureau looked with less favor on raising the taxable wage base than did Ball and his agency. The third question under debate was whether or not to propose automatic cost-of-living adjustments, with Ball in favor and Burns opposed.[41]

The debate resembled the discussion of welfare reform that took place at exactly the same time and among many of the same people. Arthur Burns and his deputy Martin Anderson argued that domestic counselor Daniel Moynihan's plans for a guaranteed income would greatly expand the welfare rolls and lead to a reduction in the number of hours people at the bottom of the labor market would work. Burns played the role of the defender of the traditional system and Moynihan the role of the innovator. In the Social Security debate, Burns also defended the traditional system and Ball, like Moynihan a Democrat, played the role of the innovator. Unlike Moynihan, who worked in the White House, Ball had to operate through surrogates in the Department of Health, Education, and Welfare. Unlike Moynihan, a flamboyant figure described by one of his policy rivals in the White House as a "playful porpoise," Ball tried not to call attention to himself.

Despite these differences in bureaucratic position and personality, Moynihan and Ball made similar arguments. As Democrats, they put forward proposals that they felt represented good political plays for the Republicans, even though they knew that key congressional Democrats would oppose them. The two proposals had similar sources of appeal to the Republicans in that both would cut down on the discretion of traditionally Democrat operators in the policy process. In the case of welfare reform, a guaranteed income would reduce the power of inner-city social workers. In the case of Social Security reform, automatic cost-of-living adjustments, similarly remote and mechanistic measures, would undercut the power of congressional barons such as Wilbur Mills and Russell Long. Both proposals, although designed to appeal to the Republicans, would, in fact, make the programs under debate more liberal, giving Moynihan and Ball what they wanted and earning the disapproval of Burns, who argued that, in the end, neither proposal served the Republicans' best interest.[42]

The Nixon Proposals

Because the argument was so difficult to resolve, Nixon delayed putting forward Social Security and welfare reform measures; then he decided in favor of the innovators in both cases. On April 14 he sent a strong signal that he would shortly recommend a Social Security increase, and the White House geared up to send out a Social Security message that would have included the 7 percent increase and little else.[43] Rather than send this message, Nixon decided to pull it back and to consider the matter further.

By the end of the summer, Nixon had resolved to make the bold play on both welfare reform and Social Security and to link the two measures together. On August 8, 1969, Nixon unveiled the Family Assistance Plan in a nationally televised talk, and on September 25 he released a special message on Social Security. In the interim Nixon's White House staff told him he should not formally submit the welfare reform legislation without also submitting the Social Security legislation. If the administration did not take the initiative on Social Security legislation, noted Senator John Williams (R–Delaware), then Mills would do it for him. Congressman Byrnes said he would not be interested in sponsoring the family assistance bill unless it had a Social Security increase tied to it.[44]

On September 17 Nixon signed into law an amendment to the Older Americans Act and announced that he would send Congress a Social Security message in a week. By delaying from the beginning of the year, the administration had paid a price. New cost estimates, made from more recent data on wage increases, indicated a larger surplus in the Social Security trust funds than had been anticipated. That had the effect of ratcheting up the amount of a benefit increase that the administration felt obligated to recommend from 7 to 10 percent, and even then the administration realized that Mills, anticipating the elections of 1970, could decide to raise the amount even more.

Nixon tried to get Congress to hold the line. In an October message on legislative programs, for example, Nixon said, "I know the political temptations here. Why not balloon the benefits now, far above 10 per cent, for political rewards in 1970? I remind the Congress that its long since time that we stopped the political over-reactions which fuel the inflation that robs the poor, the elderly, and those on fixed incomes."[45]

Nixon held out the cost-of-living adjustments as his assurance to the elderly that he would protect their interests. It was less necessary for the elderly to get all they could in the way of increased benefits in Social Security in the 1969 legislation if Social Security beneficiaries could be assured that their future benefits would be protected against the risk of inflation. As Nixon expressed this idea in his September 25 message, drafted by William Safire, "the way to prevent future unfairness is to attach the benefit schedule to the cost of living." That would "remove questions about future years," "remove the system from biennial politics," and "make fair treatment of beneficiaries a matter of certainty rather than a matter of hope."[46]

On the day that the president's Social Security proposals were released, Ball and Burns briefed the White House press corps on the issue. Burns expressed some skepticism about the proposal. He said that the automatic adjustments would, in the president's opinion, make "for a more rational revision of Social Security legislation in the future," without the need to wait for an election year and "have the two parties compete." He added, however, that "things may or may not work out that way."

Ball confined his remarks to the technical side of the legislation. He assured members of the press that the automatic adjustments would be financially sound by lecturing them, in his usual patient and effective way, on the rudiments of Social Security finance. "Wages go up more than the cost of living goes up," he explained. "So you get more income to the system with the same contribution rates than you need to pay for the cost of living increase. So, it is completely sound . . . financially to put in a provision like this and to have at the same time an automatic increase in the earnings base."[47] For Ball the increase in earnings base—the amount of a person's earnings on which the person and his or her employer paid Social Security taxes—from $7,800 to $9,000, with automatic adjustments after 1972, made the president's proposal particularly attractive.

Congressional Action in 1969

Wilbur Mills regarded the president's proposals only as a starting point. Although he rejected the idea of the automatic cost-of-living adjustment, he thought that benefits could be raised more and the earnings base raised higher than suggested by the president. The traditional supporters of Social Security expansion, such as the American Federation of Labor and Congress of Industrial Organizations, tended to agree with Mills, rather than with Nixon.

Although Ball tried to serve his superiors in the Nixon administration as best he could, he also remained in close touch with the Washington representatives of the labor movement. In

November, for example, he had lunch with three AFL-CIO staff members who told him that they believed that a 15 percent benefit increase, as favored by Mills and some, but not all, congressional Republicans was inevitable. The only question in their minds was whether the Senate would have time to act on the measure before adjournment for the year. They had many more problems with the welfare reform aspects of the legislation than with the Social Security aspects.[48]

A week later Ball and Robert Myers learned from Mills, another of the people with whom Ball remained in close touch, despite his identity as a member of a Republican administration, that Mills was considering a 20 percent benefit increase. Myers indicated that the additional 5 percent increase beyond what Mills had previously proposed would cost an additional half percent of payroll (payroll taxes would have to be raised that amount to cover the increase). Wary of Myers, who was just beginning to pull away from the agency, Ball thought this estimate a little high. Mills continued to think in terms of raising the earnings base to $12,000. So, even though Ball officially supported the administration's bill, he also worked with Mills and others to encourage a benefit increase beyond what the administration wanted.[49]

As 1969 came to a close, Social Security politics reached a climax for the year. Mills and Byrnes agreed jointly to sponsor a 15 percent benefit increase, financed out of the "favorable actuarial balance" rather than from an increase in tax rates or an increase in the earnings base. Byrnes gave up his advocacy of automatic cost-of-living adjustments, but only for the moment.

True to the usual decorum in Social Security politics, the measure passed the House unanimously. The Senate, meanwhile, attached its version of a 15 percent benefit increase, financed with a $12,000 maximum earnings base, to the Tax Reform Act of 1969, considered to be legislation that the president would not veto. Ball realized that only the 15 percent increase would stand; the rest of the Senate's significant additions, such as the $12,000 maximum earnings base, would be dropped in conference. As usual, his predictions about the course of Social Security legislation proved to be correct. The result of all of the maneuvering was a 15 percent benefit increase and no automatic cost-of-living adjustments. In the competition with the Nixon administration, Mills had won the first round.[50]

Congressional Action in 1970

In 1970, Congress continued to work on legislation in the hope of coming up with a comprehensive bill to cover Social Security and perhaps welfare as well. Although both houses of Congress ended up passing bills, a conference committee to reconcile the bills never met, and Congress completed its business without a new Social Security law, making 1970 the only year between 1968 and 1973 not to have a major increase in Social Security benefits.

Despite the apparent lack of results, the year was not without its own political significance. Wilbur Mills hoped to conduct business as usual. Toward that end he asked his committee to approve a 5 percent increase in benefits, in effect picking up the difference between the 15 percent increase that Congress had passed in 1969 and the 20 percent for which he had hoped. As usual, he left an automatic increase in the benefit level out of the legislation. His committee went along with him. As with most Ways and Means measures, the bill passed the House. On the floor of the House, however, Representative Byrnes moved that the bill be recommitted "with instructions" to add the automatic adjustments. Such motions routinely failed. In this instance, however, a coalition of Republicans and northern Democrats supported the measure, and it passed. The Committee on Ways and Means went back and changed the measure to include indexing benefits and the wage base. Even though Mills warned his colleagues that they were making a mistake and losing control over one of their most popular programs, the amended measure passed the House by a comfortable margin.[51]

Ball realized that Mills had suffered a humiliating defeat. In Ball's opinion, "Mills was a very careful man. He did not take a bill to the floor unless he knew he was going to win. . . . The papers always wrote about him as the 'powerful Chairman of the Ways and Means Committee' and he valued that very much—that he was in control. The idea of taking a bill to the floor of the House and losing on it, or even losing a major provision in it that he hadn't agreed to, was anathema."[52]

Keeping his distance from Mills, Ball turned his attention to the Senate Finance Committee. With the turn of events in the House, the actions of the Senate acquired a new significance. With Ball closely monitoring the process, the Finance Committee decided at the beginning of October that it wanted a 10 percent, rather than a 5 percent, increase—once again, the passage of time and the proximity to the election had their costs—to raise the wage base to $12,000, and to raise the minimum benefit level to $100.

In closed executive sessions that Ball attended on a daily basis, the committee members turned to Ball to suggest ways to come up with enough money to fund their proposal. In this particular case, Ball offered various technical changes, such as lowering the amount of money a retired person could earn and still receive Social Security benefits, and proposed adjusting the tax rates. For example, the House wanted the 1973 rate to be 5.2 percent of taxable payroll; Ball suggested that it be 6.0 percent.

In addition to making the committee's math come out right, Ball also needed to keep his superiors in the administration informed of how the changes affected the budget in future years. In this case, the Senate package would have added $2 billion in extra revenues to the budget in fiscal 1972 but made the 1971 fiscal year budget worse off than before. To correct that particular problem, the 1971 tax rate would have to be raised from 5.2 percent to 5.3 percent. "I don't know that we can sell this last schedule," Ball advised Veneman.[53]

President Nixon had already decided that he would continue to support what administration officials described as the "automatic escalator tied to the cost of living." Passage of the automatic adjustments looked to be very close, a matter only of fine-tuning the proposal. On October 13, the Senate Finance Committee agreed to support the House provisions but with the proviso that the automatic provisions would go into effect only if Congress failed to increase benefits, change the tax rate, or make a change in the maximum earnings base. In other words, the automatic provisions would not go into effect in a year when Congress had itself increased the benefits or changed the financing provisions. Congress could do a change by hand, so to speak, and gain the credit in the traditional manner. Only if Congress decided against that would the automatic increases become effective. "I see no problem in this nor do I see it as any significant modification of the House bill," Ball told Veneman. In fact, Ball was so pleased that he drafted a message of congratulations from the president to the committee and carried it by hand to the White House.[54]

What was striking about this process was not only that people depended on the technical expertise of Ball and his colleagues but also that he was allowed to operate from such an inside position of trust. Democrats such as Russell Long trusted him as a fellow Democrat interested in program expansion and eager to be helpful in that regard. Hence, they did not hesitate to include him in their executive sessions. Indeed, his ability to manipulate the numbers and come up with creative financing ideas made him indispensable in that setting.

Republicans such as Elliot Richardson and John Veneman also came to trust him as someone who could provide reliable information about what the Democrats in Congress would do and who could look out for, if not always actively defend, the interests of the administration. As the Senate committee met, for example, Richardson called Ball for information. In this case he asked Ball about the relationship between Senator Albert Gore (D–Tennessee), a key vote on the Family Assistance Plan, and Wilbur Cohen. Ball, who knew both Gore and Cohen, described Gore's relationship with Cohen as "friendly and easy." Richardson, who knew Gore and Cohen much less well, asked about the advisability of using the AFL-CIO and Wilbur Cohen to push Gore to support the Family Assistance Plan. "Well, what can you lose by having Gardner [the former HEW secretary], Wilbur [Cohen], and, if he's willing, Biemiller [the AFL-CIO lobbyist]? I think Wilbur would like to do something," Ball replied. Once again he had validated his worth by giving Secretary Richardson a line on a Democrat whom Richardson would need if he expected to pass welfare reform. Later in the conversation, Ball was able to predict accurately what the Senate Finance Committee would do on the wage base, something that Richardson, as a Republican and an outsider to Congress, had no real way of knowing. By providing such intelligence, which facilitated the administration's planning, Ball solidified his role within the administration.[55]

Although the Senate went on to pass its version of the bill in 1970, the process took until nearly the end of the calendar year. Because significant differences existed between the House and Senate versions of the bill, the Senate formally requested a conference and appointed conferees. Mills blocked passage of the legislation by not acceding to the Senate's request for a conference. The Congress adjourned on January 2, 1971, without a Social

Security bill. Mills had won round two in his battle to fight the automatic cost-of-living adjustments but at the cost of a personal defeat on the House floor.[56]

Congressional Action in 1971: The Conversion of Wilbur Mills

It was at this point that Ball, on his own motion, decided to intervene personally with Mills. Ball had lived through this sort of impasse before during the fight over Medicare. In that instance, too, Wilbur Mills had ignored the wishes of the Kennedy and Johnson administrations and blocked passage of a measure that constituted a high priority of the party in power. In 1964, for example, the Senate passed a Medicare bill, and Mills refused to discuss it in conference. As a result the Democrats went into an election year not only without Medicare but without an increase in Social Security cash benefits as well. Soon after the election, however, Mills realized that he did not have the votes to prevail on Medicare, and he shifted his position in time to control the legislative action that led to that measure's 1965 passage. Ball, who had vivid memories of what had happened in 1964, hoped that Mills might be brought around on automatic adjustments of benefits, just as he had been converted on Medicare.[57]

As it became clear that Mills would not agree to a conference committee at the end of 1970, Ball decided to pay him a visit. As was customary, Ball did not attack or criticize Mills; the Social Security Administration never did that. Instead, Ball accepted Mills's explanation that "When the Senate version of the Social Security bill reached the Speaker's desk on December 31, 1970, with 295 separate Senate amendments, it was clear to me that there was not enough time to hold a conference with the Senate on the bill. Indeed it would have been the height of irresponsibility for us to have attempted such a conference."[58]

On that very New Year's Eve, Ball traveled from Baltimore to Washington in a government car to talk with Mills. His mission was to convince Mills to "take over the issue and propose a cost of living adjustment himself." Ball sought a way for Mills to support the measure and still save face with his congressional colleagues. The idea that occurred to him was "to leave Congress free to decide what to do and get credit for it whenever they wanted to." If Congress voted an increase in benefits, in other words, then that vote could take the place of the automatic adjustments.[59]

Riding in the car, Ball scribbled his ideas down on paper and composed a memo to Mills. In it he urged Mills to make Social Security the first bill of the new congressional session and, if possible, to get the bill designated as H.R. 1, just as Medicare had been in 1965. He also spelled out the recommended new approach on the automatics "that would leave the initiative with Congress and be nothing but a 'fail-safe' method or minimum guarantee in the event that Congress *did not act* for *two* years and the cost-of-living rose at least some percentage (say 3%) during the period" (emphasis in original). "The theory of all this," Ball explained, "is that if the Congress acts . . . , this is the way they want it to be. Only if they fail to act for two full years because of some very unusual situation (and I doubt if it would ever happen . . .) would the purchasing power guarantee come into play. Yet psychologically the provision would give people a certain security."[60]

Primed by Ball with this new strategy, Mills did, in fact, introduce a bill at the very beginning of the Ninety-second Congress. It was ambitious in nature, incorporating a previously passed version of the Family Assistance Act and a 10 percent increase in Social Security benefits. At the same time, it was also preliminary in nature, without a provision for an automatic cost-of-living adjustment and without fully developed financing mechanisms. By the end of February, Mills set his staff to work on an automatic adjustment plan that followed the specifications of the proposal Ball had already outlined.[61]

Although the administration referred to this new plan as a product of the Ways and Means Committee staff, Ball was the real author. The appearance of this plan meant that Mills had finally given in on the question of cost-of-living adjustments. Just as on Medicare some six years earlier, he realized he no longer had the votes to hold his committee together on the question of automatic cost-of-living adjustments, and so he capitulated. Thanks to Ball, he had a way of yielding on the question without appearing to go back on his earlier stand that Congress should retain control over Social Security benefits. His change of position meant that he and Ball were once again legislative allies, leading to a congruence of objectives that the Nixon administration would find hard to oppose.

Once again, Social Security politics reverted to its usual form. The Ways and Means Committee voted for Mills's new plan on April 6, 1971.[62] Six weeks later, the committee reported out a complete bill, described by Richard Nixon as "an important landmark in the history of both social security and public welfare reform" and a "momentous step."[63] Early in the summer, the House passed H.R. 1.

The Senate had already bought itself some time in considering the legislation, a process that began at the end of July 1971. Earlier in the year, the Senate had attached an amendment to a public debt ceiling bill that provided for a 10 percent increase in Social Security benefits but that lacked cost-of-living adjustments. Anxious to get the benefit increase and mindful that none had been passed in 1970, Mills acquiesced to this maneuver. It passed in the usual bipartisan flurry. "I do not think there is anybody on this floor who would vote against the 10 percent increase retroactive to January. I think there is general agreement that this is desirable and that it is needed," said Representative Byrnes on the House floor on March 16. The measure carried by a vote of 360 to 3.[64]

In the Senate, welfare reform, rather than the cost-of-living adjustments, posed the major stumbling blocks to passage of a comprehensive bill. Russell Long, the irascible committee chairman who had been at the center of previous controversies over welfare, began the Senate Finance Committee hearings by saying the Family Assistance Plan would be the most difficult part of the bill. He described the Social Security provisions of the bill as "old friends" and doubted that the committee would need to spend much time considering them. But he threatened to hold the Social Security parts of the bill hostage as the committee made a "thorough evaluation of the welfare features of H.R. 1."[65]

The Advisory Council on Social Security

The thorough evaluation took up the rest of the year and dragged into the next, which happened to be a presidential election year. The delay made an important difference because it ultimately led to a much higher Social Security benefit than the one

Mills had originally advocated. There were both inside and outside reasons that the 20 percent increase came about in 1972. The inside reasons concerned the work of the Advisory Council on Social Security and Ball's advocacy of its recommendations to change the program's actuarial assumptions. The outside reasons had to do with the presidential politics of the year.

The story of the Social Security Advisory Council began in the spring of 1969 and lasted until 1971. In that first spring of the Nixon administration, Ball turned his attention to selecting members for an advisory council. Even though the selection process involved close consultations with HEW officials and with such umbrella organizations as the United States Chamber of Commerce, the Committee on Economic Development, the National Association of Manufacturers, and the AFL-CIO, Ball retained substantial influence over the process. If an organization delayed in sending its suggestions, Ball was happy to oblige with ideas. For example, he hinted to Under Secretary John Veneman that Gabriel Hauge, the chairman of the board at the Manufacturers Hanover Trust, might be a good name for the United States Chamber of Commerce to suggest. He had a hand in picking Arthur Flemming, a liberal Republican and the former secretary of Health, Education, and Welfare, to chair the council and met with Flemming to review who else should be on it. Douglas Brown, a perennial favorite of Ball's, found a spot as one of the public members, as did Kermit Gordon, who had already done yeoman service on the Health Insurance Benefits Advisory Council.[66]

In an illustration of Ball's close involvement in the process, Ball, rather than Flemming or Veneman, called Whitney Young of the Urban League to solicit his participation. At one point Ball asked Flemming whether their choices would be criticized as being too liberal, and Flemming reassured him that "he thought it was ok from that standpoint."[67]

Appointed in May, the Advisory Council on Social Security met for the first time in June and continued to meet throughout the remainder of 1969 and 1970. Ball attended each of the meetings. In November 1970 he sent Elliot Richardson a summary of the tentative decisions reached by the council but with the caveat that these decisions might change in the light of changes in the legislative situation. As always, the decisions appeared to be highly technical, such as one that recommended that a worker

Robert Ball testifying before Congress, with HEW Secretary Elliot Richardson at his side. Richardson greatly admired Ball, whom he described as one the greatest civil servants he ever met. Photograph courtesy of SSA History Archives.

applying for disability benefits should meet the same "insured-status requirements as now provided for retirement insurance benefits." Looking at the list, one would have had to be very alert to detect any major departures from the program as it already existed. Furthermore, despite the supposed independence of the advisory council, it was clear that the council deliberated with a close eye on the legislative situation and that it sought the approval of Ball and the administration. "If you have serious difficulty with any of the major directions the Council is taking," Ball advised Richardson, "perhaps you and Arthur Flemming and I ought to have an early discussion. The recommendations, though, seem sound to me."[68]

The council's final report did not appear until March 31, 1971, its release delayed because Flemming and Ball thought that legislation containing cost-of-living adjustments might pass at the end of 1970. Mills put a stop to that. Nonetheless, the extra time proved useful to Ball. He and Alvin David helped to draft a significant part of the report after the council had stopped meeting, an indication of the great interest that Ball took in the council's work and, to be less conspiratorial, the sheer span of time over which the council had remained in session. Indeed, by the time the report appeared, one of the members, Whitney Young, had died, and two had resigned.[69]

The 1971 report contained the usual set of detailed recommendations that made it difficult to read as any more than a laundry list. Contrary to its soporific language, however, the report represented an important point of departure in Social Security policy. Not only did the report adopt the idea of automatic cost-of-living adjustments; it also proposed a new set of actuarial assumptions for the program. Key recommendations included one that "the law should provide a guarantee that, in the absence of congressional action, social security benefits will be at least kept up to date, automatically, with increases in prices, and that the contribution and benefit base . . . will be automatically adjusted to increases in earnings levels." The council also specifically recommended that the earnings base (or wage base or contribution and benefit base—the terms tended to be used interchangeably) be increased to $12,000 in 1974.

Only at the very end of the report did the council turn to the subject of financing. Here, in the usual innocuous prose, was the recommendation that the "actuarial cost estimates for the cash benefit program be based . . . on the assumptions that the earnings level will rise, that the contribution and benefit base will be increased as earnings level rise, and that benefit payments will be increased as prices rise." With these recommendations, Ball succeeded in having an advisory group ratify the ideas that he had first proposed to Alvin David in 1965 as the next steps in Social Security.[70]

The adoption of the "dynamic" as opposed to "static" actuarial assumptions reflected the fact that Bob Myers had left Social Security during the course of the council's deliberations. Before his departure he had addressed the council on this subject and argued for the necessity of maintaining the level wage hypothesis. As Martha Derthick noted, "if he had stayed the revision of the level earnings assumptions would have been much more difficult, for Myers was wedded to the technique." Only after he left did the council establish a subcommittee to take a critical look at the program's actuarial assumptions, and in Derthick's words, the charge of this subcommittee, written by Ball, "constituted the most explicit possible invitation to recommend dynamic assumptions." Not surprisingly, the dynamic assumptions carried the day.[71]

Transmitting the report to the president, Elliot Richardson put it in the most congenial possible terms. The majority of the council, Richardson reported, supported President Nixon's recommendations, and he should feel gratified. Still, Richardson hesitated to interject the council's proposals into the ongoing Social Security debate. He thought it best to postpone taking a position until the administration developed its legislative program in the fall of 1971.[72]

Ball did not hesitate. He wasted no time in pushing to have the dynamic assumptions adopted as administration policy. He portrayed the policy changes as neither liberal nor conservative, one of his common tactics when he was attempting to forge a consensus on a particular issue. "Actually," he told the Senate Finance Committee, "you can argue this either way." Once the council's approach went into effect, he asserted, it would provide a "better control on costs" than the existing system.

Explaining why this situation should be so, Ball first pointed to the council's decision not to build up huge reserves but rather to operate on a current cost basis. Simply put, the program would take in only a little more than it needed to pay out in a given year, leading to what Ball described as "the recommended contingency level of 1 year's benefit payments." Second, he noted that the dynamic assumptions would be another inhibiting factor in Social Security's growth because the program would not keep stumbling on unexpected surpluses. Instead, the existence of rising wages would already be factored into the projections of future revenues. "Under the new approach," Ball explained, "additional financing will have to be provided at the time the benefits are increased above those necessary to keep up with the cost of living." The old approach made constant expansion possible without raising taxes; the new approach would make it impossible to raise benefits, beyond the level of the automatic increase, without also raising taxes.[73]

The debate over the actuarial assumptions took place in settings such as the Office of Management and Budget (OMB) and other agencies whose inner workings lay hidden from public view. Within the circle of economists and actuaries who followed the arcana of Social Security financing, however, Ball's ideas were not without controversy. For one thing, a switch to the dynamic assumptions would give the system a jolt of money in the form of anticipated future revenues that would suddenly appear on the books as the result of recognizing that wages would rise. This new money, which Ball described as a "one-time opportunity," could be spent in the form of increased benefits, even before putting the system on automatic pilot and linking future benefits to the rate of inflation. Or it could be spent in the form of reduced taxes to maintain benefits at their current levels.

For another thing, a switch to the dynamic assumptions made it necessary to estimate the future rate of real wage growth, a function of nominal wage levels and the general rate of inflation. That had been much less important when one simply assumed that wage levels would remain the same. Even Ball expressed some uncertainty about the course of real earnings over time. The growth in the labor force appeared to be taking place in services, rather than in industries, and productivity improvements, and hence higher wages, were more difficult to achieve in settings where people served other people rather than attending a machine. Similarly, the trend toward increased environmental protection implied a slower rate of productivity growth.[74]

Some of the economists in the administration, such as Arthur Laffer, at the time an assistant to OMB Director George Shultz and later to be a player in President Reagan's economic policies, objected to the effects of the dynamic assumptions on economic policy. Reserve financing, a feature of the old system, presumably increased the rate of savings in the economy and facilitated future growth. Laffer believed that the new system would make it less easy to use Social Security for fiscal purposes.[75]

Then there was the matter of Robert Myers's opposition to the idea. According to Paul O'Neill, an OMB official in the Nixon administration and later the secretary of the Treasury for George W. Bush, Myers favored current-cost financing (not building up large reserves) but not the dynamic wage assumptions and "would be expected to be involved in the public debate." Ball, for his part, said that the administration need not worry about Myers. His opposition to the idea of "shifting from the level-wage assumption in the cash benefit program to a rising wage assumption" would seem "to the public a highly technical matter and can hardly be a matter of public debate. It seems to me that the burden will be on him to argue that it makes sense to base cost estimates on level wages when everybody knows that wages are going to rise." Besides, Ball noted that Wilbur Mills and Russell Long favored the idea. "I think what argument there is on the rising wage assumption will be confined to highly technical circles, mostly actuarial, and that we will win and that there won't be much argument about the current cost idea." As Ball correctly forecast, his campaign, first within the advisory council and later within the administration, changed the climate of the Social Security debate, despite lingering opposition from some administration economists.[76]

Mills and the 20 Percent Increase

As the 1972 legislative year began, Ball continued his efforts to get the administration and Congress to accept the advisory council's notions of the contingency reserve and dynamic earnings assumptions. In January he indicated to Alvin David that he personally wanted to be present at a discussion of these ideas with the staff of the Ways and Means Committee. The trouble was that he had not received a firm signal from the administration on what attitude it would take toward the recommendations, even though these recommendations had been discussed in Washington circles for nearly a year.[77]

The recommendations on financing had relevance to Social Security politics because they had the potential to yield a lot of money. In a key development, the Social Security actuaries, led by Charles Trowbridge, who had replaced Myers, now estimated that if one retained the contribution (or tax) rate of the present law and adopted the new actuarial assumptions, then it would be possible to have a 20 percent increase in Social Security benefits. That figure was 15 percentage points higher than the 5 percent increase that was in the bill passed in the House and under consideration in the Senate. Thus within actuarial circles was born the 20 percent increase that became the object of Social Security politics in an election year.[78]

Ball did not try to hide the possibility of a 20 percent increase from the Nixon administration. On the contrary, he took the idea to Elliot Richardson, whom Ball believed was "quite sympathetic to the idea. That would have been quite a coup for the Republicans in this Democratic program to be for a 20 percent increase, and have it fully financed without having to increase taxes."[79] Richardson, in turn, took the idea to his superiors in the White House.

Richardson found that Budget Director George Shultz, among others, reacted warily to Ball's ideas when Elliot Richardson presented them to him. Shultz recommended that the administration not endorse the council's financing recommendation because that would put the administration on the record as "changing the very structure of the Social Security program."[80]

Wilbur Mills received the news about the possibility of a 20 percent increase with considerably more enthusiasm. In his customary dual role as adviser to the Republican administration and the Democratic Congress, Ball did nothing to hide the possibility of the large increase from Mills. "Well, Mills knows a lot about the Social Security system," Ball later explained. "He's really expert. So he asked me . . . what the change in the estimating procedure would produce. And I had to tell him." Toward the end of his life, Mills himself admitted in an interview with a historian on another matter that he would never have recommended the large increase without checking it out with Ball.[81]

On February 22, Mills, no doubt after talking with Ball, sent Ball a formal memo requesting that Social Security technicians check "out for me the adequacy" of financing a 20 percent increase. He asked whether a $12,000 wage base and a tax rate of 4.6 percent (each for employers and employees for the cash benefit program only) would "be sufficient for the cash benefit program under the general principles of the Advisory Council's recommendations on financing."[82]

The next day Wilbur Mills made public his Social Security proposal for a 20 increase and put the administration, if not Social Security Commissioner Ball, in a considerable bind. With Ball in his office, Elliot Richardson called up John Ehrlichman in the White House and gave him the news. It was one thing for politicians with presidential aspirations such as George McGovern (D–South Dakota) and Frank Church (D–Idaho) to propose a large increase; it was quite another for Mills, who had the power to accomplish what he suggested, to make a similar proposal.

The problem for the administration had not only to do with competition between Nixon and the Democrats over the level of Social Security benefits but also with the budgetary effect of Mills's plan, technically an amendment to his bill that he wanted the Senate to consider. Because of the particular way that the tax collections worked out, the result of moving from a 5 to a 20 percent increase meant, as Richardson put it, "a swing on the 73 budget from a small surplus of 300 million to a minus of 5.7 [billion]." "Wow," replied Ehrlichman.[83]

Ehrlichman hoped that George Shultz would have an answer to the problem. Shultz had no real answer. He agreed with Richardson that John Veneman, attending the executive sessions of the Senate Finance Committee, should do his best to get the bill written in a way that did the least damage to the 1973 budget but not to take a public position that would commit the administration to a particular position. "In the meantime," Shultz added, "we should be getting our ducks in a row and it should be something the President should see."[84] In a similar spirit, Richardson told one of Shultz's principal assistants that he did not want Veneman to give any Democrat on the Senate Finance Committee the impression that the administration was fighting the 20 percent increase.[85]

Nixon and the 20 Percent Increase

"Wilbur has temporarily upstaged us," said Arthur Flemming, now back in government as a member of the Nixon administration. Like Richardson, Flemming hesitated to come out against the 20 percent increase. "I have the feeling," he told Richardson, that "if we don't come up with some affirmative stance our house of cards will fall in on us." At the same time, Richardson worried that the Senate would raise Mills's 20 percent figure even higher, even though the 20 percent figure added about 6 billion dollars to the deficit and, according to Richardson's calculations, would mean a 45 percent benefit increase in Social Security in two years.

The Republicans speculated on Wilbur Mills's motives. Some believed that he took his action because he was worried that, if he did not, the administration would. "It's clear Wilbur got wind of the fact that we're thinking along positive lines," Flemming noted. Others attributed the size of the recommended increase and its timing to Mills's newly discovered presidential ambitions. Flemming wanted to know, for example, if there were any presidential candidates participating in the Senate Finance Committee's markup of the Social Security bill. Richardson said that Vance Hartke (D–Indiana) was involved, but that he was probably off campaigning in New Hampshire. "I am sure that Wilbur probably has in mind the Florida primary," said Flemming. Richardson replied that he might be concentrating on New Hampshire, a state with a high concentration of elderly residents. Mills had even told Richardson that he expected to get 10 percent of the vote as a write-in candidate. "The bug has bitten him. That is clear," said Flemming.[86]

In this way, presidential politics became intertwined with policymaking for Social Security. In the past, presidential politics had figured in Social Security but only indirectly. Congress liked to mesh the pattern of Social Security benefit increases with the rhythm of election years. As a consequence, significant increases tended to come in even, rather than odd, years. At times, too, the Democratic Congress used Social Security to establish an issue for a presidential campaign. In Medicare, for example, key votes in the Senate came in 1960 and 1964—the first to put John Kennedy on record as supporting the measure and the second to record Senator Barry Goldwater (R–Arizona) as being against it. In the end, though, Social Security politics accommodated the desires of the permanent members of Congress who ran the program as much as did the predilections of presidential candidates. The passage of Medicare depended on Wilbur Mills, not John F. Kennedy or Lyndon Johnson, and it occurred in 1965, rather than in the presidential election year of 1964.[87]

For all of that, it mattered that the Senate's consideration of H.R. 1 was delayed until the election year of 1972. With no competition for the presidential nomination in the Republican Party and significant competition in the Democratic Party, it meant that presidential contenders McGovern and Muskie, among others, would use their Senate positions to heighten their differences with the administration. More importantly Wilbur Mills shook up the process by his desire to change his political identity from that of a permanent member of Congress to a member of his party's presidential ticket. Ball said his real objective was not to become president but rather vice president on a ticket with Senator Edward Kennedy, but one did not campaign to be vice president during the primary season in America.[88] Hence, as Richardson and Flemming observed, Mills was an announced presidential candidate.

Ball followed the reaction to the Mills proposal with considerably less anxiety than did the Republican principals in the administration. He asked the public relations office to keep a sharp eye out for all available editorials, news stories, and cartoons about the Mills bill. More to the point, he did what he could to get the administration to accept the 20 percent idea. "I ought to send a short memo to the Secretary suggesting endorsement of a 20 percent benefit," he told Alvin David at the end of February.[89]

By March 7, Ball had come up with a way to get the 20 percent benefit increase but to lessen its impact on the budget. In particular, he suggested that the 20 percent increase take place in two stages: 5 percent to occur in June 1972 and 15 percent to take place in January 1973. He also recommended the maximum earnings base be raised to $12,000 for 1972, the fiscal year already underway. Ball claimed that, put together as he proposed, the proposals would have no effect on the budget for fiscal 1973, giving both Mills and the administration what they wanted. If the administration went along with these proposals, it could lay claim to moving nearly 2 million more Americans above the poverty line, including 1.4 million aged Social Security beneficiaries, who, as the administration well knew, tended to vote in presidential elections.[90]

Richardson accepted Ball's line of reasoning. John Veneman thought it might provide some mutual ground between the administration and the Congress, and he marveled at Ball's ingenuity. "When I read that memo of Ball's," said Veneman, "I thought how long has he had that in his hip pocket. He is like a magician. Just at the time you are at a critical point, he comes up with a solution."[91]

In this particular case, Ball failed to carry the point within the administration, although his proposals were debated at the very highest levels. On the same day Ball gave his suggestions on how to handle the Mills proposal to Richardson, President Nixon met with his top economic advisers to discuss the situation. George Shultz told him bluntly that some form of the increase would carry. Treasury Secretary John Connally said that by raising the wage base for Social Security, the administration would, in effect, be raising taxes, which it had pledged not to do. Nixon said that it was inconsistent to ask the American people to make sacrifices in an effort to fight inflation and then to raise Social Security benefits, which had already gone up a great deal, by 20 percent.[92]

Acting through Richardson and his aide Richard Darman, who would later play a lead role in the Reagan White House, Ball kept trying to get the president to change his mind. As Darman framed the alternatives, the president could reject Mills's proposal and oppose a proposal that was "very popular among the 20 million Americans over 65—a key group in your reelection strategy." Alternatively, the president could take no firm public position, but that would run the risk of him signing a major benefit increase into law and receiving no credit for it. Or the president could do what Ball wanted him to do, which was "to take a significant positive position—without causing any adverse effect on the budget" by agreeing to the 20 percent increase and Ball's financing suggestions. Some recalculations even showed that there would be a net gain to the budget of $1.1 billion. Although Richardson and Darman pitched the appeal to the president in political terms, they also argued in terms of the positive social effects the benefit increase would have. Older Americans were disproportionately poor; most retired people received no private pensions. Social Security benefits had kept up with prices but not with the standard of living as measured by wage increases. Furthermore, replacement rates, even with the 20 percent increase, would only be about 33 percent of pre-retirement take-home pay. As for the fact that a change in the wage base amounted to a tax increase, Richardson and Ball argued that most people viewed Social Security not as a tax "but as part of a contributory system which holds their future benefits in trust."[93]

On March 10, the president met with a group of high-level aides and cabinet members concerned with Social Security, including Connally, Richardson, Shultz, Flemming, and Ehrlichman, once again to flesh out the issues raised by the Mills proposal. Richardson presented the memorandum that he, Darman, and Ball had prepared. The president repeated his sentiment that he had to hold the line against inflation, but he noted, as John Ehrlichman put it, "if in everyone's political judgment successful Congressional action is inevitable and a veto would be overridden with a bad inflationary result, we'll have to find another way to dampen inflation." The president did not make up his mind at the meeting, asking Connally to study Richardson's memo and requesting that Gerald Ford be contacted and asked whether a presidential veto of the Mills bill could be sustained.[94]

The moment passed, and the administration failed to act on the Mills proposal. In a message on aging sent on March 23, the president supported a benefit increase of only 5 percent as contained in Mills's original bill.[95]

Passage of the 20 Percent Increase

That put things back in the congressional court. As the Senate Finance Committee continued to get bogged down in its efforts over welfare reform and as members of Congress began to express a reluctance to vote on that subject before the election, the possibility of attaching the benefit increase to another piece of legislation arose. Cued by Ball, Senator Frank Church took the initiative and at the end of June offered a Social Security amendment to a bill extending the ceiling on the public debt.[96]

As it turned out, Ball did not like the way that the Senate Finance Committee handled its proposals for increasing Social Security benefits. Ball remembered that the committee wanted to substitute a new approach to financing that combined raising the maximum wage base and increasing Social Security tax rates. "This was extraordinarily confusing," Ball commented, and "could have easily stymied the whole move to adopt the COLA [cost-of-living adjustment]." Since Ball could not persuade the Finance Committee staff to follow the House version, he decided "to follow the very unusual procedure of going around the Senate Finance Committee and getting Frank Church, Chairman of the Senate Aging Committee (which has no direct legislative responsibility) to sponsor an amendment to the bill providing for the extension of the public debt limitation."[97]

Church's actions prompted another round of activity by Richardson and Ball. On June 26, Richardson put in an urgent call to

John Ehrlichman in the White House. At that point, considerable confusion existed over just what Church would put in his amendment. Would it include the 20 percent benefit increase and the accompanying automatic cost-of-living adjustments, or would he also add some of the other items in Mills's original bill? What Richardson wanted to know from Ehrlichman was, if Church added only the benefit increase, financed in an actuarial sense, would President Nixon veto the bill. "My guess is that it would be a tough call and I have talked to Shultz some and he thinks so, too," Richardson noted. Ehrlichman still hoped to avoid any amendments to the debt ceiling bill, but that appeared unlikely.

Richardson did have one suggestion, and it came from Robert Ball. The idea was to make the increase effective on September 1, rather than June 1, and save having to pay benefit increases for June, July, and August, as called for in Church's amendment. "The only way of dealing with it we can see is to have Ball or Ball and Veneman talk to Mills because the indications are that Mills, Church, and Long are working together on this. . . . I think Ball can handle it since he can say this. . . . without implying the Administration is for it. I think that is the way to do it and if we don't we will regret it," Richardson said. "As long as there is no liability, I would say he should do it. I agree it would be a tough veto call and we're certainly not indicating to anybody that there is or won't be a veto," Ehrlichman replied. Richardson could not resist pointing out that the entire problem could have been avoided if the administration had followed his earlier advice to negotiate with Mills.[98]

Richardson called Ball and asked him to go ahead with his suggestion to modify the Church proposal. Richardson told him that the official administration position was that it did not want any amendments to the public debt ceiling bill, but Ball should ignore that and talk to anybody who would "do any good." "You can involve me to whatever extent you want to or need to," Richardson added. Ball indicated he would be glad to talk with Church. By the end of the day, Ball had spoken with Church, Russell Long, and the Ways and Means staff. Everyone agreed to make the change and in effect to let Ball amend a piece of legislation that he had helped to write in the first place. "We were able to act promptly enough to do some good," Richardson reported back to Ehrlichman, who replied that their action "saved a few bucks." "About 2 billion right there," said Richardson, and without compromising the administration.

On June 28, Church introduced his amendment, with the change suggested by Ball—an across-the-board increase for September that would be included in the October Social Security checks. As expected, the Church amendment also included the cost-of-living increases and the automatic increases in the earnings base, an earnings base that rose to $12,000 in 1974 and the same tax rate as in the existing program, at least through 1985.[99]

It became clear that Congress would pass the amendment, and the president would not veto it. As Nixon told a group of Republican senators, "any bill above the budget as proposed for FY '73 will be a veto candidate, but there are exceptions to every rule and Social Security is it. If I vetoed a 20% Social Security increase, you'd roll that in a minute, but I will insist that Social Security must be financed." That became the president's public stance as well: firm on the need to protect the public against inflation but eager to show his desire to help senior citizens. As Nixon told a press conference on the eve of the vote on the amendment, "there should be an increase in social security . . . It is not that we do not want an increase in social security. It isn't that we do not want as high an increase as possible. But the increase must be a responsible one."[100]

Signing the amendment into law on July 1, 1972, the president said that he looked with "special favor" on the automatic benefit increases incorporated into the law. "I am pleased that the Congress has at last fulfilled a request which I have been making since the first months of my administration," he added. At the same time, Nixon criticized the bill's funding arrangements in a political move designed to get maximum credit for the measure and still leave room to attack the Democratic Congress. The president lamented the fact that the new law added another $3.7 billion of debt to the federal budget, which threatened to exacerbate the nation's inflation problem.

Within the administration, Ball and Richardson disputed these figures; they said that $2.1 billion of the negative impact resulted from the fact that it was too late to increase the wage base so late in the year, making it impossible to realize savings on which the administration had been counting in its 1973 budget.

Nixon also denigrated the new law for reducing the level of reserves in the Social Security trust fund reserves below the 100 percent level that was considered prudent to meet unexpected economic adversity.[101] Ball and Richardson objected to that statement as well. Although trust fund reserves should be increased to 100 percent of the next year's outgo as rapidly as possible, the new law would bring the trust funds to this level by 1990. Under the financing arrangements for the new bill, furthermore, there would be no problem in meeting annual payments or paying administrative expenses, all of which implied that the bill, contrary to the president's statements, was adequately funded.[102]

It should be made clear that Ball and Richardson objected to the president's statement after the fact as a means of conditioning the administration's future rhetoric in discussing the program. Their dissatisfaction was momentary and hardly detracted from the tremendous feeling of satisfaction that Richardson, and particularly Ball, took from the new law. Ball recognized the Church amendment as a crucial step for the Social Security program, the culmination of a battle over automatic cost-of-living adjustments that had gone on at least since 1965, combined with a large rise in the level of benefits. Something of Ball's delight can be found in his directive to Alvin David, just before the Senate voted on the amendments, to prepare a special bulletin on the new law. "I am afraid that if we don't point out the significance of this the organization may miss how important a change is involved in this amendment—not only a 20 percent across-the-board increase but making the program inflation proof . . . and [the incorporation of] the new method of financing as recommended by the Advisory Council and a very significant increase in the maximum earnings base prior to the beginning of the automatics," he noted. Ball cautioned that David could not write the bulletin too enthusiastically "because the Administration is not for the bill as such but it seems to me as soon as the President signs it we can interpret it as being very good for the program."[103]

Ball had no doubt that a 20 percent benefit increase was good for the program. "You know," he observed years after the fact, "a 20 percent benefit increase is really the difference between the program just kind of limping along, as far as people were concerned" and its having "a real impact. This is the first change in Social Security that really raises the benefit levels so that it becomes a very important part of peoples' planning for retirement and a very important part of getting rid of poverty among the elderly."[104]

Stuffers

Although Ball wanted his organization to appreciate the 20 percent increase as a victory for the program, he objected to the way the Nixon administration wanted to inform Social Security beneficiaries about it. At issue were inserts that would be sent with the Social Security checks, known as stuffers. In the past, these stuffers had been strictly informational in nature, and if they mentioned a benefit increase, they contained formulaic language stating that the Congress passed and the president signed a law enacting the increase. No president or congressman got mentioned by name. Nearing the end of an election campaign that he hoped to win by a record margin and that would give him a mandate to get his program through Congress, Nixon decided to stuff the Social Security checks with a personal message claiming credit for the benefit increase. Chuck Colson of the White House staff thought an insert with red, white, and blue coloring, a series of quotations from Nixon's speeches, and the president's personal signature might be appropriate.[105]

Ball complained to Richardson that this message would politicize the program in an election year. Richardson, who tended to agree, assigned Richard Darman of his staff to negotiate with Colson. As the negotiations stretched on, Ball threatened political retaliation. "This might be flagrant enough as to precipitate legislation to prevent it and we might lose the political advantage we would have if we used the old (traditional) version," he told Richardson. How would Congress find out about it, Richardson wanted to know. "I don't see how this could be kept quiet," Ball replied. "I'm not saying it would happen but people thinking truly politically should keep it in mind."

Then there was the ultimate weapon, which was the threat of Ball's resignation. As Ball later noted, "Many people in the Administration would have been happy if I had resigned but they certainly didn't want it to be on an issue like this." George Shultz, who had been appointed Treasury secretary in the spring of 1972 and as a consequence served as a trustee of the Social Security Trust Fund, advised Richardson not to invoke Ball's name in the negotiations with the White House. If Richardson did that in the middle of September during a campaign fall, "you will lose immediately," said Shultz. "It is assumed he is doing everything to get us defeated so I would suggest you not mention it." That prompted an impassioned defense from Richardson, who replied in lawyerly fashion that "(a) I don't believe it. And (b) I think it is possible to push this to a point where Ball would go public and quit and I don't personally think it is safe to call his bluff on this." Richardson noted Ball had held his job for a long time and had been talking about retirement. If he were to retire, "the Democrats would have a field day." In the end, the White House, which probably realized that it needed little extra help to win the election, backed down; the notices went out with the traditional impersonal language about a benefit increase.[106]

Supplemental Security Income

In that same September, even as the election campaign heated up, the senators on the Finance Committee remained in Washington and worked on unfinished Social Security business. The Senate still needed to complete its version of H.R. 1, which the House had passed over a year before. Although the Church amendment disposed of the Social Security benefit increase and the automatic adjustments, issues related to disability, Medicare, Social Security benefits for widows and widowers, and, above all, welfare reform needed to be resolved between the two houses of Congress. As it had been throughout the process, welfare reform remained the most contentious item. The president appeared content to abandon his Family Assistance Plan. "The sooner this Congress is out of town the better off we will be," he told Richardson in the middle of September. With the election looking so promising, Nixon expected the next Congress to be far more responsive to his wishes. On October 3, the president put a stop to Richardson's attempts to compromise with Senator Ribicoff and reach agreement on welfare reform.[107]

Six days later, the Senate passed what became formally known as the Social Security Amendments of 1972, which the president signed at the end of October. If no previous legislation had been passed, the October law would still have stood out as an important expansion of Social Security. For one thing, it contained incremental changes in old-age benefits, such as raising the benefit received by a widow or widower to 100 percent of a basic benefit. For another thing, it brought Medicare to a group other than the elderly by providing disability recipients with Medicare coverage. Finally, it created a major new welfare program to cover what were known as the adult categories.[108]

This last item constituted the residue of President Nixon's plan to reform the welfare system. Although the president failed to convince Congress to substitute a federally maintained guaranteed income for the Aid to Families with Dependent Children program, he and the Congress collaborated to make major changes in the adult welfare categories. For the elderly, blind, or permanently and totally disabled, the federal government offered to take over the welfare programs previously run by the states and to guarantee a federal minimum payment to those who qualified.[109]

The outlines of the plan became clear toward the end of 1970 and in the spring of 1971. One instigator was Senator Russell Long, who, although he felt unsympathetic to the AFDC program, believed that the needy elderly deserved public assistance. From the beginning of the modern public assistance program in 1935, Louisiana, under the control of Long's father and his successors, had been one of the leading states in the percentage of the elderly on welfare. Asked by Long to come up with ideas, Ball suggested, among other things, flat federal grants to the elderly, paid out of general revenues, and federal payments to the elderly conditioned on need. As Ball explained the latter idea, there should be a program "to meet the full need of all people . . . through a last resort, income-tested program which guarantees a minimum level of living."[110] The House Ways and Means Committee picked up on Ball's idea for what became known as Supplemental Security Income, a name coined by John Veneman since many of the grants would supplement Social Security checks, and incorporated it in H.R. 1. As the legislative planning progressed, the program evolved from one run by the states, but with considerable federal financial assistance, to one run entirely by the federal government, but with benefits that could vary by state.[111]

Although Ball did his best to keep his agency out of the discussions about the Family Assistance Plan, he could not easily get out of the expectation that SSA would run the Supplemental Security Income program. He told former commissioner Altmeyer in May 1971 that "there is no real alternative to SSA's running the adult programs." That followed from the facts that many of the elderly on the new program would be the poorest of those receiving Social Security. The overlap suggested that it would be efficient to have SSA add Supplemental Security Income, which quickly became known as SSI, to its portfolio. Similarly SSA, which administered the Social Security Disability Insurance program, knew how to determine if someone was disabled. Ball reminded Altmeyer that SSA was the only national organization with the requisite skills to run such a program. Unsure of just how the new welfare program would affect the older social insurance program and aware that SSA took as a sort of unofficial motto that programs for poor people made poor programs, Ball accepted responsibility for running the new welfare program anyway.[112]

Ball's superiors in HEW and Wilbur Mills in Congress concurred in the decision to let SSA run SSI. In accordance with standard operating procedures, SSA proceeded to draw up elaborate plans for the new program. The agency geared up to run a major program, just as it had once made detailed plans to develop disability insurance and health insurance programs. The difference between SSI and the social insurance program was, however, profound. Implementation of SSI meant that Ball's agency would have to take over programs previously run by the states, and because of the need to limit benefits to people who could prove they were poor, the administration procedures for SSI were necessarily more complicated than the procedures for the much less discretionary Social Security program. Nonetheless, Ball had developed a reputation for administrative competence. If he could run an administrative monstrosity like Medicare, people assumed that he and his agency could handle SSI.[113]

Conclusion

Robert Ball treated the passage of the Church amendment and the 1972 amendments as he had treated the passage of Medicare.

During the Thanksgiving season, he called together all of the SSA employees in Baltimore and gave them a sermon on their new responsibilities. "I believe that each of your jobs will be more interesting if you are able to see the whole of which you are a part and recognize both what an important program you are part of and also how important every job in Social Security is going to be in bringing a new level of security to the American people," he said. Because the 1972 changes were so sweeping and so important, it made sense to Ball to speak of a "new social security program," one that was greatly improved from the previous version. At one time the challenge had been to extend coverage; now coverage was nearly universal. The new challenge, which the 1972 legislation successfully met, involved the adequacy of the benefits. Over the course of the previous five years, benefits had risen by more than 70 percent in nominal terms. Those gains could be consolidated and sustained because benefits were now to be indexed against inflation. The program was truly inflation proof. In fact, the phenomenon of rising wages and higher benefits at every wage level meant that for people still in the workforce benefits would rise at a faster rate than the price level: they would, in fact, keep up with changes in the standard, rather than the cost, of living. Nor could benefits be eroded by a declining wage base that covered a smaller and smaller percentage of the worker's earnings because the new $12,000 wage base effective in 1974 would mean that about 85 percent of all workers would have their full earnings covered and, with automatic increases in the wage base after that, it was expected that this percentage would be maintained indefinitely into the future.

In his speech to the SSA employees, Ball dwelled on the SSI program because he knew it would meet with the most resistance and pose the greatest administrative challenges. He argued that it was necessary to establish a federal program for the needy elderly, blind, and disabled because of the low payment standards that prevailed in many states. Some of the states made payments to the elderly as a lien against the value of their homes, which reverted to the state upon their death. The new law would be free of these anachronistic practices. And because the law would be administered by SSA, "it is expected that there will be much less stigma, if any, attached to the receipt of Supplemental Security Income."

If the new program offered many advantages over the older programs, it still would be a difficult one to put in place. There were 3.3 million blind, disabled, and aged people on the state rolls, with some 3 million more who would become eligible when the program began in January 1974. It would be necessary to hire 15,000 new SSA employees, most of whom would work in the field offices taking applications for the new program. It would also be necessary to contact people about the program and to convert old state payment records into a form that SSA could use. The administrative tasks would, therefore, be as complex as any the SSA had previously attempted. Ball called implementing SSI "the greatest challenge in the history of the organization."

Ball believed that his employees were up to the task. Social Security, he told the Baltimore workers, had become a model of effective government at a time when government institutions were under constant attack. One reason was that it was a well-conceived program. Another reason was the high quality of SSA employees. "The fact is," Ball concluded, "that Social Security has been an expression of not only effective Government but *concerned* Government."[114]

Ball gave a more sophisticated version of this talk to the higher-ranking members of the organization. Here his strategic thinking became more visible. In this talk, he emphasized what he considered to be the single most important aspect of the Social Security expansion: the expansion of the wage base. He described this base as "the measure of what you can do in the program. That's the whole income base of the system." A wage base that remained stagnant inevitably meant that Social Security would replace a shrinking proportion of the worker's earnings. Here Ball's feelings about public and private power came into play. "Unless the social security system moved on this wage base matter and unless it's kept up to date on the wage base matter, as it now will be automatically, there's always the possibility of private pension plans having to move in and doing a bigger and bigger part of the combined job. Some people think that might be a good idea. I think they are a useful supplement. I think it would be . . . too bad if they had the large role and the general Government system had a shrinking role." This was bold talk coming from a government employee in the Nixon administration, particularly after that administration had now been voted back into power.

It was almost as if Robert Myers had been right and Ball was indeed an expansionist who wanted to expand the federal government at the expense of the private sector. After the 1972 amendments, Ball could be more open about his sentiments because the system had already been expanded to the greatest extent he thought politically possible, and it could not easily be shrunk down to its former size. Ball realized that the era of spectacular benefit increases was over: "I just don't see anything in the way of a near-term future of the kind of quantum jump we have just had in these recent amendments. . . . If Bob Myers was right that I was an expansionist in the past—and I guess I was—I'm really not sure that I am an expansionist in the cash benefit program now. . . . That really has been done in a way that we ought to feel quite content with it for some time."

Although Ball did not dwell on it in his speeches, other challenges now presented themselves. An obvious one was implementing SSI. In Medicare, SSA operated through intermediaries, such as Blue Cross and Blue Shield, to send out the checks. In SSI there would be no intermediaries. As Ball put it, "Either that check gets there because we send it . . . or it doesn't get there because of us." A less obvious challenge, and one not openly discussed, concerned the ongoing fight for national health insurance. By way of contrast, the cash benefit portion of the program—the very guts of Social Security—looked to be in robust shape.[115]

In the period between 1965 and 1972 Ball oversaw an agenda for the expansion of cash benefits that demonstrated his mastery of the technical and strategic details of Social Security politics. He helped shape the ideas of cost-of-living adjustments and of dynamic actuarial assumptions and guided them through advisory councils, congressional committees, and the inner policy circles of two different administrations. Although many personal and institutional threads held the Social Security policymaking system together, Robert Ball clearly was a major player, even beyond the institutional position he held as head of the Social Security Administration.

His skills went beyond merely managing programs. He had the ability to plan and shape public policy. By solving other people's problems, such as Wilbur Mills's rejection of the automatic cost-of-living adjustments or Elliot Richardson's need to defend expansive and expensive proposals in the Nixon administration, Robert Ball became an important policy actor himself. In the end, after all the particulars played themselves out, his views, rather than those originally held by Wilbur Mills or the Nixon administration, prevailed in the 1972 legislation.

5

Defender of the Faith

Early in 1973 Robert Ball left the Social Security Administration and set up a one-man operation as a consultant to anyone who might care to take his advice. A bureaucrat out of office, Ball could easily have slipped into a life of semi-retirement, celebrating past triumphs and living the present in a reverie about the past. In fact, however, Ball suffered no diminution of influence upon his departure from the government. Instead, he went from being the nation's adviser on Social Security to serving as the Democratic Party's chief strategist on the program. In this new role, he worked with Senator Edward Kennedy (D–Massachusetts) and Representative Wilbur Mills on health insurance legislation in 1974 and with President Jimmy Carter on key amendments to the program in 1977. Freed from running a large bureaucracy yet able to command its resources on behalf of key political leaders in the White House and Congress, Ball enjoyed as much success as a consultant as he had as a bureau chief (in terms of influence over policy if not in financial terms).

He achieved this success despite the fact that the cost-of-living adjustments, which he had put in place, generated more controversy than approval during the 1970s. In general, social policy failed to follow the path that Ball had predicted for it in the beginning of the decade. In place of national health insurance and a smoothly running Social Security program, the nation ended up without a national health insurance program and with a Social Security program on the brink of bankruptcy. Instead of creating new social programs, as Ball had hoped to do when he left the SSA, he ended up repairing old ones. In the process he learned how to operate in a political environment that was greatly changed from the one that prevailed in the years of Social Security's incremental growth between 1950 and 1972.

Resignation

After Richard Nixon won a landslide victory in the 1972 elections, Ball realized that the administration would want to replace him with a Republican appointee. Even though Ball hoped to stay on to supervise the implementation of the Supplemental Security Income program, he recognized that it was not a bad time to leave. The passage of the 1972 amendments marked the end of a period of major legislative activity that was not likely to be repeated in Nixon's second term. Ball also knew that, with the announcement of Elliot Richardson's departure from the Department of Health, Education, and Welfare and his replacement by Caspar Weinberger, a more hard-line conservative whose reputation rested on his ability to control expenditures, his leverage within the administration would decline. There appeared to be little alternative to resigning as gracefully as possible. Ball later noted that he could not have stayed on as Social Security commissioner, even if he had wanted to do so.[1] As journalists Evans and Novak wrote at the time, the wonder was not that Ball was forced to resign but that he had survived Nixon's entire first term.[2]

Right after the election, the *Wall Street Journal* reported that Washington bureaucrats "shudder at reports of sweeping shake-ups, sharp personnel cuts. . . . Veteran Social Security Commissioner Ball may get the axe." Part of the reason, the *Journal* implied, was that Vice President Spiro Agnew, a Maryland politician who wished to retain his power base there, regarded Ball's job as falling within his influence.[3] Ball anxiously scanned the news ticker for an announcement of personnel changes at the Department of Health, Education, and Welfare. It took nearly a month, but the White House eventually got to Ball's job. On December 13, 1972, Richardson explained to Fred Malek in the White House that Ball "would leave unless urged to stay" and bargained with Malek for Ball not to be summarily fired but rather to let him submit a letter of resignation. The next day Richardson told Ball that it was clear that Weinberger would not ask Ball to stay and that Ball should go ahead and submit his resignation. Richardson hoped that the matter would be handled in a way that got across "the understanding that your preference is to leave."[4]

As Ball waited for Nixon to announce his departure, he wrote and distributed a long essay titled "The Assignment of the Commissioner of Social Security" that served as his valedictory. Written at the request of the administration but intended as a brief on behalf of the Social Security Administration and as a guide for future commissioners, the essay envisioned an expansive role for the head of the Social Security program. Ball argued that the commissioner continually had to define Social Security through such actions as recommending legislative changes, interpreting the existing law, setting and modifying standards of service, and explaining the meaning of the program to the public. According to Ball, the commissioner, rather than the president or the secretary of Health, Education, and Welfare, shaped what was "desirable and practical in the program." Ball also reported to his readers that the program he was leaving to his successors was in good fiscal shape, ready to enjoy a long period of stability without the need for substantial legislative changes. Furthermore, the spirit of the Social Security organization was good in part because the public embraced the program that was "based on an earned right, with the protection growing out of the work one does and the contributions one makes."[5]

On the morning of January 5, the *New York Times* reported that Nixon's acceptance of Ball's resignation was imminent and would "all but complete the removal of entire top management staff of the health component of the Department of Health, Education, and Welfare."[6] In fact, Nixon had signed the internal paperwork on January 3. With the story already leaked, Ronald Zeigler, the White House press secretary, confirmed it on January 5 and released Ball's resignation letter, which stated his personal preference to leave but hinted that he might have remained because of the "great challenge and difficulty" of putting in place the new Supplemental Security Income (SSI) program. Reiterating his contention that "the social security and the organization that administers it are in excellent shape," Ball noted it had been a privilege to contribute to the program's development; he said nothing about the privilege of serving under Nixon. The president, or the people in his personnel office, chose not to engage Ball in public debate and instead wrote a graceful reply with fulsome praise for Ball. "It is to your great credit," said the letter that the president signed, "that the Social Security Administration has, indeed, become a model for other government agencies in discharging its responsibilities to the American public."[7]

Although Ziegler refused to say that Ball had been fired, the *Washington Post* reported that "Ball's office did not hide the fact that he was being dumped and had hoped to stay on at least to put the new Social Security laws into effect." Ziegler refused to elaborate on why the White House had accepted Ball's resignation, saying only that "there should be a new direction" and that Ball was returning to private life.[8]

The *Times* expected the announcement to provoke "bitterness among Social Security employees who have considered themselves to be above partisan politics." That set the tone for much of the coverage of Ball's departure: the White House was playing politics with an important social program. On its editorial pages, the *New York Times* wrote that it was hard to understand why Nixon speeded Ball's departure at a time when the Social Security Administration had so many delicate administrative tasks to undertake. According to the *Times,* Ball had made his greatest contribution in keeping the large program "totally free from any taint of politics." Wilbur Mills told the *Washington Star* that the departure of Ball, whom he called a "near-genius," could lead to the politicization of the program. The *Star* editorialized that the burden of proof fell on the administration to find someone of "Ball's stature and someone who will not politicize this key position." The *Asheville Times* praised the way the program functioned "with a minimum of waste and lost motion" and cited the "fine courtesy" of SSA staff members who had dealings with the public. The regional paper concluded that it was too bad that Ball "had to fall victim to the Nixon pruning hook." The *Washington Post* ran its editorial under the heading, "A Superb Public Servant Steps Down." The paper called Ball "fair-minded, energetic,

committed to the success of the statutes he administered and—
above all—'a-political.'"9

The editorial comments reflected an almost willful lack of
understanding about Ball's tenure at the Social Security Administration. In particular, the newspapers highlighted his role as an
administrator and ignored his role as a legislative tactician. As an
administrator, he did his best to implement social programs so
that they functioned efficiently, but the implementation of programs nearly always followed a period in which Ball engaged actively in the political process to shape the programs to his predilections, which were not always those of the president or party in
power. Ball did not keep the program free of any taint of politics;
instead he used his political talents to expand the program. In
describing Ball as nonpolitical, the newspapers were making a
political point about Richard Nixon—that he was misusing his
presidential power to undercut popular programs—and, ironi-
cally, beginning the process by which Ball would be recognized
as a partisan figure.

Ball, for his part, refused to play the martyr. On the day that
his resignation became public, Ball began a talk to the Commonwealth Club in San Francisco by confirming the rumor that the
president had accepted his resignation. His first thoughts, he
said, were to give a no-holds barred speech, and then he joked
that he still needed a few weeks to clear out his desk and so he
had decided to go ahead with his original talk.[10]

It turned out to be the usual historical exposition about the
program's development, followed by a spirited defense of the
program's present condition. According to Ball, Social Security
had reached "the level of considerable stability." In the near future, nothing like the rise in benefits and contributions of recent
years would occur. Most of the program's tasks were accomplished. Coverage was universal; benefits were "respectable,"
and provisions for the program's financing were "adequate."
Pressed on the financing question, Ball said that "on the basis of
the best estimates that could be made with conservative assumptions the program has sufficient funds to meet all its obligations
as they come due in the future. . . . it's completely financially
sound."[11] "My feeling is I'm leaving the Social Security program
in really good shape. I feel good," Ball told a San Francisco reporter who interviewed him after the speech.[12]

As for his resignation, Ball assured his audiences in California and elsewhere that it was "a mutually agreeable decision." On the *CBS Morning News,* Ball refused to say he was fired. Instead, he preferred to call his departure a "mutual decision" because he had told the president "that I would really prefer to leave the Administration at the beginning of the new term." In this version of events, the president gave Ball what he wanted by assuring him that he could find someone else to undertake the difficult administrative tasks ahead. After twenty-one years of running the program, Ball wanted a break from administrative work and the freedom to do research and write in the broad field of social policy. After so much kinetic activity, Ball craved time to reflect on his experiences.[13]

Besides, Ball believed the future action would be in health insurance, not Social Security. Since the cash benefit program was in such robust health and since the problems of health care finance were so pressing, health insurance would rise to the surface as a national concern. Passage of national health insurance within five years was "very, very likely" Ball told CBS reporter John Hart.[14]

In the usual Washington rituals that followed Ball's resignation, the Democrats praised him, the president met with him, and his colleagues at Social Security threw him a party. Walter Mondale (D–Minnesota), Edward Kennedy, Robert Byrd, Edmund Muskie (D–Maine), and Frank Church all paid tribute to Ball on the floor of the Senate and made sure that the editorials lamenting his departure found their way into the *Congressional Record*.[15] Richard Nixon invited Robert and Doris Ball to the White House for a farewell picture. The meeting took place only a few weeks before Nixon's counsel John Dean told him there was a cancer on the presidency. When the Balls walked into the Oval Office, they found Nixon, alone, looking very upbeat, but with his usual social awkwardness. The president greeted Ball as "Mr. Social Security" and then fell back on routinized social responses. As the photographer snapped pictures, Nixon remarked that such sessions were the only times he came between a man and his wife. He then showed the Balls some framed embroidery that one of his daughters had done. "I took the occasion to make a quick pitch for national health insurance," Ball recalled, "a way of operating that I am not sure is approved of at such ceremonial occasions but when would I see him again?" He later wrote his sister-in-law that, according to his wife, he had spent the entire five or six minutes "lecturing the president on the principles and virtues of social insurance."[16]

Ball approached the future without much trepidation. Whatever his insecurities, they seldom took the form of worrying about his next job. He simply instructed his assistant to start a folder of job leads. Within two weeks of Ball's resignation, the file contained no fewer than twenty-six prospects, ranging from being a professor at the Maryland School of Social Work to working on a congressional staff to administering a health insurance plan to entering the foundation world.[17]

As the job file grew thicker, Ball attended a round of parties and ceremonies in his honor, culminating in a cocktail party and buffet held in the Diplomatic Suite of the State Department. This occasion was to be his official Washington send-off. Ball, who treated the reception not as a gala at which he could relax but rather as a working session designed to show off the agency to best advantage, paid exquisite attention to the composition of the guest list. He made sure, for example, that Ted Sorensen, President Kennedy's staffer, received an invitation, and he wrote memo after lengthy memo to ensure that anyone with a stake in the Social Security program was invited. "I think we might include George Bush, the new head of the Republican National Committee," he told his assistant, "I knew him from the Ways and Means Committee." He was less sure about whether or not to put Bob Myers on the list, "That's kind of a close question it seems to me."[18]

John Veneman, the under secretary of HEW under Elliot Richardson, served as the master of ceremonies for the party, and former secretaries Wilbur Cohen, Arthur Flemming, and Richardson each gave tributes. Richardson described Ball as the "finest embodiment of public service," someone with all the moves who exercised "skill without compromising integrity." In Ball's rejoinder, he chose to reprise a point he often made about public service. Working for the government was a "great pleasure as well as a privilege—there is no business in the world as exciting or as important."[19]

By the evening of the State Department reception, Ball already knew what he would do next. In the fall of 1972, he had given a talk to an organization, begun at the end of 1970, that operated in the field of health policy. The Institute of Medicine (IOM) lacked deep financial resources and much Washington expertise, yet as a component of the National Academy of Sciences, it hoped to marshal the academy's prestige and scientific authority to influence public policy on health care. Ball's talk established a relationship between him and Dr. John Hogness, the former dean of the University of Washington's medical school who headed the IOM.[20] A few months later, Ball met Hogness at the International Club, one of his favorite places to take people to lunch in Washington, and they talked about Ball's coming to the Institute of Medicine as a scholar in residence. By February 5, 1973, they had reached an agreement. His new position, Ball hoped, would allow him to make "frank comments on policy matters, a luxury denied appointive officials," and would give him time to write a book. Hogness, who wanted Ball to keep the IOM informed of developments in Social Security and Medicare, thought Ball could position the IOM in the national health insurance debate.[21]

Ball's decision to affiliate himself with the Institute of Medicine indicated his personal preference to work in Washington, rather than near his home in Baltimore or at an academic center. The IOM maintained offices close to the White House and near George Washington University. Whereas Ball had previously divided his time between his Washington and Baltimore offices, he would now work exclusively, along with an administrative assistant, in Washington. Furthermore, the choice of job demonstrated Ball's firm belief that future action in the field of social policy would come in health insurance. To be affiliated with the medical division of the National Academy of Sciences would give him an appropriate base from which to participate in the debates.

By locating in the heart of official Washington, Ball broke a pattern that had been set by previous Social Security officials in retirement. None of the four commissioners who had preceded Ball had chosen to settle in the nation's capital. Most retreated to academia. After leaving the commissioner's job, for example, Arthur Altmeyer went back to Madison, Wisconsin, and lived in Washington again only very briefly. Wilbur Cohen, another Social Security insider, took academic posts first in Ann Arbor and then in Austin after his service in the Johnson administration. Only Ball decided to stay in Washington. Although designated a scholar in residence with "considerable amount of freedom to do research and writing," he also expected "to remain active in the area of social policy development." In other words, he hoped to be an activist, engaged in making policy, every bit as much as he expected to be a scholar, engaged in retrospective contemplation.[22]

The Kennedy-Mills Bill

Ball spent his last day at SSA on March 17, 1973, leaving things in the hands of Deputy Commissioner Arthur Hess, and began at the Institute of Medicine on April 1. He experienced little or no decompression in the new job, even though he no longer had the excitement of coping with practical problems on a daily basis. Instead, he "was alone with one secretary figuring out where I wanted to take an initiative." The only things he missed were the support services that went along with being commissioner, in particular a chauffeur to ferry him from place to place. As he moved about Washington now, he took taxis or hunted for his own parking spaces. He also drove the daily commute between his Baltimore County home and downtown Washington, a tedious prospect under any circumstances and particularly challenging in inclement weather. Within a year, he decided to shift his residence to the Washington area as well, buying a house in suburban Virginia that would, along with his New Hampshire vacation home, be where he stayed until moving to a retirement community in the spring of 2002.[23]

Ball made national health insurance his first major project at the Institute of Medicine. That fit both his surroundings and his sense of social welfare politics. The small IOM staff contained more health services researchers than it did medical doctors, and the organization concerned itself as much with health care finance and health manpower needs as it did with the treatment of specific medical conditions. In 1973 and 1974, furthermore, the politics of national health insurance appeared to be at a critical point of development, with a real chance for the passage of significant federal legislation. Ball advised his correspondents during this period that "the greatest needs in social security . . . are probably in the health field and I would like to see us get started with a national health insurance plan."[24]

Ball made his chief contribution to the health insurance debate by creating the Kennedy-Mills bill. Although this bill did not appear until April 1974, work on the measure began on the morning of Ball's resignation from SSA. While staying in a California hotel, Ball received an early morning telephone call from Senator Edward Kennedy, who invited Ball to join his staff and work on health insurance. Ball declined the invitation but agreed to help Kennedy from the outside. As Ball realized, Kennedy, working in coalition with organized labor, had become the Democratic Party's major spokesman on national health insurance, proposing a liberal version of the measure that would pay nearly all of people's medical expenses and that relied on the government, rather than private health insurance companies, to operate the health financing system.

At some point the possibility occurred to Ball and others that Kennedy might be brought together with Wilbur Mills on behalf of a health insurance bill that both could support. Mills, as head of the committee that would consider health insurance in the House, played a key role in the health insurance debate. The trouble was that the fiscally conservative Mills took different positions from Kennedy on such questions as how much a person should pay out-of-pocket for medical care and whether private companies should play a role in a national health insurance plan. To get the two of them to agree on a proposal would be a significant step in forging a consensus bill and getting it through Congress.[25]

Ball met intermittently during 1973 with Stan Jones, Kennedy's chief staff member on health policy, and with Bill Fullerton, the Ways and Means staff member and former SSA staffer whom Ball knew well and who represented the interests of Wilbur Mills. For the most part, the meetings proved unproductive, as did direct meetings between Kennedy and Mills. According to Fullerton, Mills and Kennedy would start to talk politics and never get around to the subject of health insurance.[26]

As Ball contemplated strategy on national health insurance, he also attended to concerns related to Social Security, but he managed to tie one subject to the other. At the Institute of Medicine he continued to write essays on Social Security, just as he had as commissioner of Social Security. As always, he wrote his essays with a purpose in mind—to influence legislation—rather than to engage in a purely academic exercise.

One piece in particular played a part in the creation of the Kennedy-Mills bill. In it Ball argued that Social Security should not be thought of as a typical government expenditure but rather as one that was part of a closed system in which the government collected contributions from workers and used the contributions to pay benefits. The money in the Social Security trust fund, Ball believed, was unlike other money that the government collected through taxes because it already had a dedicated purpose. Hence, it was misleading to consider a surplus in the Social Security trust fund in the same way as a surplus in the rest of the federal government's budget. Because he wanted to protect "the values of contributory insurance," as he explained to Wilbur Mills, Ball favored separating Social Security finance from the rest of the federal budget.[27]

Ball tried to place his essay as an op-ed piece in a newspaper. He did not much care which paper took it because his main interest was "to use it with the Congress and with organizations, and newspaper publication is just a first step to reproduction."[28] In fact, the article marked a step in a related campaign not just to remove Social Security from what was called the unified budget but also to make the Social Security Administration an independent agency, as it had been when the program began in 1935. Frank Church in the Senate and Wilbur Mills in the House agreed to introduce Ball's Social Security Administration Act. "It is always reassuring to know that someone as competent as you is available to provide sound and sensible counsel," Church told Ball. Eventually, this piece of legislation became part of a Kennedy-Mills health insurance bill.[29]

Ball thought of national health insurance in terms of political positioning. At least three distinct approaches appeared to be in play at the beginning of 1974. One was Senator Kennedy's liberal plan. A second proposal, from the legislative tandem of Senators Russell Long and Abraham Ribicoff (D–Connecticut), would use the federal government to cover catastrophic medical expenses. The idea was that, after the individual spent a reasonable amount of money on health care, the government would pay for costs that were beyond the individual's reach. It was last-dollar rather than first-dollar coverage. The third distinct approach to health insurance came from the Nixon administration. In February 1974 the administration introduced the

Comprehensive Health Insurance Plan, which relied on the strategy of mandating private employers to provide health insurance for their employees.[30]

Ball believed that the appearance of the administration bill changed the nature of the debate. It gave the Democrats "no place to go since Kennedy's bill was too far out for many of them and . . . Long-Ribicoff was not enough to meet the competition of what the Administration was proposing."[31]

In response to these strategic stimuli, Ball created a new proposal for Kennedy that was more conservative than Kennedy's previous liberal proposal and, at least in Ball's opinion, superior to the Long-Ribicoff and the Nixon administration plans. To do so, he joined his ideas of an independent Social Security agency and the special nature of Social Security financing from his op-ed piece and the legislation sponsored by Church and Mills with an amendment to Long-Ribicoff that he, Stan Jones, and a staff member at the Institute of Medicine were already working on for Kennedy.

As Ball read the situation, part of the appeal of the administration's bill was that it relied on tax expenditures, rather than direct federal expenditures, for much of its financing. It mandated the private sector to spend money on health insurance rather than collecting federal taxes for that purpose. Because of the way that employers could write off their expenditures on health insurance, that meant that federal revenues would be reduced, but the net effect was the same as if the federal government had in fact collected the money and spent it to buy health insurance. This practice provided a way of effecting social expenditures without having those expenditures show up in the budget.[32]

Ball sought a similar way of taking out of the budget the expenditures in the bill he was preparing for Kennedy. He came up with the notion of making health insurance expenditures separate from the rest of the budget, in conjunction with the creation of an independent Social Security agency that would run both the cash benefit and medical care programs. To keep expenses roughly comparable to the administration's plan, he decided that Kennedy's new bill would have deductibles (a level of expenditures that had to be reached before the insurance kicked in) and co-insurance (an amount that the patient would have to pay out-of-pocket for a doctor's visit or procedure, even with health insurance). The administration bill contained such charges; Kennedy's liberal bill did not. Having made those basic decisions, Ball "took the same amount of money that would have been needed privately to carry out the Nixon plan and proposed that that amount be spent for a government plan."[33] The result was about half of the benefits as in Kennedy's more liberal bill but more benefits than in either the administration bill or the Long-Ribicoff bill.

Convinced that his plan was superior to the administration's proposal, which he called "unnecessary, complicated and ineffective," Ball needed to put it in legislative language, and, most important of all, sell it to Kennedy and Mills. The key difference between Ball's plan and the administration's plan was that Ball's plan would be administered by the federal government with coverage made compulsory. The administration's plan would be run by private insurance companies, with elective coverage on the part of employees. Ball argued that if the federal government were to impose an obligation on employers to pay up to 3 percent of their payrolls for heath insurance, then it "would make much better sense to have that 3% contributed to a plan which follows the employee from place to place as social security does." And for the same amount of money, the government plan could yield potentially better benefits, such as a lower deductible, services to children and pregnant women that were free to the patient, and greater control over health care cost inflation.[34]

At the end of February, Ball met Stan Jones at the International Club and tried to get Jones to present the idea to Kennedy. For an ensuing meeting with Kennedy himself, Ball wrote up a six-point memo that contained the basic strategy for what Ball called "a new approach to national health insurance." The lead idea was to "accept the general structure of the Administration's benefit proposals" but "adopt a compulsory social insurance approach instead of a mandated voluntary approach through private insurance." As in Medicare, the new plan would allow private insurance and Blue Cross–Blue Shield plans to perform administrative tasks for the federal government, but they would not be allowed to set premium rates. Finally, the plan would call for separating "the financial transactions of the contributory social security program including the new National Health program from the financial transactions of the general budget." After listening to

Ball, Kennedy endorsed the plan.[35] Ball believed that the senator "was getting tired of nothing happening in the field where he had been pushing now for a long time."[36]

Kennedy talked to Mills about Ball's idea. The Arkansas congressman, suffering from back pain that kept him away from Washington for much of the time and that contributed to the alcoholism that would ultimately cost him his job, told Kennedy that he had already been in touch with Ball about the proposal and thought it was a good idea. Ball doubted, however, that Mills understood all of the implications of the plan and made his own appointment to see him. The meeting took place in the middle of March. Although Mills bought most of the points, he expressed concern that the plan not wipe out the private insurance industry or dictate the terms of medical treatment to doctors. Mills gave Ball the green light to work with Stan Jones and Bill Fullerton on a bill that Kennedy and Mills could introduce jointly at the beginning of April.[37]

At this point, Ball dedicated nearly all of his time to supervising the creation of legislation. Unlike at the Social Security Administration, he no longer had an army of people at his disposal to assist him in the legal, actuarial, editorial, and public relations tasks that accompanied introducing a bill. Instead, he used his position as Mills's surrogate to command the resources of the House Legislative Reference Service and the Library of Congress. Through Mills's offices, for example, he got an actuary assigned full-time to the project at congressional expense. Fullerton described the next two weeks as a "fairly hectic period of time," with the trio of Ball, Fullerton, and Jones meeting constantly.[38] As the process unfolded, the measure acquired heft by incorporating other bills that had already been introduced. One was the bill to create an independent agency. Another was a bill that Fullerton had prepared for Barber Conable (R–New York) that dealt with long-term care.

As the April 2 deadline for the press conference approached, the group worked with "increasing intensity." Ball, for his part, did not do any of the real drafting but rather "approved most of the major policy decisions." Just as at the Social Security Administration he was the executive in charge, only now he played to an audience of Democrats, rather than also having to include the Nixon administration in the deliberations.[39]

Most of the work took place in relative secrecy, but as the date for the measure's unveiling drew closer, Ball, Kennedy, Fullerton, and Jones began to discuss it with key politicians and representatives of important organizations so as to launch it with a groundswell of support. At the very end of March, Kennedy took Ball and Stan Jones to see Senator Long in the Senate dining room. Talking to Long, Kennedy mentioned how he had worked closely with Ball on the proposal and noted that President Kennedy had greatly respected Ball. "Well, he wrote my bill, too," Long replied with his characteristic pungency. Ball tried to sell Long on the new proposal, arguing that with the appearance of the administration's bill, the Democrats needed a new place to go. Noncommittal, Long said he would ask "his boys" to go over the memo that Ball had prepared. After "his boys" on the Senate Finance Committee staff discussed the measure with Ribicoff's "man," Long decided to stand pat and not endorse the new measure.[40]

Another group equally critical to the measure's success was organized labor. The strategy depended on using Kennedy's sponsorship of the new bill to pry labor away from his old liberal health insurance bill. To get labor's reaction, Ball met with the members of the AFL-CIO staff who worked on congressional relations and social insurance policy on the same day as the Mills-Kennedy press conference to introduce the bill. The AFL-CIO staff did not celebrate the bill as an important political breakthrough. Instead the union officials raised objections to the way that the measure included co-payments and deductibles. Ball read the situation as labor's unwillingness to abandon the measure that they had supported for the past four years as well as the unspoken sense that the next Congress would be more liberal and hence more amenable to Kennedy's original bill.[41]

After listening to George Meany explain to Senator Kennedy why labor could not support the bill, Ball headed off to Mills's office, arriving only thirty-five minutes before the scheduled press conference and hoping to give Mills a last-minute briefing. The congressman still seemed a little befuddled on the fine points of the proposal. Ball did not want to be seen at the press conference, deferring to the political principals and not sure that his imprimatur on the bill would improve its chances for success. It was, however, too late to escape because the cameramen were already

setting up their equipment. During the press conference, therefore, Ball hid in a back room of Mills's office and stayed there
until the press left.[42] A major inside player in Social Security politics, Ball did not mind being relatively anonymous in public.

Introducing the bill, Mills and Kennedy noted that its benefits
were similar to those in the administration bill but with improvements at either end of the life cycle and slightly lower out-of-
pocket costs. Prenatal care, well-child care, and dental care for
children would all be provided without any deductibles and co-
pays in order "to remove any possible barrier to the receipt of
such care by children." The bill would also initiate a new long-
term care program "as a separate part of medicare over and
above anything in the administration's proposal" as a way of
"assuring a comprehensive approach to the health needs of all
Americans."[43]

In a separate statement, Kennedy noted that he regretted the
inclusion of deductibles and co-insurance. "Nevertheless," he
added, "I believe this proposal, far more than any pending proposal, is a major step toward guaranteeing good health care as a
right—and can be built upon in future years." Both Mills and
Kennedy invited other members of Congress to join them in support of the legislation, with Kennedy making the point that the
measure accepted the concept of catastrophic coverage that was
in Long and Ribicoff's bill and added more basic coverage to it.[44]

"I think things went very well on the Kennedy-Mills bill," Ball
told Wilbur Cohen. Co-sponsors were signing on to the legislation. Organized labor "has taken the view that they are devoted
to the principles of S. 3 [Kennedy's earlier bill] but that they have
great respect for Kennedy and Mills and will take a close look at
the bill. They haven't done much beyond that." The sponsors of
S.R. 3 were waiting to take their cues from labor before supporting the new legislation. Wishing to create a sense of momentum,
Ball made plans to talk with a large contingent of potentially
sympathetic senators including Ribicoff, Long, Walter Mondale,
Gaylord Nelson (D–Wisconsin), Robert Byrd, Harrison Williams
(D–New Jersey), Warren Magnuson (D–Washington), and Frank
Church. He also reached out to liberal Republicans, such as
Charles Mathias (R–Maryland) and Elliot Richardson, and,
through his old friend Doug Brown, to Marion Folsom and Sena-
tor Clifford Case (R–New Jersey). In addition, Ball contemplated

forming a group of experts—social insurance experts, Brookings economists, and people he had met at the IOM, such as lawyer and social policy expert Adam Yarmolinsky—to support the measure. He wanted to talk up the Kennedy-Mills bill and talk down Long-Ribicoff because he believed that the introduction of the new measure had "substantially moved up the timetable for serious consideration of a comprehensive national health insurance program."[45]

The initial press reaction reinforced Ball's optimism. The *Wall Street Journal* reported that "prospects for Congressional action this year" had improved considerably, because the Kennedy-Mills bill was not much different from the administration bill in concept or cost. The story quoted Senator John Tower (R–Texas) as saying that President Nixon was "very pleased" with the appearance of the bill. John Rhodes, the minority leader in the House (R–Arizona), called the measure "a breakthrough which I think can certainly advance the date of enactment of this legislation." The *New York Times* characterized the legislation as "a sensible compromise between President Nixon's proposal and the earlier, more costly Kennedy plan." The paper admonished that "a consensus on the need for effective protection of the nation's health is so widespread and bipartisan that partisan and ideological conflict can no longer be allowed to delay legislative action." The *Washington Post* added that "in recent weeks the prospects for national health insurance have brightened suddenly and unexpectedly."[46]

What mattered far more than a good word from the *Washington Post* was the endorsement of the AFL-CIO, and that never came. A month after the appearance of Kennedy-Mills, the Executive Council of that organization issued a negative report on the new bill. "While on balance Mills-Kennedy is an improvement over the Nixon bill," the council stated, "it falls short of meeting the needs of America. Frankly, we are disappointed by the bill and are surprised the sponsors didn't do better."[47]

The situation soon deteriorated. Ball went to see Senator Kennedy at the end of July and argued that it would be good strategy to get a bill passed that year. The reason was that President Nixon, who was fighting for his political life in the midst of the Watergate scandal, wanted to show his ability to govern by signing a major piece of domestic legislation. This situation might not exist in 1975 or 1976. Labor believed that the next Congress would be veto-proof and that the Democrats would be able to move on national health insurance on their own initiative. Ball dismissed that idea as "highly unlikely." Recognizing that it was late in the session, Ball told Kennedy that the only hope for a bill was one "that had such overwhelming support that the Congress would be willing to pass it without extensive consideration and modification." Ball thought that either an expanded version of the Long-Ribicoff bill that the next Democratic administration could expand upon or a bill that used the framework of Kennedy-Mills but with a greater role for the states and private insurance companies might be possible.[48] Despite considerable effort to lobby Kennedy and Mills, Ball proved unable to broker a deal.

"At this point everything seems to be going toward the plan that we liked the least," Ball told Cohen in the middle of August. He believed that Secretary Weinberger, Wilbur Mills, and Richard Nixon had agreed to back a mandated health insurance plan that also contained catastrophic protection. "If this is the way it comes out, I will be very much disappointed," Ball added. "It seems to me that we ought to do much better than this."[49] In the end neither the administration nor Kennedy nor Ball got his way on national health insurance, and as it had so many times before, the movement toward passage of a comprehensive measure simply stopped.

In retrospect, the failure of Kennedy-Mills represented the end of an era of liberal legislation in Social Security that had begun in 1950. For one thing the cast of characters changed substantially after that year. Fanny Fox would take her dive into the Washington Tidal Basin in October 1974, and Wilbur Mills's career would never recover. He soon lost his chairmanship and retired from Congress at the end of 1976. After the departure of Mills, no head of Ways and Means would run the committee without permanent subcommittees, and power over Social Security policy would become more diffuse. Richard Nixon left office in August 1974, modifying the climate for negotiation between the White House and the Congress. For another thing, the economy underwent a substantial and enduring decline in the middle of the 1970s. In 1974, for example, the percentage increase in the consumer price index reached 11.0, compared with 3.3 in 1972, and the unemployment rate hit 8.5 percent for 1975. With the economy

functioning at less than full capacity and with the constant presence of inflation, which did not return to its 1972 level until 1983,
the ability of the federal government to finance massive new entitlement programs like national health insurance declined.[50]

It took the prosperity of the postwar era to expand Social Security and pass Medicare. It took the stagflation of the 1970s to shat-
ter the apparent consensus over national health insurance. This
meant that Ball had been right: 1974 was the year to have made a
deal. A conversation that Ball had with Bill Fullerton and Stan
Jones at the beginning of 1975 captured the mood of the times.
Jones said that Kennedy realized that the only health insurance
bill that could possibly pass Congress that year would rely on the
mandating idea "since they are not going to be able to get support
for raising government revenues." Fullerton reported feelings
were "running strong in Ways and Means. . . . Discipline is being
lost and open challenges are the rule of the day." Already the committee had lost its jurisdiction over the Medicaid program.[51] The
decision to speculate in political futures and wait until next year
turned out to have been the wrong one. The window for health insurance closed at the historical conjuncture of Mills's departure,
Nixon's resignation, and the economy's deterioration.

The Ford Years

Contrary to Ball's expectations, the issue for the 1970s turned out
to be the cash benefit program, not health insurance. As the
Nixon presidency ended and the Ford presidency began, a crisis
developed in the Social Security program related to the program's financial solvency. In June 1974 in the waning days of the
Kennedy-Mills bill and the Nixon administration, Social Security
Commissioner Bruce Cardwell reported that, according to the
trustees who oversaw the Social Security trust funds, a "long
range actuarial imbalance" in Social Security had developed. The
reason was that demographic data from the 1970 census, as analyzed by the actuaries, made it prudent to assume a lower birth
rate than had earlier been projected. That meant that the proportion of aged persons to workers in the twenty-first century
would be larger than in previous predictions. It was, to be sure, a
future concern, one that would not affect developments for many

years to come. Of more pressing import was the assumption of continuing high rates of inflation and of larger than expected rates of disability.[52]

Ball did not dispute the fact that the program faced both long-range and short-range funding problems. "The rate of inflation is so high," he explained, "that it is no longer reasonable to expect that rising payrolls over the next several years will increase sufficiently to fully offset the benefit increases arising from the automatic provisions." Rather than question the automatic provisions, Ball chose to minimize the extent of the problem. The size of the short-range problem, he advised, "is easily manageable." Ball believed that no one would be worrying about the short-term problem if it were not for the long-range problems associated with the lower birth rates.[53]

Early in 1975 Ball reassured Congress and others in the policy community that "the fact that social security benefit payments will exceed contribution income for fiscal year 1976 is not a cause for concern." To meet such contingencies, the system maintained over $55 billion in reserves. Certainly, the short-term deficit should not supply the pretext for blocking the program's cost-of-living increases and in particular an 8.7 percent increase that, barring adverse congressional action, would go into effect in July. At the same time, the deficits could not be allowed to continue, and as an easy way to remedy the problem Ball suggested that in calendar year 1977 the contribution base—the amount of a worker's salary on which Social Security taxes were payable—be raised to $24,000 and that money for a tax increase scheduled for 1978 be allocated for cash benefits rather than the over-financed Medicare program. As for the long-term deficit, Ball said it would be met either by a future tax increase or by "gradually introducing general revenue financing into the system."[54]

Ball saw it as his mission to "counter the loss of public confidence" that stemmed "from the notion that the program is greatly under financed for the long run." He thought that the reports from the trustees of the Social Security Trust Funds were getting "everyone pretty excited about what may only be a possibility rather than a probability."[55] One way to counter the loss of confidence was to remind people just how many people the Social Security system reached. In the spring of 1975 Ball told a congressional committee that nearly 100 million people would contribute to the program that year and 31 million people would draw a check from it. Contributions to the program would amount to $63 billion, and the $46 billion held in reserve would earn over $2.8 billion in interest. Such a large system, sustained by so many people, could afford to pay out $67 billion. A $6 billion shortfall, such as projected for 1977, could easily be handled. Precisely because the system was so large and its revenue-generating capacities so abundant, Congress would not allow it to go bankrupt.[56]

The fact that Ball got his message across was evident in an April 1975 *New York Times* editorial that chastised "critics of this widely and deservedly admired program" for "doing their utmost to undermine confidence in both its fairness and its actuarial soundness." The *Times* warned that the recession must not become a pretext for destroying Social Security. The $46 billion dollar reserve provided "a cushion against any break in payments as a result of short-term dips in the economy." And, no less an authority than former commissioner of Social Security Robert Ball believed that deficits in Social Security acted to stimulate the economy by "pumping money into the spending stream."[57]

If the *Times* supported Ball's position, others with influence in the policy process opposed it. Within the Ford White House, William Simon, the conservative secretary of the Treasury, offered a different view of Social Security's effect on the economy. At the end of 1975, Simon reported that Social Security had come under "persistent attack in the news media for its inequities, its financial uncertainties, and its complexity. And economists have called attention to its negative effects on capital formation, employment, and economic activity generally." Should such a system need to be scaled back in response to the fiscal crisis, Simon would raise no objections. "We must not lose this chance to plan a basic financial reform," he told a key White House staff member. HEW Secretary Weinberger shared many of Simon's views. At the end of 1974 he wrote the president that "Today, perhaps more than at any time in the program's history, there are growing expressions of concern about its financing and stability—whether the system will have sufficient funds to meet its future liabilities; its treatment of men versus women; regressivity of the tax; . . . whether the so-called minimum benefit is tantamount to welfare in social security." Weinberger, unlike his predecessor Richardson, was no fan of Social Security.[58]

With conservatives such as William Simon and conservative institutions such as the editorial page of the *Wall Street Journal* on one side and liberals such as the AFL-CIO, the United Auto Workers, and Bob Ball on the other, a debate over Social Security took place in the middle of the 1970s.[59] With the fiscal crisis in Social Security and the inflation-ridden economy as a subtext, the conservatives wanted to scale the program back; with the sheer size of the program and its past record of success as a template, the liberals hoped to maintain or even expand it.

As a player in this debate, Robert Ball found a new role for himself. No longer cast as the skilled administrator or the legislative technician, he now became the partisan defender of the Social Security faith. If he would not make his name as the creator of national health insurance, he would instead gain a reputation as the man who saved Social Security. What gave him impressive credentials in this regard was not only his sense of politics but also his total dedication to the program and his comprehension of its technical details and subtleties. Having created the system of automatic benefit increases, he appeared to be the only one who could keep it running in the face of substantial criticism.

One thing that aided the performance of his new role was his proximity to power. As conditions in Washington changed, other Social Security advocates, such as Wilbur Cohen, faded from the scene. Cohen, employed full-time as an academic dean in Ann Arbor, could fly into Washington only when his schedule permitted. He could not keep as close an eye on Social Security politics as when he worked night and day in Washington as an HEW official in the Johnson administration. Arthur Flemming, the former HEW secretary and Nixon administration official, did not have sufficient grasp of the program details to be of much help to congressmen, despite his great interest in the defense of the program. Others, such as Alvin David and Arthur Hess, had always functioned as staff to Ball and lacked his political connections. Still others, such as Nelson Cruikshank, remained powerful program advocates, yet they were so obviously partisan in their outlook as to be of limited use in working out delicate compromises with Republicans. Only Robert Ball lived and worked in Washington and held a job that reinforced his standing as an expert, rather than a mere partisan advocate, and gave him the flexibility to devote all his time to Social Security as the attacks on the program mounted. As if to underscore how much time he would need to devote to his Social Security activities, Ball scaled back from full-time to part-time on the IOM payroll in 1975.[60]

Another thing that aided Ball in his new role as a Social Security advocate was his willingness to master the new institutional structure of Congress.[61] When Wilbur Mills lost his chairmanship, Wilbur Cohen lost much of his influence over the legislative process because Mills had relied on him for advice. Unlike Cohen, Ball, with sufficient time to cultivate his congressional contacts from his Washington base, moved on and made connections with the congressmen who held positions of influence in the expanded structure of subcommittees that developed after Mills's downfall.

A January 1975 visit to James Burke, a veteran Democratic congressman from Massachusetts who became the first head of the new Social Security subcommittee of Ways and Means, showed how the Ball treatment worked. Ball wanted to recruit Burke as a strong program advocate. Toward that end he gave Burke his home and office phone numbers and urged him to call at any time for help or advice. He suggested that Burke might like to recommend increasing Social Security benefits twice a year, rather than once, to keep up with inflation and offered to write him a memo containing all of the things "I think would be desirable for him to be for." Burke appeared grateful for Ball's help, remarking that Ball knew all of the political pitfalls in Social Security—all of the booby traps and where the bodies were buried, as the congressman put it. "I think he needs to start identifying himself as a spokesman for the system and to benefit from the success of the program and to be advocating improvements and interpreting them," Ball wrote in a note to himself.[62]

Ball's web of political clients extended well beyond Burke, as the names of the people on his "to do" lists indicated. In July 1975, he jotted down that he should contact Burke, Congressman Joe Waggonner (D–Louisiana), former HEW under secretary John Veneman, Walter Mondale, and Russell Long on Social Security financing. He also wanted to set up a meeting with Wilbur Cohen, Bert Seidman of the AFL-CIO, and Nelson Cruikshank on the next steps in the strategy for defending Social Security. He made a note to keep track of the hearings that Senator Mondale was holding on Social Security and to stay in touch with Al Ullman (D–Oregon), Dan Rostenkowski (D–Illinois), Abraham Ribicoff, Phil

Burton (D–California), Claude Pepper (D–Florida), and Tim Wirth (D–Colorado). In addition, he made it a point to remain current with the congressional staffers in charge of Medicare and to think of ways for "promoting interviews with popular media on the future of social security (Today Show, CBS etc)."[63]

During the presidency of Gerald Ford, Ball and the advocates of program preservation won more battles than they lost, even in the absence of an improved outlook for the economy.[64] On the contrary, the actuaries came to believe in 1976 that a permanent climacteric had been reached and that future productivity increases would not match those in the past. Accordingly, they decided to change their assumptions in favor of a declining trend in the rate of real wage growth. The previous assumption had been that average real wages would increase at a rate from 2 to 2.25 percent per year. That fit the historical pattern of the preceding twenty years. In changing the assumption in 1976, Social Security's chief actuary commented, "it is doubtful that an economy characterized by energy and resource cartels, pollution abatement requirements, and sustained inflation could generate real wage rates experienced in the relatively expansionary period of the last 25 years." Such factors as declining birth rates, improvements in mortality rates, runaway inflation, unemployment well above its postwar average, and the fact that there had been no real growth in real wages since 1971 had "a significant impact on the way we view the future."[65]

Ball did not buy all of the analysis, such as a long-range assumption of unemployment at 5 percent. He believed—correctly, as it turned out—that the low fertility rates would eventually cause the high unemployment rate to abate. Ball also objected to the way in which the trustee reports were prepared, feeling that too much discretion was left to the actuaries. "The result of leaving it entirely to the actuaries has not been very good," he said. He recognized, however, that there was little he could do about the situation without making it seem a matter of "political pressure versus technical expertise." As a result, he had to accept projections that made Social Security's future look worse than he believed it would turn out to be.[66]

Early in 1975 President Ford, worried about the immediate effect of inflation, asked that the automatic benefit increases be limited to 5 percent. Just as Ball hoped, the proposal went nowhere.

"There appears to be no chance that Congress will act to restrain the increase to five percent," Labor Secretary James Lynn told the president in May. Lynn personally called Representative Herman Schneebeli (R–Pennsylvania), who was on the Ways and Means Committee and who bluntly told him that no Republican would dare introduce the legislation.[67]

At the end of 1975 the president decided to sponsor a bill to deal with the short-term financing problem that would raise Social Security taxes in 1977, change the allocation of benefits to shore up the disability insurance trust fund, and phase out benefits for Social Security beneficiaries between 18 and 22 years of age who were full-time students. By May 1976, President Ford knew his proposal was dead, despite his desire that Congress face up to the Social Security problem, even in an election year. Congress preferred to postpone the matter until after the 1976 elections. If anything were to be done, the preference was to raise the taxable wage base, as Ball favored, rather than raise taxes, as Ford preferred.[68]

The Double-Indexing Problem

A convergence developed between the views of Ball and those of the Ford administration on the most important question related to Social Security financing. The issue, highly technical in nature yet consequential in its effects, concerned what became known as the double-indexing problem. The benefit formula adopted in 1972 determined a person's initial Social Security benefit by computing his or her average monthly earnings and paying a percentage of that. Once on the rolls, that person's benefit rose with rises in the consumer price index (CPI). The problem stemmed from the fact that the percentages in the benefit formula that determined initial benefits for people not yet on the rolls also changed to reflect rising prices. If, for example, the CPI rose by 5.9 percent in 1976, then, instead of a person's benefit being based on 137.77 percent of the first $110 of average monthly earnings (and lesser percentages of average monthly earnings above that), it would instead be based on 145.90 percent of the first $110 of average monthly earnings. In a period of rapid inflation both the CPI and wage rates (and hence average monthly earnings) would go up, with the result of producing larger than antici- pated initial benefit levels for future beneficiaries. These large benefits would come both from the increases in average monthly earnings and from increases in the percentage by which average monthly earnings were multiplied to yield the benefit level.[69]

It was not an easy matter to explain. Even Ball, a master of the simple, lucid explanation, had difficulty. "The present problem," he told his longtime friend Eveline Burns, "is that prices are fully taken into account in the change in the benefit formula and then on top of that any increases in wages raises benefits further by in- creasing the average monthly wage on which the benefit formula is calculated." Under the economic conditions of the mid-1970s, the result was benefit levels that ran considerably ahead of rises in wage levels and produced what Ball believed were irrationally high replacement rates. "I don't believe that people would toler- ate the very high level of benefits in relation to wages that would result," he said.[70]

Ball could explain his solution far more easily than he could describe the problem. He wanted to change the formula for com- puting benefits so that the system remained adequately financed whatever the condition of the economy. Instead of tying initial benefits to the rate of inflation, he proposed relating them to changes in average wage levels.[71]

The double-indexing problem became a concern of the Social Security Advisory Council appointed by the Ford administra- tion, which met for the first time in May 1974. This council, headed by W. Allen Wallis, the chancellor of the University of Rochester, contained very few of the regulars who served on past advisory councils and was the first since 1938 not to be staffed by Robert Ball. The council accepted the double-indexing problem as the most important one before it. This matter, said Wallis, had "overriding importance because it protects the social security program against instability caused by unpredictable variations in the economy."[72]

When the advisory council's report reached the president in the spring of 1975, he was advised that most of its recommenda- tions should be opposed, except for those that concerned stabiliz- ing the benefit structure. "Almost all of the Council's . . . benefit recommendations involve additional program costs," warned presidential adviser Jim Cannon. As the staff director of the council recalled, the White House immediately disowned the report, which, among other things, called for financing Medicare through general revenues. Instead, the president issued a statement: "In my view the most important recommendation of the Council calls for the stabilization of the benefit structure so that future benefits will maintain a constant relationship to the earnings and will not be so vulnerable to changes in the economy."[73]

At the end of 1975 the president made a decision to recommend a solution to the double-indexing problem that paralleled that of the advisory council and Robert Ball. This solution was described as a "neutral decoupling scheme with constant replacement rates."[74] In other words, the formula was designed to yield benefits that replaced the same percentage of real wages over time. If workers who retired in 1975 received 30 percent of their real wages in their Social Security benefits (which were then indexed for inflation during the worker's retirement), then those workers who retired in 2010 should receive a similar percentage.[75]

On June 17, 1976, the White House released the Social Security Benefit Indexing Act. "Very simply stated," said Commissioner Cardwell in briefing the press, "the President's proposal is intended to stabilize the replacement rates under a Social Security system that is indexed, as the present one is, for the cost of living for the retired person." Asked why the president should recommend such legislation so deep into a presidential election year when the chances for passage were virtually nil, Cardwell replied that the president "is attempting to call attention to the public and the Congress the fact that we are just sitting here doing nothing while the System experiences deficits and I agree with him."[76]

Uncommented on by Cardwell was the fact that Jimmy Carter, the Democratic candidate for president, also supported Ford's solution to the double-indexing problem. One link between the two campaigns on this issue was Robert Ball.

The Carter Years: The 1977 Legislation

Robert Ball, like most sophisticated Washington observers of the political scene, thought little of Governor Jimmy Carter's chances to get the 1976 Democratic presidential nomination. In the early

Robert Ball at the May 1977 White House meeting in the Cabinet Room with President Jimmy Carter. Ball is at the left end of the table; on his left is HEW Under Secretary Hale Champion and on his right is Commerce Secretary Juanita Kreps. HEW Secretary Joseph Califano sits on Champion's left. Photograph courtesy of Robert Ball.

days of Carter's candidacy, Ball would have ranked him about fifteenth or sixteenth on a list of likely nominees. Nonetheless, Ball offered to help Carter and ended up as an influential adviser to President Carter on Social Security legislation in 1977.

In general, Ball maintained the policy that he would help any Democratic candidate who asked him. That reflected his new partisan character as a Democrat but also the ethos of service he had inherited from his father and from the Social Security Administration: one helped anyone who was kind enough to ask. So when Carter's campaign requested help from Tom Joe, whom Ball had known as an assistant to John Veneman in the Nixon administration, and Joe suggested that they contact Ball, Ball obliged.

At the request of Stuart Eizenstat of the Carter campaign, Ball prepared a memo that gave Carter the same sort of advice he was giving everyone else. In particular, he pushed the ideas that increased revenues should be raised through increases in the wage base, rather than from contribution increases, and that the Democrats should think about expanding the program, rather than contracting it, as Ford wished to do. A working relationship developed between Ball and Stuart Eizenstat that carried over into the Carter White House, when Eizenstat became the domestic counselor to the president. In terms of the history of Social Security, this relationship paralleled that which had developed some twenty years earlier between Wilbur Cohen and Ted Sorensen, John F. Kennedy's speechwriter and alter ego: it created an important link between the program and the White House.[77]

Ball had personal contacts with Carter even before the election. Right after Carter's nomination, Ball, along with people representing other social welfare programs, went to Plains, Georgia, for a day-long consultation with the candidate. Ball thought that he was influencing Carter toward accepting his positions on Social Security and health insurance. Carter was, however, a different candidate than Lyndon Johnson or John F. Kennedy. For one thing, his nomination and eventual election broke a cycle that had persisted since 1948 in which people who had worked for the federal government became president (and by his third term FDR qualified more as an incumbent president than as a former governor). As the first governor to be successful in a presidential election since Franklin Roosevelt, Carter brought a different perspective to the job than did his immediate predecessors. For another thing, Carter ran at a time when, even more than usual, it was popular to rail against the evils of Washington, which included Watergate, inflation, and an energy crisis. Hence, it was tempting, and maybe even necessary, for Carter to run as the anti-government candidate, as a southern, conservative, yet racially progressive candidate who was untainted by the Great Society. That meant keeping more distance from the troubled Social Security program than either Kennedy or LBJ had.[78]

During the campaign, Ball tried unsuccessfully to get Carter to drop his attacks on Washington. Although he failed at that, he nonetheless took pride in being asked by the campaign to accompany Carter on a visit to a nursing home in Baltimore. During that visit, if not at other stops on his campaign, Carter reached out to senior citizens by emphasizing the party's links to Social Security and Medicare.[79]

Although Ball played no special role in the Carter transition, he stayed in touch with Eizenstat and with Joseph Califano, the former adviser to Lyndon Johnson who was Carter's choice to serve as secretary of Health, Education, and Welfare. Eizenstat apparently mentioned Ball as a possible candidate for a job in the Carter administration to Califano, but Ball downplayed the possibility of returning to the government. Thanking Eizenstat for his kindness, Ball indicated that he wanted to be "as helpful as possible to the new Administration and will be available to talk with you and Joe about the areas of my special interest: social security, national health insurance and welfare." "When you have time," he wrote Califano, "I would be pleased to talk with you about . . . health insurance and social security financing."[80]

Social Security financing loomed as an important early issue for the Carter administration for several reasons. First, much time had already been spent on the double-indexing problem in the advisory council and in the congressional committees. Second, the program faced short-term financing problems that, in the unlikely event of no congressional action, could cause the program to go bankrupt in the early 1980s. Third, if painful measures needed to be taken to curb the program's growth and to change the benefit formula to pay less generous benefits to future retirees, then both the administration and the Congress preferred to take those actions at the furthest possible point from the next election. Hence, Social Security financing was an issue for 1977, not 1978.

An appropriate moment to announce such legislation was soon after the May 1 Social Security trustees report, which, according to Eizenstat, would "almost certainly show both long and short term financing problems for the Social Security trust fund." If the administration moved quickly enough, it could soothe the public about the soundness of the system and give the president, rather than the Congress, control over the solution. Although the administration could wait for a year without adverse effects in the program, it seemed appropriate to act quickly.[81]

Califano and HEW Under Secretary Hale Champion, a former California state government official, relied upon two different tracks within the department to develop legislation, setting up two teams. Social Security Commissioner Cardwell headed one team. He was a Nixon appointee from the last days of his administration and a career civil servant who had been asked to stay on in the Carter administration, in part to demonstrate the bipartisan nature of the program and in part because Social Security was not considered as high a priority issue as welfare reform or health insurance. Henry Aaron, an economist from the Brookings Institution and an assistant secretary for planning and evaluation at HEW during the Carter administration, captained the other team. Aaron presumably would have less loyalty to the status quo and, as a member of the secretary's bureaucracy, more loyalty to Califano than would Cardwell and the SSA bureaucrats. Aaron could also be expected to analyze the program on an economist's terms. In place of politically accepted routine, an economist might instead think in terms of efficiency, under the supposition that there were better or worse ways of spending any level of money.[82]

Another interested party to the creation of Social Security legislation was Robert Ball. Having waited out the Ford administration, he hoped to do better with Carter. As the Carter administration set to work, Ball attended meetings with Champion and Cardwell.

In time a consensus developed on Social Security legislation that was acceptable to the HEW people, the SSA people, and Ball. The proposal relied on collecting more money for Social Security by raising the level of the payroll on which workers and their employers paid Social Security taxes. The alternatives, rejected by Ball and the HEW planners, involved raising Social Security tax rates or cutting benefit levels. The emerging plan went further than previous proposals by gradually getting rid of the maximum on the employer's payroll but raising the maximum for employees only a little. In the traditional Social Security arrangements, workers and employers paid the same amount of tax for a given employee. Under the proposed new arrangement, employers would pay more in Social Security taxes than would employees. If the plan were put into effect, benefit levels would not rise beyond what was already planned because benefit levels were based on the level of wages on which employees paid taxes, but revenues to the system would increase because employers would pay more. In addition, the plan contained a feature that would add general revenues to the system if the unemployment rate exceeded 6 percent. In other words, if the economy continued to cause the program trouble, then the federal government would add money both to maintain the system's solvency and to boost the economy through counter-cyclical spending.[83] Finally, the plan picked up the decoupling provisions that had been developed in the Ford administration.

At some point, before the completion of the negotiations at the end of April, Ball ate lunch with Eizenstat and other White House staff members. Eizenstat told Ball that the president would want a confidential memo from him at the end of the process. In other words, the president sought Ball's independent opinion of proposals prepared by the president's own bureaucracy. Ball came to realize that he was included in the negotiations with HEW at the particular insistence of the president or at least of Eizenstat. Sensitive to the feelings involved, Ball went out of his way to credit Champion with good work, but he realized that Califano and Champion were, at best, ambivalent about his role in the process.[84]

As an individual, Ball had far fewer institutional resources at his command than did the HEW planners. To compensate, Ball used what might be described as his back channels to the Social Security Administration. Mary Ross of the Social Security Administration's Office of Program Evaluation and Planning, with whom Ball had often worked on legislative proposals, reviewed his work, checking the figures and making suggestions. In addition, he called upon other contacts in the research and planning and the actuarial offices at SSA for help. That allowed Ball, in effect, to amplify his voice and to speak with the authority that comes from inside knowledge. When one factored in his grasp of Social Security politics and his long experience with the program, Ball became a formidable figure in the debate, particularly compared to the novices in Califano's office who were just beginning their periods of government service.

In the end Califano wrote one memo to the president and Ball another, although the two memos contained complementary messages. The HEW memo noted that "organized labor advocates and key individuals (such as Robert Ball and Wilbur Cohen) support the HEW proposal. Support of these individuals and organizations is essential for any plan for financing social security." Ball, for his part, called the HEW plan "an excellent one."

Nonetheless, complete unanimity did not prevail on what the president should recommend. The idea of adding general revenues to the program, even on an emergency basis, was not congenial to business groups. Within the administration, officials from the Office of Management and Budget (OMB) and from the Department of Commerce objected to aspects of the plan. OMB did not like the notions of general revenue funding or what amounted to a large tax increase on employers and preferred to accept lower reserve levels in the trust funds. The Department of Commerce wished to move toward a more straightforward use of general revenues as a permanent part of Social Security financing. Ball quibbled about the small tax increases that were proposed for 1979 and 1981 and the failure to eliminate completely the long-range actuarial imbalance.[85]

To resolve the remaining questions, Carter called for a brief meeting to reach a specific consensus. Preoccupied with preparations for an important trip abroad, Carter told Eizenstat, "I can't study this much." Two things about the Social Security issue attracted the president's attention. One was the rising cost of disability payments and the apparent ease with which people received such benefits, regardless of whether they were unable to work. The president knew about this issue because of publicity over the rising costs of disability benefits and because, as a governor, he had been responsible for running Georgia's workers' compensation program and for administering the state office that made disability determinations for the Social Security Administration. The other thing that caught Carter's attention was the double-indexing problem, which he linked with efforts to control inflation. "My support for better financing is predicated on decoupling inflation factor," he told Eizenstat. Significantly, the president also advised Eizenstat to "assess Ball's comments."[86]

The president's meeting on Social Security took place on May 4, 1977. That day Ball had taken his car to be repaired and, in the era before cell phones, was out of touch for much of the morning. By the time he came home, it was 11:00, and Betty Dillon, his personal assistant, reached him with word that the White House wanted to talk with him. He soon learned that he was invited to the meeting with the president, which was scheduled for noon.

Ball put in a hasty call to Champion, who asked if there was any way for Ball, Champion, and Califano to meet before going to the White House. Moving as quickly as he could through the traffic between his Alexandria house and HEW headquarters,

Ball parked in the HEW garage by 11:30. He then went up to the secretary's private dining room where Califano and Champion were having an early lunch. The three agreed that the OMB memorandum objecting to the financing aspects of the HEW plan was, according to Ball, "very bad staff work and almost incomprehensible." Together they left in Califano's car for the White House. On the ride, Ball pushed the idea of using the savings that would be realized, if the president's plan for cost controls on hospitals were passed, to shift money from Medicare to the rest of Social Security and thus forestall the need for increases in the contribution rate.[87]

The president began the meeting on time, with Ball, Champion, Califano, Vice President Walter Mondale, Labor Secretary Ray Marshall, Commerce Secretary Juanita Kreps, and Treasury Secretary Mike Blumenthal all in attendance. Ball sat at the table in the cabinet room with the principals, not along the wall with the members of the staff. He had reached the inner sanctum of the Carter administration, a position he had rarely, if ever, found himself in during previous administrations and certainly not since Lyndon Johnson's days in the White House. It was, by any measure, an unusual situation to have an outsider—a private citizen—sitting in on deliberations related to a very sensitive political issue at the very highest level.

Ball knew most of the players. Before the president entered the room, Juanita Kreps cornered him and asked if he supported her plan to draw one third of the program's finances from general revenues. Ball replied that because there was such a pressing need for general revenues for other purposes and because Social Security's problems could be solved without them, he preferred the HEW approach. Although Ball had approved of the idea of partial general revenue financing in the past, he did not support it in this instance. Shortly afterward, when the president walked into the room, he kissed Juanita Kreps and made a point of shaking Ball's hand. He told Ball that he had been a great help in the campaign, and Ball mentioned how glad he was to see Carter in the cabinet room.

Califano led off the meeting by outlining the HEW plan. In Ball's opinion, Califano finished "without having contributed greatly to people's understanding of the total plan," nor did Hale Champion "add very much." Carter wanted to know if the slight tax increase in the HEW plan violated his campaign pledge not to raise taxes.

Ball took that as his cue to press his case. He reminded the president that he had indeed promised not to raise the contribution rate over the present law and that there was a way to accomplish this result by assuming the passage of the hospital cost–control bill. Carter asked Califano about the idea, and Califano replied that it was acceptable.

Juanita Kreps, who held the portfolio of the Commerce Department, pointed out that employers would oppose the plan because of the way it raised the taxable wage base and ended the tradition of having employers and employees contribute equally to Social Security. Ball took it upon himself to reply to Kreps. Business would not like the plan, but its leaders would object to Krep's plan to introduce general revenue even more. In Ball's reading of history, the employer's contribution had never been thought of as attached to a particular employee but instead was regarded as a contribution to the whole system. Hence, the HEW notion of raising the wage base for employers, but not for employees, constituted "a perfectly acceptable idea from the standpoint of social security principles." When it came to a discussion of Social Security principles, no one in the room could match Ball's pedigree.

The president appeared to seal the matter and to side with the outsider Ball rather than his own cabinet member by remarking that "the last thing" he wanted to rely on for Social Security financing was general revenues. Ball figured that except for Califano, Champion, and possibly Ray Marshall most of the people in the room either opposed the plan or supported it in a very half-hearted manner. Nonetheless, the president accepted the plan, with Ball's modifications and with the need to reexamine the financing for the period between 1984 and 1990.

After the president left the room, Stuart Eizenstat told Ball that he had "certainly pulled Califano's chestnuts out of the fire." According to Ball's own estimates, he had spoken three times as much Kreps, Califano, or Carter. It had become his meeting, and he dominated it.

Present at the creation of the Carter bill, Ball became, in effect, a member of Carter's administration as the Social Security bill was completed and sent to Congress. Fighting hard to keep tax increases out of the bill, Ball managed to get the HEW officials not to schedule an increase in the Social Security contribution rate until 1985. Once having reached agreement with HEW, he "enlisted full time in the Carter administration."[88]

It was clear that Ball had more enthusiasm for the bill than did Califano and Champion. Champion said that the Social Security financing problem stemmed from the government's inability to face difficult situations and instead to postpone decisions about them. He saw the president's proposal, in a theme that formed a major motif of social policy in the Carter era, as the product of "hard choices." In language that could have been lifted from Gerald Ford, Champion said that there was no "happy way" to deal with a $80 billion problem, but "social security is to [*sic*] important to too many people to let slip."[89]

A few days later, Ball met with Al Ullman, who had succeeded Wilbur Mills as head of the Ways and Means Committee, and tried to explain the plan to him. The reception, less cordial than Ball had hoped it would be, indicated that passing the Carter plan would be difficult. Ullman had no difficulty in accepting the notions of stabilizing the replacement rate, increasing the maximum earnings base a couple of times, shifting part of the health insurance tax rate to the cash benefit program, and possibly raising taxes in 1985. Ullman objected to the innovative parts of the president's proposal that broke from Social Security tradition, in particular the use of general revenues if economic conditions deteriorated and taking the maximum off the employers' earnings base and applying the tax to the whole payroll. Ullman worried that business organizations such as the Chamber of Commerce would lead a major campaign against those two proposals and prevent them from clearing the House. Ullman, like his counterpart Russell Long, who headed the Senate Finance Committee, wanted to get through the short run and wait to solve larger problems until a larger crisis forced the action. Ball told Ullman not to underestimate the short-run problems and not to lock himself into opposition to the president's plan. As the business community considered the alternatives, Ball believed that it would eventually come around to the president's point of view.[90]

More than a backroom operator, Ball also became a public presence in the Social Security debate. In June, for example, he testified on the administration's behalf before the Senate Committee on Finance. He noted that Social Security would pay out $5.6 billion more than it took in for fiscal year 1977. The combination of

inflation, which raised benefits, and unemployment, which reduced revenues, created a situation that would leave the system
permanently underfunded. Hence, something like the president's plan was necessary.[91]

By August the president's bill appeared to be in trouble. "The
Administration's Social Security plan has hit on hard days with
both Congressman Ullman and the House Ways and Means
Staff and Senator Long and the Senate Finance Committee staff
opposing key elements. It now appears clear that neither Committee favors any use of general revenues, even in the limited
counter-cyclical fashion in the Administrative proposal," Eizenstat wrote the president.[92]

Eizenstat's solution was the same as Elliot Richardson's had
been in similar situations when Congress refused to go along
with an administration plan. He sent for Robert Ball, whom he
described to Carter as "the former Social Security Commissioner
and your adviser during the campaign, who was also helpful in
developing the Administration's proposal for Social Security financing," to meet with Senator Long and affect some sort of
compromise. Ball saw things in brighter terms. "We have come
through House and Senate passage very well and there is a
good chance that what is adopted will be very close to the main
recommendations of the President," he reported back to the
White House in November. The administration's solution to
the double-indexing system would be adopted; the finances of
the system would be stabilized, mainly from increases in the
wage base. In this regard, Ball hoped that the conference committee would follow the Senate's lead in taxing practically the entire
employer's payroll.[93]

By the time the protracted legislative process concluded in
December, the administration got neither its general revenue
scheme nor the Senate's version of a higher wage base for employers than for employees. Instead, Congress decided to add
revenues to the system by raising the contribution and benefit
base for employers and employees beginning in 1979 and to increase the combined tax rates for Social Security and Medicare
also beginning in 1979.[94]

Passage of the bill showed the lengths to which Congress was
willing to go to preserve the system that Ball had created in 1972.
As Stuart Eizenstat explained to the president in urging him to

sign the bill, the legislation "moves the social security system out of a deficit situation in 1980 and maintains a current surplus until about the year 2030."[95] Although not on the exact terms that Ball preferred and at the cost of a considerable tax increase that would make it harder to achieve other social policy goals by crowding out the available money, the bill nevertheless accomplished the basic objective of keeping the program solvent. Or so it seemed at the time.

Ball's influence on the 1977 amendments extended beyond issues related to financing to peripheral issues. One was the retirement test, an issue that was as old as the Social Security program itself.[96] To get Social Security benefits, which functioned as protection against loss of income, a person needed to retire. Almost from the beginning, however, pressure arose to allow people to collect Social Security benefits because they had reached a certain age, regardless of whether they had retired. That idea followed the form of the Townsend Plan that had been so popular in the early years of Social Security. Administrators such as Arthur Altmeyer had fought against abandoning the retirement test, but over the years Congress had liberalized the requirement so that, for example, people over age 72 could work and earn as much as they liked and still receive Social Security benefits. In 1977, Senators Barry Goldwater (R–Arizona) and Robert Dole (R–Kansas) planned to introduce an amendment that would do away with the retirement test altogether.

Ball did not want the Goldwater-Dole amendment to pass for two reasons. One was that it would be expensive to implement. In the next century, many people between age 65 and 72 would be working, and paying them Social Security benefits would be costly. Another reason was that it would deprive the system of money that it would need to fund the retirement of the baby boom generation. Instead of paying money into the system, working people between age 65 and 72 would instead be drawing money from it.

To prevent passage of the Goldwater-Dole amendment, Ball believed it would be necessary to offer a compromise and sell it to Congress. He proposed that, instead of eliminating the retirement test altogether, the age at which the retirement test stopped be lowered from 72 to 70. Senator Gaylord Nelson (D–Wisconsin), the floor manager for the bill in the Senate, encouraged Ball to talk with Senator Frank Church, chairman of the Senate Committee on Aging, whose position had begun to waver from his usual opposition to changes in the retirement test to accepting the Dole-Goldwater amendment as a political necessity. Ball reminded Church that the senator had recently come out in favor of raising the mandatory retirement age to 70, and hence it would be consistent to retain the retirement test at age 70, an admittedly "superficial" connection but one that Ball believed "might work." "That seems like a very good idea, thank you very much," said Church.

This bit of inside politics played out as Ball had hoped it would. On the Senate floor, Goldwater insisted on an up or down vote on his proposal, threatening to filibuster the whole bill if his amendment were tabled. Goldwater then moved his amendment, and Church moved to amend the Goldwater amendment by abolishing the retirement test at age 72 and moving it to age 70. Church's amendment carried by a narrow margin, and then the Goldwater amendment, as amended by Church, carried as well.

Some administration officials believed they could have defeated the Goldwater amendment without Ball's compromise. As Ball noted, however, Senator Nelson thought the vote would have been too risky, and Ball agreed. Hence, in the middle of the larger battle over Social Security financing, a small change was made in the nation's retirement policy that, like the rest of the 1977 amendments, featured a strategic defeat to preserve the program's basic framework.

Relations with the Carter Administration

As an unpaid worker for the administration, Ball believed he had earned certain perks. One was membership on the Social Security Advisory Council that Califano appointed in 1977. Although Ball liked to think that whatever appointments he received were not the results of his campaigning for them and thought of service on an advisory council as hard work, rather than a reward, he nonetheless lobbied hard to be included on the council. Ball wrote to Stuart Eizenstat in May 1977, when Ball's influence over administration policy was its height, and asked that the president tell Califano to pick him for a slot on the council. He reiterated the request in July, writing Eizenstat that "it would be useful to you and the President for me to be a member of the Advisory Council on Social Security, and I hope it works out. I'm not sure it will without your continuing attention; my guess is that I make some of the second and third level people at HEW uneasy." In September he pressed his case yet again, explaining to Eizenstat that it "was customary for HEW to clear its advisory council appointments with the President . . . in order to be sure that I am appointed it would seem to be necessary for the President to mention to Joe that he would like to see me on the Council or to ask you to talk to Joe on his behalf." Ball got his appointment, joining his friend Douglas Brown as a frequent participant on the advisory councils that met for the rest of the century.[97]

Another perk that Ball requested and received related to the president's ceremonial duties in signing the 1977 amendments. "If there is to be a group invited to the signing of the social security bill, I would very much like to be included. Can you arrange it?" he asked his friend Tom Joe. The White House did invite Ball to the ceremony, but the president's staff chose to make it a low-key occasion in the Indian Treaty Room of the Executive Office Building, without the usual souvenir pens and the other paraphernalia of political triumph. Wilbur Cohen, who also attended, did not like the low-key way in which the White House handled the occasion, a harbinger of the strained relations that would develop between the Carter administration and the traditional supporters of Social Security. The fact was that the administration did not want to celebrate the 1977 amendments, with their tax increases. As Joseph Califano's press secretary told him on the way back to the office from the ceremony, "Don't get too far out in front on the Social Security bill. Those taxes are too heavy."[98]

A third perk that Ball attempted to obtain from the Carter administration was an endorsement for the book he was finishing on Social Security. Ball had begun to write the book, under contract to Columbia University Press, in the spring of 1974. He saw it as the distillation of his accumulated wisdom on Social Security, and he decided to compose it in an unorthodox manner. Instead of creating a seamless narrative, Ball elected to adopt a question and answer approach, giving the final product the quality of a catechism or one of the chapters from James Joyce's *Ulysses*. Although even his editor had doubts about the question and answer approach, Ball took great pride in the final product, which he characteristically delayed, both because of his perfectionism and because he wanted to include the results of the 1977 amendments. Hence the dust jacket of the completed book boasted that it answered "your questions about the new social security law." "I rather like it," Ball later said of the book, claiming that its format forced him to confront the weaknesses in his argument. The title, *Social Security: Today and Tomorrow,* reflected Ball's desire to make the book as much about the future as the past.[99]

In drafts of the book and in correspondence with former SSA employees whose comments he sought, Ball came as close as he ever would to setting down his basic philosophy of social policy. "I am searching for a general philosophy of the relationship of social insurance to private pensions, on the one hand, and means-tested assistance, on the other," he wrote former SSA actuary Charles Trowbridge. "Social insurance," he noted, "needs to be able to do practically the whole job of providing replacement of income on retirement to those who work regularly but who earn less than average wages, and on the other hand, social insurance serves as the base for the above-average earner, leaving a stronger and stronger role for private pension plans the further up the wage scale you go. Means-tested assistance seems to me a necessary supplementation for people with relatively slight attachment or no attachment to work. . . . I am also quite resistant to the idea that private pensions should be mandated for everyone so that social security wouldn't have to be more than just a base for workers at all earnings levels."[100]

The book, useful as a guide to Ball's thinking, makes for very hard reading. The questions that Ball poses to himself often reflect the subtlety of his reasoning but not the questions or concerns of the average person at whom the book is supposedly aimed. "But why didn't the Congress make this provision retroactive when changing it to provide equal treatment for men and women in the future?" Ball asks in a typical passage, even though such a thought might not have occurred to anyone else. An even more fundamental problem is that the question and answer format interrupts the flow of the narrative and makes the often quite technical material even more difficult to read. The reader seeking basic information about the program or a coherent political argument is repeatedly stopped by Ball's questions, such as, "Do you really think that a two-pronged approach such as you are describing is superior to a uniform negative income tax?" The premise of the question and the answer depends on a familiarity with the negative income tax that most readers do not have. For Ball, used to the give and take of congressional testimony and primed by his years of recitation and response in Social Security training sessions and meetings with regional representatives, the question and answer format might have seemed natural. For the reader, the format is off-putting and ultimately renders the book little more than a curiosity. Nonetheless, the book achieved a measure of success, winning awards from organizations such as the American Association of Risk and Insurance (which perhaps appreciated the book's rational tone and had little ear for language) and selling 20,000 copies—a very significant sale for an academic publication.[101]

The book went to press with blurbs from the usual group of liberal suspects, Ted Kennedy, Wilbur Cohen, and Bert Seidman of the AFL-CIO, but without an endorsement from President Carter. That was one perk that Ball failed to obtain despite pushing hard for it. The timing of the book's publication, he told Eizenstat, would make it useful for "building support for the Administration's proposals, which the book explains and strongly endorses." In fact, it came out after the passage of the amendments and at a time when the administration was already in retreat on the Social Security issue. "I presume the president has a policy against outright endorsement of a book but is there anything he would be willing to say that would help get the book read." Ball continued, "Something appropriately modest perhaps along the lines of 'Bob Ball is America's foremost expert on social security and I have sought his advice both before and after [the election].'" Later Ball turned to Tom Joe in the hope that he would write Carter and get him to do the foreword to the book. Whether anyone in the White House pressed Carter on this matter is unclear. In the end, though, the book appeared with a foreword by Senator Gaylord Nelson, who, as the head of the Senate Finance Committee's subcommittee on Social Security, figured largely in Robert Ball's world but who was not very visible outside of Wisconsin. Like the book itself, Nelson was a creature of Washington. And in Washington style, Ball no doubt took a hand in drafting Nelson's foreword, which boasted, "Until now no one has put together in such readable style so coherent a picture of what social security is all about."[102]

Deteriorating Relations with the Carter Administration

As things turned out, passage of the 1977 amendments turned out to be a high-water mark for collaboration between Ball and the Carter administration. Relations with Eizenstat and with Carter himself, to the extent that Ball had contact with the busy president, remained cordial to the end of the term. Toward the very end of Carter's administration, the HEW Secretary Patricia Harris, at the president's urging, even asked Ball to come back to the government and serve as Social Security commissioner. By this time, however, Califano, Champion, and Stanford Ross, Carter's commissioner of Social Security appointed in 1978, had separated themselves from Ball and the others who defended the program as it had evolved between 1950 and 1977. Ball, for his part, drew closer to Edward Kennedy, whose views were much closer to his own than were Carter's and who mounted a challenge to Carter's renomination in 1980. Overshadowing the entire discussion was the deterioration of the economy that put pressure on Social Security finances, even though the 1977 amendments were supposed to have solved the problem.

A good example of the differences between Ball and the Carter administration concerned their respective views of the disability insurance program. At the May 1977 meeting with President Carter that Ball dominated, the president brought up his concerns about the disability insurance program: too many people were getting benefits and, as a consequence, costs were rising out of control. In his memoirs, Joseph Califano wrote that Carter had told him that the disability program was being "ripped off" by "drug addicts and alcoholics." When the president mentioned the problem in the May meeting, Hale Champion agreed that he was absolutely right: disability costs were rising, and something needed to be done about them. Ball held his tongue, since he realized that the solvency of the Social Security program, not the administration of disability insurance, was the subject under discussion. Privately, however, he worried that the Carter administration was trying to disassemble the disability program he had helped to create in 1956. In Ball's opinion, the disability insurance program was "extraordinarily successful," and all that was required to fix it was to enact "some minor administrative changes and some liberalizations in the law." The problem was that worsening actuarial experience in private and public disability programs was leading people "to throw up their hands," thus creating "the potential for serious harm."[103]

Officials in the Carter administration tended to see the problems in the disability insurance program in the same way as they looked at the double-indexing problem. Both involved flaws in the benefit formula that required correction because they led to higher than anticipated costs. In the case of disability, the problem was that replacement rates were too high. The solution was to limit the amount of money that a family could receive from disability benefits and to change the way in which disability benefits were calculated (known in the policy vernacular as the cap on family benefits and a change in the way of computing average wages). By lowering the replacement rates, the argument went, the incentives to go on the disability rolls would be less, and the rate of people aged 45 to 64 who chose to withdraw from the labor force because of disability (which had been going up considerably between 1969 and 1978) would decline.

Ball saw the problem quite differently. Most of the people on the disability rolls, he believed, belonged there; they were not lured there by the high replacement rates and permitted to stay there by lax administration. Unlike the double-indexing problem, which was a technical matter in which a policy failed to work as Congress had intended it to work, the disability insurance problem was not a problem at all. To change the method of calculating disability benefits would change the program from what Congress had intended and would mean going back on a promise that had already been made. In Ball's view, then, fixing the double-indexing problem in a way that lowered future benefits represented a technical correction; altering the replacement rates in disability insurance constituted a true benefit cut and amounted to tampering. To the administration, both actions constituted responsible acts to cut unintended costs.

Ball's feelings to the contrary, Joseph Califano highlighted the issue of disability insurance reform, and the administration joined forces with the staff of the Ways and Means Committee to make changes in the disability insurance program. In 1980, after a tortuous legislative debate, Congress passed amendments to the program along the lines that the administration had suggested. The actions confirmed Ball's fears that "there are, or will be, a lot of people running around HEW (not necessarily the best informed) thinking of things that turn out to be damaging to people."[104]

The attitude of Carter administration officials toward the disability insurance program reflected, among other things, their growing disdain for the competence of the Social Security Administration. Whereas previous administrations, Republican and Democrat, had entrusted the Social Security Administration with increasingly complex tasks, the Carter administration cut back on the agency's responsibilities and worried about the agency's ability to handle those that remained. At the very beginning of the Carter years, for example, Califano decided to strip Medicare away from the agency in favor of uniting Medicare and Medicaid and creating the Health Care Financing Administration. To be sure, Califano's actions reflected his reading of health politics, his desire to separate Medicaid from the welfare bureaucracy, and his need to make a personal imprint on the design of the department. Still, the effect on Social Security was to remove the agency's second largest responsibility from its control.[105]

Other Carter officials voiced overtly negative opinions about the Social Security Administration. When Stanford Ross, a tax lawyer who had served in the Johnson administration and who had close ties to Califano, got to SSA in 1978, he could not believe what he found: "I was stunned at my first executive staff meeting at how elderly it was and how people had kind of gotten there by slow emergence through the ranks and then stayed there for a long time. There was just a kind of stultifying atmosphere." Hale Champion, who had entertained the prospect of heading SSA himself, offered a similar assessment. "When we got there," he later recalled, "Social Security was really rocky. . . . As you looked over there you saw what was once a great organization that still had a lot of substantial ability at the third and fourth levels coming up, but all blocked off by people who had stopped wanting to change with the time or take on new missions and so on, wanted to stand around and light votive candles. . . . they weren't moving, they weren't adjusting . . . I think it was an organization that was over the hill."[106]

Although Ball realized that much of what happened since he left SSA had affected the agency negatively, he still defended his organization and criticized the way in which Ross ran it. In particular, he cited the trauma of implementing SSI, the financing problems induced by the bad economy, and the "general public reaction against government agencies." Still, he felt that Ross had made these problems worse through his lack of confidence in the program and through his efforts at reorganization. Under Ross's new scheme, the operational bureaus no longer had responsibilities for major programs, such as disability insurance. Instead, a functional pattern prevailed that Ross hoped would break up some of the inner-agency fiefdoms that he believed contributed to the agency's inefficiency. Ball charged that Ross's actions, in particular the "reliance on a small group of intimate staff members unacquainted with the social security program," were "seriously damaging to the morale of the organization."[107] Ball still preferred the organizational arrangements he had adopted in 1965 and worried that in the Carter administration the agency had "lost control over its destiny and is subject to a stream of directives from staff personnel at other levels of [the department] who are engaged only part-time on social security and who come and go as the Secretary's change."[108]

Ball never did understand the ambivalence of the Carter administration toward Social Security. He knew, for example, that Califano, Champion, and Ross made jokes about "true believers" and the high priests of Social Security and that they prided themselves as being able to separate the myths about the program from the realities. The Carter officials, mired in a view of policy in which each year the economy yielded less tax revenues than they had hoped to spend on social programs and each year the high inflation rate increased the Social Security system's liabilities, took no particular solace from the notion of workers earning their benefits through the contributions they made. The idea that workers established individual Social Security accounts fell under the heading of myth. According to Califano, it was a "misconception to call Social Security benefits an 'earned right.'"[109]

To use the language of academia, Califano did not want to privilege Social Security, and Ball did. Each could not understand how the other could so completely miss the point. According to Califano, Ball and his allies needed to realize that the "days of expansion were over, that Social Security costs had to be measured against other social needs in an era of limited resources, that the program was now very much a part of the federal budget, and that over the long haul, maintaining support for the heavy taxes necessary to provide adequately would require a sensitive disciplining of the system."[110]

Ball did not want to discipline the system. He wanted to celebrate it. In this vein, he tried to convince Stuart Eizenstat that the 1977 amendments constituted one of the administration's greatest achievements. Instead of running from the issue in the campaign with Ronald Reagan, the administration should brag about preserving inflation-proof benefits: "Social security is a program of Democratic origin and has been developed by Democrats; it is extremely popular and we ought to do nothing that associates the Democratic administration with those who would cut the programs back," he counseled Eizenstat.[111] Ball's views paralleled those of former HEW secretary Wilbur Cohen. "Neither Secretary Califano nor President Carter," complained Cohen, "have really gone all out to defend and explain the program. It is a good program. And someone at the highest level of political leadership should be willing to say that repeatedly."[112]

Confrontation in 1978

Instead, what Califano and company said led to a sharp break between them and Ball in 1978, even after they had made common cause over protecting the tax increases legislated in 1977 from a congressional effort to roll them back.

Nelson Cruikshank, the former AFL-CIO staff member who worked inside the Carter White House as an adviser to the president on policy related to the elderly, linked the need to stand by the Social Security taxes with the effort to enact energy legislation. "If members of Congress who faced up to the long-term demands of the Social Security system and assumed the political risk involved in that stance see spokesmen for the Administration now yielding to the media distortion and criticisms of the measure, they will clearly get a signal that there may be no advantage in taking the risks involved in supporting the energy legislation when there is no immediate short-term crisis," he told Carter. The president agreed and said that the administration should take a positive attitude toward the 1977 legislation. Still, he kept himself at arm's length. "I see no reason for me to start a new campaign," he noted. By April Treasury Secretary Blumenthal reported that there was increasing evidence that "the drive to reduce Social Security taxes this year can be stopped." By May the administration had succeeded in stopping it.[113]

As the fight over Social Security taxes unfolded, routine processes of policy development continued in preparation for the 1979 legislative program. In connection with annual program reviews and the development of annual budgets, HEW officials proposed that some aspects of Social Security be changed in order to save money. In particular, Califano pushed three proposals. One was to eliminate the early retirement provisions of Social Security so that 65 became the first age at which a person who was neither disabled nor a survivor of a Social Security beneficiary could claim benefits. Another was to eliminate the so-called "student benefit" that allowed survivors and other Social Security beneficiaries to receive benefits until they reached age 22, if they were attending college. A third was to eliminate the lump-sum death benefit that was intended to help with funeral expenses.

As Califano pushed his proposals through the budget process, Ball and his allies became alarmed. At first they attributed Califano's moves to routine ploys that secretaries used to protect their programs—proposing cuts that they knew would be overturned at higher levels in order to bring in their budget proposals at the desired levels. By the late fall, Ball saw the necessity to fight against the proposals and to persuade Carter that they were bad politics and bad policy.[114]

Ball pushed his case with Eizenstat, who shared many of his concerns, and used Eizenstat and Cruikshank to secure an appointment with President Carter. Eizenstat warned Carter to go slowly on cutting back Social Security since "it has an enormously powerful and large constituency and it is a program which many Americans regard as sacrosanct." Eizenstat's memo unconsciously echoed the themes of a similar memo prepared for President Ford that noted, "Protection of the system is fostered by one of the largest and strongest constituencies in the public policy arena, including the elderly, organized wage earners, and all of the wage earners who are contributing to the system and expect to benefit from it in the future." Eizenstat believed that it would be better to handle the matter in the traditional manner and ask the advisory council—the one that Ball had used his White House leverage to be appointed to—to study the situation. According to Eizenstat, the cuts would be viewed as taking away money from the elderly in order to spend it on defense programs, and eliminating the early retirement provisions would be received particularly badly.[115]

The president received another long memo, composed by Ball but also signed by Cohen and Cruikshank, that also argued against the Social Security cuts. "We cannot realistically act now as if we were designing a new program without taking into account the benefit rights that people are counting on," Ball wrote. He noted that there were a number of ways in which Social Security benefits might be pruned, but the "main point is that if such modifications are to be made in the social security program, they should be carefully worked out, gradually introduced and have sound program rationale, not short-term budget advantage. The issue at stake is no less than the confidence of people in the promises of government." Meanwhile, Cruikshank reinforced the message by explaining the political downside of cutting Social Security: "From 25 years of experience of lobbying on Capitol Hill for social legislation, I have no hesitancy in advising you that these proposals have practically no chance of being adopted. The net result therefore would be the Administration arousing all of the potential political opposition without improving the budget situation or deriving any other advantage."[116]

Carter appeared moved. "These arguments are very persuasive," he wrote on Ball's memo.[117] Because of the president's concerns, he agreed to meet with Ball, Cruikshank, and Cohen to discuss the situation. The meeting took place on December 20, 1978, in the late afternoon as night began to fall on one of the shortest days of the year and Washington prepared to get away from its official duties for the Christmas break.

Because Ball believed he was the one with the closest relationship with the president (Cruikshank, although the president's counselor, deferred to Ball), he did most of the talking. According to notes that Cohen took, Ball called the HEW proposal "horrendous." Ball remembered that the president seemed surprised by the intensity of his opposition to the cuts. Asked by the president which of the cuts he favored, Ball replied, "None of them. . . . the Administration should not recommend any cutbacks in Social Security." The president wanted to know if the group members had told Califano of its opposition. Although word had undoubtedly reached Califano, they responded that they had not. So the president recommended that Ball, Cohen, and Cruikshank meet with Califano.[118]

At that meeting, which took place on the evening of December 22, away from the White House setting that tended to induce a sense of decorum, the gloves came off. Califano used a boxing metaphor to describe the occasion, with Wilbur Cohen "moving sideways and back and forth on the balls of his feet like a fighter ready to uncork a barrage of jabs." The secretaries waiting outside wondered if Califano, Champion, and Ross were exchanging blows with Ball and his boys, like the two gangs rumbling in *West Side Story*. Although Ball prided himself on remaining calm, the meeting itself was "very hot," with both Cruikshank and Cohen "very, very tough, very excited." Califano, tired after a long year, announced that he had interrupted his vacation in order to argue his department's case with the Office of Management and Budget. "Better you should have stayed where you were," said Cruikshank. In order to get adequate funding for his programs, Califano believed he needed to include the Social Security cuts. For Ball that was exactly the trouble. Califano, and to a certain extent Carter as well, failed to see that Social Security was different from the other programs that depended on general revenues; its special nature as a contributory program with an earned benefit meant that it could not be traded off with those other programs in a political negotiation. To assume otherwise meant a breach of trust with America's workers and retirees.[119]

The meeting marked a point of demarcation in American social policy. Ball defended the program that he had inherited from the New Deal and expanded in the eras of Harry Truman, Dwight Eisenhower, Lyndon Johnson, and Richard Nixon. Califano, Champion, and Ross believed that the program could no longer be given a free ride, that it should be subject to cuts in the same way as other social programs. Simply maintaining the program, with its benefit levels that went up with inflation, strained the government's fiscal capabilities, not to mention the burden that the program put on future generations. As Carter said at the end of his meeting with Ball and his allies, Social Security was not sacrosanct.[120] Aspects of its design could be changed. Of course, Ball had immersed himself in political negotiations in order to change the basic design of the program not once but several times. He was, however, engaged in the politics of expansion or, as was the case in 1977, of program preservation; the Carter administration officials wanted to start a new politics of subtraction. In this division of opinion lay an important rift between liberals and neoliberals in the Democratic Party, between the party of Franklin Roosevelt at one end and the party of Bill Clinton at the other.

Much of the conflict lay buried below the surface and was expressed in personal rivalries that did not reach the surface of public notice. Califano backed away from advocating changes in the early retirement provisions, and Carter retreated from the other proposed changes and even kept his distance from the ongoing battle over disability reform. Carter fired Califano in the summer of 1979, and Califano's successor asked Ball to succeed Ross. It appeared, then, that Ball had won the battle. In fact, however, the Social Security issue failed to recede or to resolve itself in a satisfactory manner. If Carter had won a second term, his administration would almost certainly have revisited the cuts he proposed in the first term. Reagan, who did win the election, made many of the same proposals as did Carter's men.

Conclusion

The reason that the Social Security problem persisted was that the program was subject to the vagaries of the economy. Although the benefits were guaranteed, the means of funding them were not. By the end of 1979, it became clear that something needed to be done to shore up Social Security's finances, and in this instance, unlike in 1977, the timing was not right for propitious political action, with the elections looming and with Carter locked in a primary battle with Senator Edward Kennedy. Robert Ball found it his painful duty to let Eizenstat know that, with the increasingly pessimistic economic projections, the "financing for social security is inadequate in the near term. . . . The amounts needed are so large that there is no way to deal with the problem by a series of minor adjustments." What Ball recommended was letting the payroll taxes for Social Security and Medicare rise, as prescribed in the 1977 legislation, but to use half of the money intended for Medicare to fund Social Security, and making up the difference with general revenues. Or, if Congress objected to general revenues, then using all of the money for Social Security and finding a new way to finance Medicare.[121]

It was not reassuring news for the Carter administration, and it only got worse. The administration hoped to sneak through with the stop-gap device of having the Old-Age and Survivors trust fund borrow from the Disability and Hospital Insurance trust funds, but Ball did not think that would be enough. In July 1980 he advocated setting the Social Security tax rate at 6.13 percent for employers and employees and following a complicated plan that had been devised by the advisory council for Medicare funding. Under this plan one half of the costs of Medicare would come from a dedicated portion of the individual income tax and the other half from money raised through the corporate income tax. At the same time, Ball recognized that there were problems with this plan, not the least of which was that the AFL-CIO opposed it.[122]

In the meantime, Carter administration officials learned that the system would experience cash flow problems in 1984 and possibly earlier. Since recent economic projections had all proved too optimistic, the situation could be even worse than the estimates indicated. Indeed, the 1977 projections had turned out to be quite wrong, quite quickly. For the financing in the 1977 amendments to have worked out right, wages would have had to go up faster than prices by about 2.5 percent per year. As two economists noted, "That proved to be disastrously optimistic. Whereas the prediction had been that 1981 real wages should be 12.9 percent above their level in 1976; they actually were 6.9 percent lower." As an indication of the economy's poor performance, the unemployment rate reached 7.1 percent, and the inflation rate was 13.5 percent in 1980. A *Washington Post* editorial that appeared in the summer of 1980 caught the mood of the times. It noted that until that spring, and contrary to previous experience, prices had risen more rapidly than wages, a true recipe for disaster. Because "wages determine how much gets paid into the fund and because benefits are indexed to the Consumer Price

Index, prices determine the amount going out." And no one quite knew when the process would end. The *Post* predicted more economic turbulence ahead, advising that "people might be wise to arm themselves psychologically for more surprises."[123]

In the face of this near hysteria, Ball took it as his responsibility to remain calm, a traditional pose for authority figures in times of financial panic. In response to a conservative critic, for example, he countered that "it is quite likely that the cash benefit program could be financed for a 6 percent contribution rate on employees with a matching amount by employers into the next century and with something less than an 8 percent contribution on each from then on. I consider these figures quite conservative. The very short-term situation is quite manageable." As for the long run, one had to recognize there were many unknown contingencies. If older workers remained in the labor force, that would reduce long-run costs. If disability rates went down, that, too, would ease the problem, as would a new baby boom or an influx of immigrants. In other words, the future was not certain, and opponents should not use the mere possibility of a problem in the long run to exaggerate the difficulties in the short run.[124] In a similar vein, Ball reassured a congressman who had sent him an anxious letter from a constituent. "It is just not true that the social security program is in the kind of deep trouble that the enclosure you sent me implies," Ball noted, adding that "the modest recommendations of the Advisory Council are quite sufficient to handle the problem."[125]

Ball spread his message of reassurance during the difficult primary season of 1980 in which he worked with Peter Edelman of Senator Kennedy's campaign on issues related to Social Security and health insurance and tried to keep his ties with the Carter administration as well. Ball even went to the August Democratic Convention held in New York and appeared before the platform committee on Kennedy's behalf, arguing that the cost-of-living features in the program should be retained. Social Security, said Ball, was "a popular program and we must be vigorous in our defense of it;" conservatives inside and outside the party should not be allowed to tamper with the program's cost-of-living guarantee. Without it, some 60 percent of the elderly could find themselves living on incomes that put them below the poverty line.[126]

Robert Ball with President Jimmy Carter on Air Force One during the final days of Carter's futile reelection campaign in 1980. Carter was trying to save the election with a last-minute push on the Social Security issue. Photograph courtesy of Robert Ball.

In this way, Ball rode out the Carter years, just as he had ridden out the Ford years. When Carter defeated Kennedy for the nomination—something that was obvious by the time of the California primary—Ball returned to the fold and campaigned on Carter's behalf. During the last week of the campaign, Ball accompanied Carter in Air Force One on a trip through Florida, hoping to whip up support among senior citizens. He also tried to dig up damaging evidence from Reagan's past, looking for a recording of a speech in which Reagan had opposed the passage of Medicare and finally finding it and playing it for newsmen at the very end of the campaign. Nothing that Ball did changed the predetermined outcome. Carter joined his four predecessors in not serving two full terms.[127]

Despite financial pressures and growing criticism of Social Security as a financially unwieldy and burdensome program, Ball's 1972 legislation held together during the Ford and Carter years. Even Wilbur Cohen, a staunch Ball ally, had his doubts about whether the 1972 switch to the automatic increases in benefits was a good thing. Cohen thought there should have been a few more years of ad hoc adjustments, with the automatic provisions put into the law in 1977 or 1978. Cohen called the 1972 legislation "the most ill-fated legislation of the first 37 years of the program."[128]

Ball disagreed. Without the large benefit increase and the automatic provisions introduced in 1972, "social security would still be a relatively unimportant program which could be readily bypassed by other approaches such as income-tested assistance. Without the 72 and 77 amendments, social security wouldn't have much to sell. And there is no way, in my opinion, that we could get automatic provisions and a 20 percent benefit increase into the law today with the attitudes that people now have toward government programs. . . . It may be that given the combination of inflation and unemployment facing the program recently, the 20 percent benefit increase plus the automatic provisions can be said to have given rise to the bankruptcy discussion. On the other hand, without these provisions, the system would have greatly deteriorated during this period." For Ball, then, the 1972 amendments had rescued the program, just as the 1950 amendments had, and the 1977 amendments and the victory in the argument with Califano had saved the 1972 amendments.[129]

As Social Security became a more partisan issue in the 1970s, Ball became a more partisan figure. He began the decade as the competent administrator who had put the gargantuan Medicare program in place. He ended the decade as the chief adviser to the Democrats on the Social Security issue who believed that the expansionist spirit of the 1972 amendments should be retained. In 1974, he had hoped to create a final large structure that would complete the American welfare state. Disappointed in the goal of creating national health insurance, he was pressed into service not to start new programs but to maintain old ones. Some of these programs, such as disability insurance, were modified, yet the Old-Age and Survivors Insurance program, with benefits indexed to the rate of inflation, remained.

An outsider during the Ford administration, Robert Ball became an inside player in the Carter administration and managed to keep the administration's policies more consistent with his recommendations than with those of the president's own secretary of Health, Education, and Welfare. During the Carter administration he completed the process of shedding his identity as a staff member (the one who had hidden from the cameras when Kennedy and Mills had introduced their health insurance bill) and becoming a principal player (the one who became a member of the advisory council appointed by the Carter administration and who testified before Congress as an independent authority). With the congressional wing, rather than the presidential wing, of the Democratic Party dominant for the next twelve years, Ball's stature as a principal player would only increase.

6

Savior

Robert Ball reached the apex of his career with the passage of Social Security amendments in 1983 that preserved the program through the end of the century. The amendments marked the climax of the Social Security discussion that had taken place in policymaking circles since 1974. Despite Ronald Reagan's popularity and the desire of many of his domestic advisers to attack what Budget Director David Stockman called the "inner fortress" of America's welfare state, the amendments left such features of Social Security as cost-of-living adjustments and dependents' benefits largely intact.[1] As a consequence, the Reagan revolution made only a small dent in the Social Security program. By 1983, Ronald Reagan, like Dwight Eisenhower before him, could celebrate the program as one that he, in combination with Democrats in Congress, had helped to maintain.

Ball's significant contributions to the process included getting the Democrats to resist efforts to cut Social Security in 1981 and serving as Speaker Tip O'Neill's surrogate in negotiations with the Reagan administration in 1982. As much as anyone, Ball could take credit for the 1983 amendments, another example of his influence over a crucial point of decision for the Social Security program, another liberal victory in a conservative age.[2]

The Reagan Proposals

Much as Ball fought with Joseph Califano and Hale Champion and preferred Edward Kennedy as a presidential candidate, he very much regretted Carter's defeat in 1980.[3] The election could not have turned out worse for Ball and others with an interest in saving the Social Security program from changes. First and foremost, the White House contained a person who took more interest in Social Security than did Carter and approached the subject with more of an ideological disposition to limit its growth. "The 1980 election not only defeated Jimmy Carter," one liberal analyst later wrote, "but for the first time since the beginning of Social Security it brought to the presidency a long and determined foe of social insurance." Reagan saw Social Security as a coercive program that taxed America's workers to finance a welfare program and offered them worse returns on their money than did the private market. In addition, the Republicans gained control of the Senate, leaving only the House as a friendly base of operations for Ball.[4]

During the Reagan years, therefore, changes in Social Security politics accelerated. The Social Security Administration, from which Ball had essentially run the Social Security program, lost influence to the White House. That reflected a continuing deterioration in the agency's administrative capability, increased congressional oversight of the agency, and the fact that it was the budget process, run through the White House, that predominated in the policymaking process.[5] Robert J. Myers, the former chief actuary brought back into the government to serve as one of Reagan's deputy commissioners of Social Security, caught the tone well when he said that he and his fellow bureaucrats "weren't all there as equals" in key policy discussions. "It was clear from he beginning," he wrote, "that the shots were being called by OMB and the Executive Office of the President."[6]

As Myers's comment implied, fundamental differences existed in the approaches of the Reagan and Carter administrations toward Social Security. Carter's people saw Social Security mostly as a problem in cost control. Reagan's advisers sought more fundamental reform of the program. "I couldn't help but think that [FDR] had to be spinning in his grave at what they were trying to do to Social Security," Myers thought to himself during one White House planning meeting.[7]

For Ball these differences were particularly stark. So far as Ball was concerned, the sins of the Reagan administration were similar to those of the Carter administration after 1977, only far worse. Instead of exempting the program from the furious effort to cut social spending, the administration instead proposed $2.5 billion in cuts for fiscal 1982. That would inevitably mean reductions in benefits for people already receiving them, something that had never been done. And there seemed to be little that Ball could do to influence the administration. No longer did he have access to the White House, through someone like Stuart Eizenstat, and no longer did he know many of the people in the Social Security Administration and at the newly created Department of Health and Human Services (HHS), the successor to the Department of Health, Education, and Welfare. It was no wonder, then, that the first months of the Reagan administration found Ball on the defensive. "This is a period of defense and we are doing what we can to contain any possible losses," he told Doug Brown in April.[8]

To show how much the policymaking scene had changed since the days that Ball ran SSA, he even found Bob Myers's presence in the new administration consoling. "It is perhaps a measure of the times to say that I am extremely glad to have Bob Myers in the Social Security Administration," he noted. If nothing else, Myers had more institutional knowledge of the program than did any of the other Reagan appointees, and Ball believed that "Bob essentially wants to make the system much as it is today and in this administration that makes him very liberal."[9]

In fact, however, the first cuts that the Reagan administration suggested in 1981 were nothing new for Social Security policy. One example concerned the so-called student benefits that went to young people between the ages of 18 and 22 who were attending school and who were the dependents or survivors of deceased, retired, or disabled workers. These benefits had been legislated in 1965, during the heyday of Social Security expansion, with the rationale that a person did not reach adulthood and end dependency on a guardian at age 18. For college students and others receiving postsecondary education, the need for support persisted until age 22. It therefore seemed reasonable to extend dependents' benefits up to age 22 for students. Even this minor benefit soon began to cost a significant amount of money—more than $2 billion in 1981. As policymakers in the Ford and Carter

White Houses cast around for ways to reduce Social Security expenditures, they quickly spotted the student benefits. In the 1977, 1978, and 1979 budget proposals, first Ford and then Carter proposed phasing them out. When Reagan came into office and sought ways of reducing Social Security benefits, the proposal to eliminate student benefits had already been vetted by the two previous administrations. It took little imagination for Reagan's people to insert it into the administration's Omnibus Budget Reconciliation Act of 1981, and this time it became law.[10]

Ball, who realized that the student benefits and other relatively innocuous cuts marked only the beginning of the administration's efforts to cut Social Security, prepared for a fight. He explained to Brown that he and Cohen were working hard "to gear up the SOS organizations to take good stands on Social Security with the Congress." SOS, or Save Our Security, began in 1979 during the disputes with the Carter administration over changes in disability insurance. Headed by Wilbur Cohen, it consisted of a very loose coalition of labor unions and other advocacy groups that wanted to defend the size and scope of the Social Security program. Ball took a less visible role in the organization than did Cohen, yet he agreed to chair its advisory committee and ended up influencing nearly all of it stands on substantive issues. Ball thought it necessary to resort to such a naked display of political force, rather than exercising his usual behind-the-scenes political agility, because he worried that the administration was prepared to announce much greater cuts (the trustees' report that would appear in the summer of 1981 showed that, without further action, the trust funds might be exhausted in 1982).[11]

In the fight that followed, Ball received only limited comfort from what should have been an important institutional ally: the House Committee on Ways and Means. Many of the Democrats on this committee, the traditional steward of the Social Security program, refused to attack the Reagan administration's Social Security proposals in the same partisan way as the rest of the Democrats in the House. Jake Pickle (D–Texas), who headed the Social Security subcommittee, took a far more vigorous role in Social Security politics than his predecessor James Burke, whom Ball had befriended. Pickle had worked with the Carter administration on the disability amendments of 1980, against the wishes of Ball, Cohen, and the SOS coalition. In 1981, Pickle wanted to prepare his own Social Security bill that, he hoped, would solve the financial crisis and earn the approval of Dan Rostenkowski (D–Illinois), the head of the full Ways and Means Committee. Ball did not disagree with Pickle's basic objective, which he described as putting the "system in the position where people will again consider it soundly financed and get it off the front pages," but he objected to some of his specific proposals.[12]

A visit with Pickle early in February 1981 showed some of the differences in approach between Pickle and Ball. Pickle encouraged Ball to remain flexible and not commit himself to any particular proposal and sought Ball's help in moderating the stance of SOS. He told Ball that he wanted to produce a bill that year that would reassure people that Social Security was soundly financed. Such reassurance, according to Pickle, could not come from adding income to the system. No matter how much more money the system received, it would still remain vulnerable to a period of rampant inflation and high unemployment. Instead, the benefit formula needed to be fixed in a way that prevented the system from spending beyond its means. Pickle also showed interest in raising the retirement age, thus lessening the system's future obligations.[13]

Ball disagreed with nearly all of that. He continued to think of ways to add money to the system in order to tide it over its period of vulnerability in the 1980s. In the 1990s, the low birth rate from the 1930s would result in a period when the growth of the aged population compared to the working-age population would stabilize. The problem was getting through the 1980s, the decade before that stability arrived. One promising approach to tide the system over was to shift money from Medicare to Social Security and to use general revenues to fund Medicare. But even Ball recognized that more might be needed, such as limiting the size of the cost-of-living adjustments and changing the student benefit so that it ran until age 21, rather than 22. As for the long-range problem, Ball wanted Congress to keep its options open and not succumb to the politically motivated attacks on Social Security's solvency.[14] He viewed the proposal to raise the retirement age, for example, as simply another way to cut benefits.[15]

Pickle asked Ball to remain in touch with the committee staff, and Ball reassured him that he would, even going so far as to promise that he would help produce what he described as "the best provisions of an approach that I didn't fully approve of." When Ball talked separately to the subcommittee staff members, he discovered that they, too, were focused on the benefit formula. As Ball explained their thinking, "regardless of how big a contribution rate you put in the cash program, if the economy behaves badly for long enough, then tying (benefits) to the CPI can create a problem." It was not just a matter of politics, in other words. In the minds of the staff members, economics dictated some policy outcomes. They favored a proposal attributed to Bob Myers for basing benefit increases on either wages or prices, whichever was lower. "They are not trying to save money by this device," Ball noted, "they just want a provision that will prevent the system from having to pay out more than it takes in during what we hope are unusual periods of prices exceeding wages."

Not unsympathetic to this line of reasoning, Ball thought he might work out an arrangement with the subcommittee that included a modification of the benefit formula, the introduction of general revenues into Medicare, and more money for the cash program in return for Pickle agreeing to drop his call for a rise in the retirement age and for specific benefit cuts. At the same time, he recognized that Pickle saw his subcommittee as an independent force, separate from the administration and the Senate, that might broker a deal on Social Security.[16]

After securing the approval of his subcommittee, Pickle introduced his bill on April 9, 1981. By failing to satisfy either the administration or Robert Ball and the SOS forces, the bill set into motion a series of events that led to the 1983 amendments. The bill contained suggestions for both short-term and long-term changes. For the short term, the bill included such items as a delay in the cost-of-living adjustments and provisions for interfund borrowing between the separate trust funds that had been established for the old-age and survivors, disability, and hospital insurance programs. For the longer term, the bill featured a rise in the retirement age from 65 to 68. The bill also contained a provision that substantially increased the financial penalty for taking early retirement (which would remain available at age 62).[17]

From his vantage point in the Office of Management and Budget, David Stockman decided that the Pickle bill did not provide enough savings for the administration to meet its economic targets. The very next day he set out to produce a reform package that would yield greater savings. Stockman saw Social Security, the largest component of America's welfare state, as posing an extreme test for the Reagan revolution. If the administration could not tame the Social Security program, then it would not be able to deal with uncontrollable social spending.

As a way of thinking about the situation, Stockman developed a critique that fit a more general view of social policy within the administration. A major part of its appeal was that Ronald Reagan himself found it congenial. The line of argument held that Franklin Roosevelt had created a safety net of social programs that met people's needs but, at the same time, satisfied their equally important desires for autonomy and independence. Politicians had, however, corrupted Roosevelt's relatively simple programs and, in so doing, made some people dependent on government programs and worse off than they would have been in the absence of such programs. The Great Society, in particular, marked a period of debilitating expansion of government welfare programs that sapped people's initiatives. Hence, it fell to Reagan to restore integrity to social policy. The political subtext of this critique was that people who voted for Franklin Roosevelt, as had Ronald Reagan four times, but who felt that the government had lost its way during the permissive era of the 1960s would recognize Reagan as a kindred spirit and vote for him.[18]

In taking this line on Social Security, Stockman noted that Social Security had started during the New Deal "as a minimum, state-insured retirement pension. That idea was noble. But over the decades, the system had evolved into a capricious hybrid of out-and-out welfare benefits and earned pension annuities, which were hopelessly tangled together and disguised under the fig leaf of social insurance." Stockman objected to what Social Security traditionalists called the adequacy, as opposed to equity, provisions of the program. It made no sense to him that the program treated people who had made similar contributions to the program in disparate ways, as happened when one worker had a wife and the other remained single. He thought that the disability provisions in the program dangerously mixed benefits for people who were truly incapacitated with benefits for people who were merely unemployed or who did not wish to work. He saw a benefit formula that indexed initial benefits to changes in wage levels and that raised benefits as prices rose as providing people with windfalls that they had not in any sense earned. All of the shifts toward adequacy cost the system money, but the costs had been masked by the initially small number of people receiving benefits and the large number of people paying into the system. By 1980, Stockman believed, "Social Security had become a giant Ponzi scheme." Now, as the bills started to come due, politicians needed to exercise the necessary discipline to prune back the system and restore it to its original objectives.[19]

What was so striking about the Stockman critique was how much of it could be read as an indictment of Ball's hold over the program. Ball had not been present at the creation and had not been in a position of influence when Congress added dependents' benefits to the program in 1939. Although that had happened on FDR's watch and with FDR's active approval, both Stockman and Reagan chose to ignore that disparity between their idealized picture of FDR as the pre-Reagan and the reality of FDR's political performance. Many of the subsequent tilts toward adequacy, such as disability insurance and particularly benefits indexed to the rate of inflation, could be attributed to Robert Ball. This view of history implied that, as Ball gained sway over the program, it had departed further and further from its original goals and become more and more of a Ponzi scheme. Hence, Stockman attacked not just Social Security but the way Ball had run it.

As Stockman sat down with other administration advisers in April 1981 to come up with further cuts for Social Security, Robert Ball remained very much on the outside, with waning influence in the White House and even in the congressional committee that mattered most. The period coincided with a change in Ball's working conditions prompted at least in part by the advent of the Reagan revolution. Because he realized that the action in social policy no longer centered on national health insurance and because he did not wish to cause the Institute of Medicine the embarrassment of being associated with a liberal figure in a conservative age, Ball decided to set up shop elsewhere. He found offices for himself and his assistant Betty Dillon on Massachusetts Avenue, near the Capitol, conveniently close to the place where he did most of his business. Tom Joe, Ball's policy partner from the Nixon and Carter years, shared the quarters with him.

Like Ball, Joe was a consultant with policy connections and an interest in influencing social welfare legislation, and he had managed to create a loose bond between his Center for the Study of Social Policy and the University of Chicago. Ball was able to move in with Joe in part because he had some money from Elizabeth Wickenden, an old Ball ally who ran something called the Study Group on Social Security, to help defray the cost.[20]

Stockman met with the administration's Social Security advisers on April 10 and began the meeting by saying that raising the retirement age had become a fetish among conservatives and a substitute for more serious action.[21] He also objected to proposals, such as often put forward by Robert Ball, to expand Social Security coverage as a means of increasing the number of people paying into the system and, at least in the short run, increasing the available revenues. "Our job," he said, "is to shrink the Social Security monster. Not indenture millions more workers to a system that's already unsound." In the end, departmental and SSA technicians received instructions to come up with options that would produce the $75 to $100 billion necessary over the next five years to keep the program solvent. In particular, Stockman wanted to attack what he called the "redistributionist elements of Social Security" that he believed people had not earned and received simply as a form of political largesse.

On May 1, the group reconvened to review its progress. Stockman felt thwarted by the Social Security bureaucracy that, he said, "came up with monkish texts that were so dense and unreadable" that few of the people in attendance understood them. It was a traditional way for the bureaucracy to exert influence over the policy process, but Stockman, who had learned just enough Social Security policy-speak to follow the discussion, pressed SSA to come up with additional cuts. Through such measures as changing the benefit formula and tightening up the disability program, the bureaucrats responded to Stockman's invitation. Still, the group realized that certain items, such as changes in the program's early retirement provisions, required the president's personal approval.

A climactic meeting with the president took place on May 11. This May 1981 meeting with Reagan resembled the May 1977 meeting with Carter that Ball had attended. In both cases, the president reviewed a Social Security program in serious financial difficulty at a similar point in the budget review process. In both cases, someone outside the Social Security Administration dominated the meeting. Only in this case, David Stockman, the key figure, had no allegiance to either the agency or the program. Where Carter hoped to shore up the program, if necessary by increasing the amount of money that supported it, Reagan and his advisers entertained the possibility of real benefit cuts.

In trying to get Reagan to support cuts in the program's early retirement provisions, Stockman appealed to the president's sense of history. The early retirement features dated not from the 1935 Social Security Act and the legacy of FDR but rather from changes that had been made for women in 1956 and for men in 1961, the first to reflect the fact that women left the labor force earlier than did men and the second to provide some relief against unemployment caused by automation. In theory, the provisions cost nothing, because those who elected to retire before age 65 had their benefits actuarially reduced to reflect their early departure from the labor force. If one viewed Social Security's current costs, however, then early retirement, a seemingly discretionary part of the program, involved the payment of real benefits to real people and hence cost a great deal. Early retirement benefits, therefore, seemed costly and not entirely necessary and thus made logical targets for the budget cutters. President Reagan seemed to agree. "I've been warning since 1964 that Social Security was heading toward bankruptcy," Reagan said. "This is one of the reasons why." The meeting resulted in an agreement between HHS Secretary Richard Schweiker, a former Republican senator from Pennsylvania, and Stockman that early retirement be accompanied by a substantial penalty that would greatly reduce the benefits paid. After being assured by domestic adviser Martin Anderson that he would be the first president to fix Social Security, the president accepted the package of Social Security cuts on the spot.[22]

Just as Stuart Eizenstat and others in the Carter White House remained wary of changes in Social Security, so the political advisers to Ronald Reagan reacted with caution to the new package of proposed changes. Many of these changes took the usual arcane form of Social Security discourse, such as the proposal to "increase the dollar bend-points in the primary insurance amount (PIA) benefit formula for each year during the period

1982–1987 by 50 percent of the increase in the average annual wage, instead of by 100 percent." Some, however, were more transparent, as in a change in the definition of disability that would make it harder to get disability benefits or in a provision that would make beneficiaries wait from June to September to receive the cost-of-living adjustments in their benefits. To be sure, a few of the recommendations came from Pickle's bill, but most stood out as the work of the Reagan administration. In particular, the recommendation that early retirement benefits be reduced from 80 to 55 percent of a primary benefit amount was easy to understand. When Reagan's Legislative Strategy Group met to consider the Social Security package, chief of staff James Baker made it clear that Secretary Schweiker, rather than President Reagan, would announce the changes.[23]

On May 12 Secretary Richard Schweiker gave a press conference and unveiled the Reagan Social Security proposals to the public. An immediate storm of protest erupted. Speaker of the House Thomas P. O'Neill (D–Massachusetts), who had taken his lumps from a popular president made all the more popular by an assassination attempt that occurred at the end of March, read about the cuts on the way to work and instructed his staff to call Representative Rostenkowski and find out about them. Told that "Danny doesn't want to play politics with it," O'Neill decided to press the issue on his own. At his May 13 press conference, O'Neill pointed out that the proposals, if passed, would affect people who had already made plans to retire and would now receive much less than they had been promised. "I consider it a breach of faith to renege on that promise," said O'Neill, who called the Reagan proposals "rotten" and "despicable." O'Neill vowed to fight the measure. "Reagan has finally made a wretched mistake," recorded Majority Leader Jim Wright (D–Texas) in his diary. Even David Stockman realized that, in the administration's haste, it had erred. "The lack of warning was devastating," he later wrote.[24]

Fighting the Cuts in Congress

After May 13 the politics of Social Security shifted considerably in Ball's favor. On May 20 the Republican-controlled Senate

Robert Ball was House Speaker Tip O'Neill's representative in the negotiations with the White House on the Greenspan Commission—one of many times Ball worked closely with O'Neill on Social Security matters. Photograph courtesy of Robert Ball.

passed a resolution offered by Senator Robert Dole (R–Kansas) to the effect that any solution to the Social Security problem not "precipitously and unfairly penalize early retirees." The vote of 96 to 0 sent a message with little ambiguity. In retrospect, Stockman saw it as the beginning of the end for the administration's Social Security proposals, as indeed it was. "The centerpiece of the American welfare state," wrote Stockman in flamboyant prose, "had now been overwhelmingly ratified and affirmed in the white heat of political confrontation."[25]

Ball began to work with the leadership of the House of Representatives and with Senators Daniel Moynihan (D–New York) and Russell Long (D–Louisiana) to shape the newly invigorated Democrats' response to the Reagan proposals. In the Democratically controlled House, Ball's desire to leave the program intact meshed nicely with Speaker O'Neill's desires to use Social

Security as a political club against the Republicans. In the Senate, Ball realized that the Democrats had less leverage, but he still advised Moynihan to highlight the fact that the "Administration has been exaggerating the financing problem in OASDI."[26]

Ball's substantive message changed little. He portrayed the administration as "trying to scare the American people into supporting [cuts] by presenting a picture of impending doom both for the short run and the long run." The truth according to Ball was that the cash benefit program of Social Security faced a four-year window between "1986 and 1989 where there could be financing difficulty. Hence we need back up general revenue borrowing." The administration, according to Ball, should not be allowed to make permanent cuts because of the possibility of funding difficulties for those years. As for the longer run, in the next century, "There will be more older people. But what is important is the ratio of old people to working people. But the size of the labor force that far off depends on impossible to predict factors such as the fertility rate, immigration rates, the extent to which older people continue to work as against taking benefits, labor force participation rates by women. So it is plausible that the 1990 [tax] rate will be adequate but equally plausible that more money will be needed in 2020."[27]

Ball objected particularly to Stockman's distinction between "earned benefits" or "basic benefits" in Social Security and "welfare benefits," saying, "They seem to feel that supporters of Social Security can be divided and that somehow retirement benefits for the worker have a superior standing to spouses' benefits, disability benefits, survivors' benefits etc. This is nonsense. We have to make sure it doesn't work as a tactic."[28]

At some point after the announcement of the administration's May proposals, the Democrats decided to make an issue of the administration's desire to cut the minimum benefit from the program. They also chose to highlight the unfairness of the administration's May 1981 proposals without, at the same time, endorsing an alternative of their own. Most of the ensuing political action centered on the House, where, as Newt Gingrich (R–Georgia) put it, "O'Neill took Social Security and just drove it home ruthlessly and in some respects dishonestly."[29]

In fact, the minimum benefit appeared to be an unlikely item over which to stage a major fight. For one thing, the pedigree of this benefit differed from that of the other things on Reagan's hit list. It stemmed from Roosevelt's 1935 Social Security Act, not Lyndon Johnson's Great Society. For another thing, the views of conservatives such as David Stockman and liberals such as Robert Ball converged on this matter.

The measure owed its origins to the realization among Roosevelt's planners that some older and poorer people would not be able to contribute a great deal toward their pensions. Instead of paying meaninglessly low amounts, they decided to set the minimum level at $10 a month. It remained at that amount until 1950, when it was raised to $20. By the time Richard Nixon became president, the minimum benefit had reached $64 per month. Neither Arthur Altmeyer nor Robert Ball had been entirely comfortable with the minimum benefit because its existence tended to sever the link between contributions and benefits and presented a tempting target for politicians to raise without adequate consideration of the facts. One of the reasons that Ball had supported the creation of Supplemental Security Income was that it removed some of the political pressure to raise the minimum benefit. As part of the 1972 amendments, he had helped to engineer a new form of benefit called the "special minimum" that went to people who had paid into the system for at least ten years. The rationale was that, by the 1970s, the regular minimum mainly reached people who had already worked for a job not covered by Social Security, such as government employment, and who in fact received two public retirement pensions. Because the regular minimum benefit went to people who often did not need it, because it was subject to political manipulation, and because it undermined the structure of contributory social insurance, Ball believed that, with the special minimum in place, it could be abolished. Nonetheless, he objected to the Stockman-Reagan proposal to abolish the minimum benefit for what might be described as tempered political reasons. "Actually, I thought this was ok for the future," he later confessed, "but they did it in such a way that it actually cut benefits for people currently being paid."[30]

The House leadership knew that the distinction between the special and regular minimum was too subtle and involved too much inside knowledge about the program to be meaningful to most Americans. On the surface the administration's desire to cut the minimum benefit appeared to symbolize David Stockman's indifference toward the fate of the nation's worthy poor.

The proposal to cut the minimum benefit could be made to serve as an illustration of how the Reagan administration wished, in the words of the old cliché, to balance the budget on the backs of the poor. The fact that someone as reputable as Robert Ball agreed with the tactic, if not the reasoning, gave added support to the Democrats' cause.

To fight the minimum benefit, Ball practiced a new sort of politics that had come into existence during the Carter years. The minimum benefit proposal formed part of a much larger proposal, known as the Omnibus Budget Reconciliation Act, that contained, in a single package, all of the measures that the federal government would take to meet its domestic spending target. Ball had tried and failed to get the Ways and Means Committee to exclude the minimum benefit cuts from the comprehensive bill. At some point in the spring, he turned his attention to the next level up on the legislative chain: the leadership of the House of Representatives. The idea was to work through the Rules Committee to allow the House to vote on the Reconciliation Act in such a way that would permit the House to record its disapproval of the cut in minimum benefits and possibly to eliminate the cut altogether. Such a procedure would certainly be opposed by the Reagan administration, since one of the points of the bill was to bundle popular and unpopular budget cuts and provide political cover for taking tough stands on programs such as Social Security. Such a procedure, therefore, would also require the assent of the House leadership, since it involved starting what surely would become a contentious political debate.

Ball's point of entry to the leadership on this matter was Representative Richard Bolling (D–Missouri), who headed the Rules Committee. Bolling told Ball that he went through Ari Weiss to get to Tip O'Neill. Ivy-League educated, Weiss, who had come to O'Neill's office as an intern and worked his way up to become the Speaker's chief policy analyst, understood the substance of policy, but he also had a good feel for politics. "Ari is the nearest thing I've ever seen to a legislative genius," said Bolling. In the spring of 1981, Ball described Weiss as "very knowledgeable and smart and very young." Jack Lew, another capable member of the Speaker's staff who later served as director of OMB for President Clinton, functioned as Weiss's chief assistant.[31]

An expert in cultivating staff members, Ball began to work with Weiss and Lew on a suitable way to handle the issue of minimum benefits. Weiss seemed enthusiastic about the idea of getting the House to vote on the minimum benefit proposal and advised Ball to talk with Richard Gephardt (D–Missouri) and James Shannon (D–Massachusetts) about the strategy. It was a sensitive matter, in part because O'Neill had persuaded Pickle to assume the chairmanship of the Social Security subcommittee and was therefore "reluctant to dictate to him concerning the social security solutions he might come up with."[32]

Ball knew O'Neill but only in an impersonal Washington way. Indeed, what personal friendships he had among his working associates he restricted pretty much to people from Social Security, such as Alvin David. "I have never been an intimate friend of any members of Congress," Ball said, and "I was not one of those who was in the habit of having a few pops with Tip." Nonetheless he developed a close working relationship with O'Neill and his staff and came to admire the Speaker as a "completely sincere advocate of and defender of Social Security," a "personally attractive Boston-Irish politician."[33]

The political strategy for Social Security in 1981 did not come together until the legislative process was far along. After the Senate debated eliminating the cut in the minimum benefit bill at the end of June and the Democrats lost to the Republicans on the issue, both the Senate and the House passed the Omnibus Budget Reconciliation Act (OBRA) by the end of June. On July 21, the House passed a nonbinding resolution to "ensure that Social Security benefits are not reduced for those currently receiving them." David Stockman, for his part, dismissed this vote as a mere "gesture, a symbolic sense-of-the-House resolution." He proved to be wrong. Richard Bolling held up the final Reconciliation bill, which had already cleared a conference committee, until he could forge an agreement that allowed the House also to vote on a separate bill that would restore the minimum benefit before the cut went into effect. By the end of July, the House had approved both the Reconciliation bill and the new Social Security bill that nullified the effects of cutting the minimum benefit. That allowed President Reagan to sign OBRA into law on August 13, 1981; the question of the minimum benefit now depended on what would happen to the new Social Security bill that the House had passed.[34]

At this point, Social Security politics returned to something like normal. In the fall, the Senate Finance Committee reviewed

the House-passed bill and offered its own proposal on the minimum benefit. The committee's idea was to restore the minimum
benefit for those currently receiving it but to eliminate it for future beneficiaries. In addition, the committee's bill contained a
few more cost-saving measures, such as lowering the cap that a
family could receive from the death of a wage earner to 150 percent of a basic benefit. More ambitious proposals, such as raising
the retirement age, an action that Senator Dole favored, fell victim to Senator Moynihan's argument that "there is no crisis in
Social Security." This line clearly reflected the coaching that
Moynihan had received from Ball, who sent him memoranda
that argued, as Ball put it, "the Administration has been exaggerating the financing problem in OASDI." "I believe the stand you
have been taking against cuts in Social Security is clearly the correct one," Ball told Moynihan.[35]

By this time, neither the president nor the Speaker wanted
to push the legislation much further. On September 17, O'Neill
called Pickle into his office and, along with Bolling, instructed
Pickle not to put together a comprehensive Social Security reform package and instead to let the issue play itself out in a way
that maintained the Democrats' political advantage. As if to con-
firm that advantage, the president, speaking before a national
television audience on September 24, signaled his willingness to
drop the minimum benefit issue and made a gesture to remove
Social Security from the immediate glare of partisan politics by
calling for a bipartisan commission to study the issue and come
up with bipartisan recommendations.[36]

That still left the matter of agreeing on some sort of Social Security legislation for 1981. Ball urged his supporters in the SOS coalition to "concentrate on a limited number of objectives," the first
of which was the restoration of the minimum benefit. The coalition should not "waste its time" fighting peripheral battles, such
as measures designed to create equality for women in Social Security benefits.[37] Ball advised House Democrats to oppose the cuts
that the Senate wanted to make, such as the maximum in family
benefits, and to insist on the House version of the minimum benefit provision. In language that showed his new ties to the House
leadership and his involvement in partisan politics, he argued
that "the Democrats should avoid joining in with one more cut in
benefits. This is another chance to keep the Democratic sense of

the system clearly apart from the Republicans' attempt to cut. The Senate provision is a Reagan proposal."[38]

At the same time that Ball advocated leaving the system alone, he also realized that some sort of provision needed to be made for Social Security financing. He admitted, "using the intermediate projections, OASDI would have difficulty making full benefit payments as early as 1983 under the present law." Ball thought that the Senate provision, which would postpone the problem until 1989 by allowing interfund borrowing among the various Social Security trust funds, provided the acceptable response, particularly if it could be tweaked a little to raise the contribution rate for OASDI beyond what the Senate wanted and lower it for hospital insurance.[39]

Ball understood that the minimum benefit issue, which could be portrayed as a matter of Republican fairness, made a much better issue for the Democrats than did Social Security financing, which could be portrayed as a matter of Democratic extravagance and mismanagement. To make the case that Social Security was well funded for the rest of the century at a time when the trust fund managers said that the program might not be able to meet its obligations in 1983 was harder than arguing that the Reagan proposals hurt the poor and penalized the elderly. Nonetheless, Ball tried. He told Senator Carl Levin (D–Michigan), for example, that for the past few years "too much of the social security contribution was going into the disability insurance fund and into the hospital fund as compared with old-age and survivors insurance." To say, as the Reagan administration did, that Social Security was on the verge of bankruptcy was like saying to a person "who had three bank accounts and was low in one bank account" that he was bankrupt. Ball believed that the administration's real motivation in highlighting the Social Security financing issue was to use "Social Security reductions as a way of balancing the general budget" and to "cut back on the total role of the Federal government by having a less adequate, less effective social security system."[40]

With emotional charges being made on both sides, it took a conference committee a long time to reconcile the Senate and House versions of what became the Social Security Amendments of 1981, even though many issues had been removed from the table by President Reagan and Speaker O'Neill. At the end of November,

Ball told a correspondent that the conferees were deadlocked.[41] In the end, the conferees agreed to restore minimum benefits for those already receiving them and to eliminate the minimum for new eligibles in 1982, as the Senate wanted, but to drop the provision for changes in the maximum family benefits, as the House wanted. On the sensitive financing issues, the compromise agreement permitted interfund borrowing among the old-age and survivors insurance, disability insurance, and hospital insurance trust funds but only until December 31, 1982. That provision meant that further legislation would almost certainly be required in a lame-duck session after the 1982 election or early in 1983.[42] The president, aware of Social Security's emotional charge, did not sign the bill until the very end of the year.

As the 1981 fight over the minimum benefit unfolded, Ball became something of a public celebrity. "The vast majority of the 36 million receiving Social Security checks have never heard of him but Robert M. Ball is probably more responsible than any other individual for persuading Congress to ignore Ronald Reagan and make only minor adjustments to the retirement system," wrote Warren Weaver in the *New York Times*. The laudatory piece quoted Ball as saying, "We feel that the Social Security bill is a victory, but it's a battle and not the war. The reason President Reagan wants a commission to study Social Security for a year or more is to get the issue out of the 1982 Congressional elections. He'll be back after that."[43]

To reinforce the message of how the Democrats saved Social Security from Reagan's clutches and how they needed to control Congress in order to fight further encroachments that were sure to come, Ball appeared on television with congressional Democrats, such as Senator Paul Sarbanes (D–Maryland) and Representative Dick Gephardt. In private, Ball sent the Democratic leaders encouraging messages about how effective their work on Social Security had been. In an echo of Warren Weaver's laudatory story in the *New York Times*, Ball wrote Bolling, "Although not many of them know it, millions of people getting social security benefits owe you a great deal this Christmas." He noted that it was Bolling who had started the fight to restore the minimum benefit through his "decisive leadership" as head of the Rules Committee. That fight was "largely won, and I hope next year we can build on the victory and restore the benefit for those coming on the rolls in the future," Ball added.[44]

The National Commission on Social Security Reform

Ball reserved his most effusive praise for Speaker O'Neill and for a very good reason. As a reward for Ball's efforts on behalf of the Democrats in the House, O'Neill named Robert Ball as one of fifteen members of the National Commission on Social Security Reform that Ronald Reagan had announced in September.

It was not something that O'Neill was in any way obligated to do, as the commission's composition made apparent. The president divided the responsibility for naming members equally among the White House, the Senate, and the House of Representatives. Under the arrangement, Speaker O'Neill and Majority Leader Senator Howard Baker (R–Tennessee) each got to appoint three members (with their minority counterparts in their respective houses each allowed to name two members), and the president selected five members, including two Democrats. Baker named Senators Robert Dole, William Armstrong (R–Colorado), and John Heinz (R–Pennsylvania) to the commission. In contrast to these powerful sitting senators who held key positions on the Senate Finance Committee and the Senate Committee on Aging, Ball held no elective or appointed office and described himself as little more than a consultant on Social Security and Welfare. Nor did he represent an important constituency as did fellow commission members Congressman Claude Pepper (D–Florida), considered an important spokesman for the nation's elderly, Lane Kirkland, the head of organized labor in the United States, or Robert Beck, a Prudential Insurance Company executive who chaired the single most important committee of private businessmen concerned with Social Security. Ball, in fact, had arguably the thinnest political credentials of all of the commission members. Furthermore, if he had not been named as a commission member, he would undoubtedly have shadowed its work and offered advice to the liberal members. It was, therefore, not necessary to make him a commission member in order to induce his participation.

Still, once it became clear that neither Rostenkowski nor Pickle was interested, O'Neill turned to Ball. No wonder, then, that O'Neill elicited such lavish praise from Ball, who told the Speaker that he greatly admired his handling of Social Security. "I very much appreciate your appointing me to the new National Commission on Social Security," Ball added. "I consider it a very important responsibility."[45]

Ball's appointment to the national commission marked a key step in his transformation from an invisible government functionary to a visible public figure. As he made this transformation, he became perceived as both more partisan and more liberal. Between 1973 and 1977, he went from being a competent administrator, officially nonpartisan, to serving as a sort of unofficial trustee for Social Security on President Carter's behalf, still more of a technician than a political figure. As an inside strategist for the House Democratic leadership in 1981, however, he functioned in an openly partisan way on behalf of the liberal wing of the Democratic Party (rather than, as before, someone who worked with the highly stable, issue-oriented membership of the Social Security committees in Congress). Along the way, he changed from someone who sat in on congressional sessions as a staff member to someone who served President Carter and later Speaker O'Neill in the more elevated position as adviser and then to someone who worked with congressmen as an equal, at least in one important public forum.

If Robert Ball lacked political stature, he brought other important attributes to his work on the national commission. In the first place, he could act as a surrogate for the Speaker without compromising O'Neill in any important way. Ball, unlike an ambitious Dan Rostenkowski who was eager for a place in the House leadership, could subordinate himself completely to the Speaker's desires. "Bob didn't make a move that we weren't aware of," said O'Neill's staffer Jack Lew. "He would leave the meeting and call me or if I needed to I would call the Speaker. And it was all very safe in the sense that we were never negotiating directly."[46] In the second place, Ball, almost alone among the commission members, could devote all of his time to it. In contrast to the three sitting congressmen and four sitting senators, Ball did not have to run for reelection or do the many things required of a member of Congress. Indeed, all three of the representatives and at least two of the four senators (Moynihan and Heinz) would have to run in 1982, right in the middle of the commission's work.

In the third place, Ball brought a lot to the table. He knew more about Social Security than any other commission member, an obvious advantage in the often highly technical discussions. He was the commission's expert in a group of generalists. Furthermore, he had more experience than anyone with Social Security advisory councils and knew how to function effectively around them. He had a particular gift for bringing contentious groups to consensus, as he had demonstrated with the Hobby lobby in 1953. According to O'Neill's biographer, therefore, Ball, who functioned as the Speaker's "personal guru" on Social Security, became O'Neill's "most important appointee" on the commission.[47] Another commentator, close to the situation, wrote of Ball's "total mastery of the history and provisions of the Social Security system; . . . reputation for absolute integrity; . . . nonconfrontational style and, not least, . . . ability to subordinate his role to that of others."[48]

These words were written in retrospect. At the time, no one knew how the commission's work would turn out and, in the months leading up to the commission's launch, many of its members made disparaging comments about it. Barber Conable, the ranking Republican on the Ways and Means Committee appointed to the commission by the Republican minority leader in the House, called the commission a "cop out," and even Ball, who had as much reason as anyone to take it seriously, had told the *New York Times* that the president was only using the commission as a means of getting through the 1982 congressional elections.[49]

Both sides had something to gain and something to lose from the commission. As Ronald Reagan put it, "Saving Social Security will require the best efforts of both parties and of both the executive and legislative branches of government."[50] For the Democrats, a good outcome would mean that the Republicans would accept the fact that Social Security was securely financed for the rest of the century and not turn the program's financial crisis against the Democrats. As Ball put it, the Democrats needed to keep the Republicans "from continuing to talk about the system being near bankruptcy and doing all the background business of preparing the country for cuts."[51] For the Republicans, a good outcome would mean that the Democrats would stop using Social Security as a political issue against them.

In both cases, a good outcome required that the other side give something up. If the Republicans agreed that the program was securely financed, that would, in all likelihood, foreclose cuts and make it harder to cut government spending and balance the budget. If the Democrats agreed to drop the Social Security "fairness" issue, they would have to let go of something that brought them considerable political advantage at a time when they had few political advantages. Hence, as Reagan noted, reaching an agreement on Social Security would take "bipartisan cooperation and political courage."[52]

Nor could the issue be looked at as having only two sides. If the commission reached an agreement, it could be viewed as a victory for Tip O'Neill and the congressional leadership but not for the House Ways and Means Committee that sought its own credit for "solving" Social Security. Senator Robert Dole had to make his own independent set of calculations based on his sense of where Social Security would be as an issue in 1988 when he might well run for president, and no doubt Senator Moynihan toyed, at some level of consciousness, with a presidential run as well. Robert Ball, for his part, worried not just about the political perceptions of the program but also about its ability to deliver on its promises and the possibility of adding new features, such as national health insurance, to it. All members of the commission had to decide whether it was in their interests to have the commission reach an agreement, whether it was better to fight out the Social Security issue in Congress, or whether the Social Security issue should remain just that—an unresolved issue.

Although Robert Ball made these sorts of calculations as knowingly as anyone, he took his job as a commissioner, to which he devoted nearly all of 1982, extremely seriously. He went about his tasks quite deliberately. First, he sought to establish a working relationship with commission chairman Alan Greenspan, the former head of President Ford's Council of Economic Advisers. Before the commission even held its first meeting, Ball asked for private time with Greenspan.

It was typical of Ball that, where others might have regarded a visit with Greenspan as a social occasion, he saw it as important business and prepared a lengthy note to himself on how he wished to handle the conversation. Ball wanted his spontaneity to be scripted. In the script for Greenspan, he would emphasize his desire to control some of the staff appointments and would encourage Greenspan not to take Stockman's line about "how social security ought to get back to its original purpose." He also wanted Greenspan to establish objective boundaries on Social Security's financing problems, rather than engaging in politically charged speculation. In other words, the commission should determine "What inflation rate, wage increase rates, unemployment rates are the most likely and what is a reasonable outside limit on the pessimistic ones and what does this do to the combined social security funds between now and 1990?" But even the objective boundaries, it seemed, involved subjective judgments, underscoring the difficulty of the commission's work.[53] The atmosphere was so politically charged that, before Ball met with Greenspan, he sought the approval of his commission colleagues Claude Pepper and Martha Keys (a former member of Congress from Kansas and one of the Speaker's appointees).[54]

The meeting with Greenspan and two of his associates took place over breakfast in the Watergate Hotel on January 30, 1981.[55] It was not a totally one-sided occasion. Greenspan, as the head of the commission, needed to meet with and take the measure of someone who clearly was destined to play an important part in the commission's work.

Ball arrived early and chatted with Robert Carlson, the official White House liaison to the commission, who had worked with Reagan in California and played a role in the welfare reforms that Governor Reagan had instituted there. Ball saw Carlson's presence as a distraction and an annoyance. He "talked more than he should have . . . and frequently elaborated the obvious." When Greenspan arrived, the group got down to business. Well prepared, Ball knew just what he wanted to say. With his sharp sense of strategy, he moved by indirection. He deliberately set out to establish a "background of uneasiness on the part of the five Democratic appointed members," so that it seemed reasonable that they be allowed to have some staff members of their own. Ball told Greenspan that many people in Ball's political camp remained skeptical about the commission, seeing it only as a way to put off the Social Security issue through the fall elections. The administration, in its public statements, continued to inflame the situation by noting, for example, that it would never accept raising taxes or dipping into general revenues. If Ball said that he wouldn't accept benefit cuts, then, he told Greenspan, the discussion would end before it could even begin. Still, Ball had to assume that there was a chance of "something happening." Greenspan, who put the chances of reaching an agreement at perhaps one in three, added that one in three was not zero.

Ball next worked on his initiative to get Greenspan to think about the financing problem in ways that implied that it could be solved without tearing down the entire Social Security structure. Betraying his pessimism about the economy, Greenspan said that the commission needed to look at what would happen to Social Security if the economy collapsed. Ball put the matter in less pessimistic terms: what would have to happen to the economy to cause problems with interfund borrowing. According to Ball, Greenspan appeared to accept his approach.

Working methodically through the points that he wished to raise, Ball turned to an instruction he had received from Martha Keys to make sure that women's issues were on the commission's agenda. Using his inside knowledge of Social Security politics, Ball told Greenspan that both the women on the commission, Keys and Mary Falvey Fuller (a California businesswoman appointed by Reagan), favored an earnings-sharing plan. This policy proposal allowed husbands and wives to share their contributions to Social Security and served as a means of ending some of the disparities in benefits received by men and women and between one-wage-earner and two-wage-earner families. The fact that Ball felt obligated to mention this issue, which was current in Social Security discussions throughout the 1970s, showed how the commission had to consider more than just the Social Security financing issue. It needed at least to take notice of the other reform currents that were swirling around the program.[56]

Ball also offered Greenspan his share of practical advice. He suggested, for example, that not all of the meetings take place near the White House but instead be held on Capitol Hill. That would facilitate participation by the members of Congress. As someone who had served as Congress's servant for many years, Ball also advised against Saturday meetings because he realized that the congressmen went home every weekend, particularly in an election year. If the commission were to succeed, it would need to engage in sensitive negotiations, and these were best carried out by the congressmen themselves, rather than by their staff surrogates. If Greenspan wanted the congressmen, rather than their staff members, to attend, he would need to facilitate their participation by holding the meetings at convenient times, dates, and locations. Since both Ball and Greenspan hoped to create an atmosphere suitable to serious negotiation, that meant fostering private discussions among the people who counted and downplaying public hearings.

Only after touching on all of these topics and many more besides did Ball and Greenspan return to the matter of staffing. Because the Democratic members of the commission needed reassurance and because the facts could be presented in so many different ways, the five liberal Democrats "would feel better if at least two or three of the senior staff people were individuals whose point of view about social security was close to our own." Ball argued that often "it is not just a question of facts but of values in staff work," and Greenspan readily agreed. Having laid an elaborate background, Ball suggested that Merton Bernstein, a law professor at Washington University and a close Ball ally on causes such as Save Our Security, be made a consultant to the commission and that the Democrats be allowed to pick one or two more staff members.

Within a few weeks, the Democrats firmed up plans to hire Bernstein, Betty Duskin, and Eric Kingson. Bernstein, who had responsibilities back in St. Louis, served part-time, flying back and forth for the commission meetings. Betty Duskin, associated with organized labor (and hence with ties to Lane Kirkland) and the National Council on Senior Citizens, worked full-time, as did Kingson, a young professor of social work at a nearby university appointed because of his connections to Claude Pepper's staff. Ball described Kingson as a "generally knowledgeable person" who would "stand up for what he believes regardless of who is staff director and his own views are liberal Democratic." These three staff members joined a group of SSA employees detailed to the commission and others, such as Carolyn Weaver of Robert Dole's staff, who had ties to one of the commissioners—all crammed into a townhouse on Jackson Place, around the corner from Blair House and across from the White House.[57]

The townhouse, which had access to the New Executive Office Building, looked elegant from the outside and had "high ceilings, cornices, marble fireplaces and crystal chandeliers" on the inside. Still, there was something decidedly makeshift about the commission headquarters. It resembled nothing so much as a stage set. Presidential commissions quartered in the row of townhouses on the west side of Lafayette Park came and went, each bringing its own furniture, each setting up temporary offices for busy commissioners who flew in for an afternoon, and then each folding like a play ending its run. Most produced a report, sometimes received with great ceremony, but then nearly always filed away in the National Archives and forgotten.[58]

The commission reunited Ball and his old nemesis Robert Myers, who headed the staff from a second-floor office. The former chief actuary quit his job as deputy commissioner of Social Security for programs in the middle of December in the hope of being named to the commission. Because he had alienated David Stockman during his service in the Reagan administration, he did not expect an appointment from President Reagan, but he held out hope that he would be named by Senator Baker as a Senate Republican appointee. The Senate might wish to repay him for his faithful staff work over the years. As it turned out, Baker appointed three senators, and as Myers ruefully noted, "I wasn't a Senator." Failing to win first prize, he set out to gain the position of staff director, and this time, with the backing of Senator Dole and others, he succeeded.[59] Once again, in a competition that Ball refused to acknowledge, he had bested Myers, securing appointment to the commission at the behest of his political principals while Myers settled for a subordinate position as head of the staff. Once again, Robert Myers would work for Robert Ball during a Republican administration.

Ball realized he would need to establish a working relationship with Myers, just as he had with Greenspan. "Bob and I had our differences about . . . what were the right recommendations," Ball remembered some eighteen years after the fact. He went to see Myers, who had attended the earlier breakfast meeting with Greenspan but remained relatively quiet, in the middle of February, before the commission's first formal meeting. The conversation between Ball and Myers exposed differences in their attitudes toward the program's future. Ball perceived that the strategy of Myers and Greenspan was to pick a series of pessimistic economic assumptions and then to cut the benefits to meet those assumptions in order to make it through the critical short-term time period without difficulty and, if things turned out better than expected, to build up the size of the trust funds. As the conversation proceeded, Ball realized that he and Myers would have to negotiate "a picture of what the present financing situation" looked like so as to avoid "precipitating a donnybrook at the very first meeting." It might be that Ball would have to make one presentation and Myers another.[60]

The appointment of Myers to the staff and Ball to the commission created a situation in which Myers directed the commission's work but Ball served as a de facto staff director to the commission's five liberal Democrats. Without being asked, Ball simply assumed that he would oversee the work of what he called the liberal or Democratic caucus, consisting of Moynihan, Pepper, Kirkland, and Keys, and direct the caucus's three-person staff. He took it upon himself to get the group to meet, to prepare an agenda for the group to consider, to moderate the group's discussions, to formulate a strategy to follow at commission meetings, and, most importantly of all, to bargain on the group's behalf with other commission members. If a minority report needed to be written, it was understood that Ball, working with the staff specially recruited to serve the liberal Democrats, would draft it.

Ball stepped into the commanding role with his usual sense of deference. If a caucus of the liberal Democrats were to be held in Claude Pepper's office, for example, Ball would ask Pepper to chair, and only after Pepper demurred would he step in and moderate the discussion. Although Ball maintained decorum, his role as leader and facilitator of the group "was never questioned by the principals." In this sense he served as a full-fledged commission member but also undertook staff duties, just as he had done for nearly every Social Security advisory council since 1948.[61]

The general contentiousness of the issues created an initially tense working atmosphere for the commission. The first meeting concerned largely procedural matters, and the second featured long background lectures by Robert Myers on how benefits were computed and by Social Security actuaries on the assumptions used to make cost estimates. By the middle of April, Ball, who had a keen sense of not wanting to waste the time of the congressmen in the room, felt that the members were "getting restless at what seems to be the slow pace of the study and the content of the Commission meetings." He told Nancy Altman, a former aide to Senator John Danforth (R–Missouri) who served as Greenspan's chief assistant, that no more than half of the time of the meetings should be devoted to the "education" of the commission members, and the remainder should be spent discussing the "most fundamental issues."[62]

As a way of stimulating discussion, Ball sent each of the commissioners a report he had prepared that mentioned a possible change in the way that cost-of-living adjustments (COLAs) worked. Instead of tying benefit increases to prices, Ball suggested the possibility of linking benefit increases to the average of wages and prices. He raised this matter as a deliberate means "to get us away from the kind of lengthy period of orientation and academic discussion that the staff seems to have in mind." Instead, he wanted to probe the question "of whether there is any possibility of agreement on a core set of recommendations."[63]

The appearance of the 1982 Trustees Report on April 1, 1982, and the lack of progress on a budget agreement in Congress further soured the commission's mood. The regular May meeting of the commission produced a situation in which, according to Myers, "the members were calling each other names and once nearly sank into an uncontrollable shouting match." What precipitated this shouting match was a demand from the Senate Budget Committee that Social Security's annual spending be cut by $40 billion. If that were the case, the liberal Democratic members of the commission felt that the work of the commission had been compromised. Moynihan used the occasion to launch a tirade against the Reagan administration, to which Senator Armstrong took exception. With his caustic wit, Robert Dole managed to diffuse the situation. He told the audience not to pay too much attention to the heated exchange because that was the way the Senate usually operated. With Greenspan's soothing style as chair, the commission managed to maintain its dignity for the rest of its deliberations.[64]

At about the same time, a subtle shift in Ball's position occurred that was visible in a report he sent to the commission members at the beginning of May. Even with interfund borrowing, he now believed, the system still required more money or authority to borrow from general revenues in order to get through the period from 1984 to 1989. He conceded that a "structural change" in how automatic benefit increases worked "should be considered in order to reduce the system's vulnerability to short-term variables." In a confidential note, he admitted that "the automatic provisions for current beneficiaries are too vulnerable to short-term changes in the economy. The automatic provisions should be related to the income source, such as wages." Ball also realized that Medicare's rate of growth should be reduced and explored the notion of reimbursing hospitals on a prospective, rather than retrospective basis. At the end of the commission's June meeting, he expressed these ideas in public. "It now seems to me quite clear," he said, "that inter-fund borrowing does not solve the short-term problem; it does not get OASDI to 1990. So there is some action that needs to be taken for the cash benefit part of the program between now and 1990."[65]

If something needed to be done beyond interfund borrowing, which already existed in the legislation and could be extended beyond the current deadline, then Ball and his group of liberal Democrats had more of a reason to bargain with the others on the commission. Ball turned his attention to the many possibilities for raising revenues or cutting costs, making long lists that he could share with the others in the liberal caucus and, if he could get the liberal Democrats to agree, eventually with the entire commission. The list he prepared on May 5, for example, including such items as postponing cost-of-living adjustments to put them on a fiscal-year basis, making coverage of state and local government employees compulsory, and moving up the tax increase scheduled for 1990.[66]

He began a round of meetings with the people in his caucus to see what they would be willing to accept. One of the most important meetings occurred on June 11, when Ball met with Lane Kirkland and two of his key staff members at the AFL-CIO.[67] Like Ball, Kirkland felt that there might be some sort of negotiation with the Republicans, and like Ball he accepted the idea that the system required additional revenue for the next seven years. Kirkland reported that Greenspan wanted a substitute for a COLA based on prices, favoring something like a COLA set at 1.5 percentage points lower than the increase in average wages. With the help of AFL-CIO staff member Larry Smedley, Ball persuaded Kirkland that this proposal might be part of a larger package. Ball began to think that it might be possible to fashion an agreement that combined Greenspan's idea of a change in the COLA with raising the Social Security tax rate. Talking with Kirkland, Ball noticed that Kirkland was more flexible on many of the issues than was Bert Seidman, his principal staff member for social insurance issues. As a consequence, Ball believed that the meeting served "to open up future possibilities."

Flexible as Kirkland might be, he still needed to follow the general policy lines that organized labor had established over the years. For example, Kirkland ruled out of hand the notion of raising the retirement age because "the labor movement had been going in exactly the opposite direction too long," and he and Ball realized that, in a similar sense, the use of general revenues to prop up Social Security would be unacceptable to Greenspan. Kirkland's position as a labor leader representing government employees (and public employees constituted one of the few vibrant areas in the labor movement at the time) meant that he was obligated to oppose bringing federal employees into the Social Security system. He told Ball that he might have to dissent from the other members of the liberal caucus on this issue.

For the most part, though, Kirkland's position meshed with Ball's. "Lane Kirkland is thinking about this problem in exactly the same way I am in terms of posture," he noted. Like Ball, Kirkland wanted to reach an agreement with Greenspan and the conservatives "but not to give on benefits now or in the future, ruling out an increase in the retirement age, not really hoping for general revenue as a solution but willing to increase social security taxes on workers and employers and solving the problem generally in traditional terms."

In the public meetings of the commission Ball carried the ball for the other liberal members, expressing in public the ideas that they had reviewed in private. At the June meeting, for example, the commission listened to talks about morbidity and mortality trends and how they affected people's ability to work. Ball resisted all suggestions that, because elderly Americans, as a group, were healthier and living longer than previously, the retirement age be raised. He said that elderly Americans formed such a diverse group that few generalizations could be applied to them. Instead of raising the retirement age, Ball preferred to collect Social Security taxes from the elderly people in the labor force. He noted, also, that most people retired before age 65 and just bringing the average age of retirement up to 65 would be an accomplishment. Although people should be given the chance to work longer, raising the retirement age, inevitably an arbitrary act, would not do much to restore people's faith in the system, particularly among the younger workers who were the ones who had the most doubts about Social Security. In the June meeting, as at many of the others, Ball tended to dominate the discussion.[68]

At the July meeting, which consisted of long discussions of the women's equity issue and of the investment policies followed by trust funds, Ball stressed that "there's nothing excessive about our present replacement rates. . . . I'd hate to start focusing on a reduction when I see really no evidence . . . that anything that has been promised [is] excessive." Greenspan replied that the 42 percent of pre-retirement income that Social Security replaced on average was "not a sacrosanct number . . . clearly other things equal, the higher the better. But the trouble is that not all other things are equal."[69]

In private, Ball continued to test the right mix of cost cuts and revenue enhancements that might form the basis of a deal. He went so far as to prepare "talking notes" that he could distribute to his patrons in Congress, such as Representatives Gephardt and Shannon and Senator Long. One idea that appealed to Ball involved the taxation of the income that beneficiaries received from Social Security. This money might be channeled back into the Old-Age, Survivors, and Disability Insurance (OASDI) trust funds, which amounted to a way of using tax expenditures and general revenues to fund Social Security.[70] Unlike many of his fellow liberals, Ball saw nothing wrong with taxing Social Security benefits. Treating Social Security like other retirement income made it seem more like normal income and less like welfare.

Told by Ball that "there is no question now given the way the economy has behaved that inter-fund borrowing would not be enough to see the system to 1990," Ball's Democratic political patrons concurred that more taxes were needed. The 1977 amendments, which had included tax increases for 1985, 1986, and 1990, provided political cover. The increases already legislated could simply be moved up and made effective in an earlier year. Russell Long, for example, took the position that the increases were already scheduled, "that the heat had already been incurred in the '77 amendments . . . and that moving them up should not be considered that big a deal and if that's what it took we should do it." Long doubted that Robert Dole, the head of the Finance Committee, would want to reduce benefits or bring general revenues to the system. "What came through loud and clear" to Ball was "that we could meet the problem by a straightforward increase in the contribution rates through the device of moving up already scheduled rates."[71]

Alan Greenspan remained less convinced that more taxes were the answer to the problem.[72] He told Ball that he did not particularly like the idea of moving up the tax increases, although Ball surmised "that he might come to it as the least bad of alternatives." Still, Greenspan worried that more taxes might not be sufficient to save the program. As it turned out, Greenspan remained very pessimistic about the economy's short-term and long-term prospects. In a variant of an idea shared by many conservatives, Greenspan believed that during the 1960s and 1970s policymakers made an over-optimistic assessment of the economy's future growth and, as a consequence, made "too large a commitment to retirement income" and left too little for society's other needs. Hence, the situation required some corrective discipline, such as raising the retirement age. Greenspan thought that the differences between people like him and people like Ball might be too wide to bridge and that the commission's report might consist of a statement of the two separate philosophies. Ball disagreed. Such an approach was not a good way to negotiate. As Ball had learned in many Social Security forums, "frequently people could come to the same conclusion about a specific recommendation for a variety of different reasons and from different philosophical points of view and one didn't want to shut off that kind of agreement by stressing the philosophical at the beginning of the negotiation."

Ball thought Greenspan underestimated the commission. He realized that its composition differed from that of other Social Security advisory councils, since it contained influential congressmen, the president of the National Association of Manufacturers, the head of the labor movement, and the chief executive of the largest insurance company in the world. If this group could reach agreement, "it would be extraordinarily influential, particularly because from a political standpoint all parties concerned had a stake in a quick resolution." An agreement from this group had a good chance of being adopted.

Instead, therefore, of stressing the issues that divided the commission, Ball preferred to start with the items on which there was wide agreement. That would give the group "some sense of the possibility of agreeing and some momentum for moving ahead." In a list of such items, Ball included extending coverage, crediting the trust fund for checks that had not been cashed, and making minor modifications in the way the trust fund invested its money. Ball carried a list of such items around with him as he went from meeting to meeting.[73] To facilitate the discussion of these items, he asked Myers and the Social Security actuaries to estimate how much each of the items would save in the hope of creating "building blocks" for subsequent negotiating packages.[74] The entire exercise was reminiscent of the way in which he had handled other sensitive political negotiations at a time of political division, whether it was convincing Secretary Hobby of the efficacy of Social Security or working with the Nixon administration looking for little ways to save money and still achieve big goals.

By August Ball thought he had made some progress in moving the commission closer to an agreement. That month's meeting featured a stylized showdown between two economists. Henry Aaron of the Brookings Institution, chosen by the liberals, outlined one view of the program, and Michael Boskin of Stanford University, chosen by the conservatives, presented another. Aaron pointed out that the rates of return for people who would retire in the future would be much lower than for previous retirees. Ball countered that there were benefits to Social Security that could not be calculated in the rates of return, such as people being able to depend on receiving benefits ahead of time (a defined benefit plan, in the pension jargon), not having to submit to a means test, and knowing that their parents would be taken care of, thus lessening the painful trade-off between providing for the welfare of their children or their parents. Boskin emphasized the large windfalls for early retirees that would be followed by a "very bad yield by younger workers and those who are not yet in the labor force when they retire in the next century." Boskin favored eliminating the subsidies built into the Social Security system and allowing more opportunities for private savings accounts and other forms of private investments.[75]

The breakthrough for Ball occurred at the very end of the meeting. Joe Waggonner, a former Democratic congressman from Louisiana with a conservative outlook who had been appointed to the commission by President Reagan, reacted to Boskin's talk with a rambling, southern-style comment: "I felt that you were going to offer us a number of alternative proposals that had to do with certain aspects of the Social Security program, but it does appear to me that what you have recommended to us, which is an alternative in the overall, a rather new program, a substitute program for the existing Social Security program. . . . It looks like apple and pie to agree to these points that you've listed which look [like] the personal savings accounts. I think we all want to do those things [but] they're going to raise an awful lot of questions, and I personally would like to see them because I'm of the opinion right now that maybe the end result of what you propose is for the President to create another commission to study that plan. . . . Because with the time that's ours, we're not going to have any real opportunity to evaluate that plan, as good as it might well be."[76] In other words, Waggonner believed that radical reform of the type advocated by Boskin was off the table. The commission would have to concern itself with saving the existing Social Security program, not radically reforming it. Greenspan told Ball much the same thing. Although Greenspan indicated he had some personal sympathy for Boskin's ideas, "he does not intend to press them in this Commission but rather to concentrate on making the kind of system we have financially viable."[77] That put the negotiations squarely in Ball's court.

The results of the midterm elections of 1982 gave the commission no easy outs. Neither party gained a victory decisive enough to provide a comfortable working majority to deal with the issue. The Democrats gained twenty-six seats in the House, but the Senate remained under Republican control. Since neither side enjoyed a clear advantage in Congress, that increased the risks of leaving the problem for Congress to handle. Even liberal commissioner Claude Pepper worried about fighting out the issue in Congress because he feared that Reagan might allow things to deteriorate to the point where full benefits might not be paid on time. The president also remained wary of a confrontation with Congress because he thought that the longer the issue remained alive, the more benefit the Democrats would receive from it. The idea of a lame-duck session to deal with the problem lost its appeal to Democrats because they preferred to wait until the new congressional session and the arrival of more Democrats in both Houses. At the same time, a deadline loomed. Something needed to be done before July 1983, when the money from interfund borrowing would run out, if the Social Security system were to pay full benefits on time.[78]

Because of Ball's staff work, the five liberal members of the commission now functioned as a cohesive group, determined to stay together on the commission report. This outlook followed from the realization that a report signed by Ball, Keys, and Moynihan, but without Pepper or Kirkland, would not amount to much. In the first post-election meeting, held in Alexandria, Virginia, Ball's caucus made its first serious gestures to Greenspan and the Republicans. In the first place, Ball and the other liberals agreed on target numbers for the short-term and long-term Social Security deficits. Ball believed it was good politics to pick a high number for the short-term deficit, and the group agreed that the system would have to come up with $150 to $200 billion to solve that problem. Ball's strategy surprised the Republicans, who thought that it was natural for the Democrats to favor as small a target number as possible, since that would make the problem seem as small as possible. Although he was glad to have the Republicans think that way, Ball, in fact, preferred a large number. Having a large number meant that the Republicans could not easily solve the problem with benefit cuts—they had, after all, assured voters that they would take no precipitous action and cut the benefits of the people already receiving them— and would instead have to accept some sort of tax increase. In fact, moving up the tax increase scheduled for 1990 to 1984 generated an estimated $136 billion in revenues, leaving little to be done by benefit cuts.

For reasons of political strategy, Ball also reached a deal on the size of the long-term deficit. In the past he had argued that the situation some fifty to seventy-five years in the future remained too indeterminate to predict with any certainty. At the Alexandria meeting, Ball, with the concurrence of his liberal caucus, accepted that the long-term deficit was, in the Social Security jargon, 1.82 percent of payroll. That committed the conservatives to endorse the "II-B" estimates from the actuaries, even though many of them had been arguing that the long-term deficit was, in fact, much larger than those estimates implied. It was, however, the short-term that mattered the most to the Democrats.[79]

Ball believed that Greenspan, Dole, Heinz, and Conable might be willing to come to an agreement with the liberal Democrats. During the course of the Alexandria meetings, Ball asked Dole, who was seated next to him, how he would react to a modification of the proposal already made by Ball's group so that it also included a three-month delay in the cost-of-living adjustment and, in the long run, a 5 percent reduction in replacement rates (that would not start to take effect until 2020). Dole showed some interest. Ball got his caucus together, and they agreed to the concessions. Claude Pepper suggested that they get the Speaker on the phone, and he, too, liked the idea. He urged a modification so that, instead of the change in the cost of living being phased in over three years, it be made all at once, so that adjustments to the cost of living would be put on a fiscal-year basis. Between 1983 and 1989 such a move would save the system $25 billion and in the longer run save 0.14 percent of payroll. Ball's group asked Dole to come up to the room where they were meeting. Next Greenspan got brought into the conversation, and he, too, showed interest. Greenspan agreed to call Jim Baker in the White House. There the matter ended. Baker could not find agreement within the White House for the proposal, since some of the White House staff did not feel it went far enough in cutting benefits. Greenspan reported back that the White House had not had time to consider the position of Social Security in the 1984 budget carefully enough to close the deal.[80]

Although the Alexandria meeting ended on November 15 without a formal agreement, the press reported that "political circumstances may be improving for a comprehensive solution to the retirement program's financial problems." The story in the *Wall Street Journal* quoted a Republican staff member to the effect that, "This was the first time there was any real willingness to look at benefits, as small as it may be." Still, there were signs that a limit had been reached. "I don't see any real possibility of the Democrats agreeing to any reduction in benefits that goes beyond this," Ball said. The president said that he opposed the notion of raising payroll taxes. "I don't think there's much room," the president said. The commission meeting for December lasted only fifteen minutes.[81]

The Commission Reaches a Deal

Although public avenues of compromise appeared to be closed, the process of negotiation continued in private. Essentially, what happened was that, although the commission was approaching the end of the year and the end of its appointed term, the Republicans decided to invite the Democrats to hold further discussions. The political faction of the White House, and in particular James Baker, Richard Darman, and Kenneth Duberstein, along with Budget Director David Stockman, who was a former congressman, continued to believe that it would be better to reach a deal through the commission apparatus than through Congress. The president appeared to agree. As a consequence, the White House staff initiated highly informal contacts with Ball. In particular Darman, a White House counsel and Baker's top assistant, called Ball and asked if they could have a conversation that never took place. Used to such subtleties and eager to advance the process, Ball agreed to meet with Darman on December 17, 1982.[82]

In a long and rambling conversation, they probed each other's positions.[83] Because they knew each other from their common service working for Elliot Richardson, they talked easily with one another. Darman brought with him the sixth iteration of a proposal that had been crafted by Alexander Trowbridge, a nominal Democrat and former member of Lyndon Johnson's cabinet but the current head of the National Association of Manufacturers and a Reagan appointee to the commission. The copy contained annotations that had been made by President Reagan, indicating his degree of interest in the negotiations. Darman reported that the White House remained divided over the wisdom of using the commission to solve the problem. Ed Harper, the head of the Domestic Policy Council, Baker, Edwin Meese, and Stockman wanted to reach an agreement through the commission and had managed to persuade the president of that approach. Still, even within this group, Harper and Meese took their positions only for political reasons and not out of any real desire to settle the issue. Others, such as economic adviser Martin Feldstein, hoped to make major cuts in the program over the long term and welcomed an open fight in Congress over the issue. And Darman believed that the president, whom he thought truly wanted to return to an earlier, simpler era, could, if no agreement were reached, launch an educational campaign to convince the nation that Social Security should be phased out or greatly reduced.

Darman and Ball agreed that, to a great extent, the argument was over numbers, rather than principle, since the president had agreed to around $45 billion in tax increases, and Ball's group had agreed to a postponement of the COLA. The two also understood that there were more disagreements over the long-run solutions to the problem than over the short-term measures. Still, as they both realized, the differences in the numbers even for a short-term solution were enormous. The president remained adamant that the tax increases proposed by the Democrats were too high.[84]

As for specific concessions, Ball raised the idea of a further delay in the COLA so that it was put on a calendar basis. That meant that instead of getting increased benefits at the end of June, beneficiaries would have to wait until the beginning of January—a six-month delay that would be phased in over three years. The White House, Darman reported, thought in terms of a one-year moratorium and then switching over to a fiscal-year basis (a fifteen-month delay) or lowering the amount of the COLA by two percentage points for five years. They also wanted to lower the replacement rate beginning in 1990 and raise the retirement age to 68 by 2011. As for Ball's idea about taxing a portion of Social Security benefits and returning the money to the trust fund, Darman thought the president might reject it because it was a tax. Showing the intellectual agility that made him so effective in negotiations, Ball countered that instead of a tax it could be thought of as a benefit cut for the higher-paid. Darman agreed that such an argument might strike a chord with Reagan, who often said that it made no sense for him or his wealthy friends to get Social Security checks.

Although Darman and Ball did not reach agreement on a specific plan, Ball thought it a good sign that the White House staff had become involved in the negotiations. Darman had told him that "it might well be to the advantage of the Democratic Party as such not to settle the issue, that it would be the Republicans and the President who would be hurt the most but that the social security system would also be hurt." This intelligence convinced Ball that the White House staff would pursue the negotiations.[85]

Another line of communication developed between Robert Dole and Daniel Moynihan, the two politicians who, more than any others, carried the Social Security brief for their parties in the Senate. On January 3, Dole published an op-ed article in the *New York Times* in which he stated that the problem could be solved in a pragmatic manner through some combination of benefit cuts and tax increases. Moynihan, who according to Paul Light had been brought into the discussions by David Stockman at the same time that Darman had contacted Ball, tapped Dole on the shoulder during a Senate ceremony on January 3 to swear in the members of the new Congress. He urged Dole not to let the commission die and instead to extend the negotiations.[86]

The two of them brought Ball, already anointed by Darman, into the discussions. As Ball recalls what happened next, they asked him if it would be worthwhile to continue the negotiations. Ball said it would. "They evidently had this set-up before," said Ball, because Greenspan appeared to know about it and quickly became a member of the group, and James Baker immediately invited the group over to his house. They realized that they needed someone from the House to participate and so they added Barber Conable to their group. "And that's what started two weeks of real negotiation, really between the Speaker and the President of the United States," said Ball, "But, we were the proxies for negotiation that reversed the usual Advisory Council thing . . . coming to an agreement first with the two principals, and then getting the Council to endorse what we had already decided."[87]

The first meeting between the five members of the commission and the members of the White House staff who had been pushing for a negotiated settlement took place on Wednesday, January 5, 1983, in James Baker's comfortable home on Foxhall Road. As in the commission meetings, Ball quickly assumed the role of chief negotiator for the Democrats and the Speaker. Many of the proposals had already been developed over the long course of the commission meetings. To track the group's progress toward a mutually acceptable agreement in what had now become a straightforward, pragmatic negotiation, removed from the commission's earlier flighty discussions of the Social Security problem, Ball kept a series of score sheets. These listed the items proposed and tallied the amount of money each would save in the period between 1983 and 1989 and over the long term of seventy-five years.

The big-ticket items on Ball's first score sheet were the shift in the COLA payment to a calendar basis by 1987, which he had discussed with Darman and which saved $46 billion, and the acceleration of previously scheduled taxes, which brought in $53.2 billion. The taxes on the Social Security benefits of wealthier OASDI recipients would produce $30 billion in revenue, and extending coverage to all nonprofit employees and newly hired federal workers would add $23.6 billion. A change in the tax rate for the self-employed, so that they paid the same rate as the combined rate for employers and employees, would yield $19 billion.[88]

The proposal that would have the most long-term impact featured a tax increase that would go into effect after 2000 but only if the trust funds fell below half of the next year's outgo. The score sheet also contained a 5 percent reduction in replacement rates, under terms that were only vaguely stated. Together these items amounted to 0.75 percent of payroll over the seventy-five-year period. They remained tentative, however, and clearly would be the object of future bargaining.[89]

In a testament to the influence of the commission's earlier discussions, some of the items on Ball's score sheet would actually cost the system money. These consisted of measures that had been pushed by Martha Keys to create gender equity in the program, such as allowing a divorced spouse to receive benefits regardless of whether the insured spouse had retired. Although none of these items accounted for much money; they indicated how the national commission continued, in a very limited way, to advance the sort of Social Security reform that had been discussed in liberal circles for the past ten years. The high testosterone environment of the negotiating sessions—in which the participants, all of whom were male, played political hardball and took Sunday afternoon breaks to watch the Redskins play football—was not the place to advance complicated and likely costly proposals such as earnings sharing in Social Security. Modest accommodations to the feminist agenda could, however, be made.

The details of the negotiations that were conducted in this locker room atmosphere remained secret, but the press soon learned about the group's existence. Efforts to elude the press added a cloak-and-dagger element to an already clandestine operation. On January 7, for example, Ball looked out his window and saw that members of the press were camped out in front of his house. They expected, mistakenly as it turned out, the negotiating group to meet at Ball's house. As it happened, the group was scheduled to gather at Baker's house, but Ball did not want the reporters to follow him to the meeting. As John Trout details in his excellent account of the 1983 amendments, Ball first sent his wife to the door, dressed in jogging clothes, to signal to the press that she was not expecting company. Whether the extremely casually clad press members got the message, which lost something in translation across the generations, was unclear. That gambit having failed, Ball called Darman at the White House. Using the powers of the presidency, Darman arranged to have a car sent, not to Ball's house, but to a spot on the well-traveled George Washington Parkway, close to Ball's back door. To get there, however, Ball needed to climb down a steep slope and travel through thick woods, all over the snow-covered winter terrain. Ball, a veteran climber from his summers in the White Mountains, snuck out the back door, down the hill, through the woods, and into the White House car.[90]

For the following week, the group continued to meet, most often at Blair House, the official government guesthouse that had once been the temporary quarters of President Truman while the White House, directly across the street, was undergoing repairs. Ball kept making changes on his score sheet. By January 11 the group had achieved an important element of symmetry in its proposals that the negotiators, accustomed to battles in which there were winners and losers, assumed was crucial to gaining a final agreement. In the period between 1983 and 1989, $39 billion would come from tax increases and $39 billion from putting the COLA on a calendar-year basis. That gave at least the appearance that both sides were making equal sacrifices in the negotiations. It made for the "win-win" condition that the group was seeking. In fact, however, the score sheet contained its share of ambiguous items, such as collecting income taxes from wealthier Social Security recipients and devoting the proceeds to the Social Security tax funds. As Ball had pointed out to Darman, that was either a benefit cut to the wealthy, a win for the Republicans, or a form of general revenue financing, a win for the Democrats. These ambiguities allowed the group to count the money that the move generated but not to score it as a victory for either side. Similarly, having the self-employed pay as much as did employers and employers together could be regarded as a tax increase to the self-employed or a simple matter of equity designed to correct a previous defect. It, too, could be counted in a neutral way.

Although neither side cared to admit it, the Republicans gave away far more ground than did the Democrats in the negotiations, reflecting their impression that the Democrats held the upper hand. Despite Ball's careful way of phrasing the proposal to tax Social Security benefits, for example, the fact remained that it was something he favored and that the Republicans, wary of tax increases and general revenue financing, should have opposed. Extended coverage so that the program reached new groups of workers, as David Stockman surely recognized, represented an expansion of the system that he had argued against in previous White House meetings. The gender-equity items, similarly, appealed mainly to a constituency that was more important to the Democrats than to the Republicans.

Then there were items that Ball had been collecting over the life of the commission and having the Social Security actuaries refine for use in just this sort of situation. They brought money into the system in somewhat the same way that a collection agency could squeeze out money for a hard-pressed business. If people failed to cash their Social Security checks, for example, then Ball proposed that the value of those checks not be carried forward into eternity. Instead, those debts should be taken off the books and the money credited to the trust funds. This "found" money came to the trust funds with few political complications.

The January 11 score sheet also included an item known as military service wage credits. Beginning in 1957 members of the armed forces received Social Security coverage. At the same time, they also received credit for their previous military employment in the calculation of their ultimate Social Security benefits. Ball suggested that the trust funds be reimbursed for the credits that had been extended to the military in this manner. At the very end of the negotiations, Bruce Schobel, a Social Security actuary, added a new item to the military credits—something known as "payments in lieu of subsistence." That was money that the Defense Department was supposed to have paid into the trust funds to account for the fact that the nominal wages of servicemen did

Robert Ball, along with other members of the Greenspan Commission, looks on anxiously as Claude Pepper addresses the press conference announcing the commission's final report. Ball was privately afraid that Pepper might say something that would undermine the carefully crafted deal he had negotiated with the Reagan administration. Staff director and long-time Ball colleague Robert J. Myers stands at the far right. Photograph courtesy of Robert Ball.

not reflect their true salaries because of the free room and board they received and enabled them to collect benefits on amounts higher than their nominal wages. It all made for a complicated item to explain, expressed as it was in nearly impenetrable prose. Paul Light, in his book on the commission's work, dismisses these payments as "accounting games," but they were consequential ones, yielding $6.3 billion on the January 11 score sheet and even more on subsequent ones.[91]

By Thursday, January 13, Ball had changed the heading on his scorecard from "compromise proposal" to "potential solution." The new set of negotiated items included some things of interest to the Republicans. One was a provision, such as had been recommended by Greenspan, that if the prices increased at a greater rate than wages, then the cost-of-living adjustment would be based on wage growth, rather than the consumer price index.

Another was to increase the benefits of those who waited past the age of 65 to retire and, over a period between 1990 and 1999, to decrease the benefits of those who retired early.

Significantly, the January 13th "potential solution" provided enough money to meet the system's short-term problems but left some of the long-term problem unsolved. Instead of a definite provision, the scorecard included a statement that the majority would propose meeting the rest of the long-term problem by increasing the normal retirement age, and the minority would find some other means to solve the problem.[92]

On Saturday, January 15, the "potential solution" morphed into the "recommended bipartisan solution to the social security problem." At the center of this solution, as before, stood the agreement to cut $40 billion of benefits by shifting the cost-of-living adjustment to a calendar-year basis and providing for $40 billion worth of tax increases. The agreement protected Lane Kirkland by not charging workers for the first tax increase that would take effect in 1984 and raise the OASDI tax from 5.4 percent to 5.7 percent. When the tax rate hit 6.06 in 1988, however, Kirkland and the workers he represented would have to pay the tax increase or seek further relief from Congress. The accommodation to Kirkland represented the sorts of concessions that both sides needed to make in order to keep one of more of their members happy. Robert Beck, the Prudential Insurance executive and an important constituent for the White House negotiators, disliked providing tax relief to workers, arguing that it amounted to little more than a general revenue subsidy. Hence, the group made a concession to Kirkland by providing one year of relief and to Beck by providing only one year of relief. In another subtle bargain, the final agreement dropped the decrease in early retirement benefits and the possibility of a 5 percent reduction in the replacement rates in return for Ball's faction agreeing to implement the six-month delay in COLAs immediately, rather than phasing it in over a period of time.[93]

As in the previous iteration, a significant amount of the long-term problem, nearly a third of it, remained unsolved. The two sides agreed to disagree over how best to handle this problem. That meant that the two sides would fight about it in Congress. Unlike in the debate over short-term benefits, however, the Republicans could face the Democrats on more or less equal terms on this aspect of the Social Security issue. It was not a matter of taking benefits away from current workers but rather conditioning the benefits for future workers. And if the Democrats opposed a rise in the retirement age, they would have to make some sort of counterproposal, if only a vague promise to raise taxes in the future.[94]

The negotiators held their last meeting at Blair House on Saturday morning, January 15, and reached what they hoped would be the final agreement. Around noon the group broke up. The White House negotiators went back to their offices, presumably to talk with some of the more recalcitrant conservative members of the commission and to brief the president on what had happened. Ball stayed behind at Blair House with Moynihan. Together they called Jim Wright in Texas, and Moynihan called Robert Byrd. Moynihan then left, leaving Ball behind to check with Kirkland, Pepper, and then the Speaker on whether the agreement would be acceptable.

Everyone, it seemed, was away. Kirkland was on a train from New York to Washington, unreachable until 4:00 in the afternoon. Ball called him the minute he got back to his Washington apartment. Kirkland said that if Pepper agreed to the six-month delay in the COLA, then he would accept the whole package. Ball telephoned Pepper in his apartment and talked with the congressman and his assistant, Richard Lehrman. Lehrman said it was a good deal and that Pepper should take it. Pepper took it. Ball now realized that his side would back the agreement because he had kept the Speaker fully informed throughout the negotiating process, and O'Neill had said that if Kirkland and Pepper supported the agreement, then he would as well. O'Neill, as it happened, was on the West Coast at a celebrity golf tournament, and Ball spoke with him there.

By now others who had sat in on the negotiations—Moynihan, Dole, Conable, Pepper—had started to come back to Blair House. Around seven, Baker, Stockman, Darman, and Duberstein walked back across the street to Blair House and reported that the president would agree to the deal if the Speaker would. Symptomatic of the stress under which all the negotiators had labored and of the long hours that the process had consumed, a flap then developed over the White House's insistence that the president and the Speaker sign a common statement. Although

O'Neill objected, loudly and profanely, to what he regarded as a last-minute imposition, the two sides managed to smooth it over with separate statements that had a common theme of support for the commission agreement.[95]

It remained for the agreement to receive the blessing of the full National Commission on Social Security Reform. The negotiators now walked around the corner to the commission's plush townhouse. The commissioners, who had been assembled there in anticipation of voting on the agreement, listened to an explanation of what the agreement contained. Then, by a vote of twelve to three, they accepted the agreement. Those who opposed it represented the commission's extreme conservative wing—Senator William Armstrong, who had attended many of the negotiating sessions but said very little, Representative Bill Archer (R–Texas), who sat on the Ways and Means Committee, and former representative Joe Waggonner. The votes of those who favored the agreement clearly counted more than the votes of those who opposed it. On the Senate Finance Committee, for example, Senator Dole outranked Senator Armstrong, and on the Ways and Means Committee Barber Conable carried more seniority and authority than did Bill Archer. Even more importantly, the agreement had the endorsement of a conservative like Greenspan and a liberal like Pepper.[96]

Conclusion

It was a moment of some exaltation for Ball. As soon as the commission voted, he raced up a flight of stairs with Baker and Greenspan to reach the telephone in the second-floor offices. Baker called the president and reported that the commission had reached agreement. In an autobiographical fragment that Ball prepared about the episode and intended for one of his biographers to use, he wrote, "it was a moment for which Ball had been preparing all his life."[97]

Robert Ball regarded his work on the National Commission on Social Security Reform as his supreme accomplishment. In fact, it was a synthesis of much that he had learned in such settings as the 1948 advisory council about moving a disparate group toward consensus and, over the course of a long career as a bureaucrat, about the inner workings of Social Security. No one else had Ball's combination of interpersonal skills and impersonal knowledge, and he used both to maximum advantage on the commission. Even Robert Myers, no admirer of Ball's and resentful of the way in which many commentators played up the confidential negotiations and de-emphasized the rest of the commission's work, lauded Ball's performance. "As far as the Democrats went, he put the package together," he said. "It was common knowledge that he was representing the speaker." "I didn't agree with a lot of what Ball was doing," added Senator Armstrong, "but it was quite a thing to watch him work."[98]

The commission's agreement produced a sense of euphoria in Washington. Moynihan published an article in the *Washington Post* under the headline "More than Social Security Was at Stake." Instead, the agreement showed the capacity of the political system to function in an effective way on an important issue. It took politics beyond gridlock toward meaningful compromise. "There is a center in American government. It can govern," wrote Moynihan. When Moynihan introduced Ball to a meeting of Senate Democrats, they gave him a standing ovation. The president added his congratulations. On January 22, he put in a personal phone call to Ball. "I called to thank you and salute you for all you did to help bring about the social security agreement. I know how important your role was in getting this agreement and I know how heavily the Speaker relied on you," said the president, who thought the agreement was "a real shot in the arm to the American people to show we can all work together."[99]

The agreement meant nothing if Congress failed to pass it, yet seldom did a piece of legislation start with more political blessings. In the Republican-controlled Senate, it had the support of Dole, the chair of the key committee, and, beyond that, the support of Ronald Reagan, the unquestioned head of his party. In the Democratic-controlled House, it had the backing of Speaker O'Neill and Claude Pepper, who headed the important Rules Committee. Many of the liberal groups that could be expected to have problems with the legislation had already had a chance to consider it before it was adopted; that was the point of putting Kirkland and Pepper on the commission.

Furthermore, the supporters of the measure stressed that it was a package that needed to be accepted or rejected in its entirety. If any part of the compromise came undone, the whole plan would unravel as both sides scrambled for political cover. In addition, opponents of the legislation could not easily defeat it through the familiar process of delay because a real deadline loomed. Something had to be done about Social Security or, under the interfund borrowing measures that had been agreed to in 1981, the system would not be able to send out checks for the full amount on July 3. The media had a way of making this point dramatically, if somewhat inaccurately, as in a *Newsweek* story that reported that, without an agreement, "the checks owed to 36 million retirees . . . would simply not be mailed." If ever Congress faced an action-inducing deadline, that situation applied to the 1983 Social Security law.[100]

Passage came quickly but not effortlessly. Ball shifted his role from negotiator to commission spokesman and legislative lobbyist without slackening his pace.

One revolt that needed to be quelled came from Pepper. When representatives from the American Association of Retired Persons went to see Pepper to protest the six-month delay in the cost of living, they pointed out that the cut was, in effect, permanent. Once the COLAs were delayed, that money would never be made up. The situation was analogous to skipping an interest payment in a bank account; whatever the subsequent rate of interest, the total amount would always be lower than if the payment had been made. The full force of this point hit Pepper for the first time, even though it was clearly illustrated on the commission's score sheet by the fact that, over the seventy-five-year period, the measure saved 0.27 percent of payroll. Pepper, in high dudgeon, called Ball and told him that he had never agreed to such a thing and the whole deal was off. Ball realized that Pepper's defection would spoil the agreement. Like an emergency room doctor, Ball went right to work. He told Pepper not to do anything until he got there. In an effort to forewarn others whom Pepper might contact, Ball immediately called Ari Weiss and Jack Lew in the Speaker's office as well as Wilbur Cohen and Lane Kirkland. When he arrived in Pepper's office, he and staff aide Richard Lehrman tried to talk Pepper down. After many phone calls and pleadings, what appeared to turn the trick was a conversation with Richard Bolling, Pepper's predecessor as head of the Rules Committee, who was embarking on a new career as a teacher at

Boston College. Bolling flattered Pepper, telling him what an important contribution he had made on the Social Security agreement. Because Pepper, who was hard of hearing, kept the volume on the telephone so high, Ball could hear the whole thing. Fortified in his resolve, Pepper announced to the AARP that the COLA delay was the price of the agreement but that it was a good agreement and he stood behind it.[101]

In addition to this sort of hand-holding, Ball also engaged in a certain amount of legislative tinkering. One problem that developed in the legislative process was that some actuaries feared that the agreement did not afford enough of a margin for error in the middle 1980s. In part, that had stemmed from the way in which Ball had jury-rigged the tax increases in an effort to appease both Kirkland and Beck. As he looked at the numbers again, Ball admitted that "the money in those middle years did look pretty close to the line." Seeking help, Ball called Darman, who consulted with Stockman and his people in OMB. They came up with the idea of crediting the trust funds with all the money that would be received in a given month at the very beginning of that month. That compensated for the fact that checks went out at the beginning of the month but revenues came in throughout the month. It improved the financing situation enough to overcome the actuaries' objections, even though, as Bob Myers pointed out, it amounted to a loan from the general Treasury to Social Security—more accounting games but necessary ones to keep the legislation moving.[102]

Beyond tinkering, Ball actively lobbied to pass the bill. Even on a fast-track bill that qualified as must-pass legislation, public disputes developed. One stemmed from the opposition of federal employees to Social Security coverage. Like all the parts of the plan that brought in a substantial money for the system, this provision was crucial to the survival of the package. Ball wrote memos to Pickle and Dole on why new federal employees needed to be included in the system and met with a coalition of federal employees in an effort to mollify them. The problem was that the federal civil service plan functioned as an amalgam of a public and private pension, just as regular workers often received both Social Security and private pensions, and hence discontinuing it meant, in effect, a cut in retirement benefits. The Democrats in the Senate appeared particularly willing to placate the federal employee unions, as well as the AFL-CIO that stood behind them, and Senator Long agreed to sponsor an amendment that made Social Security coverage contingent on the development of a supplementary civil service plan, so that new workers would enjoy the same benefits as old workers. But if Congress waited for the adoption of a supplementary civil service pension, it could wait forever, and the Social Security agreement would stall. Hence, Ball saw Long's bill as a barrier against ever bringing federal employees into the Social Security system and, at Senator Dole's urging, offered an alternative. In the end, although Ball's alternative failed—"had I worked harder on some Democratic liberals it might have passed," he lamented—the House carried the point in the conference committee, and the federal employee issue came out the way that Ball wanted.[103]

The fact that this issue arose in the legislative process reflected one of the weaknesses in the commission agreement in that bringing federal employees into Social Security did not have the full endorsement of Lane Kirkland. Another, more important shortcoming concerned the fact that no agreement had been reached on solving all the long-term financing problem. That left room for the majority to press for an increase in the retirement age. Of all the arguments advanced by Ball in the commission, the conservatives on the commission and in the White House had the most difficulty in understanding his opposition to raising the retirement age. Furthermore, Pickle and Rostenkowski, who had pointedly removed themselves from membership on the commission, favored this measure and had included it in their 1981 Social Security reform bill. Even Jim Wright in the House leadership agreed with Pickle on this matter. Hence, preventing the retirement age from being raised would require a considerable lobbying effort.

Ball knew that, on this issue as compared to nearly all the others, some compromise would be necessary because agreement had not been reached within the commission. Ball believed that, although it would be impossible to pass Pepper's liberal proposal, it might be possible to defeat Pickle's conservative proposal to phase in a rise in the retirement age to 67. He had in mind a compromise provision that would set the retirement age at 66 and include some minor reduction in replacement rates. What prevented this outcome was that organized labor concentrated on the federal employee issue and neglected the retirement age, even though Ball told Kirkland that Pickle's amendment had a real chance of passing. The Speaker, for his part, refused to make the retirement age a leadership issue. Freed to vote as they wished, the Democrats in the House chose to raise the retirement age. In conference, Pepper rejected Dole's entreaties to compromise along the lines suggested by Ball, preferring to preserve the issue for a future legislative battle. On this matter, then, Ball lost, and the forces that had been pushing for a pared-down Social Security program ever since the Carter administration won.[104]

For the most part, though, the agreement held, although with the window for legislative change open, Congress could not resist shoving some additional items through it. The most important add-on to the commission agreement concerned Medicare and involved a fundamental change in the way the government compensated hospitals for the services they provided to the elderly. The key innovation involved something called diagnosis-related groups. When a person went to the hospital, this individual would receive a diagnosis. Hospitals would bill the government according to this diagnosis, turning the system into one of prospective payment rather than retrospective reimbursement.

Although both Ball and key figures in the Reagan administration favored this provision, Ball had not had an opportunity to concentrate on it during the commission negotiations. Others in the government and Congress, however, saw the Social Security legislation as the perfect vehicle to advance the cause of the diagnosis-related groups (DRGs). Both the Medicare and Social Security proposals provided a means of shoring up the system and ensuring its future survival. At some level, both were about controlling costs. "It became clear that after the Social Security deal was cut that this was the vehicle that we could put the DRGs on," said Robert Rubin, an assistant secretary in HHS. Like everyone else in Washington, Rubin knew that the Social Security legislation was the closest thing to a sure thing as existed in Congress. As he recalled, it was "veto-proof, fail-safe—this was gone. It had the blessings of the Speaker, the majority leader, the minority leader, the President—I mean nobody was fussing with this. . . . the skids were really greased on this baby."[105]

Certainly, by previous standards, the legislation just raced through Congress. In 1981 the legislative process for Social

Security began in January, and it took until the very end of the year to produce a bill that did little more than postpone the substantive decisions. In 1983 the process began in January and yielded a bill of considerable consequence that the president signed on April 20.

One could look at the 1983 law in a variety of ways. Without a doubt it helped to bolster public confidence and get Social Security through the difficult period between 1983 and 1989. It enabled the program to pass through the Carter and early Reagan recessions to the prosperity that lay beyond. Remarkably, the amendments took much the same form as the 1977 amendments, relying largely on taxes and other forms of revenue enhancement. To be sure, the 1983 law included some benefit cuts, such as the COLA delay that Ball had negotiated and the rise in the retirement age that Congress had imposed. It also left behind some vulnerabilities, such as tax increases from which Congress might retreat as the dates for their imposition drew near and lingering doubts about the program's future that President Clinton and the second President Bush would exploit. Still, Social Security escaped the Reagan revolution largely unscathed. It lost a very few of what David Stockman called its welfare features, such as the student benefit, but gained gender-equity features and expanded the percentage of the labor force that paid into it. One might almost view the 1983 amendments as a treaty of surrender in the conservative project to dismantle the welfare state. The basic structure of Social Security, which Stockman had termed the inner fortress of the welfare state, remained unchanged and as a consequence strengthened.

When two Harvard professors, writing in the 1980s, wanted to find an example of a success in domestic policy, to match the Cuban missile crisis as a foreign policy success, they chose the 1983 amendments. Both cases featured skillful negotiation and effective group dynamics that saved the postwar world from destruction. In the case of the Cuban missile crisis, the "ex comm," or executive committee working within the White House, ended a crisis without causing a nuclear war. In the case of the 1983 amendments, a small group of negotiators working on the edges of the White House defused a crisis without causing the Social Security checks to stop. Although the Harvard professors did not push the point, both cases relied on establishment figures to reinforce the conventional wisdom of the time: the cold war framework of foreign policy and a domestic policy anchored by contributory social insurance.[106]

It was a testimony to Robert Ball's skill in the work of the national commission that the Reagan administration capitulated to the 1983 amendments, not grudgingly but with a smile and even a feeling of triumph. The White House decided to hold the signing ceremony outside, despite the unseasonably cold temperatures, and to treat the occasion as a high-profile event. In contrast to Carter, who signed the 1977 amendments with some reluctance, Reagan appeared to relish the passage of the 1983 amendments. The president claimed the bill as a great victory and as a "clear and dramatic demonstration that our system can still work when men and women of good will join together to make it work." He regarded the bill's passage as concluding a "tumultuous debate about Social Security" that "has raged for more than two decades in this country." Now, according to the president, Social Security would be preserved, reaffirming "the commitment of our government to the performance and stability of Social Security." To reinforce the bipartisan nature of the legislation, Reagan invited Speaker O'Neill and Senator Baker to speak. Ball, on the platform with the president as a commission member, could not help admiring the president's vigor as he watched the ceremony with a feeling of pride.[107]

7

Closing Time

Robert Ball never matched his 1983 triumph. The circumstances of a well-defined crisis and the willingness of both sides to make a deal never repeated themselves. For a time in 1983 television cameras trailed Ball as he made his round of public appearances, but he regained his anonymity within a few months. He returned to being part of the inner workings of the policy process, his status much improved as result of his work on the 1983 amendments but his job as an adviser to the Democrats on Social Security much the same. After 1983 and for the rest of the century, he served as Social Security's principal defender in the face of attacks on its financial viability and its relevance to modern conditions. Despite two bouts with cancer, he remained exceptionally active, as involved in the politics of Social Security as anyone in the country.

Reaching milestone birthdays, Ball passed into the category of elder statesman. When he became 80 in 1994, the *National Journal*, an important Washington publication for those who followed the fine points of public policy, reported that Ball was "widely considered one of [Social Security's] last living patron saints." It described the 1983 amendments as "his crowning achievements" but noted that some eleven years later he still came into the office at least several days each week. Ball may have contemplated retirement, but then "'somebody attacks social security and I have to go back to work.'"[1]

Five years later, the *New York Times* headlined a piece on Ball "A Great Defender of the Old Social Security Battles On." It featured a quote from Brookings economist Henry Aaron, who said, "I don't know of any other 85-year-old who's wrestling with what he's going to do, new." Confronted by challenges to Social Security that provoked new actions, Ball acknowledged that his retirement had been "less than restful." John Rother, the chief lobbyist for the American Association of Retired Persons (AARP) described a visit to Ball's summer home at Lake Winnepesaukee in New Hampshire, at which Ball spent an increasing portion of each year. "Usually I find him in a lounge chair on a sunny dock with a cell phone, and there is a fax machine in the house," said Rother.[2]

The only subtle difference one could detect was in the pictures that accompanied the various elder statesmen stories. In 1994, at age 80, Ball posed in a suit and tie in an office setting. The 85th birthday stories featured Ball clad in a comfortable blue cardigan, sitting on the front porch of his Virginia home, seemingly at ease.

1984 Campaign

After the 1983 amendments, Ball remained as tightly identified with the Democrats as ever. In the ill-fated 1984 campaign, in which Ronald Reagan trounced former vice president Walter Mondale, Ball worked hard for Mondale. Ball owed his influence on the campaign in part to the past work he had done with Mondale and in part to Ted Marmor, a Yale academic who specialized in health and Social Security policy and who had previously worked at the University of Minnesota and established connections with Mondale. Marmor, eager to extend his reach beyond academia into the realms of politics and policy, became a member of the issues staff on the Mondale campaign. An extravagant admirer of Ball's, Marmor brought in Ball, just as Tom Joe had hooked Ball up with the Carter campaign some eight years earlier. As Ball told his old White House patron Stuart Eizenstat, "I did have a chance . . . to do most of the social security work for the Mondale campaign and, at least, we did succeed in pushing the President into a very strong commitment [for Social Security]."[3] During the election, noted Marmor, Ronald Reagan "finally embraced social security with a clarity previously reserved to legatees of the New Deal." Ball could take a little credit for that.[4]

On the campaign, Ball showed his political ability by advising Mondale to raise Social Security as an issue under the guise of making Social Security a non-issue. In a script that Ball drafted, Mondale was to say that Ronald Reagan should "leave social security out of it." Mondale would then go into detail on Social Security's robust fiscal health in the wake of the 1983 amendments and then quote from Reagan's less than total endorsement of the program. That, in turn, would set the stage for bringing up Reagan's past actions, such as his 1981 proposals to trim the program and his harsh administrative actions cutting people off the disability rolls. As Ball explained to Mondale's advisers, "My idea is for WFM to put RR on the defensive by proposing a joint pledge to honor social security commitments in present law. . . . In working up to the proposed pledge, we must detail RR's anti-social security record. . . . If RR agrees to such a pledge (which I doubt) it tightens the noose on the secret plan to raise taxes [something that Mondale had agreed to do but that Reagan adamantly refused to do]. If he tries to explain why he won't make such a pledge we have a social security issue and the press ought to keep after him on any weasel worded attempt to explain." None of this maneuvering affected the outcome of the campaign, yet Mondale enjoyed some of his best moments on the Social Security and Medicare issues.[5]

National Academy of Social Insurance

When Ball worked on the Mondale campaign, he was 70 years old and mindful of his personal legacy. His desire to leave something substantive behind led, over the course of the next two years, to the creation of a new organization that occupied much of his time and attention for the rest of the decade. It was to concern itself not just with partisan politics but also with broader issues related to social insurance.

"It occurred to me," Ball wrote right after the campaign in a letter to Nancy Altman, Greenspan's assistant on the National

Commission on Social Security Reform, "that it would be desirable to have an informal network of people who are both devoted to the social security program and very knowledgeable about it. I have nothing more in mind than keeping in touch with one another and exchanging papers, ideas, etc." In this idea lay the seed for the National Academy of Social Insurance, but as Ball later noted, "it was a pretty amorphous idea at first."[6]

The people whom Ball thought of as appropriate members of the network included nearly everyone on the Democratic staff of the 1983 commission, Brookings economists with whom Ball had worked and who had proved helpful to him, and old-line bureaucrats and labor union officials. Ball initially thought that such a group might write op-ed pieces and letters to the editor on Social Security. Hence, although the group would engage in academic speculation, it would, as he had told Altman, be devoted to Social Security and no doubt defend it in politically salient terms.[7]

The transformation of the informal network into a formal academy owed something to an article that Ted Marmor published on Robert Ball and Wilbur Cohen. Lavishing effusive praise on the two, the piece detailed their heroic efforts in building and preserving Social Security and Medicare. At the very end of the article, Marmor mentioned that Cohen and Ball, for all their sterling qualities, did have a crucial failing: they were unable "to ensure the supply of similarly gifted and wide-ranging leaders to follow them. . . . they did not produce their own institutional children."[8] Ball, who had worked closely with Marmor on the article to get the details of his life right, took the criticism to heart. Although he thought he had tried hard to find a successor, his efforts "obviously hadn't been successful." That became painfully obvious when it came time to suggest a commissioner of Social Security. Try at he might, Ball could only come up with "very, very few names."[9]

So one point of the National Academy was to draw new people into the field who might make it their career and eventually fill the top jobs. Hence, an informal network of experts already committed to Social Security would not be enough. Something would need to be done to make the field itself more attractive. In time, the National Academy of Social Insurance took on this task through such means as offering a prize for the best doctoral dissertation on the subject of social insurance and running a paid Washington internship program that put bright students in touch with the leaders of the field over the course of a Washington summer.[10]

Another source for the National Academy was Ball's experience during the 1970s with the Institute of Medicine. This organization, as part of the National Academy of Sciences, took its honorific responsibilities very seriously and elected its members, rather than merely inviting those interested in its activities to join. At the same time, it encouraged members to get involved in the practical projects, on real issues in the fields of medicine and health policy, that it sponsored. The IOM, then, was a prestigious organization, and to be made a member constituted a substantial honor. At the same time, it prided itself on being an activist organization that brought balanced, impartial views to important questions and sought to have influence in Washington. Ball saw something similar for the National Academy of Social Insurance.[11]

As the ideas gelled in Ball's mind, he sought the advice of others whom he trusted. He turned first to Alicia Munnell, a gifted economist who, as Ball put it, "may come closest to a successor." Part of Ball's attraction to her stemmed from the fact that he had converted her to his views. Munnell began her involvement in the field as a research assistant at the Brookings Institution, working for tax policy expert Joseph Pechman. At the time, Pechman, along with two younger economists, was writing a book about Social Security, published in 1968 and critical of the way in which Social Security mixed income redistribution and retirement protection. Ball, who saw the manuscript before publication, sent the authors sixty pages of comments trying to modify the book's argument. The person at Brookings who had the responsibility for checking out the comments and bringing them to the attention of the authors was Munnell.[12]

After Brookings, Munnell received a Ph.D. at Harvard, working under the direction of Martin Feldstein, a prominent public finance economist who criticized Social Security for, among other things, lowering the savings rate. In time, Munnell returned to Brookings and eventually wrote her own book on the future of Social Security that followed the economist's line that it was wrong to combine the elements of equity and adequacy within one program.[13] At one point, she became the staff director for a project that considered questions related to Social Security coverage for state and local employees and others employed by the government. "While many people were giving her quite a hard time in relation to her proposed report, I was supportive," said Ball, "and we got to know each other that way." After this exposure to Ball, she became a defender of the program. She illustrated, according to Ball, "the conversion of several pro–Social Security economists who first found the program confused by the inclusion of several objectives at once, but who later became staunch supporters of just this approach."[14]

It was an extremely important conversion, reuniting liberals who might have favored measures such as the negative income tax in the 1960s with older New Deal liberals such as Ball, who realized that Social Security provided as efficient and effective a form of income distribution as the political system was likely to yield. Furthermore, as more of the arguments in Social Security centered on the program's effect on the economy's behavior, people like Ball had more need for economists to come to the program's defense. In starting the National Academy, therefore, Ball put economists that he could trust, such as Alicia Munnell, at the head of the list.

Ball also reached out to Henry Aaron, one of the collaborators on Pechman's study and another of the economists to experience a conversion. Ball knew Aaron, among other contacts, from Aaron's service as assistant secretary for planning and evaluation in Joseph Califano's Department of Health, Education, and Welfare during the Carter administration and through their joint service on the advisory council that met at the end of Carter's term. From a wary beginning on the Pechman book, their friendship developed into a close one. Among other things both had rather unassuming, if somewhat remote, manners, a devotion to hard work, and razor-sharp analytical minds. They discovered that they could work with one another on op-ed pieces and other essays in persuasion.[15]

Alicia Munnell became the first president of the National Academy of Social Insurance, Aaron the first vice president, and Ball the first chairman of the board. Ball and Munnell usually took the lead in performing the tasks required to start up an organization, such as visiting foundations in an effort to get money, finding office space, and hiring staff.

For outreach to the philanthropic community, Ball depended on David Hamburg, a former head of the Institute of Medicine who had come to the job with little or no Washington experience. He quickly saw Ball, still in residence at the Institute of Medicine at the time, as an asset in learning how Congress functioned and how the government worked and made Ball one of his close advisers. After leaving the institute, Hamburg became a professor at Harvard and then head of the Carnegie Corporation, which ended up funding Ball's work and the work of the National Academy. Hamburg gave Ball access to some of the leading foundations. "Your leads have proven to be quite productive, yielding possible support in some cases and stimulating ideas in others," Ball told Hamburg.[16]

In addition to the large foundations, Ball also sought support from business organizations, relying on his business contacts from Social Security advisory councils. Both Alexander (Sandy) Trowbridge and Robert Beck, members of the National Commission on Social Security Reform and the heads of the National Association of Manufacturers and the Prudential Insurance Company, respectively, were enlisted to work on the academy's behalf.[17]

The first support for the academy came neither from Hamburg nor a private company but from money controlled by Elizabeth Wickenden. Someone with deep liberal roots and many Washington connections, Wickenden, a friend of Lyndon Johnson's, had worked for the National Youth Administration in the 1930s and as a Washington representative of the American Public Welfare Association in the 1940s. Unique among those whose interests centered on welfare, rather than Social Security, she appreciated the importance and promise of Social Security, even before it emerged as America's most important social welfare program in the 1950s. Her collaboration with Wilbur Cohen and Robert Ball had always been a tight one, and through money that she controlled she supported Ball's work after he left the Institute of Medicine. Using funds from the Marshall Field Foundation, which was liquidating its principle, Wickenden gave $10,000 to the Academy and enabled it to get started.[18]

With the money from Wickenden, the trio of Ball, Munnell, and Aaron set up an organizing committee that, in turn, invited the first, or founding, members to join. Among the people involved in the effort were Wilbur Cohen, Robert Myers (once again acting in a secondary role to Ball), Bert Seidman of the

AFL-CIO, Ted Marmor, Eric Kingson (from the commission staff) and Howard Young, an actuary with liberal tendencies and labor movement connections who had been useful to Ball on the national commission. Ball also secured the support of Senator Moynihan and asked him to suggest a Republican who would be helpful. Moynihan approached Senator John Heinz. "We are moving along well with the Academy," Ball reported to Heinz toward the end of 1986. "We have some money, not yet enough, but we've done most of the nuts and bolts things from incorporation to by-laws and are now ready to hire an executive director and get moving."[19]

Alicia Munnell helped to hire Pamela Larson as the National Academy's first staff director. At first Munnell and Ball tried to find someone for this particular position by placing an advertisement in the *Washington Post,* with no particular success. Then they used their own Washington contacts and ended up interviewing, among others, a local academic and an AFL-CIO staff member with whom Ball had worked closely. Neither seemed right for the job. Then Munnell found out about Larson, who had worked in the field of social services for the aged and was about to take a job with the American Public Welfare Association. During Larson's interview with Munnell and Ball, Munnell became convinced that Larson was the right person for the job, and Ball soon agreed. Larson had the requisite organizational abilities, energy, and enthusiasm for the job. She also had an exquisitely good touch with people, flattering some and needling others, so that people felt comfortable with her and wanted to work with her. "She has been just right in this kind of job and we were very fortunate to have found her at the beginning," said Ball.[20]

With offices in a small and secluded quadrangle located within easy walking distance of Union Station and the Capitol, the National Academy of Social Insurance, started in 1986, was in full operation by 1988. In an important change of routine that occurred in that year, Ball shifted his office from Massachusetts Avenue to the Academy offices at 505 Capitol Court NE. In the first years of the academy he was a constant presence, interested in every detail of the academy's existence and patiently pushing his own ideas of what the academy should be about and the projects it should undertake.

Increasingly, Robert Ball saw the National Academy as an important part of his legacy. "I hope to leave the National Academy of Social Insurance as a more or less permanent institution when I finally retire and consider its development over the next five years one of my highest priorities," he told David Hamburg.[21] Since Ball did such a disproportionate amount of the work and because the academy was his idea, it inevitably became his organization.

That sometimes gave concern to his collaborators, even Alicia Munnell, who worked in Boston and had to fly to Washington for academy events. Ball realized that he tended to function as the academy's chief executive, even though Munnell was nominally the president. As a result, she experienced "considerable uneasiness . . . from time-to-time, feeling that I was racing along and she was hurrying to catch up." She eventually resigned as president, and Ball had to scramble to find someone else for the position. This time he settled on Stanford Ross, Carter's Social Security commissioner and someone who was outside the ranks of Ball's close collaborators. Although Ross helped open up the academy to new influences and to new areas of focus, his appointment created tension with Ball and even with the accommodating Pamela Larson. Still, Ball appreciated the fact that Ross moved the academy into the area of national health insurance, despite Ball's initial caution.[22]

According to the academy's mission statement, it functioned as "a nonprofit, nonpartisan organization made up of the nation's leading experts on social insurance" that conducted research and enhanced "understanding and informed policymaking on social insurance."[23] For Ball, who had operated for so long as a partisan figure in Washington, it was difficult to separate research in the academic sense and advocacy in the Washington manner. Ball's inner conflict between the academy's research mission and his desire to advance the cause of Social Security came through most clearly in the choice of members.

One issue concerned whether or not to admit Haeworth Robertson, the former chief actuary of Social Security who, like many in his role, became a prominent program critic. Eventually he attacked the very idea of social insurance and advocated that a system of flat benefit take its place. Ball did not want to admit him because he thought a minimal requirement for membership should be "support for the general idea of social insurance." Munnell and Myers, among others, disagreed, arguing that the academy would be viewed as too exclusive, open only to liberals and hence not representative of the range of opinion in the field, if it rejected Robertson. Despite Ball's extraordinary influence over the academy's affairs, he lost the argument, and Robertson joined the academy. The admission of Carolyn Weaver, another noted program critic who had worked for Robert Dole on a number of important Social Security assignments, raised similar issues. She, too, received an invitation to join. On the one hand, Ball thought the presence of Robertson and Weaver led to a situation in which the academy was "afraid to take strong stands for social insurance principles because that wouldn't represent the views of all the members." On the other hand, he realized that having a broadly representative membership increased the organization's operational capacity. Ball remained uncharacteristically ambivalent on this matter.[24]

As the National Academy's founder, Ball cast a long shadow. He remained heavily involved in the academy's affairs, a constant figure at its annual meeting and at many of its functions, a dominant figure on its board, until he decided to give up his office at the academy, now moved into grander quarters on Massachusetts Avenue right across from the Brookings Institution, in 1997. Henry Aaron, Alicia Munnell, and Pamela Larson, among others, remained behind to continue the academy's work. In that sense, Ball felt the academy was a success. "There was a time when I felt a lot of pressure on the basis that there wasn't anybody else really working on" Social Security, he told the *New York Times* in 1999. "Now there's a whole group. They'll carry on whether I die tomorrow and do as good or better job."[25]

Long-Term Care

As Ball attended to the future by starting the National Academy in 1986, he also paid attention to the concerns of the present day. Responding to the perceived needs of the public and the political possibilities for new programs, he launched a new project. It began with David Hamburg, who was the sort of person who liked to keep in touch with his professional associates by sending them things to comment on and by involving them in projects that came his way. As head of the Carnegie Corporation, Hamburg became associated with a wide range of activities that extended well beyond his original interests in medicine. One Carnegie project, in which he asked Ball to participate, concerned retirement provisions for college professors. The distinguished panel associated with this study included the presidents of Wesleyan University and the University of Michigan, the head of CBS, and people such as Alicia Munnell and Robert Ball. Through this study, Ball gained an interest in the subject of long-term care and worked up a plan to finance long-term care for college and university personnel that appeared in print as part of the commission's work.[26]

His interest in the subject engaged, Ball spent a substantial amount of time on long-term care in the period leading up to the 1988 election. During this time, Medicare became an item on the policy agenda as Otis Bowen, a medical doctor and former governor of Indiana who served as a secretary of Health and Human Services for President Reagan, sought to expand the program to include better coverage for catastrophic health expenses. As usual, Ball played a role in the legislative consideration of this measure that resulted in the Medicare Catastrophic Coverage Act of 1988. In the spring of 1987, Ball told his liberal allies that he expected long-term care to become a major issue over the course of the next two years. When he testified on Bowen's Medicare bill, he made sure "to discuss the issue of long-term care insurance." The Ways and Means Committee appeared to be moving toward what Ball described as a "catastrophic, acute care program this year, but I am of course in favor of keeping the question of a new long-term care insurance program on the agenda of the primaries and beyond." He thought Senator George Mitchell (D–Maine), the head of the Finance Committee's health subcommittee, might be a useful ally.[27]

As Ball expected, the Medicare legislation passed in 1988 contained some items related to long-term care but not a comprehensive long-term care plan. The new Medicare law featured the new financing provision of a dedicated tax, based on a person's income, which proved to be so unpopular that Congress took the unusual step of repealing the legislation in 1989. During the law's brief time on the books it included such benefits as 150 days of treatment in a skilled nursing facility in a given year, up to 38 consecutive days of home health care for the acutely ill, up to 80 hours of in-home care in a given year for "chronically dependent individuals," and more than 210 days of hospice care for the terminally ill. Neither Ball nor his allies believed that these features were enough to cope with a problem that made many elderly and disabled people feel vulnerable and that threatened to disrupt the lives of their families. Hence, long-term care emerged as one of the issues in the 1988 campaign.[28]

In the summer of 1988, as George H. W. Bush faced Michael Dukakis in the presidential election, groups such as the American Association of Retired Persons, the Villers Foundation, and the Save Our Security Coalition joined together to create "Long Term Care '88." Throughout the campaign, the group tried to highlight the issue, pressuring each of the candidates to declare his approval of new long-term care legislation. According to the coalition, long-term care was "an idea that can elect the new president."[29]

Ball maintained active ties to each of the groups involved in this effort. In particular, he came to know Ron Pollack, the head of the Villers Foundation, who proved to be an important supporter of the National Academy and of Ball's own work. Pollack asked Ball to write a report on long-term care that the Villers Foundation, later known as the Families United for Senior Action Foundation, published and distributed in 1989.

At this point, George Bush had already defeated Dukakis, but Ball still saw long-term care as an important issue. Working on long-term care provided Ball with an opportunity to recapitulate many of the important ideas and concerns of his working life. In the 1930s and 1940s, Ball had concentrated on getting the Social Security program to provide sufficient retirement income to senior citizens. Long-term care figured into that. If a retiree faced an illness such as Alzheimer's that would rob him of his ability to live independently, then the costs of retirement became much greater than could conceivably be covered through Social Security's regular cash benefit program. In the 1950s, Ball concentrated on disability insurance, and the need for long-term care frequently followed from the circumstance of disability. In the 1960s, Ball made health insurance a principal area of endeavor, but the system he had helped to create focused on the provision of acute care in a hospital setting. Long-term care was vitally connected to retirement, disability, illness, and health care provision, yet it differed in important ways, since the objective was not cure so much as care, not cash income so much as social services. Long-term care as a social problem, therefore, touched on issues to which Ball had devoted his working lifetime, but the problem could not be solved through the specific programs that Ball had worked so hard to create. The solution required an expansion of America's welfare state.

Ball recommended an expansion of the nation's social welfare policies to accommodate long-term care in ways that were analogous to his recommendations for solving previous problems. In the book for the Villers Foundation, Ball, writing with Thomas Bethell, a Washington freelance writer and editor who would assist Ball on many future writing assignments, began by highlighting the demographic changes that made long-term care such a challenging issue. In the past, women had taken time from their lives to care for dependent elderly relatives or spouses. In the present, women worked outside of the home and no longer were available to fill the caretaker role. Many elderly people lived alone, far away from relatives of any sort. Even if the nearest relative lived right down the block, that relative, a child of someone in the old-old group, might already be in his or her 6os or 7os and unable to cope with the stressful demands of providing care to someone with Alzheimer's or another debilitating illness. As a consequence, the only alternative was to put the relative, even one with relatively mild dementia who could live at home with the proper kind of assistance, in an expensive and often forbidding nursing home.

Ball realized that Medicare was not designed to handle the problem. It covered home care and nursing home expenses only in connection with a recovery from an acute illness. It limited reimbursement for home health care to people under the active treatment of a physician who required intermittent skilled nursing care as part of a convalescent plan. Such things as homemaker services and the preparation of meals fell outside of Medicare's purview. The only key change in the 1988 law was the provision of respite care for people who needed a break from attending to a dependent individual at home.

In the absence of better long-term coverage within Medicare, Medicaid, a welfare program run by the states, had become the nation's major payer for long-term care by default. Not only did that skew the Medicaid program toward chronic care and leave less money available for other forms of illness, but it also led to what Ball regarded as an inherently unsatisfactory policy result. In language echoing that of many of his other reports, Ball wrote, "people who have worked and supported themselves all their lives resent deeply the notion of being forced to submit to close financial scrutiny before they qualify for help. They would much prefer to have the opportunity to plan ahead and protect themselves in advance by contributing to a social insurance program such as Social Security." In this passage, Ball reasserted the truth of the old social policy epigram by which he lived: programs for poor people made poor programs.[30]

Could people salve their dignity by buying a private insurance policy to cover the risk of one day having to pay for long-term care? In Ball's opinion, no. Just as he had once pointed out the failure of private insurance to provide disability and health insurance at a cost that people could afford, he now devoted the bulk of the long-term care report to showing the shortcomings of private insurance in that area. Policies existed, but they were expensive, restricted in their eligibility, not easily renewed beyond their term, limited in the benefits they covered, and unprotected against inflation. A policy that paid $100 a day for nursing home care might cover only a small portion of the risk by the time a member of generation X needed a nursing home. Although private insurers could devise better policies, it was not clear they could sell them at the price they would have to charge.

Could a way be found out of the dilemma posed by great public need and high private cost? In Ball's opinion, the answer lay in socializing the cost through social insurance. As in nearly everything Ball wrote, he touted the virtues of social insurance: "Social insurance derives its unique strength from the principle that the best form of self-protection is mutual aid on a universal scale; when everyone contributes, everyone can be protected." Through this form of collective action, nearly everyone, old or young, sick or well, could be covered, and everyone would be in the "same boat," creating "broad support for maintaining the well-being of the program and protecting the quality of benefits." Problems would disappear. There would be no need to screen out bad risks; low-income people could be covered at a reasonable cost; full inflation protection could be provided.[31]

Even Ball admitted that the design of a long-term care social insurance program posed considerable challenges. He realized that any plan should emphasize home care, but he knew that Congress would be wary of a plan that paid for housekeeping services. To keep costs down and the caseload under control, it would be better to focus on those who met "reasonably severe disability criteria—such as inability to perform unassisted a specified number of the activities of daily living." Even so, Ball must have known how subjective a concept disability of any sort was, and if he forgot, he had only to look at the volatility of the disability insurance program or be reminded of that fact by one of his actuarial critics such as Robert Myers. He therefore felt compelled to hedge his proposal with many safeguards. There would be co-payments and the strict management of individual care plans to "avoid the use of unnecessary services." There were administrative complications as well. Ball thought that the states should run the home care program but with close supervision at the federal level, even though he knew that such a distribution of responsibility had not worked out well in the disability program.[32]

Then came the formidable problem of designing a benefit for nursing home care. Most people who went into a nursing home would have some income from Social Security. Ball saw no reason why some of this money should not be spent to pay part of the cost of the nursing home. After all, the person got room and board inside the nursing home and no longer needed to use Social Security benefits for that (unless there was a dependent who remained at home, in which case alternate rules would apply). But even if one agreed on an acceptable amount that a person would pay out-of-pocket, one still needed to consider just what sort of nursing home benefit social insurance should provide. Here Ball thought that social insurance's contribution might be to protect the assets of people who would one day go back into the community or who had a spouse or other dependent still living in the community. After making several alternative suggestions, he settled on a nursing home benefit of only a year but one that could be extended indefinitely for someone with a spouse or dependent living in a community. He read the data to show that few people who lived in a nursing home for more than a year ever returned home. For single people who would never return to the community, the protection of assets that would make it possible for them to live independently did not constitute a pressing social need. Such people could spend down their assets and, if necessary, fall back on Medicaid. Hence, Ball put the first emphasis on home care, rather than institutional care, and provided a limited but nonetheless socially meaningful nursing home benefit as part of his proposed package.[33]

Even limited home care and nursing home benefits that came with co-payments would cost a substantial amount of money. Hence, even more than on the design of the program, Ball's proposals foundered on the issue of cost. According to the terms of the 1983 amendments, 15.3 percent of taxable payrolls would be dedicated to Social Security and Medicare in 1990. For many the employee share of the Social Security tax would be the highest tax they would pay. Ronald Reagan liked to boast of how he had cut taxes, and George Bush offered television viewers the chance to read his lips on the issue of no new taxes. Still, the taxes from the 1983 amendments continued to affect the nation's employers and employees. Far from being tolerant of new taxes, members of Congress, including Senator Daniel Patrick Moynihan in a serious break with Ball that continued to escalate in the years ahead, thought in terms of repealing the Social Security tax increase set to go into effect in 1990. It took considerable political effort to preserve the 1990 taxes at their scheduled levels; coming up with an additional $20 billion dollars to pay for long-term care benefits in 1990, with costs sure to rise in the years ahead, turned out to be impossible.[34]

Ball made many financing proposals, none of which worked. One could enact dedicated personal and corporate taxes, but that approach had proved less than popular in the 1988 Medicare amendments. One could remove the cap on earnings subject to Social Security taxes for both employers and employees or for employers alone. One could increase the estate tax, but George Bush wanted to repeal it. One could tax Social Security benefits more heavily for wealthier individuals and dedicate the proceeds to long-term care, yet the wealthy showed little inclination to reduce their retirement income. Because of these difficulties, the long-term care proposal, to use show business slang, opened well during the 1988 campaign but did not have legs.[35]

The 1991 Advisory Council

Other problems, such as those associated with Medicare and the long-term funding of Social Security, crowded out long-term care from the policy agenda. Ball had a chance to look at Medicare and broader issues associated with health care finance as part of his service on a Social Security advisory council that was created by the Bush administration in June 1989.[36]

Ball owed his appointment to this council, at age 75, to his association with John Rother of the AARP. Rother had once worked for Senator John Heinz on the staff of the Senate Committee on Aging and had gotten to know Deborah Steelman, another Capitol Hill staffer. Steelman had gone on to serve as an adviser to Vice President Bush on health affairs, and later President Bush named her as the chair of the advisory council created in 1989. Given a chance to choose between two people by Steelman, Rother chose Ball as the council's representative of older Americans.

Ball's appointment marked the third time he had been asked to serve on a Social Security advisory council since his retirement as commissioner. He was becoming a perennial, much like his friend Douglas Brown, who served repeatedly from the 1930s through the 1960s. Even more than Brown, Ball took a leadership role on advisory councils. In 1989 he once again became the head of the liberal faction that also included the labor representatives and, on most occasions, John Dunlop, the distinguished Harvard professor of labor relations and former secretary of Labor in Republican administrations.

The council that reported in 1991 conducted itself with much less decorum than had the Greenspan Commission. The initial staff director was eased out and replaced by Anne LaBelle, whom Ball described as a politically oriented person who considered him her enemy and whose "suspicions were easily aroused." Steelman, Ball believed, wanted a radical restructuring of Medicare, converting it into a catastrophic plan with a very high deductible. She hoped to encourage the spread of private insurance and to use the savings from Medicare for other health care expenditures. She also wanted the states to experiment with health insurance plans and to become, in the old Brandeis expression, laboratories of reform. Ball saw things completely differently. He and his allies sought to negotiate over a national health insurance plan with universal coverage. The two sides talked past one another in a contentious atmosphere that, according to one staff member detailed by SSA to the commission, often resembled a food fight. Although Ball remained his affable, polite, and courtly self, he realized that the council would not be the vehicle to advance the health care finance discussion.

For all of the difficulties, Ball worked as hard or harder on the advisory council as anyone associated with it. He sent Anne La-Belle long lists of questions for the council to consider and long critiques of the council's draft report. He also drafted a plan that he circulated first to the council and later to his friends and associates with an interest in health insurance. The contents of the plan showed Ball's attempt to face the fiscal and political realities of the 1980s. Instead of creating health insurance on the European or Canadian model, he suggested instead that it be based on the American experience and utilize the strengths of existing employer-based health insurance, Medicare, and Medicaid.[37]

The keys to the plan were an expansion of Medicare and a new mandate that all private employers provide their employees with health insurance. This approach represented something of a reversal for Ball. Despite his adherence to the idea of social insurance and his strong belief that benefits should be preserved, he had, almost from the beginning, criticized Medicare for its failure to control health care costs. He wrote in 1984, for example, "There is no inherent reason to fear greater and greater expenditures for medical care as compared to other types of expenditures if the results add to the length and quality of human life and the medical care is efficiently provided. But there is reason to try to eliminate useless, harmful or even marginal practices and to try to deliver services at costs that are as low as is consistent with reasonable compensation of health professionals, quality care, and the encouragement of practice improvements." Medicare, he argued, needed "cost control measures."[38] As for mandated approaches such as President Nixon had proposed in the early 1970s, Ball had always thought that a Social Security approach, such as in the Kennedy-Mills bill, was superior. In 1991, however, he shifted directions, using Medicare and a mandated approach as important bases on which to build adequate health insurance coverage.

In his new health insurance plan, Ball proposed extending Medicare so that coverage began at age 60, combining the payments to hospitals and doctors into one program with a new way of paying for doctors' expenses, reinstating the catastrophic coverage passed in 1988, and even including a few long-term care benefits. Most importantly of all, he suggested that Medicare become a catastrophic program for people of all ages by taking responsibility for all expenditures above $25,000 a year per individual. That would make it easier to mandate coverage of a standard benefit through private insurance for all workers and their dependents from age 1 to age 60. Infants and pregnant women would have their needs met by expanding state-administered programs already legislated for that purpose so that such programs covered all who were eligible regardless of income.

As for paying for the new plan, Ball thought that employers, who would be grateful for the way that the expanded Medicare program relieved them of expenses, might be asked to pay a higher payroll tax for Medicare. Retired workers would be required to pay higher taxes on their Social Security benefits, and employers would pay Social Security taxes on their entire payroll. Ball also sought to tap some of the surplus in the Social Security program that had developed as a result of the increased taxes in the 1983 amendments, combined with the robust economy after 1982 and the fact that new retirees in the 1980s came in large part from the relatively small cohort born in the 1930s.

This suggestion met another political need of the moment. As Ball knew, key political figures, such as Senator Moynihan, objected to the growing surplus in Social Security. Advised by Bob Myers, who had never liked large surpluses in the Social Security trust fund, Moynihan had wanted to roll back the Social Security tax scheduled for 1990. Aware of that political pressure, Ball now argued that Social Security might be changed to a pay-as-you-go basis as Moynihan and Myers wanted. Instead of rolling back taxes, however, Ball wanted to spend the extra money to expand Medicare. The strategy resembled previous efforts to expand the program that had been so successful in the period between 1950 and 1972, an effort to harvest the 1980s prosperity to produce national health insurance.[39]

Ball held out some hope for his plan as an entering point in discussions that centered on extending health insurance coverage to the more than 35 million people, the majority of whom held regular jobs, who did not have health insurance. But he failed to gain endorsement for the plan in the advisory council. Instead, the advisory council ended in disarray, its work neglected by President Bill Clinton when his administration began to explore the health insurance issue in 1993. With typical tenacity, Ball kept refining his health insurance plan after the advisory council concluded its work in 1991. He joked with his friend John Trout, who was starting to write a biography of Ball, that the health insurance plan, once passed into law, might be a fitting last chapter for the book. Much to Ball's regret, that last chapter never got written.[40]

The 1994–1996 Advisory Council

Instead of working on Bill Clinton's health insurance program, Robert Ball spent much of that administration engaged in a fight for the survival of the Social Security program. His chief point of entry into the discussion consisted of his service on yet another Social Security advisory council, convened in the spring of 1994, which issued its report in January of 1997. Later, as the Clinton administration grappled with specific Social Security recommendations, Ball participated indirectly in the White House discussions.

If one followed the history of Social Security finance, there should have been no heated discussions of Social Security's solvency in the 1990s. The problem had been faced repeatedly and repeatedly solved. After the passage of the 1972 amendments, the actuaries certified that the program was soundly financed for the next seventy-five years. Then, in a short time, inflation caused by the first oil crisis threw the system out of balance. Congress came to the rescue of the program in the 1977 amendments only to have the second oil crisis disrupt the program's financing. That led to the Greenspan Commission and the 1983 amendments and the assurance that, once again, the system was sound for the next seventy-five years. Ball did his part to spread confidence in the system after the 1983 amendments. When the Committee on Economic Development issued a report with the unsettling title "Social Security: From Crisis to Crisis," Ball enlisted

Greenspan and Myers to write a piece with him in which they stated, "We believe that it is highly probable that the social security system will be financially healthy over at least the next two decades." It would take double-digit unemployment and high inflation to throw the system out of whack, and once beyond the mid-1980s, even that would not be enough to disrupt it. Meanwhile, the surpluses kept accumulating. As Ball told the Joint Economic Committee in 1989, the trust funds were "building at an astonishing rate." By the end of 1989, the OASDI trust fund level would reach $168.3 billion, and the system would continue to pay out less than it took in and to grow, according to the experts, for the next forty years.[41]

For all of that, a little more than a decade after the 1983 amendments, the trustees reported that, once again, the program faced a long-term deficit. That announcement, combined with concerns over how to finance the retirement of the baby boomers and a general sense that the system could never be fixed, led to new discussions about how to save Social Security. In this round, proposals that had previously been off the table, such as replacing Social Security with a mandated private savings plan, gained new legitimacy.

It was only reasonable to ask what had happened, particularly given the repeated assurances that the system was in good financial shape and the surprising news that, in the short run, the system had done better than expected since 1983. Nor was the problem the result of a sudden discovery that the baby boom would disrupt the system. To be sure, the ratio of workers to beneficiaries would fall in the future from about 3.3 in 1995 to 1.8. That explained why the cost per individual and hence the tax rate that each individual must bear would rise in the future, but the declining ratios had already been figured into the 1983 calculations, and nothing had happened in the interim to change those ratios. The sources of the expected shortfall of 2.17 percent of taxable payroll lay elsewhere. For one thing the mere passage of time shifted the 75-year-period one more year into the high-cost period, so the simple passage of time made the estimates deteriorate. That explains part, but only part, of this deficit. For another thing, disability rates continued to rise beyond expectations. The actuaries also made their assumptions about real wage growth more pessimistic and changed some of their methods of estimating costs. The result, despite favorable factors such as increased immigration and fertility rates, was a projected long-term deficit.[42]

That meant Ball would have to save Social Security again, only this time without the stimulus of a short-term deadline for action and in the face of a much more distrusting public worried that expert predictions often failed to come true and concerned about the retirement of the baby boomers. A neoliberal president such as Bill Clinton did not have the same policy enthusiasms as did FDR, and his pre-Carter Democratic successors. At least since the Carter era, substantial doubts had developed, even among Democrats, that the Social Security payments could be as generous in the future as they had been in the past. The year 2000, a magnet for people's attention as the new millennium approached, would mark the sixty-fifth anniversary of the Social Security Act. The fiftieth anniversary had been a year of celebration and self-congratulation after the passage of the 1983 amendments, but even then there had been questions among those who were 25 to 34 years old about whether Social Security would be there for them. The *New York Times* led its story on the fiftieth anniversary by mentioning the "erosion of public confidence in social security." In 1994, as Ball prepared at age 80 to serve on another advisory council, those doubts remained, and ahead loomed the year 2000, when Social Security would reach retirement age and possibly be replaced by something else.[43]

For Ball the differences among Democrats on Social Security were illustrated by his disagreements with Lawrence Thompson. Ball had known and worked closely with Larry Thompson, an economist with superior analytic skills, at least since the Carter administration when Thompson had directed the Office of Research and Statistics at the Social Security Administration and helped Ball with the 1977 amendments. "I thought he was the one person in government," Ball remembered, "with the knowledge, experience and skills to make an outstanding commissioner." When the Democrats returned to power in 1993, Ball lobbied for Thompson's appointment and nearly got it. In the White House background checks, a problem developed concerning Thompson's payment of Social Security taxes for someone who worked in his home. It was a minor matter that Thompson had rectified, but in the political climate at the beginning of the Clinton administration it was enough to derail his appointment. He settled for the position of deputy commissioner and in effect ran the agency for a number of years. As a consequence, he exerted a major influence over selecting members of the 1994 commission.

Despite his admiration for Ball, Thompson's view's on the future of the program now differed from Ball's. He decided that with Social Security taxes so high after 1990 (15.3 percent of taxable payroll), they could not be raised further. There might be minor adjustments such as bringing all state and local employees into the system but not much else. If no more money came in, that meant that benefits would have to be cut because of the long-range financing problem. To make up for the shortfall between the benefits the system could afford and the benefits the system had promised, Thompson thought workers should be required to invest additional amounts that would be deducted from their paychecks and put into individual private accounts. The additional deductions would, he hoped, not be considered tax increases. Ball disagreed. It was a disagreement between two Democrats with a close working relationship.[44]

In selecting nominees to serve on the advisory council, Thompson gravitated toward people who held his point of view: Democrats who understood the political realities and economic constraints facing Social Security. To chair the council, he picked and gained approval for Edward Gramlich, known as Ned, who was a public finance economist with a policy bent. Although currently the dean of the School of Public Policy at the University of Michigan, Gramlich had substantial Washington experience, having served, among other posts, as acting director of the Congressional Budget Office in 1987. Like Thompson, Gramlich did not favor using the Social Security contributions for private accounts but wanted some mechanism to make up what he saw as the inevitable shortfall.[45]

As for Ball, he had to fight to get on the council. "They really didn't know how to turn me down when I made clear that I would like to be on it," he said. Conveniently forgetting his efforts to get appointed to the Carter era advisory council, Ball noted, "That is something I have almost never done in the past but I felt I needed to be on the Council to have my point of view strongly represented." Once on the council, he found the usual assortment of people who represented organized labor and sympathized with his point of view. He also made common cause with Edith Fierst, an attorney who specialized in women's issues as they affected Social Security and, surprisingly, with Thomas W. Jones, the president and chief operating officer of TIAA-CREF. "He and I hit it off real well," Ball recalled, and "he joined the labor people and Edith Fierst to make up the five people who more or less followed my lead." Once again, Ball found himself the head of a caucus, and once again he did more than his share of the work in formulating positions and negotiating with other council members.[46]

If Ball could count, more or less, on the support of six people, that still left seven others with whom he disagreed. Carolyn Weaver, a public choice economist who believed that Social Security required fundamental revision and reform and who felt that Ball and his allies often manipulated public opinion to achieve a less than optimal result, joined the advisory council through her ties to Senator Dole, who was at the peak of his influence and about to be the Republican Party's presidential candidate. Ball regarded her as an ideologue and an unrelenting critic of Social Security. Sylvester Schieber, the vice president of a private pension consulting company, also thought that Social Security should be privatized. Since Ball decided there was little possibility for compromise with Weaver or Schieber, he regarded the other five members as swing votes.

Unlike Alan Greenspan in 1983, Ned Gramlich abandoned the effort to come to a consensus. He decided instead that it would be best if he put the major alternatives before the country. His attitude infuriated Ball, who refused to recognize substituting a private plan for Social Security as a legitimate alternative. Nonetheless, five members of the council, led by Schieber and Weaver, backed what they called personal security accounts. Ball and his allies wanted to preserve the present system and provide it with sufficient funding so that it could be sustained indefinitely into the future. Gramlich, along with Marc Twinney, a retired Ford Motor Company executive, offered an intermediate proposal, similar to Larry Thompson's notion, that he called publicly held individual accounts. Hence, when the report appeared, it did not recommend a particular plan but instead laid out three options among which policymakers should choose. "A deeply divided Social Security advisory council yesterday put forth several

drastic and controversial changes to the giant retirement system
as a means of saving it from the severe financial shortfalls it faces
starting in the next century," the *Washington Post* reported.[47]

Ball regretted that he could not reach a compromise with one
other member of the council, such as Gramlich, Twinney, or Joan
T. Bok, a New England business executive and a devoted Democrat, yet he realized that the advisory council report was just a
step in the process and not a blueprint for legislation.

Despite Ball's misgivings, the group agreed on a number of
important findings and principles that Ball helped to write up in
the final report. For example, the council endorsed traditional objectives of Social Security, such as benefits adjusted for inflation,
universal coverage, family benefits, and benefits that protected
the lowest wage earners against poverty. Even in the contested
realm of finance, the council came to some agreement. Because
the council concluded that "little support exists today for increasing payroll tax rates by 2.17 percentage points to provide long-
term balance," all of the members agreed that alternative sources
of revenue would be required. In one key recommendation, the
council backed away from the pay-as-you-go approach to Social
Security financing, which Ball had supported in the previous advisory council as a means of freeing up money for health insurance, and instead came out in favor of "partial advance funding."
That implied an effort to collect money in advance to prefund
some of the system's future liabilities.[48]

More specific recommendations proved harder to reach. Despite the best efforts of the AFL-CIO representatives, the council
came out against general revenue financing for Social Security, a
significant omission in light of subsequent efforts to spend part
of the budgetary surplus to "save" Social Security. The council
also arrived at two recommendations that could be regarded as
benefit cuts. One was to increase the number of years used in
computing indexed average wages (which would lower those
wages), and the other, which Ball opposed but his ally Edith
Fierst supported, was to accelerate the transition of the "normal"
retirement age, at which full benefits would be paid, to age 67
and to raise the age "in line with overall longevity."[49]

Throughout the discussions, the council put a new emphasis
on workers receiving their money's worth from Social Security.
Benefits for each generation of workers should "bear a reasonable

relationship to total taxes paid, plus interest."[50] The council met at a time when the great bull market appeared to be enriching millions of Americans who put stocks and mutual funds into their private investment accounts or who participated in retirement funds such as TIAA-CREF. Even previously threadbare professionals, such as professors and rabbis, began to speak of the inevitability that they would have hundreds of thousands of dollars, if not more, at their disposal upon retirement. Social Security, by way of contrast, offered a much poorer rate of return and could not compete with the appeal of private alternatives such as 401-K accounts. In the past, Ball had pointed out that Social Security offered many compensating advantages, such as defined benefits indexed to the rate of inflation and life insurance and disability protection, yet these advantages no longer seemed so compelling as the rate of inflation fell and as the rate of return on private investment rose.

Tom Jones of TIAA-CREF provided Ball with a way out of the dilemma. He proposed that some of the money in the Social Security trust funds be invested in stocks, just as his organization invested the money it received from teachers, universities, and others in stocks. Despite the many practical difficulties, Ball saw the attractiveness of the suggestion: "The response to the money's worth argument among the six of us on the Council who favored traditional Social Security was to argue for partial reserve financing and the investment of part of the fund build-up in stocks with their greater return and thus a bigger bang for the buck from Social Security contributions. When you factored in the administrative advantages of Social Security, then Social Security came out well in the money's worth comparison." Unlike the personal savings accounts advocated by the conservatives that would result in many private accounts, some of them very small, Ball's proposal would keep the Social Security money together and avoid the transactions costs that drove up the price of private investments. At base, then, Ball wanted to preserve Social Security as a defined benefit plan and use the stock market as a means toward that end.[51]

Although the Ball group hedged on its recommendation to meet Social Security's financing problems by investing part of the Social Security trust funds in private equities, the proposal was nonetheless an audacious one.[52] For one thing it violated much of what Ball had previously said and believed. In 1984, for example, he wrote that stocks "that produce high yields do so because investment in them involves high risk. . . . The various Advisory Councils on Social Security . . . have concluded in the past, as I have, that investing large amounts of Social Security funds in common stocks would raise serious questions about the governance of private industry. . . . [T]he managers of the Social Security Trust Funds, as representatives of the new owners of a large part of American business, could hardly avoid responsibility for the management decisions of private industry. I believe this would be an undesirable result and inconsistent with a free enterprise economy."[53] Ball now reversed course. In thinking about how to come up with the 2.17 percent of covered payroll to reduce Social Security's long-term deficit, he relied upon familiar devices, such as increasing the taxation of benefits and putting some of the money from one trust fund (for Medicare) into another (for OASDI). He also went along with the increase in the computation period to determine average wages and recommended the extension of coverage. For the remaining 0.80 percent of payroll, however, he suggested that "Social Security should have the . . . freedom to invest part of its funds in the broad equities market representing practically the entire American economy." Ball thought that as much as 40 percent of the accumulated Social Security funds might be invested in private equities through an expert board charged with investing "solely for the economic benefit of Social Security participants and not for any other economic, social, or political objective."[54]

It made for tricky politics. It required the general public or Congress to recognize the distinction between a defined benefit program, in which future benefits of a specified amount were guaranteed, and a defined contribution program, in which one put a specified amount of money into a fund and took one's chances. Ball thought that the advantages of a defined benefit plan were self-evident. If, however, people lost sight of that difference between Ball's plan and the other plans, then they might argue that it would be better to invest their money on their own, rather than let the government do it for them. The plan also had to face the objections that Ball had previously raised against investing public funds in private companies. Would Congress or the public tolerate putting billions of dollars into a tobacco company or a corporation accused of discriminating against blacks or women, whatever the rate of return from that investment? Would the government be able to protect against insider trading in which people with advanced knowledge of the government's investments could make a killing? Would the investment of so much money in the stock market create adverse economic effects? Would the government be able to obtain a sufficient rate of return to keep the system solvent? One could only make educated guesses at the answers to these questions. It was no wonder, then, that even Ball's allies on the advisory council had doubts about the stock market strategy. They lacked his mental agility and his nerve, his ability to reinvent himself at age 82.

Aware of the departure that the plan represented, Ball accompanied it with the reassuring boilerplate about Social Security, as if the words that had appeared in so many of his reports—the Social Security bureaucrats used to call this boilerplate in congressional reports "the guff"—could be used as a talisman to ward off his enemies. Social Security was "universal; an earned right; wage related; contributory and self-financed; redistributive; not means-tested; wage-indexed; inflation protected; and compulsory." Although the statement implied that these ideas developed from the ideals of Social Security's founders, many of them, such as the system being wage-indexed and inflation protected, came from Ball. If he had his way, Social Security would now get a new twist.[55]

To the Present

The advisory council report mattered only to the extent that it influenced public policy. Ball realized that the next level of discussion would be at the White House. First, Clinton needed to get through the 1996 election, and then he could think about his legacy. One part might be saving Social Security and making it safe for America's baby boomers and their children, people like Bill Clinton and his daughter, Chelsea. In the fall of 1997 Ball set to work writing memos on Social Security to Gene Sperling, the director of Clinton's National Economic Council. Sperling sat on a committee of eight that included the secretary of the Treasury, the head of the Office of Management and Budget, and the commissioner of Social Security, and that was charged with the task of recommending a course of action on Social Security to Clinton. Sperling assured Ball that he would distribute the memos to all of the committee members. Ball knew that many of the eight started out with sympathy for the plan devised by Ned Gramlich, whom Clinton had appointed as a governor of the Federal Reserve Board. Larry Summers, a high Treasury official and an acclaimed economist who would later become president of Harvard, was "all out for Gramlich," according to Ball. That meant that Ball's first task was to discredit the Gramlich plan and only after that to promote his own. At the end of the year, Ball confessed that "win, lose or draw, this is about the best I can do."[56]

Ball noted that the proposal put forward by Schieber and Weaver had always struck him "as a stalking horse but I fear that the IA plan [Gramlich's plan] might be taken seriously. I am deeply concerned about it." Ball had deep reservations about this plan, beginning with the fact that it would reduce guaranteed Social Security benefits by 30 percent on average. Making up the difference depended on the returns a worker received from an individual account. For the average investor, the plan would protect the status quo, but those with less than average investment returns would receive less than they would have under the present law. Nor did the harm end there. Ball suspected that many workers would figure out ways to gain access to the funds in their accounts before they reached old age, leaving them with inadequate savings for retirement. The Gramlich plan would also undermine support for the Social Security system by producing lower and lower benefits, causing the more successful investors to demand that more of their payroll taxes be shifted over into private accounts. That would put the redistributive features of Social Security at risk. Because the plan took more out of worker's wages than did the present system, it would leave less money to solve Medicare's financial problems.[57]

Then there were the administrative problems. Advocates of the Gramlich plan expected workers to choose among five to ten plans, with the government responsible for each fund's investments. At the very least, therefore, employers would have to deduct the additional 1.6 percent from wages every pay period and then send the proceeds to the government in a way that allowed the government to put each worker's contributions into the correct account. It was a formidable administration task that, if the government performed inefficiently, would discredit the program.[58]

Having argued against the Gramlich plan, Ball made proposals of his own. Rather than suggest any one plan, he gave the Clinton administration a large table with many options in a manner analogous to the approach he took on the Greenspan Commission. The table contained some nine items. Among them were a very modest tax increase of half a percentage point in the tax rate and a proposal to "correct" the consumer price index so that it more accurately reflected the cost of living and presumably lowered future cost-of-living adjustments. The list also included the notion of investing part of Social Security's surplus in stocks. Ball then mixed and matched the items in three different ways, coming up with three packages that would solve the problem. The point was to show that the problem could be fixed in politically viable ways that did not involve taxes as high as in the Gramlich plan. As Ball noted, the Gramlich plan "relies on higher deductions from workers' earnings to buy higher benefits for some participants . . . at the cost of lower benefits for others, along with less certainty for all about which group they might end up in."[59]

As Ball waited for the president to decide on what approach he should take, he continued to refine his own plan. In the summer of 1998, he distributed a plan that he believed to be the best, with no benefit cuts and the only tax increases coming from raising the wage base on which employers and employees made contributions to Social Security. By far the largest savings in the plan came from investing Social Security funds in stocks. He added a new wrinkle by permitting workers, on a voluntary basis, to have their employers deduct an additional 2 percent of their earnings covered by the Social Security earnings base and having the employer forward this money to the IRS. Workers would have three choices about how they wished to invest their money in what Ball called "supplemental savings accounts." The plan, according to Ball, both restored Social Security to long-term balance and also established what he described as a "simple, effective way for individuals to set up savings accounts supplemental to Social Security."[60]

When the president made his own proposal in January 1999, he added another twist. He suggested that more than half of the federal budget surplus be transferred to Social Security over the course of the next fifteen years. That would add, according to Social Security Commissioner Ken Apfel, some $2.8 trillion to the Social Security trust funds. The president appeared to accept the points that Ball had made during the long debate over Social Security financing. In particular, he used the idea of investing some of the Social Security trust funds in private stocks, and he created his own form of a supplemental savings account that he called Universal Savings Accounts. Although it was difficult to measure the degree of Ball's influence over the Clinton proposals, it was clear that Ball's activities had affected the debate.[61]

Ball accepted the president's proposal with his customary agility. One of the nine guiding principles that Ball held so dear and repeated so often was that Social Security was "contributory and self-financed." That meant that the system did not rely on general revenues. The 1996 advisory council had endorsed that idea as part of its report. In the face of Clinton's proposals, however, Ball put that scruple aside. In fact, Ball had once been an advocate of general revenue financing, as had Douglas Brown and the other members of the 1938 advisory council. Although support for a general revenue contribution diminished in the late 1950s, Ball "kept advocating it as late as 1978." Then he changed his mind. "I just could not see a Commissioner of Social Security, as I had been, successfully arguing before Congress" for general revenues, Ball said. Then along came the Clinton proposal that left Ball "astounded" but "pleased" at the return of a policy he had once advocated and then abandoned.[62] Ball's May 2001 "Social Security Plus" plan contained the notion of paying off about half of the unfunded obligations of the present system by "making transfers from the general fund of the Treasury of $100 billion in 2002, and in amounts that are the same percentage of GDP (about 0.9 percent) for subsequent years through 2023."[63]

Ball also kept after the Clinton administration not to abandon the idea of what he called "direct Social Security investment in equities." He wanted to make sure that it was included in the budget for fiscal 2001 that the Clinton administration would present to Congress early in 2000. He sent a memo to key officials in the Treasury Department and the White House that reflected his continued engagement in the politics of Social Security. Although Ball understood that the idea of investing Social Security funds in stocks had no chance of being adopted in the near future, he believed it was important to condition the long-run policy environment. "It is important to keep this policy option alive for the longer run," he wrote. Just transferring part of the budget surplus to Social Security would not be enough to offer Republicans in negotiations. If the idea of investing Social Security funds in stocks was not included in the budget, it would not be taken seriously. "This leaves us with one less way—and an important way—of closing the long-term gap between the final transfer and full Social Security financing," he concluded. After high-level discussions and consultations with other experts who reinforced Ball's message, the Clinton administration decided to include investment of Social Security funds in its budget, just as Ball wanted.[64]

At the beginning of 2000 Ball looked forward as often as backward. On the one hand, he attended to producing a book of his essays that he had written between the early 1940s through the end of the century—including a piece meant to influence the 2000 election. He also worked on organizing his papers so that they could be sent off to the State Historical Society in Wisconsin. On the other hand, he wrote a report that dealt with the fine points of the assumptions that lay behind the seventy-five-year estimates for the cost of Social Security. He remained very involved in discussions of Social Security reform, so much so that he regretted he did not have more time to spend on Medicare. Still, he remained in touch with Senator Kennedy and his staff, making strategy over the next steps in the fight for national health insurance. At the same time, the work of the National Academy of Social Insurance engaged his attention, and he continued to make proposals for projects it might undertake.[65]

The Clinton years ended, and the Gore years never began. Ball did his part to assure Gore's election by taping a commercial that called attention to Gore's commitment to the Social Security program. The commercial received substantial air time in battleground states, such as Pennsylvania, and might have accounted for some of the vice president's late campaign bounce in those states. In the end, though, it was George W. Bush, rather than Al Gore, who became president, and Ball prepared for another Republican regime.[66]

A new president took up the cause of privatizing Social Security. In an effort to create the necessary momentum, he appointed a commission, headed by none other than former senator Daniel Patrick Moynihan, to come up with a specific proposal. It was Ball among others who considered the Democrats' response. When Senator Tom Daschle (D–South Dakota) received an invitation to join Bush's commission, he consulted with Robert Ball, who helped draft his letter of refusal. Unlike previous commissions, Ball wanted the Democrats to have nothing to do with this one because he did not want to legitimize the privatizing of Social Security. When Bush announced his commission, CBS News dispatched its White House correspondent to interview Ball and used a sound bite from the interview on the evening news.

It was an act that could not be sustained indefinitely. Ball spent more and more time in New Hampshire, although he no longer drove from Washington to get there. Now he took the plane. He had more difficulty remembering names, although he retained a wide range of information about Social Security and retained his keen sense of political strategy. Ball watched as his friend Arthur Flemming, the former secretary of Health, Education, and Welfare and constant presence in Social Security affairs, remained active well into his nineties. He also saw that Flemming had lost some of his flexibility, his edge, and ultimately his effectiveness. Ball hoped that he would know when to get off the stage, although in his case disengaging from current affairs might mean leaving the backstage. Still, the battle over Social Security's future raged, and people turned to Ball for advice. Even in the era of the second George Bush, Robert Ball, who had done so much to determine the course of Social Security politics for more than half a century, was a player.[67]

Conclusion

The life of Robert Ball illuminates key developments in the history of Social Security.

The program's founding legislation, passed in 1935 and 1939, happened without him. The next major piece of legislation, passed in 1950, raised benefit levels and extended coverage, enabling Social Security to surpass welfare as the nation's primary approach to maintaining the income of people who were not in the labor force. As the director of the advisory council that wrote the report that led to the 1950 amendments, Robert Ball, in effect, wrote the script for the 1950 amendments. The main theme of the script was that contributory social insurance represented a form of social protection that was superior to welfare. The nation should aid not only those who could prove they were poor but all those who had participated in the labor force. Social protection followed from social participation, defined as having worked in a paying job, maintaining the home of someone who worked, or being dependent on someone who worked. The genius of this notion lay in the way it enabled the welfare state to be broadened beyond a small class of people who considered themselves to be poor so that it could reach nearly everyone. The receipt of social welfare benefits became not something exceptional but

357

something normal. Robert Ball saw the potential to achieve this goal in the late 1940s and took the first successful steps toward reaching it.

In laying the groundwork for the 1950 amendments, Ball used the conservative means of social insurance, with its emphasis on contributory benefits and its close links to the labor market, toward the liberal ends of an expanded welfare state. Again and again in his career, he emphasized the compatibility of social insurance with American values. With this emphasis he pressed repeatedly to expand the powers of the federal government. The result was a Social Security program that included disability benefits (1956) and medical care (1965) and a Social Security program in which the basic level of benefits rose with the American standard of living, as amendments in 1952, 1956, 1958, and 1967 demonstrated. The program linked benefit levels to wage levels, so that someone who earned more money in his working lifetime received more money in retirement than someone who had earned less. Yet Ball also did a great deal to soften the terms of this relationship in the name of social adequacy. Hence a poorer person received a greater return on his Social Security contributions than did a richer person. Ball also worked hard to extend benefits beyond the basic social unit of a working man and his wife so that, for example, a child in a family in which the breadwinner had died could receive benefits until she reached the age of 21. Always, however, the conservative rhetoric of contributory social insurance accompanied the pleas to expand the welfare state.

In 1972 Ball orchestrated a complex process of consultation with the Nixon administration and with Democratic congressional leaders that led to the passage of the most important law in the program's development since 1950. Congress agreed to raise basic benefit levels by 20 percent and to create a new system in which benefit levels rose automatically, without the intervention of the president or Congress, according to changes in the consumer price index. This legislation enabled the level of program benefits to surge with the great wave of inflation in the 1970s and facilitated the program's major expansion. For the 1972 legislation Ball did not write a philosophical rationale, as he had for the 1950 amendments, so much as he conditioned the policy environment to accept a major new approach to Social Security. The

Nixon administration did not favor the 20 percent increase in benefits but, under Ball's tutelage, came to accept them. Wilbur Mills, the central congressional figure, did not favor linking benefits automatically to the cost of living but, again under Ball's influence, came to play a major role in its eventual passage.

The 1972 amendments, coming as they did at the beginning of the stagflation era with its attendant rises in prices and in unemployment, ushered in an era of fiscal crisis for the Social Security program. Economic crisis required strategic adjustments in the program. These needed to be made in a political environment in which each party looked with great suspicion on the motives of the other. House Speaker Tip O'Neill wanted to use President Reagan's desire to stem the growth of the Social Security program as a political weapon against him. President Reagan hoped to discredit the program, and the party that had nurtured it, as an example of profligate social spending that could not be sustained into the next century. The situation required the skills of someone with considerable negotiating abilities and a keen strategic sense to reach a solution acceptable to both sides. Robert Ball proved to be that person. As much as anyone, he worked out the terms of a 1983 deal in which both sides agreed to cuts in the program but left intact the basic program structure, including benefits that rose automatically with changes in the consumer price index. In this way, he preserved the program for the rest of the century and into the next.

The life of Robert Ball illustrates changes in the policymaking structure for Social Security over the course of the program's history. The founding legislation of 1935 occurred before the creation of a bureaucracy with a vested interest in the program's survival and expansion. Its passage set in motion the policy dynamic that led to the program's being altered even before it had begun to pay benefits. The 1939 amendments, and the attendant creation of family benefits, occurred at the instigation of Congress, concerned about the adverse economic effects produced by the 1935 legislation. There followed a period of hiatus in which Congress showed relatively little interest in Social Security, a period that ended with the passage of the 1950 amendments. After that the appearance of Social Security legislation became a regular event, usually timed to coincide with congressional elections. This pattern ended shortly after the 1972 amendments. For the rest of the century, the passage of a major Social Security law was usually the product of a fiscal crisis.

In the period between 1950 and 1972 a consensus developed that the Social Security program should be expanded as the economy expanded. To work out the terms of this expansion, Congress and the president relied heavily on the Social Security bureaucracy. In this period, therefore, bureaucratic influence over Social Security policy reached its height. Congress made legislation with Social Security personnel in the room as the responsible committees marked up drafts of a bill. The extent to which benefits were raised resulted as much from decisions made by the Social Security Administration as from political advocacy on the part of members of Congress or the president. Benefits rose to the level that the system could afford, and Social Security bureaucrats decided just how much that was. To be sure, the bureaucracy consulted with all the concerned parties in Congress and in the White House and in such Washington locations as the headquarters of the AFL-CIO. The leaders of the Social Security Administration met repeatedly with officials in the Department of Health, Education, and Welfare and in the Bureau of the Budget. Yet it was the Social Security Administration, as much as any single entity, that controlled the process.

Within the Social Security Administration, Robert Ball served as the chief operating officer for nearly the entire period between 1950 and 1972. Beyond running the agency so that it accomplished its routine tasks, such as sending out checks on time, he also made strategic program decisions. He determined the sequence of Social Security's expansion, from the victory over welfare to disability insurance, to health insurance, to benefits indexed to the rate of inflation. He steered advisory councils in the direction that he wanted Social Security to go. He sat in on nearly all the important closed congressional sessions that were devoted to fashioning legislation. He became, in effect, the program's Washington ambassador—the person from the bureaucracy who shuttled back and forth between the program's operational center in Baltimore to offices in the nation's capital where he met with important officials in the Department of Health, Education, and Welfare and influential members of Congress and their staffs. In these meetings, he made actuarial and other technical data politically comprehensible. He also gave the political establishment a sense of whether a particular change in the law was administratively feasible.

Then, with the legislative process over, he would go back to Baltimore and supervise the process of putting the new law into operation. That involved making elaborate timetables and plans so that massive social programs, such as Medicare and disability insurance, could be implemented with a minimum of bureaucratic snafu and a maximum amount of favorable notice for the agency. That involved interpreting the new legislation to people working in Baltimore and in field offices across the nation so that they understood its importance. Energized and inspired, they would then work hard on the agency's behalf. Ball, in turn, would report back to Congress and to the Bureau of the Budget that the new law had been put into operation successfully. That, in turn, would encourage Congress to take the next incremental step on the road to Social Security's expansion, and the process would continue.

After 1972 conditions changed. No longer did Congress legislate and the Social Security Administration implement massive social programs. Instead, Social Security became a controversial issue. People disagreed over how to secure the program's financial future and even over whether the program was worth saving. If President Bill Clinton wanted to change welfare as we knew it, the same could be said for President George W. Bush's plans for Social Security. He wanted to change a defined benefit plan into a defined contribution plan, with private companies, rather than the Social Security Administration, at the center of the nation's retirement system. As such notions became more respectable, the locus of policymaking shifted. Decisions once made by the Social Security Administration were now being made at higher levels. Presidents from Gerald Ford to George W. Bush needed to decide important issues related to Social Security that their predecessors had not had to face. Decisions once made within congressional committees, with Representative Wilbur Mills the dominant figure, were now made by the congressional leadership. No longer did representatives of the Social Security Administration sit in on closed sessions in which congressmen marked up legislation. No longer was there a pattern of active collaboration between Congress and the Social Security bureaucracy. The perceived crisis in Social Security could not be handled in that manner.

As the policymaking system for Social Security changed, so did Robert Ball's job. He worked in the Social Security bureaucracy from 1939 until 1973, a period of thirty-four years. He spent the second part of his career, a period of nearly equal length, as a freelance Social Security consultant. During his second career, his influence over Social Security policy increased. Stepping outside a large bureaucracy and its often confining routines, he was able to offer his advice freely to President Jimmy Carter in the period leading up to the 1977 amendments. In 1983, with the Democrats out of power, he worked effectively with the congressional leadership to produce the "rescue" legislation of that year.

Ball's effectiveness in his second career depended on his extensive knowledge of the program, his continuing ability to gather information from actuaries, legislative analysts, and researchers in the bureaucracy, and his assiduous cultivation of members of Congress responsible for Social Security policy. His clients knew they could rely on his strategic sense and his political tact to produce congenial results. He was a full-time student of the program without daily responsibilities to distract him from working on a special project for a Stuart Eizenstat in the White House or a Jake Pickle in Congress. He was someone who was already retired from his government career. That meant that if he were appointed to an advisory council, one could be certain that Robert Ball would work as hard as anyone else on that council, and that, if necessary, he would devote full time to that council, unlike the other members who had to fly in and out of Washington for meetings and who had to juggle government service with their normal jobs. And unlike many Washington players, he sought no special recognition beyond respect for his Social Security expertise. He was not positioning himself to run for office, get a presidential appointment, or receive a research grant that would sustain his consulting business. For him program preservation and making strides toward new social programs such as long-term care were the ultimate rewards. If one shared those goals and was in a position to influence public policy, one could depend on Bob Ball's help.

The life of Robert Ball demonstrates the qualities of leadership in the Social Security field in the last half of the twentieth century. Unlike his predecessors as commissioner of Social Security, Ball devoted nearly his entire career to Social Security. The others worked in state government and with other programs, such as public assistance and workers' compensation, before running the Social Security program. Ball came straight to Social Security. Once in the agency, he spent only a short time in the field before arriving at the central headquarters. He gained a wide knowledge of the program in the training division and then went to the part of the agency concerned with policy analysis and legislative affairs. This branch functioned as an elite corps of Social Security employees who guided the program through its era of expansion and supplied many of the agency's top administrators, including Ball and his deputy Arthur Hess.

What separated Ball from his colleagues was his ability to combine basic administrative competence with social vision. As he once told a reporter, "I guess I'd have to plead guilty to being a social planner, a social reformer, at least as much as an administrator. I really think that to head an organization of this kind it's best to be able to combine program skills—what the program should be and where it is going—with being able to lead the administration of the program after it is in effect."[1] Others had narrow and highly specialized program skills, such as the ability to do research in the program's legislative history or devise routines that would enable applications for benefits to be processed quickly. Many in the agency had a sort of mechanical ingenuity that made them invaluable in solving practical problems. Ball's talents extended far beyond that. He could concentrate on the fine points of administration, but he also had the knack of always keeping the big picture in mind and knowing how to use short-run strategy to reach long-term goals.

Furthermore, he projected the image of the leader. There was something mature about him, with his tall stature and his graying hair. Although he could make jokes, he maintained a sense of dignity and made people believe that what he said should be taken seriously. He never appeared strident or out of control. He might have been a social reformer, but there was nothing of the zealot about him. His posture toward his adversaries was always one of respect, and whatever he said, even as he pushed for major expansions of the welfare state, always appeared to be well considered and, above all, reasonable. In his approach toward Congress and toward others in positions of authority, he was relentlessly reasonable, the sort of person who did not want to change the world but rather one who wanted to make practical suggestions to reach widely held social goals.

The ease with which Ball moved in the highest policy circles belied the inordinate amount of time he spent in preparation for a meeting or a public appearance. Before he testified in Congress, he studied background materials for hours and rehearsed his answers to the questions he thought he might be asked. Often he dictated notes to his subordinates asking them for specific pieces of information or requesting them to locate documents that might be helpful. Arriving in the hearing room, he carried a brief case crammed with background reports that he had read. Before his agency released a report or sent an important memo to someone in authority, he critiqued draft after draft, trying to get the nuances of the agency's message exactly right. Where others might decide that something was good enough—close enough for government work, as the old expression had it—Ball never parted with material easily. He wanted to get it right. Yet unlike others who fussed over reports, Ball could also be decisive, quick to see if a particular amendment or proposal fit in with the agency's plans or benefited his political allies.

Ball was earnest without being sanctimonious. One of his greatest talents lay in his ability to inspire others. Perhaps he acquired this talent from his minister father, or perhaps it was innate. A hallmark of his leadership of his agency was his ability to give an inspirational speech that enabled workers at all levels in all grades to feel that they were part of something important. Their own job in the mail room or at a desk in a payment center might be modest, yet they knew from listening to Ball that they played a role in a program that made a vital difference in many people's lives. Ball somehow enabled them to see the larger purpose in their mundane tasks.

After he left the agency, Ball remained a leader in the Social Security field, even without thousands of employees to exhort to greater goals. His strategic skills remained with him, as did his encyclopedic knowledge of the program and his willingness to work hard on projects that did not promise an immediate payoff. He knew how to be helpful to the politicians who called on him for aid, such as Jimmy Carter and Tip O'Neill, because he understood the constraints under which they operated. He also sharpened his skills as a negotiator, able to close the deal that led to the

1983 amendments. He became an extraordinary resource that defenders of Social Security had at their disposal.

Finally, the life of Robert Ball reveals the limitations of some of the current accounts of Social Security's history. Too much of this literature concentrates on the founding legislation of 1935 and 1939 and not enough on the era of Social Security's expansion after 1950. In their role as social critics, historians and other social scientists have been quick to notice the program's tendency toward racial exclusion in 1935 and toward excluding women from their fair share of benefits in 1939. Whatever one might think of this social criticism, it is difficult to deny the tremendous growth in Social Security benefits after 1950. Social Security's expansion has made it the closest thing that this country has to a universal program, one that benefits blacks and whites, men and women. The liberal project undertaken by Ball and others has produced its share of success. Robert Ball's use of the conservative means of social insurance toward the liberal ends of an expanded welfare state has left an indelible mark on American social policy.

Notes

Preface

1. Edward Berkowitz and Kim McQuaid, *Creating the Welfare State: The Political Economy of Twentieth-Century Reform*, 2d ed. (New York: Praeger, 1988), p. xiii.

2. Hence in President's Commission for a National Agenda for the Eighties, *Government and the Advancement of Social Justice: Health, Education, and Civil Rights in the Eighties* (Englewood Cliffs: Prentice Hall, 1981), there is no mention of Social Security financing.

3. See Edward D. Berkowitz, *Disabled Policy: America's Programs for the Handicapped* (New York: Cambridge University Press), pp. 41–104.

4. James W. Singer, "It Isn't Easy to Cure the Ailments of the Disability Insurance Program," *National Journal*, May 16, 1978, p. 718; Joseph A. Califano Jr., *Governing America: An Insider's Report from the White House and the Cabinet* (New York: Simon and Schuster, 1981), p. 384; Donald O. Parsons, "Disability Insurance and Male Labor Force Participation: A Response to Haveman and Wolfe," *Journal of Political Economy* 92 (June 1984), pp. 542–49.

5. Edward D. Berkowitz, *Mr. Social Security: The Life of Wilbur J. Cohen* (Lawrence: University Press of Kansas, 1995).

6. Edward D. Berkowitz, "Introduction: Social Security Celebrates

an Anniversary," in *Social Security after Fifty: Successes and Failures*, ed. Edward D. Berkowitz (New York: Greenwood Press, 1987), pp. 7–8.

7. Eric R. Kingson and Edward D. Berkowitz, *Social Security and Medicare: A Policy Primer* (Westport, Conn.: Auburn House, 1993).

8. Edward D. Berkowitz, *To Improve Human Health: A History of the Institute of Medicine* (Washington, D.C.: National Academy Press, 1998), p. 81.

9. One of his legacies, for example, was a book about readings on Social Security, an idea that he pushed repeatedly over the course of several years before the project reached fruition. See Eric R. Kingson and James H. Schulz, eds., *Social Security in the 21st Century* (New York: Oxford University Press, 1997). Among the blurbs on the back cover is one from David Hamburg, the president of the Carnegie Foundation and one of Ball's great patrons and friends.

10. Robert J. Myers, with Richard L. Vernaci, *Within the System: My Half Century in Social Security* (Winsted, Conn.: ACTEX, 1992).

11. Robert M. Ball, *Social Security: Today and Tomorrow* (New York: Columbia University Press, 1978).

Introduction

1. Social Security Advisory Board, *Why Action Should Be Taken Soon* (July 2001), pp. 1–2; Office of Policy, Office of Research, Evaluation and Statistics, *Facts and Figures about Social Security* (Washington, D.C.: Social Security Administration, 1999); Congressional Budget Office, *Social Security: A Primer* (Washington, D.C.: Government Printing Office, September 2001), p. 2.

2. Marilyn Moon, *Medicare Now and in the Future* (Washington, D.C.: Urban Institute Press, 1993); Board of Trustees of the Social Security and Medicare Trust Funds, *2000 Annual Report of the Board of Trustees of the Federal Hospital Insurance Trust Fund* (Washington, D.C.: Government Printing Office, 2000); Joseph White, *False Alarm: Why the Greatest Threat to Social Security and Medicare Is the Campaign to "Save" Them* (Baltimore: Johns Hopkins University Press, 2001), pp. 53–69.

3. Arthur Altmeyer, Edwin Witte, Douglas Brown, Wilbur Cohen, and William Haber all played key roles in the formation of Social Security, but they came to that subject through an interest in labor relations. The Wisconsin connection, as nurtured first by John R. Commons and later by Selig Perlman and Edwin Witte, was important here. See John R. Commons, *Myself: The Autobiography of John R. Commons* (1934; reprint, Madison: University of Wisconsin Press, 1963); Lafayette G. Harter Jr., *John R. Commons: His Assault on Laissez-Faire* (Corvallis: Oregon State University Press, 1962); Leon Fink, "A Memoir of Selig Perlman and His

Life at the University of Wisconsin: Based on an Interview of Mark Perlman, Conducted and Edited by Leon Fink," *Labor History* 32 (fall 1991), p. 520; Theron Schlabach, *Edwin E. Witte: Cautious Reformer* (Madison: State Historical Society of Wisconsin, 1969). For a broad view of the labor movement's importance see Nelson Lichtenstein, *State of the Union: A Century of American Labor* (Princeton: Princeton University Press, 2002), pp. 20–53.

4. Jerry Cates, *Insuring Inequality: Administrative Leadership in Social Security, 1935–1954* (Ann Arbor: University of Michigan Press, 1983); Sheryl R. Tynes, *Turning Points in Social Security: From "Cruel Hoax" to "Sacred Entitlement"* (Stanford: Stanford University Press, 1996), pp. 64–98; Edward D. Berkowitz, *America's Welfare State: From Roosevelt to Reagan* (Baltimore: Johns Hopkins University Press, 1991), pp. 40–64; Edward D. Berkowitz, "The Historical Development of Social Security in the United States," in *Social Security in the 21st Century,* ed. Eric Kingson and James Schulz (New York: Oxford University Press, 1997), pp. 25–29; Edward D. Berkowitz, "History and Social Security Reform," in *Social Security and Medicare: Individual versus Collective Risk and Responsibility,* ed. Sheila Burke, Eric R. Kingson, and Uwe E. Reinhardt (Washington, D.C.: National Academy of Social Insurance, 2000), pp. 33–42.

5. Arthur J. Altmeyer, *The Formative Years of Social Security* (Madison: University of Wisconsin Press, 1966), p. 185; W. Andrew Achenbaum, *Social Security: Visions and Revisions* (New York: Cambridge University Press, 1986), pp. 38–44; Edwin Amenta, *Bold Relief: Institutional Politics and the Origins of Modern Social Policy* (Princeton: Princeton University Press, 1998), chapter 6; Bartholomew H. Sparrow, *From the Outside In: World War II and the American State* (Princeton: Princeton University Press, 1996), pp. 33–66; Jill S. Quadagno, *The Transformation of Old Age Security: Class and Politics in the American Welfare State* (Chicago: University of Chicago Press, 1988).

6. Robert Ball, interview by Larry DeWitt, Alexandria, Va., interview 2, March 12, 2001, Social Security Administration History Archives, Baltimore (copy available on the Web at http://www.ssa.gov/history/orals/ball2.html).

7. 80th Congress, 1st sess., S.R. 141, July 7, 1947 (submitted by Eugene Millikin and Walter George); Robert M. Ball, "Social Insurance and the Right to Assistance," *Social Service Review* 21 (September 1947), pp. 331–44; Advisory Council on Social Security, *Old-Age and Survivors Insurance: A Report to the Senate Committee on Finance,* 80th Cong., 2d sess., 1948, S. Doc. 149 (Washington, D.C.: Government Printing Office, 1948).

8. Carolyn L. Weaver, *The Crisis in Social Security: Economic and Political Origins* (Durham: Duke University Press, 1982), calls attention to

the founders of Social Security as "zealots." According to Theodore Marmor, Ball "could have posed for pictures of executive presence in *Fortune* during the 1950s and 1960s" (Theodore R. Marmor, "Public Management: Wilbur Cohen and Robert Ball," in *Leadership and Innovation: A Biographical Perspective on Entrepreneurs in Government*, ed. Jameson W. Doig and Erwin C. Hargrove [Baltimore: Johns Hopkins University Press, 1987], p. 253).

9. Martha Derthick, *Policymaking for Social Security* (Washington, D.C.: Brookings Institution, 1979), pp. 62–80.

10. Tynes, *Turning Points in Social Security*, pp. 99–132; Quadagno, *Transformation of Old Age Security*; Edward D. Berkowitz, *Mr. Social Security: The Life of Wilbur J. Cohen* (Lawrence: University Press of Kansas, 1995), pp. 71–93.

11. Historical sociologists have done a great deal of work linking the American political system and the lack of bureaucratic competence in a government dominated by patronage appointees. See Ann Shola Orloff, "The Political Origins of America's Belated Welfare State," in *The Politics of Social Policy in the United States*, ed. Margaret Weir, Ann Shola Orloff, and Theda Skocpol (Princeton: Princeton University Press, 1988), pp. 37–80; Amenta, *Bold Relief*; Ann Orloff, *The Politics of Pensions: A Comparative Analysis of Britain, Canada, and the United States, 1880s–1940* (Madison: University of Wisconsin Press, 1993); Stephen Skowronek, *Building a New American State: The Expansion of National Administrative Capacities, 1877–1920* (New York: Cambridge University Press, 1981).

12. Deborah A. Stone, *The Disabled State* (Philadelphia: Temple University Press, 1984), pp. 68–89; Derthick, *Policymaking for Social Security*, p. 73; Edward D. Berkowitz, *Disabled Policy: America's Programs for the Handicapped* (New York: Cambridge University Press, 1987), pp. 73–78.

13. Gilbert Y. Steiner, *Social Insecurity: The Politics of Welfare* (Chicago: Rand McNally, 1966), p. 37; Martha Derthick, *Uncontrollable Spending for Social Services Grants* (Washington, D.C.: Brookings Institution, 1975), p. 79; Blanche D. Coll, *The Safety Net: Welfare and Social Security, 1929–1979* (New Brunswick: Rutgers University Press, 1995).

14. On Medicare see Herman Miles Somers and Anne Ramsay Somers, *Medicare and the Hospitals: Issues and Prospects* (Washington, D.C.: Brookings Institution, 1967); Moon, *Medicare Now*; Edward Berkowitz and Wendy Wolff, "The Origins and Consequences of Medicare," in *Paying the Doctor: Health Policy and Physician Reimbursement*, ed. Jonathan D. Moreno (New York: Auburn House, 1991), pp. 143–56; Theodore R. Marmor, with Jan S. Marmor, *The Politics of Medicare* (Chicago: Aldine, 1973); Richard Harris, *A Sacred Trust* (New York: New American Library, 1966); Sherri I. David, *With Dignity: The Search for Medicare and Medicaid* (Westport, Conn.: Greenwood Press, 1985).

15. Judith M. Feder, *Medicare: The Politics of Federal Hospital Insurance* (Lexington, Mass.: Lexington Books, 1977).

16. Tynes, *Turning Points in Social Security,* pp. 133–54; Derthick, *Policymaking for Social Security,* pp. 339–68.

17. On the adoption of cost-of-living adjustments, see R. Kent Weaver, *Automatic Government: The Politics of Indexation* (Washington, D.C.: Brookings Institution, 1988), and Julian Zelizer, *Taxing America: Wilbur D. Mills, Congress, and the State* (New York: Cambridge University Press, 1998).

18. Many commentators on Nixon have discussed the increasingly partisan nature of his administration. For some acerbic views, see Richard Reeves, *President Nixon: Alone in the White House* (New York: Simon and Schuster, 2001), and Anthony Summers, *The Arrogance of Power: The Secret World of Richard Nixon* (New York: Penguin Books, 2000).

19. The indispensable source on this point is Derthick, *Policymaking for Social Security.*

20. See Martha Derthick, *Agency under Stress: The Social Security Administration in American Government* (Washington, D.C.: Brookings Institution, 1990).

21. See Joseph A. Califano Jr., *Governing America: An Insider's Report from the White House and the Cabinet* (New York: Simon and Schuster, 1981), pp. 368–401, on this point. The literature on the Carter era and his style of governance is at an early stage, but see Bruce J. Schulman, *The Seventies: The Great Shift in American Culture, Society, and Politics* (New York: Free Press, 2001), pp. 121–43; Gary M. Fink and Hugh Davis Graham, eds., *The Carter Presidency: Policy Choices in the Post–New Deal Era* (Lawrence: University Press of Kansas, 1998).

22. Paul C. Light, *Artful Work: The Politics of Social Security Reform* (New York: Random House, 1985); Achenbaum, *Social Security,* pp. 81–99.

23. For a view of Social Security sympathetic to privatization see Sylvester J. Schieber and John B. Shoven, *The Real Deal: The History and Future of Social Security* (New Haven: Yale University Press, 1999), which also provides a good historical overview of the program.

24. Among the books written in defense of Social Security and against the idea of privatization are Max J. Skidmore, *Social Security and Its Enemies: The Case for America's Most Efficient Insurance Program* (Boulder, Colo.: Westview Press, 1999), Merton C. Bernstein and Joan Brodshaug Bernstein, *Social Security: The System That Works* (New York: Basic Books, 1988), and Theodore R. Marmor, Jerry L. Mashaw, and Philip L. Harvey, *America's Misunderstood Welfare State: Persistent Myths, Enduring Realities* (New York: Basic Books, 1990); Dean Baker, *Social Security: The Phony Crisis* (Chicago: University of Chicago Press, 1999); White, *False Alarm.*

25. Amy Goldstein, "Social Security Future Grim, Bush Panel Says," *Washington Post,* July 20, 2001, p. A-1. For a contrary view on the effectiveness of Bush's efforts, see Robert Dreyfuss, "Bush's House of Cards," *American Prospect,* September 10, 2001, pp. 16–19.

26. Peter J. Ferrara and Michael Tanner, *A New Deal for Social Security* (Washington, D.C.: Cato Institute, 1998), p. 1.

27. Among the best examples of historical sociology are Amenta, *Bold Relief,* and Tynes, *Turning Points in Social Security.* These and other social scientists—in particular Martha Derthick—write with an eye toward historical detail and explanation and have added a great deal to the literature. Achenbaum, *Social Security,* remains the only survey of the program's history, and it covers events only until 1985. The biography is Berkowitz, *Mr. Social Security.* Standard surveys of American social welfare history that mention Social Security include James T. Patterson, *America's Struggle against Poverty, 1900–1980* (Cambridge: Harvard University Press, 1981); Michael Katz, *In the Shadow of the Poorhouse* (New York: Basic Books, 1986); James Leiby, *A History of Social Welfare and Social Work in the United States* (New York: Columbia University Press, 1978); and Walter I. Trattner, *From Poor Law to Welfare State* (New York: Free Press, 1990). On the history of old age and Social Security's place in it see Carole Haber and Brian Gratton, *Old Age and the Search for Security: An American Social History* (Bloomington: Indiana University Press, 1994).

28. Mary Elizabeth Poole, "Securing Race and Ensuring Dependence: The Social Security Act of 1935" (Ph.D. diss., Rutgers University, 2000), pp. 165, 308.

29. The debate over coverage exclusions has floundered over the question of intent. Did administrative necessity, indifference to the program, the racist views of southern congressmen, or some other factor cause Congress to limit coverage to industrial and commercial workers on regular payrolls? The most convincing piece on this topic is Gareth Davies and Martha Derthick, "Race and Social Policy: The Social Security Act of 1935," *Political Science Quarterly* 112 (November 1997), pp. 217–35. The best empirical work is Robert C. Lieberman, *Shifting the Color Line: Race and the American Welfare State* (Cambridge: Harvard University Press, 1998).

30. Gwendolyn Mink, *The Wages of Motherhood: Inequality in the Welfare State, 1917–1942* (Ithaca: Cornell University Press, 1995), pp. 127, 136. Other key works that analyze the role of gender in the American welfare state include Mimi Abramovitz, *Regulating the Lives of Women: Social Welfare from Colonial Times to the Present* (Boston: South End Press, 1988); Clarke A. Chambers, "Toward a Redefinition of Welfare History," *Journal of American History* 73, 2 (1986); Joanne Goodwin, *Gender and the*

Politics of Welfare Reform: Mothers' Pensions in Chicago, 1911–1929 (Chicago: University of Chicago Press, 1997); Linda Gordon, *Pitied But Not Entitled: Single Mothers and the History of Welfare* (New York: Free Press, 1994); Gordon, "Social Insurance and Public Assistance: The Influence of Gender in Welfare Thought in the United States, 1890–1935," *American Historical Review* 97 (February 1992), pp. 19–54; Jacqueline Jones, *Labor of Love, Labor of Sorrow: Black Women, Work and the Family from Slavery to the Present* (New York: Vintage Books, 1986); Alice Kessler-Harris, *In Pursuit of Equity: Women, Men, and the Quest for Economic Citizenship in Twentieth-Century America* (New York: Oxford University Press, 2001).

31. Michael K. Brown, *Race, Money and the American Welfare State* (Ithaca: Cornell University Press, 1999), pp. 2, 12.

32. Alice O'Connor, *Poverty Knowledge* (Princeton: Princeton University Press, 1991), p. 57.

1. Arriving

1. Arthur J. Altmeyer, *The Formative Years of Social Security* (Madison: University of Wisconsin Press, 1966), p. ix. It should be noted that the federal supervision of the state unemployment insurance programs was transferred to the Department of Labor in 1949, where it remains (Altmeyer, *Formative Years,* p. 176). On Altmeyer see also W. Andrew Achenbaum, "Arthur Altmeyer," in *Biographical Dictionary of Social Welfare in America,* ed. W. Trattner (Westport, Conn.: Greenwood Press, 1986), pp. 25–27. Although no full-scale biography of Altmeyer exists, Larry DeWitt, the historian of the Social Security Administration, is preparing one from Altmeyer's papers, which are in the Wisconsin State Historical Society, Madison.

2. On Cohen see Edward D. Berkowitz, *Mr. Social Security: The Life of Wilbur J. Cohen* (Lawrence: University Press of Kansas, 1995), which also contains observations on Altmeyer and Ball.

3. "Dr. and Mrs. Ball, Once of Englewood, Married 50 Years," clipping from *Englewood (N.J.) Press Journal,* June 11, 1953, in Robert Ball Papers, Wisconsin State Historical Society, Madison (hereafter Ball Papers); Robert Ball to Nathan A. Clark, associate editor, *National Cyclopedia of American Biography,* September 19, 1961, Ball Papers; "Rev. Archey Ball, Minister 50 Years," *New York Times,* April 13, 1955, Ball Papers. When I looked at these papers, they had not yet been sent to the Wisconsin State Historical Society. Hence I cannot supply box numbers for the many citations to the Ball Papers in this book. Presumably, however, a finding aid in Madison will aid future researchers and enable them to make their way through the often haphazard arrangement of

Ball's papers. It was one of the ironies of Ball's life that, although a superb administrator, his own papers were in considerable disarray.

4. "Dr. and Mrs. Ball," Ball Papers; Ball to Clark, September 19, 1961, Ball Papers; "Rev. Archey Ball," Ball Papers; Robert Ball, interview by J. Halamandaris, December 1987, Oral History Collection. This interview was videotaped and intended to be distributed as a videotape, but there is a transcript available in the Social Security Administration (hereafter SSA) History Archives, Baltimore.

5. See Berkowitz, *Mr. Social Security,* pp. 39–40.

6. Ball, Halamandaris interview; Theodore Marmor with Phillip Fellman, "Entrepreneurship in Public Management: Wilbur Cohen and Robert Ball," in *Leadership and Innovation: A Biographical Perspective on Entrepreneurs in Government,* ed. Jameson Doig and Erwin Hargrove (Baltimore: Johns Hopkins University Press, 1987), p. 215.

7. On Norman Thomas, who lived from 1884 until 1968, and who became a Presbyterian minister after attending Princeton and before becoming a leader of the Socialist Party, see W. A. Swanberg, *Norman Thomas: The Last Idealist* (New York: Scribners, 1974).

8. Ball, Halamandaris interview.

9. Paul A. Raushenbush and Elizabeth Brandeis Raushenbush, *Our "U.C." Story, 1930–1967* (Madison, Wis.: privately printed, 1979), p. 3. Walter Rauschenbusch believed in such ideals as trying to achieve Christ's kingdom on earth. See William R. Hutchison, *The Modernist Impulse in American Protestantism* (New York: Oxford University Press, 1976), and Doris Robinson Sharpe, *Walter Rauschenbusch* (New York: Macmillan, 1942).

10. On the importance of birth order see Frank J. Sulloway, *Born to Rebel: Birth Order, Family Dynamics, and Creative Lives* (New York: Pantheon, 1996).

11. For impressionistic images of growing up in the depression see Studs Terkel, *Hard Times: An Oral History of the Great Depression* (New York: Pantheon, 1970); Irving Bernstein, *A Caring Society: The New Deal, the Worker, and the Great Depression* (Boston: Houghton Mifflin, 1985).

12. Ball, Halamandaris interview.

13. Information prepared for *Who's Who* (no date) entry for Robert Ball in Ball Papers. Ball's high school graduation program (in his personal possession) lists him as one of the top twenty-five members of his class in academic ranking. He told me that to be ranked any higher would risk social embarrassment (personal conversation).

14. Ball entered Wesleyan exactly one hundred years after the university's founding. See David B. Potts, *Wesleyan University, 1831–1900: Collegiate Enterprise in New England* (New Haven: Yale University Press, 1992).

15. This sketch of Ball's college career is culled from "Background of Robert M. Ball," n.d. (but one of many vitae and biographical sketches), Ball Papers; *Who's Who* materials, n.d., Ball Papers; Ball, Halamandaris interview.

16. Information on Ball's arrest can be gleaned from the federal personnel forms that he was required to fill out, such as "Standard Form 58," n.d., Ball Papers; Ball, Halamandaris interview.

17. Ball to "Dot," his sister Dorothy, n.d., but probably 1935, SSA History Archives, Baltimore; Ernest Hemingway, *The Short Stories of Ernest Hemingway* (New York: Scribners, 1938).

18. Robert Ball, "Social Security Board, Application and Personal History Statement," n.d., Ball Papers.

19. Norman Ware was a prominent labor economist in the Wisconsin school. He was an expert on the American labor movement in the nineteenth century and author of works that are still in print, including *The Industrial Worker, 1840–1860: The Reaction of American Industrial Society to the Advance of the Industrial Revolution* (1924; reprint, Chicago: Ivan Dee, 1990). See also Ware, *The Labor Movement in the United States, 1860–1895* (New York: Appleton, 1924).

20. The best modern study of the CIO is Robert Zieger, *The CIO, 1935–1995* (Chapel Hill: University of North Carolina Press, 1995).

21. Robert Ball to J. C. Shover, director of personnel, National Labor Relations Board, April 17, 1941, Ball Papers.

22. Berkowitz, *Mr. Social Security*, p. 329.

23. The institutional economics movement was associated with such universities as the University of Texas and, most prominently with the presence of John R. Commons, Selig Perlman, and Edwin Witte, the University of Wisconsin. See John R. Commons, *Myself: The Autobiography of John R. Commons* (1934; reprint, Madison: University of Wisconsin Press, 1963); Edwin E. Witte, *Social Security Perspectives: Essays by Edwin E. Witte* (Madison: University of Wisconsin Press, 1962); Wilbur J. Cohen, "Edwin E. Witte," in *Biographical Dictionary of Social Welfare in America,* ed. Walter I. Trattner (Westport, Conn.: Greenwood Press, 1986), pp. 785–87; Edwin E. Witte, *The Development of the Social Security Act* (Madison: University of Wisconsin Press, 1962).

24. Ball quoting Ware as reported in Robin Toner, "A Great Defender of the Old Social Security Battles On," *New York Times,* May 3, 1999, p. A-16.

25. Berkowitz, *Mr. Social Security*, pp. 36–37.

26. Ball to J. C. Shover, April 17, 1941.

27. "Robert Myers Ball," *Current Biography* 29, 1 (January 1968), pp. 6–8; Ball, Halamandaris interview.

28. Ball, Halamandaris interview; Ball, "Standard Form 58," n.d., Ball Papers.

29. Ball, "Application and Personal History Statement," n.d., Ball papers; J. C. Shover to Robert M. Ball, April 2, 1941, Ball Papers; Ball to Shover, April 17, 1941, Ball papers.

30. I take my description of Ball's work on the newspaper from Materials Submitted to the National Labor Relations Board, in Ball to Shover, April 17, 1941, Ball Papers.

31. Robert Ball, autobiographical memo prepared for the author between 1999 and 2001, p. 38. Ball, as I noted in the preface, prepared this memo—in essence a mini-autobiography—for my personal use in connection with this project. This long memorandum, which I cite as Ball Memoir, is available to researchers as part of the Robert Ball papers in the History Archives of the Social Security Administration in Baltimore. For other works commenting on the centrality of the labor question to the politics of the 1930s and beyond see Anthony Badger, _The New Deal: The Depression Years, 1933–1940_ (New York: Hill and Wang, 1989); Irving Bernstein, _Turbulent Years: A History of the American Worker, 1933–1941_ (Boston: Houghton Mifflin, 1971); Melvyn Dubofsky, _The State and Labor in Modern America_ (Chapel Hill: University of North Carolina Press, 1994); Lizabeth Cohen, _Making a New Deal: Industrial Workers in Chicago, 1919–1939_ (New York: Cambridge University Press, 1990).

32. Altmeyer, _Formative Years,_ p. 53; Arthur J. Altmeyer, interview by Peter Corning, June 29, 1967, Madison, Wis., Oral History Collection, Columbia University, New York (copy available in SSA History Archives and on the Web at http://www.ssa.gov/history/ajaoral4.html). See also Sylvester J. Schieber and John B. Shoven, _The Real Deal: The History and Future of Social Security_ (New Haven: Yale University Press, 1999), p. 46.

33. Charles McKinley and Robert W. Frase, _Launching Social Security: A Capture-and-Record Account, 1935–1937_ (Madison: University of Wisconsin Press, 1970), pp. 67–68; Edward Berkowitz, "The Social Security Administration," in _A Historical Guide to the United States Government,_ ed. George Thomas Kurian (New York: Oxford University Press, 1998), p. 537.

34. Arthur Hess, interview by Edward Berkowitz, July 8, 1996, Charlottesville, Va., available in the Centers for Medicare and Medicaid Services Library in Baltimore, in the National Library of Medicine in Bethesda, Md., and on the Web site of the SSA at http://www.ssa.gov/history/HESS2.html; McKinley and Frase, _Launching Social Security,_ pp. 500, 308; Ball Memoir, p. 307; Jack S. Futterman, interview by Larry DeWitt, Ellicott City, Md., March 24, 2000, SSA History Archives, p. 111.

35. Robert Ball, transcript of autobiographical notes prepared for John Trout, August 9, 1993, p. 3 (in possession of John Trout; hereafter

Trout Memoir). These were notes written for Trout when it appeared that he would write a biography of Ball.

36. Ball Memoir, p. 6; Hess interview.

37. Ball, Trout Memoir, p. 3.

38. Ball Memoir, pp. 5–7; Ball to Mr. Joseph J. Tighe, Regional Representative, BOASI, Philadelphia, February 26, 1941, Ball Papers; Ball, "Standard Form 58," n.d., Ball Papers.

39. Ball Memoir, pp. 8–9.

40. It did maintain some administrative and research offices in Washington, D.C., first as part of what became the Department of Health and Human Services and then, after 1994, as an independent agency.

41. Ball Memoir, p. 9.

42. "Social Security Administrative Order 57, Organization and Functions of the Bureau of the Old-Age and Survivors Insurance, 4/25/41," Ball Papers.

43. Ball Memoir, p 12.

44. I gathered this information on Alvin David from the various biographical items in the Alvin David file, SSA History Archives, Baltimore. David died at age 95 early in 2002. His obituary appeared in the *Baltimore Sun* on February 27, 2002.

45. Alvin David, interview by Larry DeWitt, October 27, 1997, Chicago, SSA History Archives, available on the Web at http://www.ssa.gov/history/adavidorl.html.

46. Ball, Halamandaris interview; Ball Memoir, p. 308.

47. Ball Memoir, pp. 15–18.

48. Ibid., p. 18; Ball, Trout Memoir, p. 10.

49. "Notes for Your Guidance," no author but attributed to Robert Ball, SSA History Archives; "This is the first document I wrote for general circulation in the Social Security Administration," he later wrote in an edited volume of his writings. "It reflects both the agency's official view and my own view of what I have always thought a government agency should be" (Ball, *Insuring the Essentials: Bob Ball on Social Security*, ed. Thomas N. Bethell [New York: Century Foundation Press, 2000], p.113).

50. Analysis Division, Bureau of Old-Age and Survivors Insurance, "A Program for the Development of Old-Age and Survivors Insurance, Report 2, Coverage of the Self-Employed," Social Security Board, rev. July 1945, in Ball Papers; Ball, "Standard Form 58," n.d., Ball Papers.

51. I have written about the condition of the Social Security program in the 1940s in such pieces as Berkowitz, "History and Social Security Reform," in *Social Security and Medicare: Individual versus Collective Risk and Responsibility*, ed. Sheila Burke, Eric R. Kingson, and Uwe E. Reinhardt

(Washington, D.C.: National Academy of Social Insurance, 2000), pp. 31–55; Berkowitz, "Research and Politics in Policymaking for Social Security," *Journal of Gerontology Social Sciences* 52B, 3 (May 1997), pp. S115–S116; and Berkowitz, "The Historical Development of Social Security in the United States," in *Social Security in the 21st Century*, ed. Eric Kingson and James Schulz (New York: Oxford University Press, 1997), pp. 22–38. See also Edwin Amenta, *Bold Relief: Institutional Politics and the Origins of Modern Social Policy* (Princeton: Princeton University Press, 1998), and Bartholomew H. Sparrow, *From the Outside In: World War II and the American State* (Princeton: Princeton University Press, 1996), pp. 33–66.

52. *Issues in Social Security*, chapter 1, Report to the Ways and Means Committee, 1946, reprinted in *Readings in Social Security*, ed. William Haber and Wilbur J. Cohen (New York: Prentice Hall, 1948), p. 247.

53. Analysis Division, Bureau of Old-Age and Survivors Insurance, "Program for the Development of Old-Age and Survivors Insurance," pp. 12–15; Robert C. Lieberman, *Shifting the Color Line: Race and the American Welfare State* (Cambridge: Harvard University Press, 1998).

54. Lieberman, *Shifting the Color Line*; Ball Memoir, p. 20.

55. See Elizabeth de Schweinitz, "Biographical Notes on the Career of Karl de Schweinitz," n.d., Ball Papers. In addition to his work with Ball and as a social welfare administrator, de Schweinitz was also a noted historian of social welfare who published *England's Road to Social Security* (Philadelphia: University of Pennsylvania Press, 1943).

56. Ball, Trout Memoir, pp. 11–12.

57. Berkowitz, *Mr. Social Security*, pp. 55–56.

58. Witte, *Development of the Social Security Act*, pp. 29–30; Altmeyer, *Formative Years*, pp. 296–97; William Graebner, *A History of Retirement: The Meaning and Function of an American Institution, 1885–1978* (New Haven: Yale University Press, 1980), p. 185; biographical information from J. Douglas Brown Papers, Mudd Library, Princeton University, Princeton, N.J.

59. A typical communication from Ball to Brown reads, "I feel that it would be most helpful for you to cover again some of the fundamental philosophy that you have written and talked about over the years—the significance of relating benefits to wages" (Robert Ball to J. Douglas Brown, October 4, 1957, Ball Papers).

60. J. Douglas Brown, "The American Philosophy of Social Insurance," Sidney Hillman Memorial Lecture, November 18, 1955, University of Wisconsin, transmitted in Hugh McKenna, Division of Field Operations, to all regional directors, July 5, 1956, Ball Papers.

61. J. Douglas Brown, "Developments in the Social Security Program," *Proceedings* 21, 2 (January 1945); Academy of Political Science,

Columbia University, "Shaping the Economic Future," reprinted in *Readings in Social Security,* ed. William Haber and Wilbur J. Cohen (New York: Prentice Hall, 1948), p. 127.

62. Ball Memoir, p. 23.

63. Ibid., p. 283.

64. Ball to Doris Brown, n.d., but 1987 in Chronological Files, 1987, Ball Papers.

65. Robert M. Ball, "Social Insurance and the Right to Assistance," *Social Service Review* 21 (September 1947), pp. 331–44.

66. 80th Congress, 1st sess., S.R. 141, July 7, 1947, submitted by Eugene Millikin and Walter George.

67. Mark H. Leff, "Speculating in Social Security Futures: The Perils of Payroll Tax Financing, 1939–1950," in *Social Security: The First Half-Century,* ed. Gerald D. Nash, Noel H. Pugach, and Richard F. Tomasson (Albuquerque: University of New Mexico Press, 1988), pp. 243–78; James. L. Dergay, "Independent Legitimators in a Time of Social Insurance Consensus: The 1948 Advisory Council and the Passage of the 1950 Amendments to the Social Security Act" (master's thesis, University of Maryland, 1996); Wilbur J. Cohen to Edwin Witte, September 25, 1947, Box 35, Edwin Witte Papers, Wisconsin State Historical Society, Madison.

68. Arthur Altmeyer to Eugene Millikin, September 29, 1947, and Millikin to Altmeyer, September 26, 1947, Ball Papers; Jacob Perlman to Office of the Director, BOASI, October 15, 1947, Ball Papers; Sherwood B. Stanley to Altmeyer, October 4, 1947, Ball Papers.

69. Edwin Witte to Wilbur J. Cohen, October 8, 1947, Box 35, Witte Papers. On Folsom see Sanford M. Jacoby, *Modern Manors: Welfare Capitalism since the New Deal* (Princeton: Princeton University Press, 1997), and Jacoby, "Employers and the Welfare State: The Role of Marion B. Folsom," *Journal of American History* 80 (September 1993), pp. 525–56. On the relationship between business and Social Security more generally see Sheryl R. Tynes, *Turning Points in Social Security: From "Cruel Hoax" to "Sacred Entitlement"* (Stanford: Stanford University Press, 1996), and Kim McQuaid, *Uneasy Partners: Big Business in American Politics, 1945–1990* (Baltimore: Johns Hopkins University Press, 1994).

70. Alice M. Hoffman and Howard S. Hoffman, *The Cruikshank Chronicles: Anecdotes, Stories, and Memoirs of a New Deal Liberal* (Hampden, Conn.: Archon Books, 1989); Edward Berkowitz, "How to Think about the Welfare State," *Labor History* 32 (fall 1991), pp. 489–502; Ball Memoir, p. 38.

71. Wilbur J. Cohen to J. Douglas Brown, October 1, 1947, Box 27, Wilbur J. Cohen Papers, Wisconsin State Historical Society, Madison.

72. "Meeting of the Preparatory Committee of the Advisory Council

on Social Security to the Senate Committee on Finance," Hotel Commodore, New York, October 17, 1947, Record Group 46, Senate 80A-F8, Committee on Finance, Box 3, Folder 7, National Archives, Washington, D.C.

73. Ball Memoir, p. 42; "Meeting of the Preparatory Committee of the Advisory Council on Social Security to the Senate Committee on Finance," Harvard Club, New York, November 22, 1947, RG 46, Sen. 80A-F8, Committee on Finance, Box 3, Folder 7, National Archives.

74. Ball Memoir, pp. 43, 50.

75. Ibid., pp. 47, 49; Alvin David, interview.

76. Schieber and Shoven, *Real Deal,* p. 89; Robert Ball, interview by David G. McComb, November 5, 1968, p. 16, Oral History Collection, Lyndon Baines Johnson Presidential Library, Austin, Texas.

77. "Summary of Third Meeting of the Advisory Council on Social Security to the Senate Committee on Finance," February 20–21, 1948, RG 46, Sen. 80A-F8, Committee on Finance, Box 3, Folder 7, National Archives.

78. Advisory Council on Social Security, *Old-Age and Survivors Insurance,* p. 1; Ball, Trout Memoir , cassette, side 3, transcript, p. 14.

79. "Summary of the First Meeting of the Advisory Council on Social Security to the Senate Committee on Finance," December 4 and 5, 1947, RG 46, Sen. 80A-F8, Committee on Finance, Box 3, Folder 7, National Archives.

80. "Material for Advisory Council Meeting," O. C. Pogge to Mr. A. J. Altmeyer, December 2, 1947, Ball Papers.

81. A. J. Altmeyer, "Statement before the Advisory Council on Social Security—Senate Finance Committee," December 4, 1947, Ball Papers.

82. Ibid.; Ball Memoir, p. 42.

83. Ball Memoir, pp. 45–46.

84. "Summary of First Meeting of the Interim Committee of the Advisory Council on Social Security to the Senate Finance Committee," Washington, D.C., December 20, 1947, RG 46, Sen. 80A-F8, Committee on Finance, Box 3, Folder 7, National Archives; "Summary of Second Meeting of the Advisory Council on Social Security to the Senate Committee on Finance," Washington, D.C., January 16–17, 1948, RG 46, Sen. 80A-F8, Committee on Finance, Box 3, Folder 7, National Archives.

85. "Summary of Second Meeting of the Advisory Council on Social Security to the Senate Committee on Finance"; Ball Memoir, 45. On the disability insurance issue see Edward D. Berkowitz, *Disabled Policy: America's Programs for the Handicapped* (New York: Cambridge University Press, 1987).

86. "Summary of Second Meeting of the Advisory Council on Social Security to the Senate Committee on Finance"; "Summary of Second

Meeting of the Interim Committee of the Advisory Council on Social Security to the Senate Committee on Finance," February 7, 1948, RG 46, Sen. 80A-F8, Committee on Finance, Box 3, Folder 7, National Archives; Dergay, "Independent Legitimators"; Ball Memoir, p. 44; Advisory Council on Social Security, "Questions and Answers on Old-Age and Survivors Insurance: A Report to the Senate Committee on Finance from the Advisory Council on Social Security," n.d., Ball Papers.

87. "Materials for Advisory Council Meeting," O. C. Pogge to Mr. A. J. Altmeyer, December 2, 1947, Ball Papers; Altmeyer to Robert Ball, March 11, 1948, Ball Papers.

88. "Summary of the Fourth Meeting of the Advisory Council on Social Security to the Senate Committee on Finance," March 12–13, 1948, RG 46, Sen. 80A-F8, Committee on Finance, Box 3, Folder 7, National Archives.

89. Advisory Council on Social Security, *Old-Age and Survivors Insurance*.

90. Ball, Halamandaris interview.

91. Advisory Council on Social Security, *Old-Age and Survivors Insurance*, p. 1.

92. Advisory Council on Social Security, "Questions and Answers."

93. "Summary of the Fifth Meeting of the Advisory Council on Social Security to the Senate Committee on Finance," Washington, D.C., April 9–10, 1948, RG 46, Sen. 80A-F8, Committee on Finance, Box 3, Folder 7, National Archives; Arthur Altmeyer to Oscar Ewing, March 24, 1947, RG 235, Records of the Federal Security Agency, general decimal series, 1944–1950, 500–700, Box 265, National Archives.

94. Robert Ball to Sumner H. Slichter, January 1, 1949, RG 45, Sen. 80A-F8, Committee on Finance, S.R. 141, Advisory Council Members, Box 2, Folder 11, National Archives.

95. Dergay, "Independent Legitimators," pp. 53 (quoting Cruikshank), 57; Berkowitz, *Mr. Social Security*, pp. 62–69; Wilbur J. Cohen and Robert J. Myers, "Social Security Amendments of 1950: A Summary and Legislative History," *Social Security Bulletin* 13 (October 1950), 7.

2. Bureau Manager

1. For examples of other successful social welfare efforts during the 1950s see Stephen P. Strickland, *Politics, Science, and Dread Disease: A Short History of Medical Research Policy* (Cambridge: Harvard University Press, 1972), and Martha Lentz Walker, *Beyond Bureaucracy: Mary Elizabeth Switzer and Rehabilitation* (Lanham, Md.: University Press of America, 1985). Walker's book contains an introduction by Elliot Richardson, who notes (p. ix), "We have too many biographies of elected and

appointed officials in the Federal government but too few of great bu-reaucrats." One attempt to close the gap is Jameson W. Doig and Erwin C. Hargrove, eds., *Leadership and Innovation: A Biographical Perspective on Entrepreneurs in Government* (Baltimore: Johns Hopkins University Press, 1987).

2. For more on social welfare in the 1950s see Edward Berkowitz and Kim McQuaid, "Welfare Reform in the 1950's," *Social Service Review,* March 1980, pp. 45–58, reprinted in *Poverty and Public Policy in Modern America, ed.* Donald Critchlow and Ellis Hawley (Chicago: Dorsey Press), 1988.

3. The best political history of Social Security during this period con-tinues to be Martha Derthick, *Policymaking for Social Security* (Washing-ton, D.C.: Brookings Institution, 1979), but see also Sylvester J. Schieber and John B. Shoven, *The Real Deal: The History and Future of Social Secur-ity* (New Haven: Yale University Press, 1999), particularly part 1.

4. "Social Security Aide Gets New Recognition," *Baltimore Evening Sun,* March 14, 1961, p. 17; Delia Kuhn and Ferdinand Kuhn, eds., *Ad-ventures in Public Service: The Careers of Eight Honored Men in the United States Government* (New York: Vanguard Press: 1963).

5. Robert M. Ball, "What Contribution Rates for Old-Age and Survi-vors Insurance," *Social Security Bulletin* 12 (July 1949), pp. 2–8, reprinted in Ball, *Insuring the Essentials: Bob Ball on Social Security: A Selection of Ar-ticles and Essays from 1942 through 2000 by Robert M. Ball,* ed. Thomas N. Bethell (New York: Century Foundation Press, 2000), pp. 209–24; Ball, "Old Arguments and New," in *Social Security and Medicare: Individual versus Collection Risk and Responsibility,* ed. Sheila Burke, Eric R. King-son, and Uwe E. Reinhardt (Washington, D.C.: National Academy of Social Insurance, 2000), p. 59.

6. Robert Ball, autobiographical memorandum prepared for Ed-ward Berkowitz (hereafter Ball Memoir), pp. 53, 55.

7. Ibid., p. 56.

8. Robert Ball to Karl de Schweinitz, November 15, 1949, SSA His-tory Archives, Baltimore.

9. Ball Memoir, p. 56; Alvin David, interview by Larry DeWitt, Octo-ber 27, 1997, Chicago, SSA History Archives, available on the Web at http://www.ssa.gov/history/adavidorl.html.

10. See Robert Ball's "Standard Form 57," June 24, 1953, Ball Papers, which lists his employment history and other personal information.

11. Robert Ball, autobiographical notes prepared for John Trout (hereafter Trout Memoir), n.d., cassette 5, transcript, pp. 9–10; Ball Mem-oir, p. 57.

12. Robert M. Ball, assistant director in charge of the Division of Pro-gram Analysis, "Program Development: A Status Report," delivered at

conferences of field office managers, February 19–March 21, 1951, Ball Papers, p. 10.

13. Ibid., p. 13

14. Ibid., pp. 19–20.

15. Robert Ball, "Notes from Talk to FSA Regional Directors and Regional Representatives Conference," December 12, 1951, Washington, D.C., Ball Papers.

16. Ball Memoir, pp. 54–55.

17. Ball, Trout Memoir, cassette, side 6, transcript, p. 12.

18. National Planning Association, *Pensions in the United States: A Study Prepared for the Joint Committee on the Economic Report by the National Planning Association* (Washington D.C.: Government Printing Office, 1953), pp. 25, 29.

19. Ball Memoir, p. 60.

20. For a good overview of the events leading to the 1952 amendments see Wilbur J. Cohen, "The Legislative History of the Social Security Amendments of 1952," mimeograph, June 1954, Box 249, Wilbur J. Cohen Papers, Wisconsin State Historical Society, Madison.

21. Edward D. Berkowitz, *Mr. Social Security: The Life of Wilbur J. Cohen* (Lawrence: University Press of Kansas, 1995), pp. 72–76; Derthick, *Policymaking for Social Security*, p. 431; Ball Memoir, pp. 60–61; Ball, Trout Memoir, cassette, side 6, transcript, p. 12.

22. Ball Memoir, pp. 59–60.

23. Schieber and Shoven, *Real Deal*, p. 126; Ball, Trout Memoir, cassette, side 6, transcript, p. 15; Robert Ball, interview by J. Halamandaris, December 1987, Washington, D.C., p. 14, transcript in SSA History Archives.

24. Ball Memoir, pp. 76–78.

25. Arthur J. Altmeyer, *The Formative Years of Social Security* (Madison: University of Wisconsin, 1966), pp. 211–12.

26. Nelson Rockefeller to Jane Hoey, October 27, 1953, and Hoey to Rockefeller, November 3, 1953, OF 236-B-2-Box 9092, Central Files, Eisenhower Library, Abilene, Kansas; "Mrs. Hobby Ousts Key Aide," n.d., but probably November 3, 1953, in clipping file, Box 57, Nelson Rockefeller Papers, Rockefeller Archives, Pocantico, New York.

27. Berkowitz, *Mr. Social Security*, pp. 71–93.

28. Ibid., p. 82; Robert M. Ball, interview by Peter A. Corning, Washington, D.C., April 5, 1967, Oral History Collection, Columbia University, New York; Ball Memoir, pp. 70–71.

29. Ball, Trout Memoir, pp. 14–15.

30. Derthick, *Policymaking for Social Security*, pp. 144–57; M. Albert Linton to Robert L. Hogg, executive vice-president, American Life Convention, December 17, 1952, Box 26, Oveta Culp Hobby Papers,

Eisenhower Library; Elizabeth Wickenden, "Comments on Proposed Revised Policy Declaration by the United States Chamber of Commerce on Social Security for the Aged, December 9, 1952," Box 51, Cohen Papers; Chamber of Commerce, *Improving Social Security: An Analysis of the Present Federal Security Program for the Aged and the Proposal of the Chamber of Commerce of the United States* (Washington, D.C.: Chamber of Commerce, 1953).

31. Robert M. Ball, interview by David G. McComb, November 5, 1968, p. 7, Oral History Collection, Lyndon Baines Johnson Library, Austin, Texas.

32. Ball Memoir, p. 66.

33. Ball, Trout Memoir, cassette, side 6, transcript, p. 15; Berkowitz, *Mr. Social Security*, p. 85.

34. Ball noted, "there was explicit discussion at a meeting of the consultants as whether or not my name should be included in the reports and the decision was that acknowledging my role might weaken the objectivity and force of their presentations, although they were careful to thank me profusely for my work." Ball to Edward Berkowitz, September 5, 2001, in materials I will make available to the SSA History Archives, Baltimore.

35. Consultants on Social Security, *A Report to the Secretary of Health, Education, and Welfare on Extension of Old-Age and Survivors Insurance to Additional Groups of Current Workers* (Washington, D.C.: Department of Health, Education, and Welfare, 1953), pp. 1, 7; Ball Memoir, p. 71; Ball, Trout Memoir, cassette, side 6, transcript, p. 16.

36. Eveline M. Burns, interview, February 10, 1965, Oral History Collection, Columbia University, pp. 99–100, quoted in Derthick, *Policymaking for Social Security*, pp. 98–99.

37. Ball Memoir, p. 68.

38. See Carl Curtis to Daniel Reed, December 22, 1953, Box 33, Cohen Papers, and Lewis Meriam, Karl Schlotterbeck, and Mildred Maroney, *The Cost and Financing of Social Security* (Washington, D.C.: Brookings Institution, 1950).

39. Robert Ball, interview by Larry DeWitt, Alexandria, Va., interview 3, April 3, 2001, SSA History Archives.

40. *Analysis of the Social Security System: Hearings before a Subcommittee of the Committee on Ways and Means, House of Representatives, Eighty-third Congress, First Session on OASI: Coverage, Eligibility, Benefits and Public Assistance*, November 18, 19, and 20, 1953 (Washington, D.C.: Government Printing Office, 1954), p. 500.

41. Ibid., p. 645.

42. Ibid., p. 649.

43. Ball Memoir, p. 68.

44. Ball, Trout Memoir, cassette, side 6, transcript, pp. 17–18.

45. "The appointment of John Tramburg had a little more behind it. Both Wilbur (Cohen) and I knew John Tramburg through the American Public Welfare Association and Loula Dunn, its chief executive. His support for the existing program was known before he was appointed and Wilbur particularly pushed his appointment through back channels." Ball to Berkowitz, September 5, 2001.

46. Ball Memoir, p. 69.

47. Ball, McComb interview, p. 8.

48. Ball Memoir, p. 73.

49. Ibid., p. 78; John Campbell to Bob Ball, February 22, 1954, Ball Papers; Ball to Campbell, March 1, 1954, Ball Papers.

50. "An Interview with the New Director," *OASIS* (a newsletter for Social Security employees) 14, 2 (February 1954).

51. Robert Ball, interview by Larry DeWitt, March 12, 2001, interview 2, Alexandria, Va., SSA History Archives.

52. Ball Memoir, p. 81; Robert Ball to Nancy Lupo, September 29, 1984, Ball Papers.

53. Ball, Trout Memoir, cassette, side 6, transcript, pp. 19–20; Ball Memoir, p. 92.

54. Arthur Altmeyer to Wilbur Cohen, August 25, 1954, Box 6, Cohen Papers.

55. Robert Ball, "Post Amendment Bureau Conference," November 1954, Ball Papers.

56. Ibid.

57. Edward D. Berkowitz, *Disabled Policy: America's Programs for the Handicapped* (New York: Cambridge University Press, 1987), pp. 72–73.

58. Edwin Beach, executive secretary, Advisory Committee on Selection of Social Welfare Director, to Robert Ball, September 24, 1954, Ball Papers; Ball to Beach, October 1, 1954, Ball Papers; Beach to Ball, October 11, 1954, Ball Papers; Loula Dunn, director, American Public Welfare Association, to Ball, October 14, 1954, Ball Papers; J. Douglas Brown to Ball, October 14, 1954, Ball Papers; Ball to J. Douglas Brown, November 2, 1954, Ball Papers; Ball to Nelson Cruikshank, November 2, 1954, Ball Papers.

59. Robert Ball to the Secretary, November 17, 1954, Ball Papers; Ball to Mr. and Mrs. Karl de Schweinitz, November 17, 1954, Ball Papers; Ball to Nelson Cruikshank, November 26, 1954, Ball Papers.

60. J. Douglas Brown to Robert M. Ball, November 30, 1954, Ball Papers; Nelson Rockefeller to Ball, November 18, 1954, Ball Papers; Oveta Culp Hobby to Ball, November 18, 1954, Ball Papers.

61. Oveta Culp Hobby to Robert Ball, n.d., but 1955, Ball Papers.

62. Robert Ball to Marion Folsom, July 21, 1955, Ball Papers.

63. Ball Memoir, p. 75.

64. For more on the politics of disability insurance, see Berkowitz, *Disabled Policy,* pp. 41–78; Deborah A. Stone, *The Disabled State* (Philadelphia: Temple University Press, 1984), pp. 68–89; Edward Berkowitz and Daniel M. Fox, "The Politics of Social Security Disability Expansion: Social Security Disability Insurance, 1935–1986," *Journal of Policy History* 1 (1989), p. 244.

65. Ball, interview by McComb, p. 24.

66. Ball Memoir, p. 75.

67. Ball, interview by McComb, p. 26.

68. Berkowitz, *Disabled Policy,* p. 76; Edward Berkowitz and Wendy Wolff, "Disability Insurance and the Limits of American History," *Public Historian* (spring 1986), pp. 65–82.

69. Nelson Cruikshank to Arthur Altmeyer, July 18, 1956, Box 11A, Nelson Cruikshank Papers, Wisconsin State Historical Society, Madison. For a recent description of the passage of disability insurance, see Robert A. Caro, *Master of the Senate* (New York: Alfred A. Knopf, 2002), pp. 678–82.

70. Robert Ball, "OASI's Place in the Economic and Social System," speech given at district managers' conference, November 15, 1956, Ball Papers.

71. Ibid.

72. Robert Ball, "A New Period in Bureau History," speech given at regional managers' conferences, 1957–58, Ball Papers; "Background Notes on OASI Operations," prepared by Sam Crouch, July 2, 1956, Ball Papers.

73. "The Administration's Goals and Accomplishments," January 4, 1954, *Public Papers of the President* (Washington, D.C.: Government Printing Office, 1960), pp. 2–6.

74. Robert Ball, "Bureau Objectives, presented at a series of OASI conferences, October 1955–February 1956," Ball Papers.

75. Ball, interview by Larry DeWitt, interview 2, March 12, 2001.

76. See Edward Berkowitz, "Health Care Financing Administration," in *A Historical Guide to the U.S. Government,* ed. George Thomas Kurian (New York: Oxford University Press, 1998), p. 287.

77. *OASI: Statement of Bureau Objectives,* agency pamphlet, widely distributed circa 1958, pp. 4, 17, 20, Ball Papers; a version of these objectives is reprinted in Ball, *Insuring the Essentials,* pp. 101–11.

78. OASI: *Statement of Bureau Objectives,* pp. 5, 7, 8, 10, 20.

79. Ibid., pp. 12–13.

80. Ball, Halamandaris interview, p. 20.

81. Fedele Fauri to Robert Ball, March 27, 1958, Ball Papers; Arthur Flemming to Victor Christgau and Ball, September 11, 1958, Ball Papers; Beth de Schweinitz to Ball, March 5, 1958, Ball Papers.

82. *A Report to the Secretary of Health, Education, and Welfare on the Operation of the Bureau of Old Age and Survivors Insurance by a Group of Specially Appointed Consultants* (Washington, D.C.: Department of Health, Education, and Welfare: 1958).

83. Jack S. Futterman, interview by Larry DeWitt, Ellicott City, Md., March 24, 2000, pp. 17–21, 111, 266, SSA History Archives.

84. Robert Ball to Jack S. Futterman, May 15, 1959, Ball Papers; Futterman interview, p. 126.

85. Ball Memoir, p. 95; Robert Ball to John J. Finelli, vice president, Electronic Installations, Metropolitan Life Insurance Company, March 20, 1958, Ball Papers.

86. Robert Ball to Charles Schottland, June 4, 1958, Ball Papers; Ball to Reinie Hohaus, June 4, 1958, Ball Papers; Hohaus to Ball, June 5, 1958, Ball Papers. On Hohaus see Derthick, *Policymaking for Social Security,* pp. 136–42. Widely reprinted, Hohaus's essay "Equity, Adequacy, and Related Factors in Old Age Security" can be found in *Social Security Programs: Problems and Policies,* ed. William Haber and Wilbur J. Cohen (Homewood, Ill: Richard D. Irwin, 1960), p. 62.

87. "Statement Presenting Report to Secretary," June 4, 1958, Ball Papers; *A Report to the Secretary of Health, Education, and Welfare on the Operation of the Bureau of Old Age and Survivors Insurance.*

88. Department of Health, Education, and Welfare, press release, June 2, 1959, Ball Papers.

89. Ball Memoir, p. 87; Berkowitz, *Disabled Policy,* pp. 109–10; House Committee on Ways and Means, Subcommittee on the Administration of the Social Security Laws, *Administration of Social Security Disability Insurance Program: Preliminary Report* (Washington: Government Printing Office, 1960); Subcommittee on the Administration of the Social Security Laws, *Administration of Social Security Disability Insurance Program: Hearings,* 86th Cong., 1st sess., November 4, 5, 6, 9, 10, and 12, and December 7, 1959 (Washington, D.C.: Government Printing Office, 1960); Arthur E. Hess, "Old Age Survivors and Disability Insurance: Early Problems and Operations of Disability Provisions," *Social Security Bulletin* 20 (December 1957), p. 4.

90. Robert Ball to Arthur Hess, November 20, 1959, Ball Papers.

91. Ball Memoir, pp. 87–88.

92. "Ball Named to Top Ten," item in *OASIS* (bureau newsletter), n.d., but clearly 1958, Ball Files, SSA History Archives.

93. Robert Ball to Marion Folsom, July 14, 1958, Ball Papers; Ball, McComb interview, p. 33.

94. Mr. Folsom, telephone call to Robert Ball, July 8, 1957, typescript in Ball Papers.

95. George K. Wyman to William Mitchell, November 5, 1959, RG 47, Records of the Social Security Administration, File 326.102,

Box 70, Accession 64A-751, Washington National Records Center, Suitland, Md.

96. Robert M. Ball, "Old-Age, Survivors, and Disability Insurance on its 25th Anniversary," *Public Welfare,* July 1960, pp. 151–52.

97. Arthur S. Flemming to Robert Ball, February 3, 1961, Ball Papers.

98. Ball Memoir, pp. 99–102. Ed Gibson, Center for Public Administration and Policy, Virginia Polytechnic Institute and State University, in "Tales of Two Cities: The Administrative Facade of Social Security," an unpublished paper, provides interesting detail on the physical spaces in which the Social Security program operated.

99. "Notes Used by Robert M. Ball, October 11, 1960, Talk to Region VIII Managers Conference, Baltimore Maryland," Ball Papers.

100. Robert Ball to Nelson Cruikshank, November 10, 1960, Ball Papers.

101. Ball Memoir, pp. 98–99; Berkowitz, *Mr. Social Security,* pp. 133–37.

102. Ball Memoir, p.106; Wilbur Cohen, interview by Charles Morrissey, November 11, 1964, John F. Kennedy Presidential Oral History Collection, p. 20.

103. Robert M. Ball, "Health Insurance and Government," address at the American Society of Insurance Management, Inc., Delaware Valley Chapter, Philadelphia, October 19, 1961, Ball Papers; Ball, "The Role of Social Insurance in Preventing Economic Dependency," Second National Conference on the Churches and Social Welfare, Cleveland, Ohio, 1961, Ball Papers.

104. "Income Maintenance Program after an Enemy Attack," in Victor Christgau to Charles Schottland, June 13, 1957, Ball Papers; J. S. Futterman, executive assistant to Robert Ball, to Roy Touchet, assistant manager, Division of Management, November 1, 1961, Ball Papers.

105. Theodore R. Marmor, with Phillip Fellman, "Entrepreneurship in Public Management: Wilbur Cohen and Robert Ball," in *Leadership and Innovation: A Biographical Perspective on Entrepreneurs in Government,* ed. Jameson W. Doig and Erwin C. Hargrove (Baltimore: Johns Hopkins University Press, 1987), p. 215; Robert Highton, "Robert Ball Is Boss to 34,661," *Baltimore Sun,* March 28, 1962, clipping file, SSA History Archives.

106. "Social Security Aide Gets New Recognition," *Baltimore Evening Sun,* March 14, 1961, p. 17.

107. Marjorie Hunter, "Social Security Commissioner Is Planning to Retire This Year," *New York Times,* February 28, 1962, p. 18; Charles McKinley and Robert W. Frase, *Launching Social Security: A Capture-and-Record Account, 1935–1937* (Madison: University of Wisconsin Press, 1970), p. 500.

108. Ball Memoir, p. 106.

109. "Ball Named by Kennedy," *Baltimore Sun,* March 20, 1962, and Joe Wachtman, "Federal Log: Ball Expected to Assume SS Reins Early in April," *News Post American,* April 1, 1962, both in clippings file, SSA History Archives; "Minutes of Executive Staff Meeting," March 20, 1962, Ball Papers.

110. "Remarks Made at Swearing-In Ceremony for Robert M. Ball, Commissioner of Social Security," April 17, 1962, Ball Papers.

3. Medicare

1. Robert Ball, interview by Blanche Coll, p. 6, February 2, 1988, Washington, D.C.

2. Karl de Schweinitz to Robert Ball, n.d., but circa 1963, Ball Papers.

3. Robert Ball, autobiographical memorandum prepared for Edward Berkowitz (hereafter Ball Memoir), pp. 107–8.

4. Jack S. Futterman, interview by Larry DeWitt, Ellicott City, Md., March 24, 2000, p. 141, Social Security Administration (hereafter SSA) History Archives.

5. Ball Memoir, p. 111.

6. Robert Ball, interview by Larry DeWitt, Alexandria, Va., interview 2, March 12, 2001, p. 64, SSA History Archives, available on the Web at http://www.ssa.gov/history/orals/ball2.html.

7. The passage of the AFDC-unemployed parents program on a temporary basis in 1961 and on a permanent basis in 1962 helped to ease some of the problem. See Gilbert Steiner, *The State of Welfare* (Washington, D.C.: Brookings Institution, 1971), and Blanche D. Coll, *Safety Net: Welfare and Social Security, 1929–1979* (New Brunswick: Rutgers University Press, 1995). Ball noted that if a man other than the father supported a child, it was unclear whether that would disqualify the child (Ball to Berkowitz, July 15, 2002).

8. Robert Ball, DeWitt interview, interview 2, March 12, 2001, p. 64. The development of welfare has produced a voluminous literature that notably includes, in addition to the books cited in note 7, Linda Gordon, ed., *Women, the State, and Welfare* (Madison: University of Wisconsin Press, 1990); Gordon, *Pitied But Not Entitled: Single Mothers and the History of Welfare* (New York: Free Press, 1994); Robyn Muncy, *Creating a Female Dominion in American Reform* (New York: Oxford University Press, 1991); Theda Skocpol, *Protecting Soldiers and Mothers* (Cambridge: Harvard University Press, 1993); Roy Lubove, *The Struggle for Social Security, 1900–1935* (Cambridge: Harvard University Press, 1968); James T. Patterson, *America's Struggle against Poverty, 1900–1980* (Cambridge: Harvard University Press, 1981) . I have written on this subject at greater length in Edward D. Berkowitz, *America's*

Welfare State: From Roosevelt to Reagan (Baltimore: Johns Hopkins Press, 1991).

9. Ball, Coll interview, p. 3.

10. Ball Memoir, p. 109.

11. Ibid., pp. 111–12.

12. Wilbur Cohen to Ellen Winston, March 16, 1967, Wilbur J. Cohen Papers, Wisconsin State Historical Society, Madison; see also Martha Derthick, *Uncontrollable Spending for Social Services Grants* (Washington, D.C.: Brookings Institution, 1975).

13. Ball Memoir, pp. 109–10.

14. Quoted in Edward D. Berkowitz, *Mr. Social Security: The Life of Wilbur J. Cohen* (Lawrence: University Press of Kansas, 1995), p. 152.

15. Robert Ball to Karl de Schweinitz, January 3, 1963, Ball Papers.

16. Margaret Weir, Ann Shola Orloff, and Theda Skocpol, "Introduction: Understanding American Social Politics," in *The Politics of Social Policy in the United States,* ed. Weir, Orloff, and Skocpol (Princeton: Princeton University Press, 1988), pp. 8–9. For contrary views to those expressed here on the development of Social Security and welfare see the books by Linda Gordon cited in note 8 and the work of Gwendolyn Mink, such as *The Wages of Motherhood: Inequality in the Welfare State, 1917–1942* (Ithaca: Cornell University Press, 1995) and *Welfare's End* (Ithaca: Cornell University Press, 1998).

17. A useful overview of Medicare's passage, development, and current policy problems is Marilyn Moon, *Medicare Now and in the Future* (Washington, D.C.: Urban Institute Press, 1993). On the politics of Medicare's passage, see Peter A. Corning, *The Evolution of Medicare: From Idea to Law* (Washington, D.C.: Government Printing Office, 1969), available on the Web at http://www.ssa.gov/history/corning.html; Eugene Feingold, *Medicare: Policy and Politics* (San Francisco: Chandler, 1966); Richard Harris, *A Sacred Trust* (New York: New American Library, 1966), James Sundquist, *Politics and Policy: The Eisenhower, Kennedy, and Johnson Years* (Washington, D.C.: Brookings Institution, 1968); Paul Starr, *The Social Transformation of American Medicine* (New York: Basic Books, 1982); Daniel M. Fox, *Health Politics, Health Policies: The British and American Experience, 1911–1965* (Princeton: Princeton University Press, 1986); Theodore R. Marmor, with Jan S. Marmor, *The Politics of Medicare* (Chicago: Aldine, 1973); Max J. Skidmore, *Medicare and the American Rhetoric of Reconciliation* (Montgomery: University of Alabama Press, 1970); Sherri I. David, *With Dignity: The Search for Medicare and Medicaid* (Westport, Conn.: Greenwood Press, 1985).

18. Robert Ball, interview by Peter A. Corning, April 5, 1967, p. 29, Oral History Collection, Columbia University, New York.

19. "New from the AFL-CIO," press release for August 28, 1957, Ball Papers; "Forand Calls for Major Improvements in Social Security," press release from office of Representative Aime J. Forand, August 27, 1957, Ball Papers.

20. Robert Ball, interview by Larry DeWitt, interview 3, April 3, 2001, p. 99. SSA History Archives, available on the Web at http://www.ssa.gov/history/orals/ball3.html.

21. I gathered this information on Alvin David from the various biographical items in the Alvin David file, SSA History Archives. The file contains various short biographical statements about David including one headed "Mr Alvin M. David" and dated October 31, 1968, as well as David's curriculum vitae.

22. See Alvin David, interview by Larry DeWitt, October 27, 1997, Chicago, SSA History Archives, available on the Web at http://www.ssa.gov/history/adavidorl.html.

23. Futterman interview, pp. 168, 126.

24. Jack S. Futterman to John Trout, December 28, 1992, Ball Papers.

25. For details, see the books cited in note 17. For the events that led up to Medicare see Monte M. Poen, *Harry S Truman versus the Medical Lobby: The Genesis of Medicare* (Columbia: University of Missouri Press, 1979); Daniel S. Hirshfield, *The Lost Reform: The Campaign for Compulsory Health Insurance in the United States from 1932–1943* (Cambridge: Harvard University Press, 1970); Roger J. Hollingsworth, *A Political Economy of Medicine: Great Britain and the United States* (Baltimore: Johns Hopkins University Press, 1986); Beatrix Hoffman, *The Wages of Sickness: The Politics of Health Insurance in Progressive America* (Chapel Hill: University of North Carolina Press, 2000).

26. "Memorandum of phone call from Harry Becker to Robert Ball," June 8, 1961, Ball Papers; "Health Insurance Benefits—Use of Blue Cross and Other Private Organizations to Facilitate Payments to Hospitals and Other Providers," Theodore Sorensen Papers, Box 36, Subject Files, 1961–1964, Medical Care for the Aged, June 2–13, 1962, John F. Kennedy Library, Boston.

27. Burr Harrison to Abraham Ribicoff, January 9, 1962, Ball Papers; Robert Ball to Harrison, January 26, 1962, Ball Papers.

28. Robert Ball to the secretary, May 12, 1962, Ball Papers.

29. Robert Ball, interview by John Trout, Alexandria Va., circa 1991, transcript supplied to author on floppy disk by Trout.

30. Ball, Corning interview, pp. 45–46. On Mills's role in the passage of Medicare see Julian Zelizer, *Taxing America: Wilbur D. Mills, Congress, and the State* (New York: Cambridge University Press, 1998).

31. Futterman interview, pp. 125, 137.

32. "The Government's Case on Medical Help for the Aged," *National Observer,* March 25, 1963, Ball Papers; Robert M. Ball, "Medical Care: Its Social and Organizational Aspects—The American Social Security Program," *New England Journal of Medicine* 270 (January 30, 1964), pp. 232–36.

33. Robert M. Ball, "Medicare Recollections," speech delivered July 20, 1995, Ball Papers.

34. "Remarks of Congressman Wilbur D. Mills before the Downtown Little Rock Lions Club," December 2, 1964, Box 151, Cohen Papers.

35. See Marmor, *Politics of Medicare,* pp. 64–65; Wilbur Cohen to the president, March 2, 1965, Box 83, Cohen Papers; Fred Arner, "Wilbur Mills' Three-Layered Cake—It's [sic] 25th Birthday," unpublished manuscript; Harris, *Sacred Trust,* p. 187.

36. Ball, Corning interview, p. 16.

37. Ball, Trout interview.

38. Robert Ball to Betty Dillon (his personal assistant), April 12, 1972, Ball Papers.

39. Futterman interview, pp. 155–57.

40. Robert Ball, interview by J. Halamandaris, December 1987, p. 18, transcript available in SSA History Archives.

41. National Academy of Social Insurance, "Reflections on Implementing Medicare," typescript, 1993, transcript of a discussion with Robert Ball and Arthur Hess on January 31, 1992, pp. 9, 21.

42. Erwin Hytner to John Trout, January 8, 1992, Ball Papers.

43. Wilbur J. Cohen, "FDR and the New Deal: A Personal Reminiscence," *Milwaukee History* 6 (autumn 1983), p. 74.

44. Arthur Hess, interview by Edward Berkowitz, Charlottesville, Va., July 8, 1996, Health Care Financing Administration (HCFA; now called Centers for Medicare and Medicaid Services) Oral Interview Collection, Baltimore. This interview is available on the Web sites of both the Centers for Medicare and Medicaid Services (http://cms.hhs.gov/about/history/hess2.asp) and the Social Security Administration (http://www.ssa.gov/history/HESS2.html). For more on Hess see Martha Derthick, *Policymaking for Social Security* (Washington, D.C.: Brookings Institution), pp. 29–30. For Hess's experience with disability insurance see Edward D. Berkowitz, *Disabled Policy: America's Programs for the Handicapped* (New York: Cambridge University Press, 1987), pp. 160–61.

45. Hess interview.

46. Paul Rettig, interview by Edward D. Berkowitz, August 14, 1995, Washington, D.C., p. 10, HCFA Oral Interview Collection, available on the Web at http://www.ssa.gov/history/rettig.html and http://cms.hhs.gov/about/history/rettig.asp.

47. Ball, Halamandaris interview, p. 16.

48. National Academy of Social Insurance, "Reflections on Implementing Medicare," p. 15.

49. Ball, Halamandaris interview, p. 16. For more on HIBAC and on the implementation of Medicare see Herman Miles Somers and Anne Ramsay Somers, *Medicare and the Hospitals: Issues and Prospects* (Washington, D.C.: Brookings Institution, 1967); Judith M. Feder, *Medicare: The Politics of Federal Hospital Insurance* (Lexington, Mass.: Lexington Books, 1977).

50. See Somers and Somers, *Medicare and the Hospitals,* p. 36.

51. William Fullerton, phone interview by Mark Santangelo, Crystal River, Fla., 20 October 1995, pp. 2, 18, HCFA Oral History Collection, available on the Web at http://www.ssa.gov/history/fullert.html and http://cms.hhs.gov/about/history/fullert.asp.

52. Ball, "Medicare Recollections," p. 11.

53. National Academy of Social Insurance, "Reflections on Implementing Medicare," p. 15.

54. Robert M. Ball, "The Assignment of the Social Security Commissioner," 1972, typescript of report to the Secretary of Health, Education, and Welfare, Ball Papers, p. 48.

55. Robert M. Ball, "Hospitals and Health Insurance for the Aged," speech given at the 67th Annual Meeting of the American Hospital Association, August 30, 1965, Ball Papers.

56. Robert M. Ball, "Health Insurance for People Aged 65 and Over: First Steps in Administration," *Social Security Bulletin* 29 (February 1966), p. 6.

57. Somers and Somers, *Medicare and the Hospitals,* pp. 188, 163, 180.

58. Jay Constantine, interview by Ed Berkowitz, August 24, 1995, Alexandria, Va., p. 4, HCFA Oral History Collection, available on the Web at http://www.ssa.gov/history/CONSTANT.html and http://cms.hhs.gov/about/history/constant.asp.

59. National Academy of Social Insurance, "Reflections on Implementing Medicare," p. 25.

60. Ball Memoir, pp. 141–42.

61. Ball to the under secretary, August 12, 1965, Ball Papers.

62. Ibid. For more on the problems posed by voluntary health insurance see Rashi Fein, *Medical Care, Medical Costs: The Search for Health Insurance Policy* (Cambridge: Harvard University Press, 1986); Mark V. Paul, ed., *National Health Insurance* (Washington, D.C.: American Enterprise Institute, 1981); Victor R. Fuchs, *Who Shall Live? Health, Economics and Social Choice* (New York: Basic Books, 1974); Kenneth Arrow, "Uncertainty and the Welfare Economics of Medical Care," *American Economics Review* 53 (September 1963): 946.

63. Berkowitz, *Mr. Social Security,* pp. 232–38; Derthick, *Policymaking for Social Security,* pp. 325–34; Berkowitz, *Disabled Policy,* pp. 79–104.

64. Robert M. Ball, "A Progress Report on Medicare," speech delivered at the American Management Association, March 21, 1966, Ball Papers.

65. Robert Ball, "A Report on the Implementation of the Social Security Amendments of 1965," speech delivered to regional assistant commissioners and regional commissioners of the SSA, November 15, 1965, Baltimore, Ball Papers.

66. Robert M. Ball, "Health Insurance for People 65 or Over," speech delivered at American Pension Conference, January 26, 1966, Ball Papers.

67. White House press release, May 24, 1966, containing "Progress Report to the President on the Launching of Medicare," Ball Papers; Robert Ball, "A Report on the Implementation of the Medicare Provisions of the 1965 Amendments to the Social Security Act as of May 23, 1966," Ball Papers.

68. Robert Ball, "Talk Delivered on July 7, 1966 to the Employees of the Social Security Administration in Baltimore, Maryland at the Start of the Medicare Program," Ball Papers.

69. Robert Ball, "A Report on the Implementation of the Social Security Amendments of 1965," November 15, 1965, Ball Papers.

70. The best introduction to this monumental legislation and its effects is Hugh Davis Graham, *The Civil Rights Era: Origins and Development of National Policy, 1960–1972* (New York: Oxford University Press, 1990).

71. For a perceptive history of the hospital, see Charles E. Rosenberg, *The Care of Strangers: The Rise of America's Hospital System* (New York: Basic Books, 1987).

72. John Gardner to Lyndon Johnson, May 23, 1966, Ball Papers; Robert Ball, "Speaking Points," June 30, 1966, Ball Papers.

73. Ball, "Talk Delivered on July 7, 1966."

74. Robert M. Ball, interview by David G. McComb, November 5, 1968, pp. 40–41, Oral History Collection, Lyndon Baines Johnson Library, Austin, Texas.

75. Alvin M. David to Robert M. Ball, April 18, 1966, Ball Papers.

76. "Recollections (Discussions) by Social Security Administration Officials of Knowledge and/or Involvement in Certain Stages of Early Implementation of the Medicare Program (Calendar Year 1966)," group oral interview with Arthur Hess, September 25, 1992, Atlanta, Georgia, p. 11.

77. Ibid., p. 12.

78. Ball, "Talk Delivered on July 7, 1966 to the Employees of the Social Security Administration."

79. Robert Ball, "1965: Expectations; 1975: Realizations: What Next," Medical Care Seminar, Palm Springs, Calif., March 1–2, 1979, Ball Papers.

80. Obviously this is a matter of degree; in Ball's words of "how high you set the bar." Nonetheless, Ball believed that the substantial integration of the southern hospitals was "a major, major accomplishment and most of it occurred at the very beginning." Robert Ball to Edward Berkowitz, September 5, 2001, Ball Papers.

81. Ball, Halamandaris interview, p. 16.

82. For background on the distinctions between these sorts of plans see Starr, *Social Transformation of American Medicine,* pp. 290–334, and Lawrence D. Brown, *Politics and Health Care Organization: HMOs as Federal Policy* (Washington, D.C.: Brookings Institution, 1983), pp. 3–74.

83. Robert M. Ball to the secretary, January 27, 1966, Ball Papers.

84. Ibid.

85. Robert M. Ball to the under secretary, January 21, 1966, transmitting "Inquiries and Endorsements Regarding Carriers," January 23, 1966, Ball Papers.

86. Robert Ball to Wilbur J. Cohen, February 7, 1966, and other fragmentary materials in Part B carrier materials, Ball Papers.

87. David L. Copelman, "Memorandum of a Confidential Conversation with Herman Somers," January 13, 1966, Ball Papers.

88. Robert Ball to Wilbur J. Cohen, January 21, 1966, Ball Papers; Ball to the secretary, January 27, 1966, Ball papers.

89. Robert Ball to the under secretary, January 21, 1966, Ball Papers.

90. "Group Health Insurance, Inc. of N.Y.," n.d., write-up in Part B carrier materials, Ball Papers.

91. Robert Ball to Wilbur J. Cohen, February 7, 1966, Ball Papers.

92. Ball, McComb interview, p. 42.

93. Robert Ball to the under secretary, August 12, 1965, Ball Papers.

94. Robert Ball, "A Report on the Implementation of the Social Security Amendments of 1965," delivered to SSA regional assistant commissioners and regional commissioners, November 15, 1965, Baltimore, Ball Papers; "A Report on the Implementation of the Medicare Provisions of the 1965 Amendments to the Social Security Act as of May 23, 1966," from Robert M. Ball, commissioner of Social Security, in John Gardner to Lyndon Johnson, May 23, 1966, Ball Papers.

95. Robert Ball, "Chart Talk on Implementing Medicare," spring 1966, Ball Papers.

96. Robert M. Ball, "Hospitals and Health Insurance for the Aged," 67th Annual Meeting of the American Hospital Association, August 30, 1965, Ball Papers. It should be pointed out that the Bureau of Old-Age and Survivors Benefits started out in 1937 as the Bureau of Old-Age

Benefits, since survivors benefits were not added until 1939. On the creation of HCFA see Hale Champion, interview by Edward Berkowitz, Cambridge, Mass., August 9, 1995, p. 21, HCFA Oral History Collection, available on the Web at http://cms.hhs.gov/about/history/champ.asp and http://www.ssa.gov/history/champ.html; and also Joseph A. Califano Jr., *Governing America: An Insider's Report from the White House and the Cabinet* (New York: Simon and Schuster, 1981), pp. 41–45.

97. I am grateful to the SSA History Office for supplying information on SSA's organizational structure over time. See the material reproduced from a 1983 congressional study panel that is contained on the Web at http://www.ssa.gov/history/orghist.html.

98. National Academy of Social Insurance, "Reflections on Implementing Medicare," p. 4. Using a metaphor also adopted by Lyndon Johnson, Wilbur Cohen compared launching Medicare to preparing for D-Day; see Wilbur Cohen, interview by David McComb, December 8, 1968, Oral History Collection, tape 2, transcript, page 11, Lyndon Baines Johnson Library, Austin, Texas. See also Berkowitz, *Mr. Social Security,* pp. 243–54.

99. Ball, "Talk Delivered on July 7, 1966 to the Employees of the Social Security Administration."

100. Robert Ball to President Lyndon Johnson, October 14, 1966, Ball Papers. The text of the speech is also available in Ball Papers.

101. Ball, McComb interview, p. 48.

102. Ball Memoir, p. 143.

103. Robert Ball to Douglas Brown, July 7, 1966, Ball Papers.

104. "An Interview with Robert Ball," *Hospitals,* January 1, 1967, pp. 46–52, Ball Papers.

105. Robert Ball, "Is Medicare Worth the Price?" interview, *U.S. News and World Report,* July 21, 1969, clipping in Ball Papers.

106. *Medicare and Medicaid: Problems, Issues, and Alternatives,* Report of the Staff to the Committee on Finance, United States Senate, February 9, 1970 (Washington, , D.C.: Government Printing Office, 1970), pp. 3, 9, 20.

107. Constantine, Berkowitz interview, pp. 5–6.

108. Ball Memoir, p. 143.

109. Richard Nixon to Robert Finch, January 30, 1969, and enclosures, Ball Papers.

110. Ball, "Is Medicare Worth the Price?" p. 51.

111. Robert M. Ball, "Medicare Recollections," July 20, 1995, Ball Papers.

112. Robert M. Ball, Assignment of the Social Security Commissioner, December 1972, pp. 48–49, Ball Papers.

113. "Address by Robert M. Ball," Washington Journalism Center, Washington, D.C., January 29, 1973, Ball Papers.

114. Ball, Assignment of the Social Security Commissioner, p. 49.

115. See Fein, *Medical Care, Medical Costs;* Derthick, *Policymaking for Social Security,* p. 336.

116. Wilbur Cohen to Joseph Califano, January 19, 1968, Box 95, Cohen Papers.

117. Philip Lee, interview by Edward Berkowitz, November 27, 1995, Washington, D.C., HCFA Oral History Collection, available on the Web at http://cms.hhs.gov/about/history/lee.asp and http://www.ssa.gov/history/LEE.html.

118. Ball, "Medicare Recollections," p. 2.

119. For books on the "demise" of national health insurance see Jacob S. Hacker, *The Road to Nowhere: The Genesis of President Clinton's Plan for Health Security* (Princeton: Princeton University Press, 1997), and Theda Skocpol, *Boomerang: Health Care Reform and the Turn against Government* (New York: W. W. Norton, 1996).

120. "Comments of Robert Ball on Martha Derthick's August 1989 Draft of 'Agency under Stress: The Social Security Administration and American Government,'" Ball Papers.

121. See Fox, *Health Politics, Health Policies.*

4. Expanding Social Security

1. Martha Derthick, *Policymaking for Social Security* (Washington, D.C.: Brookings Institution, 1979), pp. 346–47.

2. Despite the importance of the 1972 legislation, it has not spawned much historical research into its political origins and policy implications, but see the indispensable Derthick, *Policymaking for Social Security,* pp. 339–68; Sylvester J. Schieber and John B. Shoven, *The Real Deal: The History and Future of Social Security* (New Haven: Yale University Press, 1999), pp. 346–62; R. Kent Weaver, *Automatic Government: The Politics of Indexation* (Washington, D.C.: Brookings Institution, 1988), and Julian Zelizer, *Taxing America: Wilbur D. Mills, Congress, and the States* (New York: Cambridge University Press, 1998).

3. Robert Ball, interview, *U.S. News and World Report,* December 7, 1964, pp. 54–63, in Robert Ball Papers, Wisconsin State Historical Society, Madison.

4. Robert M. Ball, "Social Security: A Changing Program for a Changing World," *St. Louis University Law Journal* 10 (winter 1965), p. 230; Ball, "Some Reflections on Selected Issues in Social Security," June 1967, Ball Papers.

5. Ball, "Social Security: A Changing Program," p. 233.

6. Robert Ball, "Some Reflections on Selected Issues in Social Security"; Ball, notes for interview with Chris Hartman, *Baltimore Sun,* January 25, 1968, Ball Papers.

7. Robert Ball to Alvin David, March 30, 1965, Ball Papers.

8. See the classic discussion of the nature of American reform in Richard Hofstadter, *The Age of Reform* (New York: Vintage Books, 1955). Another classic narrative of this type is Eric Goldman, *Rendezvous with Destiny: A History of Modern American Reform* (New York: Random House, 1953).

9. Wilbur J. Cohen, "The Legislative History of the Social Security Amendments of 1952," mimeo, June 1954, p. 11, Box 249, Wilbur J. Cohen Papers, Wisconsin State Historical Society, Madison.

10. See Derthick, *Policymaking for Social Security,* pp. 354–55.

11. On the relationship between economists and Social Security administrators see Mark H. Leff, *The Limits of Symbolic Reform: The New Deal and Taxation, 1933–1939* (New York: Cambridge University Press, 1984); Wilbur J. Cohen and Milton Friedman, *Social Security: Universal or Selective* (Washington, D.C.: American Enterprise Institute, 1972); Michael J. Boskin, *Too Many Promises: The Uncertain Future of Social Security* (Homewood, Ill.: Dow Jones–Irwin, 1986); Leff, "Speculating in Social Security Futures," in *Social Security: The First Half-Century,* ed. Gerald D. Nash, Noel H. Pugach, and Richard F. Tomasson (Albuquerque: University of New Mexico Press, 1988), p. 268; Edward Berkowitz, "Social Security and the Financing of the American State," in *Funding the American State, 1941–1995,* ed. W. Elliot Brownlee (New York: Cambridge University Press, 1996), pp. 148–93.

12. Robert Ball, autobiographical memorandum prepared for Edward Berkowitz (hereafter Ball Memoir), p. 153.

13. Ibid., p. 154. On Mills and his attitude toward Social Security see Zelizer, *Taxing America,* and Derthick, *Policymaking for Social Security.*

14. Robert Ball, interview by Larry DeWitt, interview 4, May 1, 2001, Alexandria, Va., SSA History Archives, Baltimore, available on the Web at http://www.ssa.gov/history/orals/ball4.html.

15. Wilbur Cohen to President Lyndon Johnson, August 24 and 28, 1967, Box 93, Cohen Papers; Joseph Loftus, "House GOP Unit Backs Bill Raising Social Security Benefits," *New York Times,* August 17, 1967, p. 21; James F. Clarity, "Lindsay Tells Senators of Peril in Limits on Welfare Assistance," *New York Times,* September 13, 1967, p. 31; Wilbur Cohen to Joseph Califano, December 8, 1967, Box 94, Cohen Papers; Cohen to the president, December 11, 1967, and John Gardner to the president, Box 51, Joseph Califano Papers, Lyndon Baines Johnson Library, Austin, Texas; Edward Berkowitz, *Mr. Social Security: The Life of Wilbur J. Cohen* (Lawrence: University Press of Kansas, 1995), pp. 249–62.

16. Ball, DeWitt interview, May 1, 2001.

17. Robert Ball, interview, *American Medical News,* August 17, 1970, Ball Papers.

18. Robert Ball to Robert Burroughs, February 4, 1969, Ball Papers; Burroughs to Ball, March 27, 1969, Ball Papers; Ball to Ted and Irene Ball, March 26, 1969, Ball Papers; Ball to Burroughs, May 8, 1969; Ball Papers.

19. Ball Memoir, pp. 162–66.

20. Robert Ball, "Memorandum of a Conversation with John Byrnes," June 19, 1969, Ball Papers.

21. Robert J. Myers, with Richard L. Vernaci, *Within the System: My Half Century in Social Security* (Winsted, Conn.: ACTEX, 1992), p. 159.

22. Myers, *Within the System,* p. 162; Derthick, *Policymaking for Social Security,* p. 171. For a fuller portrait of Myers see Edward D. Berkowitz, "Introduction: Social Security Celebrates an Anniversary," in *Social Security after Fifty: Successes and Failures,* ed. Berkowitz (New York: Greenwood Press, 1987), p. 8; Jerry Cates, *Insuring Inequality: Administrative Leadership in Social Security, 1935–1954* (Ann Arbor: University of Michigan Press, 1983), pp. 92–93. The Myers interview by Larry DeWitt, conducted in Silver Spring, Md., on March 14 and July 8, 1996, in the SSA History Archives, is particularly detailed on the development of Myers's career. The Social Security History Web site includes the interview and other materials related to Myers at http://www.ssa.gov/history/myersorl.html.

23. Myers, *Within the System,* pp. 158–64.

24. Ibid., p. 164; Ball Memoir, p. 162.

25. Robert J. Myers, "The Future of Social Security: Is It in Conflict with Private Pension Plans," presented at the American Pension Conference, October 23, 1969, copy in Ball Papers (with the annotation "noted, RMB" on top).

26. "Sabotage Charged on Social Security," *Washington Evening Star,* February 24, 1970, p. A-1; Carl T. Curtis to Russell Long, March 2, 1970, Ball Papers; "Answers to Questions Raised by Senator Curtis at Hearings on Medicare and Medicaid," n.d., Ball Papers.

27. Fragment with no heading, no date, in Myers Files, Ball Papers. Whether or not Ball's statement was ever released to the press is unclear.

28. The article is reprinted in its entirety in Myers, *Within the System,* pp. 168–75.

29. Robert M. Ball to the under secretary, March 26, 1970, Ball Papers.

30. Robert Myers to Secretary Finch, April 14, 1970, reprinted in the *Congressional Record,* June 3, 1970, p. S-8267, and in Myers, *Within the System,* pp. 175–78.

31. John Veneman to Robert Ball, May 25, 1970, Ball Papers; Ball Memoir, p. 165.

32. Myers, _Within the System_, p. 182.

33. Richardson quoted in Derthick, _Policymaking for Social Security_, p. 79. For Richardson's testimonials to Ball in print see Elliot Richardson, _The Creative Balance_ (New York: Holt, Rinehart and Winston, 1976), p. 90, and Richardson, _Reflections of a Moderate Radical_ (New York: Pantheon, 1996).

34. "Myers Resigns as SSA Actuary," _American Medical News_, June 1, 1970, p. 11; John G. Veneman to the editor, _American Medical News_, June 24, 1970, Ball Papers; Tom Joe to the under secretary, n.d., but June 1970, Ball Papers.

35. Ball to Victor Christgau, n.d., but 1970, Ball Papers.

36. Robert Ball to Betty Dillon, May 15, 1972, Ball Papers; Ball to Betty Dillon, January 24, 1972, Ball Papers; Ida Merriam to Ball, "Comments on Bob Myers' article or speech on 'The Spectrum of Governmental Health Care Proposals,' as printed in the Congressional Record for October 21, 1971," November 9, 1971, Ball Papers; Alvin M. David to Ball, November 17, 1971, transmitting and commenting on "Leviathan," Robert J. Myers's review of the 1971 advisory council report in _The Actuary_, June 1971, p. 1, Ball Papers; Charlotte Crenson to Ball, October 6, 1971, transmitting Myers's letter to the editor of the _Washington Star_, October 3, 1971, Ball Papers; "Trow: Seems to Limit His Functions," Ball wrote to actuary Charles Trowbridge, May 22, 1972, transmitting a report on Finance Committee consultants (Report 92–789), appointing Myers as a consultant to the committee, Ball Papers.

37. Robert Ball to Robert Myers, n.d., but 1992, obtained from John Trout (Trout to Berkowitz, March 27, 1999). As a historian interested in Social Security I had earlier obtained a copy of this memo, because Ball wanted to distribute it to historians and to others who might eventually put their papers in an archive where it would become, Ball hoped, part of the official record.

38. Richard Nixon to Robert Finch, February 11, 1969, with enclosure, "Social Security and Veterans Programs," Ball Papers.

39. Robert M. Ball to the under secretary, February 28, 1969, Ball Papers.

40. "Draft Memorandum for the President," in Ball to the under secretary, February 28, 1969, Ball Papers.

41. "Bureau of the Budget alternatives to our social security legislative recommendations," in Ball to the under secretary, March 17, 1969, Ball Papers; "Social Security and the Consolidated Budget," in Ball to the under secretary, March 24, 1969, Ball Papers; Ball to Jim Kelly, March 24, 1969, Ball Papers; Alvin David to Ball, May 6, 1969, Ball Papers.

42. Godfrey Hodgson, *The Gentleman from New York: Daniel Patrick Moynihan* (Boston: Houghton Mifflin, 2000), pp. 149–81; Daniel Patrick Moynihan, *The Politics of a Guaranteed Income* (New York: Random House, 1974); Vincent J. Burke and Vee Burke, *Nixon's Good Deed: Welfare Reform* (New York: Columbia University Press, 1974); Martin Anderson, *Welfare: The Political Economy of Welfare Reform in the United States* (Palo Alto, Calif.: Hoover Institution Press, 1978); Edward D. Berkowitz, *America's Welfare State: From Roosevelt to Reagan* (Baltimore: Johns Hopkins University Press, 1991), pp. 120–33.

43. Robert M. Ball to the under secretary, May 28, 1969, Ball Papers.

44. Ken Cole to Arthur Burns, September 17, 1969, including memo from Welfare Working Group to John Ehrlichman, September 13, 1969, Arthur Burns Papers, Box A-20, Gerald Ford Presidential Library, Ann Arbor, Mich.

45. "Excerpts of President Nixon's Message on Legislative Programs," *Washington Post*, October 12, 1969; on the improved trust fund balance see Robert Ball to John W. Byrnes, September 25, 1969, Ball Papers, and Robert J. Myers to Ball, September 25, 1969, Ball Papers.

46. "Message on Social Security," Office of the White House Press Secretary, September 25, 1969, Ball Papers; Zelizer, *Taxing America*, p. 317.

47. "Transcript of Press Briefing," September 25, 1969, Box A-20, Burns Papers.

48. Robert Ball, "Confidential—For the Files," November 12, 1969, Ball Papers.

49. Robert Ball, "Memorandum for the Files," November 19, 1969, Ball Papers.

50. Robert M. Ball to the under secretary, December 5, 1969, Ball Papers; Zelizer, *Taxing America*, p. 324; Robert M. Ball, "Social Security Amendments of 1972: Summary and Legislative History," *Social Security Bulletin* 36 (March 1973), pp. 4–5.

51. Weaver, *Automatic Government*, p. 74; Zelizer, *Taxing America*, p. 325.

52. Ball, DeWitt interview, May 1, 2001.

53. Kenneth R. Cole to Peter Flanigan, Robert Finch, Bryce Harow, and others, March 17, 1970, Ball Papers; Robert Ball to the under secretary, October 1, 1970, Ball Papers; Ball to the under secretary, October 2, 1970, Ball Papers.

54. Robert M. Ball to the under secretary, October 13, 1970, Ball Papers; Ball, "Draft Message for President," October 13, 1970, Ball Papers.

55. Transcript, telephone conversation between Elliot Richardson and Robert Ball, October 9, 1970, Telephone Conversations File, Box 128, Elliot Richardson Papers, Library of Congress, Washington, D.C.

56. Ball, "Social Security Amendments of 1972," p. 8; Zelizer, *Taxing America*, p. 325.

57. "Remarks of Congressman Wilbur D. Mills before the Downtown Little Rock Lions Club," December 2, 1964, Box 151, Cohen Papers; Clinton Anderson to Wilbur Cohen, December 1, 1964, Box 1106, Clinton Anderson Papers, Library of Congress; Wilbur Cohen to the president, February 25, 1965, Record Group 235, Records of the Department of Health, Education, and Welfare, Accession 69A-1793, File AW-5, Washington National Records Center, Suitland, Md.

58. Committee on Ways and Means press release, January 21, 1971, Ball Papers.

59. Ball Memoir, p. 153.

60. Robert Ball, penciled note, December 31, 1970, Ball Papers.

61. Robert Ball to the under secretary, February 23, 1971, enclosing "A Ways and Means Committee Staff Alternatives for Automatic Adjustment of Benefits, the Contribution and Benefit Base, and Exempt Amount under the Retirement Test," dated February 23, 1971, Ball Papers.

62. "Ways and Means Committee Tentative Decisions on H.R. 1," April 6, 1971, Ball Papers.

63. Statement by the president, White House press release, May 18, 1971, Ball Papers.

64. *Congressional Record*, 92d Cong., 1st sess., March 16, 1971, 117, pt. 5, p. 6732.

65. "Senator Long Releases Text of Opening Statement to Be Given July 27 at Committee Hearings on H.R. 1," Committee on Finance press release, July 26, 1971, Ball Papers.

66. Robert Ball to the under secretary, March 7, 1969, Ball Papers; Ball to the under secretary, April 21, 1969, Ball Papers.

67. Robert Ball, "Note to be used in conversation with Veneman about the Advisory Council, with the main points of my last conversation with Arthur Flemming, March 12, 1969," Ball Papers.

68. Robert Ball to the secretary, November 9, 1970, and Elliot Richardson to Ball, November 20, 1970, Chronological File 1970–1973, Box 122, Richardson Papers.

69. Derthick, *Policymaking for Social Security*, p.352.

70. Advisory Council on Social Security, *Reports of the 1971 Advisory Council on Social Security*, H. Doc. 92-80 (Washington: Government Printing Office, 1971), pp. 5, 9.

71. Derthick, *Policymaking for Social Security*, p. 353. Myers later said the "increasing earnings assumptions" were an "unsound actuarial procedure—even if automatic adjustments are adopted. What it would

mean, in essence, is that actuarial soundness would be wholly dependent on a perpetually increasing inflation of a certain prescribed nature—and a borrowing from the next generation to pay the current generation's benefits, in the hope that inflation of wages would make this possible." Myers noted that an assumption that wages would rise at twice the rate of prices in the future "seems reasonable" but was not in keeping with recent trends and was "very sensitive." Myers favored rising-earnings and benefit assumptions for a five-year period, with level assumptions after that. "By this procedure, reasonable forecasts can be made as to what wages and prices will do for the short term, without there being the danger of assuming financing gains over many decades as the result of inflation continuing." Myers, "Leviathan," *Actuary,* June 1971, pp. 4–5, Ball Papers.

72. Elliot Richardson, "Memorandum for the President," April 1, 1971, White House Central Files, Subject Files, FG 23–10, SSA, January 1, 1971, Box 11, Nixon Presidential Materials Project, National Archives, College Park, Md.

73. Robert M. Ball to Bill Robinson, November 5, 1971, Ball Papers; C. L. Trowbridge to Bill Robinson, November 3, 1971, Ball Papers; Ball, "Notes for the Presentation to the Senate Finance Committee Tomorrow Morning on the Advisory Council's Recommendations Concerning Financing," March 21, 1971, Ball Papers.

74. Robert Ball to Ida Merriam, n.d., but 1971, Ball Papers.

75. Robert Ball to Ida Merriam, November 2, 1971, Ball Papers; Paul H. O'Neill to the director/deputy director, "Financing Social Security," n.d., Ball Papers.

76. Robert Ball to William Robinson, November 9, 1971, Ball Papers; Paul O'Neill, "Financing Social Security," Ball Papers.

77. Robert Ball to Alvin David, January 24, 1972, Ball Papers.

78. Robert Ball to Charles Trowbridge, February 3, 1972, Ball Papers.

79. Ball, DeWitt interview, May 1, 2001.

80. Robert Ball to Betty Dillon, February 18, 1972, Ball Papers; transcript, telephone conversation between Elliot Richardson and George Shultz, February 16, 1972, Telephone Conversations 1970–73, Box 131, Richardson Papers.

81. Ball, DeWitt interview, May 1, 2001; Ball Memoir, p. 199. I was the historian to whom Mills confided about his reliance on Ball, in a conversation that took place in 1985 in Washington, D.C.

82. Wilbur Mills to Robert Ball, February 22, 1972, Ball Papers.

83. Transcript, telephone conversation between Elliot Richardson and John D. Ehrlichman, February 23, 1972, Telephone Conversations 1970–1973, Box 131, Richardson Papers.

84. Transcript, telephone conversation between Elliot Richardson and George Shultz, February 23, 1972, Telephone Conversations 1970–73, Box 131, Richardson Papers.

85. Transcript, telephone conversation between Elliot Richardson and Paul O'Neill, February 23, 1972, Box 131, Richardson Papers.

86. Transcript, telephone conversation between Elliot Richardson and Arthur Flemming, February 24, 1972, Box 131, Richardson Papers.

87. Derthick, *Policymaking for Social Security*, pp. 62–88; Edward D. Berkowitz, "History and Social Security Reform," in *Social Security and Medicare: Individual versus Collective Risk and Responsibility*, ed. Sheila Burke, Eric Kingson, and Uwe Reinhardt (Washington, D.C.: National Academy of Social Insurance, 2000), pp. 31–55.

88. Ball, DeWitt interview, May 1, 2001.

89. Robert Ball to Alvin David, February 29, 1972, Ball Papers.

90. Commissioner of Social Security to the secretary, March 7, 1972, Aging, Social Security Benefit Increase File, Box 134, Richardson Papers.

91. Transcript, telephone conversation between Elliot Richardson and John Veneman, March 7, 1972, Box 131, Richardson Papers.

92. George Shultz, "Meeting with the President, Tuesday, March 7, 1972," March 7, 1972, President's Office Files, Box 88, Nixon Presidential Materials Project; transcript, telephone conversation between Elliot Richardson and Arthur Flemming, March 8, 1972, Box 131, Richardson Papers.

93. Richard Darman to the secretary, March 7, 1972, and Darman to the secretary, March 10, 1972 (with enclosures), both in Box 134, Richardson Papers; commissioner of Social Security to the secretary, n.d., but probably March 9, 1972, Box 134, Richardson Papers; commissioner of Social Security to the secretary, March 9, 1972, Ball Papers.

94. Memorandum from John Ehrlichman to the President's File, March 10, 1972, President's Office Files, Box 88, Nixon Presidential Materials Project.

95. Derthick, *Policymaking for Social Security*, p. 359.

96. Zelizer, *Taxing America*, p. 340.

97. Ball Memoir, p. 197. "The Senate Finance Committee staff had favored and gotten into the bill a provision that required a tax rate increase every time benefits were increased. This was not needed as wages rose and would have soon been unworkable—not compatible with the automatic reasoning. It was to get around this as much as anything that I went to the Church amendments" (Ball to Berkowitz, July 15, 2002).

98. Transcript, telephone conversation between Elliot Richardson and John Ehrlichman, June 26, 1972, Box 132, Richardson Papers;

transcript, telephone conversation between Elliot Richardson and George Shultz, June 26, 1972, Box 132, Richardson Papers.

99. Commissioner of Social Security to the secretary, June 28, 1972, Box 134, Richardson Papers; commissioner of Social Security to the secretary, June 26, 1972, Box 134, Richardson Papers; transcript, telephone conversation between Elliot Richardson and Bob Ball, June 26, 1972, Box 132, Richardson Papers; transcript, telephone conversation between Elliot Richardson and John Veneman, June 26, 1972, Box 132, Richardson Papers; transcript, telephone conversation between Elliot Richardson and John D. Ehrlichman, June 27, 1972, Box 132, Richardson Papers.

100. "Memorandum for the President's File on the Meeting with Republican Members of the Senate Finance Committee," June 27, 1972, President's Office Files, Memoranda for the President, Box 89, Nixon Presidential Materials Project; "The President's News Conference of June 29, 1972," *Public Papers of the Presidents of the United States: Richard Nixon, 1972* (Washington, D.C.: Government Printing Office, 1974), pp. 214–15.

101. "Statement of the President upon Signing HR 15390 into Law," July 1, 1972, *Weekly Compilation of Presidential Documents, July 3, 1972,* p. 1122.

102. Elliot Richardson, "Memorandum for the Honorable John Ehrlichman," July 27, 1972, Ball Papers; commissioner of Social Security to the secretary, July 10, 1972, Ball Papers.

103. Robert Ball to Betty Dillon, June 27, 1972, Ball Files.

104. Ball, DeWitt interview, May 1, 2001.

105. Ball Memoir, p. 149.

106. Transcript, telephone conversation between Elliot Richardson and Commissioner Ball, September 11, 1972, Box 132, Richardson Papers; transcript, telephone conversation between Elliot Richardson and George Shultz, September 11, 1972, Box 132, Richardson Papers.

107. James H. Falk, "Memorandum for the President's File," September 18, 1972, President's Office Files, Memoranda for the President, Box 89, Nixon Presidential Materials Project; Ken Cole to the President's File, October 3, 1972, Memoranda for the President, Box 90, Nixon Presidential Materials Project.

108. John G. Veneman to Caspar Weinberger, October 25, 1972, Ball Papers; Ball, "Social Security Amendments of 1972," pp. 15–25.

109. Historical studies of Supplemental Security Income remain few, but see Burke and Burke, *Nixon's Good Deed,* and Martha Derthick, *Agency under Stress: The Social Security Administration in American Government* (Washington, D.C.: Brookings Institution, 1990), pp. 22–33.

110. See Robert Ball, *Social Security: Today and Tomorrow* (New York: Columbia University Press), pp. 349–50.

111. I take this account directly from Ball. See Ball Memoir, pp. 176–81. It should be noted that the administration favored, as part of its original welfare reform legislation, the establishment of a federal minimum in state public assistance programs affecting the elderly, blind, and disabled. See Committee on Ways and Means, "Written Statements Submitted by Administration Witnesses Appearing before the Committee on Ways and Means at Hearings on Social Security and Welfare Proposals Beginning on October 15, 1969," Committee Print (Washington: Government Printing Office, 1969).

112. Robert Ball to Arthur Altmeyer, May 11, 1971, Ball Papers.

113. Commissioner of Social Security to the under secretary, March 3, 1971, Ball Papers; commissioner of Social Security to the under secretary, March 2, 1971, Ball Papers; commissioner of Social Security to the under secretary, March 9, 1971, Ball Papers. For a detailed look at the implementation of SSI, see Derthick, *Agency under Stress*.

114. "Address by Robert M. Ball," Delivered to Social Security Employees, Baltimore, November 20, 1972, Ball Papers.

115. Robert Ball, transcript of remarks at the National Conference, SSA Auditorium, November 14, 1972, Ball Papers.

5. Defender of the Faith

1. Robert Ball, autobiographical memorandum prepared for Edward Berkowitz (hereafter Ball Memoir), p. 246.

2. Robert Evans and Rowland Novak, "Inside Report," *Baltimore Evening Sun,* January 15, 1973, clipping in Robert Ball Papers, Wisconsin State Historical Society, Madison.

3. "Washington Wire," *Wall Street Journal,* November 17, 1972, Ball Papers.

4. Robert Ball to Betty Dillon, December 11, 1972, Ball Papers; transcript, telephone conversation between Elliot Richardson and Fred Malek, December 13, 1972, Box 133, Elliot Richardson Papers, Library of Congress, Washington, D.C; transcript, telephone conversation between Elliot Richardson and Robert Ball, December 14, 1972, Box 133, Richardson Papers.

5. Robert Ball, "Assignment of the Commissioner of Social Security," December 14, 1972, pp. 1, 6, 7, 9, 15, 26, Ball Papers.

6. "Social Security Chief Is Believed Out," *New York Times,* January 5, 1973, p. 22.

7. Robert Ball to the president, n.d.; Fred Malek to the president, January 2, 1973; Tom Jones, "Memo for the Press Office," January 3, 1973;

Office of the White House Press Secretary, "Notice to the Press," January 5, 1973—all in White House Central Files, Subject Files, FG23 (DHEW), FG23-10/A, Box 11, Nixon Presidential Materials Project, National Archives and Records Service, College Park, Md.

8. Carrol Kilpatrick, "Nixon Vows Future Hill Consideration," *Washington Post,* January 6, 1973, Ball Papers.

9. "Ouster at Social Security," *Washington Star News,* January 15, 1973; "Defender of the Aged," *New York Times,* January 8, 1973; editorial, *Riverside (Calif.) Press,* January 8, 1973; editorial, *Asheville (N.C.) Times,* January 6, 1973; "Social Security Chief Dropped, 33-Year Veteran," *Washington Star,* January 5, 1973; "A Superb Public Servant Steps Down," *Washington Post,* March 15, 1973—all in Ball Papers.

10. "Commissioner Robert M. Ball's Speech, 'Our New Social Security Program' before Commonwealth Club of California, January 5, 1973," Ball Papers.

11. A 28-minute audio file of Ball's speech is available at http://www.ssa.gov/history/sounds/ball1.ram.

12. Jerry Carroll, "Social Security Chief's Version of Resignation," *San Francisco Chronicle,* January 6, 1973, Ball Papers.

13. CBS Television Network, transcript of *CBS Morning News with John Hart,* January 11, 1973, pp. 23–24, Ball Papers.

14. *CBS Morning News* transcript, p. 25.

15. Walter Mondale, "Finding a Successor for Robert Ball," *Congressional Record–Senate,* 93d Cong., 1st sess., February 15, 1973, pp. 2625–26; Edward M. Kennedy, "Robert Ball: A Dedicated Social Security Administration Commissioner," *Congressional Record–Senate,* 93d Cong., 1st sess., February 6, 1973, pp. 226–27; Frank Church, "Robert Ball's Resignation as Social Security Commissioner," *Congressional Record–Senate,* 93d Cong., 1st sess., February 1, 1973; Robert M. Byrd, "Robert M. Ball, Commissioner of Social Security," *Congressional Record–Senate,* p. 781—all clippings in Ball Papers.

16. Ball Memoir, p. 186; Robert Ball to Irene Ball, March 12, 1973, Ball Papers.

17. Robert Ball to Betty Dillon, January 18, 1973, Ball Papers.

18. Ball Memoir, p. 185; Robert Ball to Betty Dillon, February 1, 1973, Ball Papers; Ball to Dillon, February 2, 1973, Ball Papers; Ball to Dillon, February 5, 1973, Ball Papers.

19. Audiotape of reception in honor of Robert Ball, February 21, 1973, SSA History Archives, Baltimore; text of Robert Ball's speech at the reception, February 21, 1973, Ball Papers.

20. Ball to Betty Dillon, November 7, 1972, Ball Papers; Edward Berkowitz, *To Improve Human Health: A History of the Institute of Medicine* (Washington, D.C.: National Academy Press, 1998). Harold M.

Schmeck Jr., "President of the Institute of Medicine: John Rusten Hogness," *New York Times*, March 30, 1971; "Hell of a Show Promised by Hogness for Institute of Medicine," *Drug Research Reports*, May 24, 1972, Irvine Page Papers, National Library of Medicine, Bethesda, Md.

21. Robert Ball to Betty Dillon, January 22, 1973, Ball Papers; IOM News Release, February 21, 1973, Ball Papers; *Washington Report on Medicine and Health*, February 26, 1973, Ball Papers.

22. Ball to all SSA employees, March 14, 1973, Ball Papers. On Altmeyer and Cohen see Edward Berkowitz, *Mr. Social Security: The Life of Wilbur Cohen* (Lawrence: University Press of Kansas, 1995); Arthur J. Altmeyer, *The Formative Years of Social Security* (Madison: University of Wisconsin Press, 1966); W. Andrew Achenbaum, "Arthur Altmeyer," in *Biographical Dictionary of Social Welfare in America,* ed. W. Trattner (Westport, Conn.: Greenwood Press, 1986), pp. 25–27.

23. Ball Memoir, p. 200.

24. Robert Ball to Wendell Coltin, February 12, 1974, Ball Papers. For more on the politics of national health insurance in this period see Karen Davis, *National Health Insurance: Benefits, Costs and Consequences* (Washington, D.C.: Brookings Institution, 1975), and more generally Paul Starr, *The Social Transformation of American Medicine* (New York: Basic Books, 1982), pp. 379–419.

25. Robert Ball, "Note for the Files, Sequence of Happenings on Kennedy-Mills Bill, S. 3286 and H.R. 13870—introduced on April 2, 1974" (hereafter "Sequence of Happenings"), Ball Papers; Starr, *Social Transformation of American Medicine,* pp. 382, 394.

26. William Fullerton, interview by Mark Santangelo, Crystal River, Fla., October 20, 1995, Health Care Financing Administration Oral History Collection, transcript available at the Center for Medicare and Medicaid Services, http://cms.hhs.gov/about/history/fullert.asp, and at the SSA Web site, http://ssa.gov/history/fullert.html; Ball, "Sequence of Happenings."

27. Robert Ball to Wilbur Mills, February 22, 1974, Ball Papers.

28. Robert Ball to Charles Trowbridge, January 30, 1974, Ball Papers.

29. Senator Frank Church to Robert Ball, April 2, 1974, Ball Papers; Ball to Church, April 9, 1974, Ball Papers.

30. "New Nixon Health Insurance Plan: Politics or Possibility," *Hospital Practice* (March 1974), clipping in Ball Papers.

31. Ball, "Sequence of Happenings"; Judith Randal, "National Health Insurance Gets New Lease on Life," *Washington Star News*, April 7, 1974, p. c-5; Starr, *Social Transformation of American Medicine*, p. 404.

32. See Christopher Howard, *The Hidden Welfare State* (Princeton: Princeton University Press, 1997).

33. Ball Memoir, p. 225; Ball, "Sequence of Happenings."

34. Robert Ball, "Administration's Health Insurance Plan—Employee Health Insurance Plan," February 7, 1974, Ball Papers.

35. Ball, "Sequence of Happenings"; Robert Ball, "A New Approach to National Health Insurance: Basic Strategy," draft, February 28, 1974, Ball Papers.

36. Ball Memoir, p. 225.

37. Ball, "Sequence of Happenings"; Berkowitz, *Mr. Social Security*, pp. 294–95; Julian Zelizer, *Taxing America: Wilbur D. Mills, Congress, and the State* (New York: Cambridge University Press, 1998), pp. 350–53.

38. Fullerton interview.

39. Ball, "Sequence of Happenings."

40. Ball, "A New Approach to National Health Insurance," draft, April 1, 1974, Ball Papers; Ball, "Sequence of Happenings."

41. Ball, "Sequence of Happenings." Ball says that Andy Biemiller of the AFL-CIO explicitly told him that the next Congress would be more favorable to Kennedy's original bill (Ball to Berkowitz, July 15, 2002).

42. Ball, "Sequence of Happenings."

43. "Joint Statement of Congressman Wilbur D. Mills . . . and Senator Edward M. Kennedy . . . upon Introduction of the Comprehensive National Health Insurance Act of 1974," April 2, 1974, Ball Papers.

44. "Statement by Senator Edward M. Kennedy upon Introduction of the Comprehensive National Health Insurance Act," April 2, 1974, Ball Papers.

45. Robert Ball to Wilbur Cohen, April 5, 1974, Ball Papers; Ball, "To Do List," April 5, 1974, Ball Papers; Ball, "To Do List," April 29, 1973, Ball Papers; Ball, note for the files, May 13, 1974, Ball Papers; Ball to Doug Brown, April 11, 1974, Ball Papers; Ball to Wilbur Mills, July 9, 1974, Ball Papers.

46. "New Health Bill Aids Prospect for '74 Passage," *Wall Street Journal*, April 3, 1974, p. 1; "Health Plan Progress," *New York Times*, April 7, 1974, p. 16; "National Health Insurance," *Washington Post*, April 8, 1974, Ball Papers; Richard D. Lyons, "What Can Be Expected from Health Insurance," *New York Times*, April 7, 1974, Ball Papers.

47. "Statement by the AFL-CIO Executive Council on the Mills-Kennedy Bill," May 9, 1974, attachment in Larry Smedley to Bob Ball, May 30, 1974, Ball Papers.

48. Robert Ball, "Prospects and Alternatives for National Health Insurance," notes for a meeting with Senator Edward Kennedy, July 25, 1974, Ball Papers.

49. Robert Ball to Wilbur Cohen, August 16, 1974, Ball Papers.

50. The economic data are taken from the *Statistical Abstract of the United States* between 1965 and 1985 as reported in Sheryl R. Tynes, *Turning Points in Social Security: From "Cruel Hoax" to "Sacred Entitlement"*

(Stanford: Stanford University Press, 1996), p. 134; Zelizer, *Taxing America*, pp. 350–60. For the 1970s as a turning point see William C. Berman, *America's Right Turn: From Nixon to Bush* (Baltimore: Johns Hopkins Press, 1994); David Frum, *How We Got Here: The 70s, the Decade That Brought You Modern Life—For Better or Worse* (New York: Basic Books, 2000); Bruce J. Schulman, *The Seventies: The Great Shift in Culture, Society, and Politics* (New York: Free Press, 2001).

51. Robert Ball, "Confidential Note on Conversation with Bill Fullerton and Stan Jones, Saturday Night, January 25, 1975," Ball Papers.

52. "Briefing Notes for James B. Cardwell, June 4, 1974, on reports of the Trustees of the Social Security Trust Fund," Box 3, Pamela Needham Files, Gerald Ford Library, Ann Arbor, Mich.

53. Robert M. Ball, "Issues in Social Security Financing, 1974," speech delivered at the Eighth Conference on Social Security, University of Michigan, Ann Arbor, October 16, 1974, Ball Papers.

54. Robert M. Ball, "Statement on Social Security Financing," February 19, 1975, Ball Papers.

55. Robert Ball to Kermit Gordon, August 19, 1974, Ball Papers.

56. Robert Ball, testimony before Subcommittee on Retirement Income and Employment, Select Committee on Aging, House of Representatives, May 14, 1975, Ball Papers.

57. Editorial, *New York Times*, April 3, 1975, clipping in Ball Papers.

58. William Simon to the Executive Committee, Economic Policy Board, n.d., but 1975, Box 11, Spencer Johnson Papers, Ford Library; William E. Simon to James Cannon, November 11, 1975, Box 9, Arthur Quern Papers, Ford Library; Caspar Weinberger to the president, December 9, 1974, Box 5, Needham Papers.

59. See Gladys E. Means to counselor to the vice president, April 25, 1975, Box 8, Quern Papers.

60. Donald S. Fredrickson to Robert Ball, February 28, 1975, Ball Papers.

61. On the changes in Congress see John Jacobs, *A Rage for Justice: The Passion and Politics of Phillip Burton* (Berkeley: University of California Press, 1995), pp. 248–79; Frum, *How We Got Here*, pp. 275–84.

62. Robert Ball, "Notes of Conversation with Congressman James Burke," January 17, 1975, Ball Papers.

63. Robert Ball, "To Do List," July 8, 1975, Ball Papers.

64. For background on the era of Gerald Ford and his presidency, see John Robert Greene, *The Presidency of Gerald Ford* (Lawrence: University of Kansas Press, 1995); Robert Hartmann, *Palace Politics: An Insider's Account of the Ford Years* (New York, McGraw-Hill, 1980); James Cannon, *Time and Chance: Gerald Ford's Appointment with History* (New York: HarperCollins, 1994).

65. Haeworth Robertson to Robert Ball, April 6, 1977, Ball Papers. Robertson, who served as chief actuary of the Social Security Administration from 1975 to 1978, became a noted program critic. See A. Haeworth Robertson, *The Coming Revolution in Social Security* (Reston, Va.: Reston, 1981).

66. Robert Ball to Alice Rivlin, March 1977, Ball Papers; Ball to Haeworth Robertson, April 20, 1977, Ball Papers; Ball to Wilbur Cohen, June 6, 1977, Ball Papers.

67. James T. Lynn to the president, May 14, 1975, Box 8, Quern Papers.

68. Jim Cannon to the president, December 17, 1975, Box 11, Spencer Johnson Papers; David Matthew to Carl Albert, February 11, 1976, Box 11, Spencer Johnson Papers; Bruce Cardwell and Bill Morrill, "Draft Memorandum for the President," March 10, 1976, Box 11, Spencer Johnson Papers; Gerald Ford, "Transcript of Question and Answer Session with the Northern Illinois Newspaper Association," March 12, 1976, Box 11, Spencer Johnson Papers; Jim Cannon to the president, April 30, 1976, Box 10, James Cannon Papers, Ford Library; Sylvester J. Schieber and John B. Shoven, *The Real Deal: The History and Future of Social Security* (New Haven: Yale University Press, 1999), p. 175.

69. Rudolf G. Penner, *Social Security Financing Proposals* (Washington, D.C.: American Enterprise Institute, 1977), p. 6.

70. Robert Ball to Eveline Burns, December 13, 1974, Ball Papers.

71. Ball to Burns, December 13, 1974.

72. W. Allen Wallis, statement of March 7, 1975, Box 3, Needham Papers.

73. Jim Cannon to the president, May 2, 1975, Box 33, Cannon Papers; Gerald Ford statement, March 7, 1975, Box 33, Cannon Papers; Caspar Weinberger to the president, May 2, 1975, Box 33, Cannon Papers.

74. Bruce Cardwell and Bill Morrill, draft memorandum for the president, March 10, 1976, Box 11, Spencer Johnson Papers.

75. The administration accepted this idea, even in the face of an alternative suggestion from a Congressional Research Panel led by actuary and economist William Hsiao. Instead of indexing wages in the benefit formula, Hsiao advocated linking benefit increases to increases in the cost of living. This approach would stabilize benefits in relation to their purchasing power, rather than in relation to rises in the standard of living as reflected in rising average wages. Jim Cannon to the president, April 30, 1976, Box 10, Cannon Papers; Martha Derthick, *Policymaking for Social Security* (Washington, D.C.: Brookings Institution, 1979), pp. 387–408.

76. "White House Fact Sheet, Social Security Indexing Act," June 11, 1976, Box 11, Spencer Johnson Papers; James Cardwell, "Transcript of Press Briefing," June 17, 1976, Box 11, Spencer Johnson Papers.

77. Ball Memoir, p. 211; Berkowitz, *Mr. Social Security,* pp. 114–15.

78. The presidency of Jimmy Carter is just beginning to come into historical focus. Among the key books and articles are Burton I. Kaufman, *The Presidency of James Earl Carter Jr.* (Lawrence: University Press of Kansas, 1993); Charles O. Jones, *The Trusteeship Presidency: Jimmy Carter and the United States Congress* (Baton Rouge: Louisiana State University Press, 1988); Erwin C. Hargrove, "The Carter Presidency in Historical Perspective," in *The Presidency and Domestic Policies of Jimmy Carter,* ed. Herbert D. Rosenbaum and Alexej Ugrinsky (Westport, Conn.: Greenwood Press, 1994), pp. 21–26; Stephen Skowronek, *The Politics Presidents Make: Leadership from John Adams to George Bush* (Cambridge: Harvard University Press, 1993), pp. 361–406.

79. Ball Memoir, pp. 212–13. For a good policy-related view of the Carter presidency, see the essays in Gary M. Fink and Hugh Davis Graham, eds., *The Carter Presidency: Policy Choices in the Post–New Deal Era* (Lawrence: University Press of Kansas, 1998). Significantly, though, the volume contains an essay on welfare reform but not on Social Security, reflecting President Carter's own interests and predilections.

80. Robert Ball to Stuart Eizenstat, January 17, 1977, Ball Papers; Ball to Joseph Califano, January 19, 1977, Ball Papers.

81. Stu Eizenstat and Frank Raines to the president, April 29, 1977, Box 278, Stuart Eizenstat Papers, Jimmy Carter Library, Atlanta; Eizenstat to Joseph Califano, March 18, 1977, Box 278, Eizenstat Papers; Michael Stern, Senate Finance Committee staff member, to Stuart Eizenstat, April 8, 1977, Box 278, Eizenstat Papers; Joseph A. Califano Jr., *Governing America: An Insider's Report from the White House and the Cabinet* (New York: Simon and Schuster, 1981), p. 369.

82. Califano, *Governing America,* p. 372; Jerry H. Jones, "Meeting with Bruce Cardwell," August 1, 1973, White House Central Files, Subject Files, FG23 10/A, Box 11, Nixon Presidential Materials Project, National Archives.

83. Robert Ball, "Note for File on Meeting with the President, May 4, 1977, on SS Financing," May 6, 1977, Ball Papers; John Snee and Mary Ross, "Social Security Amendments of 1977: Legislative History and Summary of Provisions," *Social Security Bulletin,* March 1978, p. 6.

84. Ball, "Note for File on Meeting with President, May 4, 1977."

85. Robert Ball to the president, April 28, 1977, Box 278, Eizenstat Papers; memorandum to the president from HEW, April 27, 1977, Box 278, Eizenstat Papers; Stu Eizenstat and Frank Raines to the president, April 29, 1977, Box 278, Eizenstat Papers (with president's comments).

86. Jimmy Carter's comments on Stu Eizenstat and Frank Raines to the president, April 29, 1977, Box 278, Eizenstat Papers.

87. I take this account of the meeting with the president from Ball's

memorandum, "Note for File on Meeting with the President, May 4, 1977," written close to the events.

88. Robert Ball, "Note for the Record on Status of Social Security Financing," May 4, 1977, Ball Papers; Ball Memoir, p. 216.

89. Hale Champion, "Notes on Social Security Message," May 6, 1997, and Carter's message of May 9, 1977, Box 278, Eizenstat Papers.

90. Robert Ball, "Conversation with Al Ullman," May 11, 1977, Ball Papers; Ball Memoir, p. 216.

91. "Testimony of Robert M. Ball before Senate Committee on Finance," June 16, 1977, Box 16, Nelson Cruikshank Papers, Jimmy Carter Library.

92. Stu Eizenstat to the president, August 12, 1977, Box 278, Eizenstat Papers.

93. "Comparison of Social Security Proposals of the Administration, Senate, and House," November 8, 1977, Box 16, Cruikshank Papers; Jimmy Carter to Al Ullman, December 1, 1977, Box 16, Cruikshank Papers; Stu Eizenstat to the president, November 2, 1977, Box 277, Eizenstat Papers; Eizenstat to the president, August 12, 1977, Box 278, Eizenstat Papers; Robert Ball to Eizenstat, November 9, 1977, Box 5, Cruikshank Papers; Ball to Gaylord Nelson, Box 5, Cruikshank Papers.

94. Snee and Ross, "Social Security Amendments of 1977," p. 18; for the administration's view of the passage of the bill see Califano, *Governing America*, pp. 380–81.

95. Stu Eizenstat and Frank Raines to the president, December 19, 1977, Box 277, Eizenstat Papers.

96. I base this account entirely on Robert Ball, "Memorandum for Files: Events Leading Up to the Reduction of age 72 to 70 in the Senate Bill," November 7, 1977, Ball Papers. For more on the history of the retirement test see Wilbur Cohen to C. B. Bragman, February 23, 1950, Box 29, Cohen Papers, Wisconsin State Historical Society, Madison, and Larry DeWitt, "The History and Development of the Social Security Retirement Earnings Test," August 1999, Special Study 7, SSA History Archives, Baltimore, available on the Web at http://www.ssa.gov/history/ret2.html.

97. Robert Ball to Stuart Eizenstat, May 20, 1977, Ball Papers; Ball to Eizenstat, July 20, 1977, Ball Papers; Ball to Eizenstat, September 7, 1977, Ball Papers.

98. Robert Ball to Tom Joe, October 19, 1977, Ball Papers; Califano, *Governing America*, p. 382; Edward D. Berkowitz, *Disabled Policy: America's Programs for the Handicapped* (New York: Cambridge University Press, 1987), p. 118.

99. Robert Ball, "Notes on a Conversation with John Moore of Columbia University Press," April 3, 1974, Ball Papers; Ball Memoir,

pp. 208–9; Robert M. Ball, *Social Security: Today and Tomorrow* (New York: Columbia University Press, 1978).

100. Robert Ball to Charles Trowbridge, December 22, 1976, Ball Papers.

101. Ball, *Social Security: Today and Tomorrow,* pp. 115, 385; Ball Memoir, p. 208; Robert Ball to David Hamburg, July 15, 1980, Ball Papers.

102. Ball to Eizenstat, July 20, 1977; Robert Ball to Tom Joe, December 3, 1977, Ball Papers; Gaylord Nelson, Foreword, in Ball, *Social Security: Today and Tomorrow,* p. ix.

103. Berkowitz, *Disabled Policy,* pp. 114–22; Ball, "Note for File on Meeting with the President, May 4, 1977"; Ball to Tom Joe, August 11, 1977, Ball Papers; Califano, *Governing America,* p. 384.

104. Berkowitz, *Disabled Policy,* pp. 111, 115–22; Ball to Joe, August 11, 1977.

105. Califano, *Governing America,* pp. 43, 45; Alan Baltis, "The Reorganization of DHEW: What Happened, Why and So What," *Journal of Health and Human Resources Administration* 1 (1979), pp. 504–25.

106. Stanford Ross, interview by Larry DeWitt, June 4, 1996, Oral History Collection, SSA History Archives; Hale Champion, interview by Ed Berkowitz, Cambridge, Mass., August 9, 1995, p. 21, HCFA (now Centers for Medicare and Medicaid Services) Oral History Collection, Baltimore, available on the Web at http://cms.hhs.gov/about/history/champ.asp.

107. Robert Ball to Mr. B. K. MacLaury, December 15, 1980, Ball Papers; Martha Derthick, *Agency under Stress: The Social Security Administration in American Government* (Washington, D.C.: Brookings Institution, 1990), pp. 122–26.

108. Robert Ball, "Comments on Futterman Report," September 16, 1980, Ball Papers.

109. Califano, *Governing America,* p. 387.

110. Ibid.

111. Robert Ball to Stuart Eizenstat, July 22, 1980, Ball Papers; "Interview with Robert Ball," March 16, 1982, no author, Ball Papers.

112. Wilbur Cohen to Alvin David, January 23, 1978, in Box 5, Cruikshank Papers.

113. Stu Eizenstat and Frank Raines to the president, April 6, 1978, Office of Staff Secretary, Handwriting File, Box 79, Carter Library; Mike Blumenthal to the president, April 7, 1978, Office of Staff Secretary, Handwriting File, Box 79, Carter Library; Nelson Cruikshank to the president, January 27, 1978, Box 277, Eizenstat Papers; Califano, *Governing America,* p. 383.

114. Califano, *Governing America,* p. 389; Wilbur Cohen to Bert Seidman, Nelson Cruikshank, Robert Ball, and Elizabeth Wickenden,

August 21, 1978, Box 247, Wilbur Cohen Papers; Berkowitz, *Mr. Social Security,* pp. 300–302.

115. Stu Eizenstat to the president, December 20, 1978, Office of the Staff Secretary, Handwriting File, Box 113, Carter Library; Jim Cannon to President Ford, November 28, 1975, Box 33, Cannon Papers.

116. Nelson Cruikshank to the president, December 19, 1978, Office of Staff Secretary, Handwriting File, Box 113, Carter Library; Robert Ball, Wilbur Cohen, and Nelson Cruikshank to the president, December 19, 1978, Office of the Staff Secretary, Handwriting File, Box 113, Carter Library; Cruikshank to the president, December 20, 1978, Office of the Staff Secretary, Handwriting File, Box 113, Carter Library.

117. Ball, Cohen, and Cruikshank to the president, December 19, 1978.

118. Ball Memoir, p. 218; "Interview with Robert Ball," March 16, 1982; Wilbur J. Cohen, "Some Notes on Social Security Proposals in 1978–1979," Box 204, Cohen Papers.

119. Califano, *Governing America,* pp. 395, 391; "Interview with Robert Ball," March 16, 1982; Ball Memoir, p. 220.

120. Berkowitz, *Mr. Social Security,* p. 301.

121. Robert Ball to Stuart Eizenstat, November 15, 1979, Box 77, Eizenstat Papers.

122. Robert Ball to Stuart Eizenstat, July 13, 1980, Ball Papers.

123. "Fact Sheet, Social Security Finance," October 30, 1980, Box 277, Eizenstat Papers; editorial, *Washington Post,* June 23, 1980, Box 277, Eizenstat Papers, Box 277; Schieber and Shoven, *Real Deal,* p. 189; Tynes, *Turning Points in Social Security,* p. 134.

124. Robert Ball to Carolyn Weaver, July 30, 1980, Ball Papers.

125. Robert Ball to Congressman James L. Oberstar (D–Minnesota), July 28, 1980, Ball Papers.

126. Statement of Robert Ball before Platform Committee, August 12, 1980, Ball Papers.

127. Ball Memoir, p. 224.

128. Wilbur Cohen to Alvin David, January 23, 1978, Box 5, Cruikshank Papers.

129. Robert Ball to Wilbur Cohen, February 13, 1978, Box 5, Cruikshank Papers.

6. Savoir

1. David A. Stockman, *The Triumph of Politics: How the Reagan Revolution Failed* (New York: Harper and Row, 1986), p. 181.

2. As a major episode in the history of American social welfare policy, the 1983 amendments have attracted attention from scholars and participants. Among the accounts on which I rely here are W. Andrew

Achenbaum, *Social Security: Visions and Revisions* (New York: Cambridge University Press, 1986), chapter 4; Merton C. Bernstein and Joan Brodshaug Bernstein, *Social Security: The System That Works* (New York: Basic Books, 1988); Paul Light, *Artful Work: The Politics of Social Security Reform* (New York: Random House, 1985); Robert J. Myers with Richard L. Vernaci, *Within the System: My Half Century in Social Security* (Winsted, Conn.: ACTEX, 1992); Edward D. Berkowitz, *America's Welfare State: From Roosevelt to Reagan* (Baltimore: Johns Hopkins University Press, 1991), pp. 73–81; Eric R. Kingson, "Financing Social Security: Agenda-Setting and the Enactment of the 1983 Amendments to the Social Security Act," *Policy Studies Journal* 13 (September 1984), pp. 131–56. Kingson, like Merton Bernstein, Robert Myers, and Paul Light, was a participant in the events that he describes. I have also looked at the unpublished manuscript by John Trout, "The Necessary Man," that forms part of his larger biography of Robert Ball. Although he decided not to write his own account of the amendments, Ball gave substantial help to the Bernsteins and to Trout.

3. Ball to Jimmy Carter, n.d., but 1981, Ball Papers, Wisconsin State Historical Society, Madison.

4. Max J. Skidmore, *Social Security and Its Enemies: The Case for America's Most Efficient Insurance Program* (Boulder, Colo.: Westview Press, 1999), p. 92.

5. See Martha Derthick, *Agency under Stress: The Social Security Administration in American Government* (Washington, D.C.: Brookings Institution, 1990).

6. Myers, *Within the System*, p. 14.

7. Ibid., p. 10.

8. Robert Ball to J. Douglas Brown, April 6, 1981, Ball Papers.

9. Robert Ball to J. Douglas Brown, May 5, 1981, Ball Papers.

10. For an excellent discussion of this matter see the research note prepared by Social Security historian Larry DeWitt, "Research Note #11: The History of Social Security 'Student' Benefits," 2001, available on the Web at http://www.ssa.gov/history/studentbenefit.html.

11. Ball to Brown, May 5, 1981. For more on the Save Our Security coalition see the materials in the Cohen Papers, such as Cohen to J. J. Pickle, August 22, 1979, Box 230, Cohen Papers, Wisconsin State Historical Society, Madison.

12. Ball to Brown, May 5, 1981.

13. Robert Ball, "Notes on a Conversation with Jake Pickle," February 5, 1981, Ball Papers.

14. Robert Ball, "Possible Approaches to Social Security Financing Problem," February 2, 1981, Ball Papers.

15. Robert Ball, "Notes for the Files on a Conversation with Senator Lawton Chiles," February 9, 1981, Ball Papers.

16. Ball, "Conversation with Jake Pickle," February 5, 1981.

17. Light, *Artful Work,* p. 118; John A. Svahn and Mary Ross, "Social Security Amendments of 1983: Legislative History and Summary of Provisions," *Social Security Bulletin* 46 (July 1983), p. 6.

18. See, for example, Stuart Butler and Anna Kondratas, *Out of the Poverty Trap* (New York: Free Press, 1987); Charles Murray, *Losing Ground* (New York: Basic Books, 1984); Martin Anderson, *Welfare: The Political Economy of Welfare Reform in the United States* (Palo Alto, Calif.: Hoover Institution Press, 1978); Edward D. Berkowitz, "Changing the Meaning of Welfare Reform," in *Maintaining the Safety Net: Income Redistribution Programs in the Reagan Administration,* ed. John Weicher (Washington, D.C.: American Enterprise Institute, 1984), pp. 23–42.

19. Stockman, *Triumph of Politics,* pp. 181–82. The classic article on adequacy and equity in Social Security is Reinhard A. Hohaus, "Equity, Adequacy, and Related Factors in Old Age Security," which is reprinted in William Haber and Wilbur J. Cohen, eds., *Social Security Programs: Problems and Policies* (Homewood, Ill: Richard D. Irwin, 1960), p. 62.

20. Betty Dillon to Emmet W. Harris, September 4, 1981, Ball Papers (terminating her employment with the Institute of Medicine); Elizabeth Wickenden to Robert Ball, April 27, 1981, Ball Papers; Harold Richman to Ball, December 14, 1981, Ball Papers; Ball to Richman, December 22, 1981, Ball Papers.

21. I base this account of the Reagan administration's actions largely on Stockman, *Triumph of Politics,* pp. 187–88.

22. On the early retirement benefits see Eric R. Kingson and Edward D. Berkowitz, *Social Security and Medicare: A Policy Primer* (Westport, Conn.: Auburn House, 1993), pp. 47–48.

23. Stockman, *Triumph of Politics,* p. 189; "HHS Fact Sheet," May 12, 1981, quoted in Svahn and Ross, "Social Security Amendments of 1983," p. 47.

24. John Aloysius Farrell, *Tip O'Neill and the Democratic Century* (Boston: Little, Brown, 2001), p. 572; Stockman, *Triumph of Politics,* p. 191.

25. Stockman, *Triumph of Politics,* p. 193; Farrell, *Tip O'Neill and the Democratic Century,* p. 572.

26. Robert Ball, "Memorandum for Daniel Patrick Moynihan," October 14, 1981, Ball Papers.

27. Robert Ball, "Notes for Democratic Caucus. White House Conference on Aging, " November 27, 1981, Ball Papers.

28. Ibid.

29. Farrell, *Tip O'Neill and the Democratic Century,* p. 579.

30. Office of the Chief Actuary, Social Security Administration, *History of Provisions of Old-Age, Survivors, Disability and Health Insurance, 1935–1996,* SSA publication no. 11–11515 (Washington, D.C.: Government Printing Office, 1997), p. 5, available on the Web at

http://www.ssa.gov/OACT/HOP/hoptoc.htm; Robert Ball, autobiographical memorandum prepared for Edward Berkowitz (hereafter Ball Memoir), p. 251.

31. Ball Memoir, p. 251; Farrell, *Tip O'Neill and the Democratic Century,* pp. 566–67, 432.

32. Robert Ball to Wilbur Cohen, June 1, 1981, Ball Papers.

33. Robert Ball, "Remarks about Tip O'Neill," in Ball to Ed Berkowitz, April 5, 2000 and available in the SSA History Archives, Baltimore.

34. Stockman, *Triumph of Politics,* p. 217. I base this legislative history on Geoffrey Kollmann and Carmen Solomon-Fears, "Major Decisions in the House and Senate on Social Security: 1935–2000," March 26, 2001, a Congressional Research Service report available on the Web at http://www.ssa.gov/history/reports/crsleghist3.html.

35. Robert Ball, Memorandum for Senator Daniel Patrick Moynihan, October 14, 1981, Ball Papers; Ball to Moynihan, November 23, 1981, Ball Papers.

36. Farrell, *Tip O'Neill and the Democratic Century,* p. 581; Light, *Artful Work,* pp. 132–33.

37. Robert Ball, note to Elizabeth Wickenden, Nelson Cruikshank, Bert Seidman, and others (writing in his capacity as a member of the advisory committee of SOS), August 13, 1981, Ball Papers.

38. Robert Ball, "Proposed Position on the Senate Social Security Bill," October 22, 1981, Ball Papers.

39. Robert Ball, "Social Security Financing Plan for House Democrats," October 15, 1981, Ball Papers.

40. Robert Ball to Senator Carl Levin, n.d., but clearly fall 1981, Ball Papers.

41. Robert Ball to Patrick Linehan, November 30, 1981, Ball Papers.

42. Light, *Artful Work,* pp. 136–37; "Congress Approves Compromise Plans for Social Security," *Wall Street Journal,* December 17, 1981, p. 3.

43. Warren Weaver Jr., "Arguing against Social Security Cuts," *New York Times,* October 17, 1981, p. 18.

44. Robert Ball to Dick Bolling, December 21, 1981, Ball Papers.

45. Robert Ball to the Speaker, December 18, 1961, Ball Papers; Light, *Artful Work,* pp. 164–65.

46. Farrell, *Tip O'Neill and the Democratic Century,* p. 601.

47. Ibid.

48. Bernstein and Bernstein, *Social Security,* pp. 38–39; It should be noted that Ball himself reviewed the Bernsteins' work, so that it can be read as one of his semi-official accounts of the commission (see the transcript of Ball's dictated cassette, November 11, 1986, headed "Facts," in Ball Papers).

49. Light, *Artful Work,* p.163.

50. Ronald Reagan to Robert M. Ball, December 23, 1981, Ball Papers.

51. Robert Ball, "Confidential Note for the File: Meeting on January 30, 1982 Concerning Plans for the New Commission on Social Security," February 2, 1982, Ball Papers.

52. Reagan to Ball, December 23, 1981.

53. Robert Ball to Alan Greenspan, January 8, 1982, Ball Papers; "Hiring Staff for Commission on Social Security Reform," January 27, 1982, Ball Papers; Ball, "Notes for breakfast meeting with Alan Greenspan, January 30, 1982," January 20, 1982, Ball Papers.

54. Robert Ball, "Note for the Record," January 27, 1982, Ball Papers.

55. I base this account on Robert Ball, "Confidential Notes for the File: Meeting on January 30, 1982," Ball Papers.

56. For more on earnings sharing and other issues of interest to women's groups see Richard V. Burkhauser and Karen C. Holden, ed., *A Challenge to Social Security: The Changing Roles of Women and Men in American Society* (New York: Academy Press, 1982); Holden, "Social Security and the Economic Security of Women," in *Social Security in the 21st Century,* ed. Eric Kingson and James H. Shulz (New York: Oxford University Press, 1997), p. 94; N. M. Gordon, "Institutional Responses: The Social Security System," in *The Subtle Revolution: Women at Work,* ed. Ralph E. Smith (Washington, D.C.: Urban Institute Press, 1979), pp. 224–26; Edward D. Berkowitz, "Family Benefits in Social Security: A Historical Commentary," in *Social Security and the Family,* ed. Melissa Favreault, Frank J. Sammartino, and C. Eugene Steuerle (Washington, D.C.: Urban Institute Press, 2002), pp. 19–46.

57. Robert Ball, "Hiring Staff for Commission on Social Security Reform," January 27, 1982, Ball Papers; Lane Kirkland to Alan Greenspan, January 11, 1982, Ball Papers; Ball to Daniel Moynihan, Claude Pepper, Martha Keys, and Lane Kirkland, February 19, 1982, Ball Papers.

58. Myers, *Within the System,* pp. 33–34. On the workings of presidential commissions see Robert H. Zieger, "The Quest for National Goals, 1957–81," in *The Carter Presidency: Policy Choices in the Post–New Deal Era,* ed. Gary M. Fink and Hugh Davis Graham (Lawrence: University Press of Kansas, 1998), pp. 29–50; Edward D. Berkowitz, "Commissioning the Future," *Reviews in American History* 11 (June 1983), pp. 294–99; Berkowitz, "Jimmy Carter and the Sunbelt Report: Seeking a National Agenda," in *The Presidency and Domestic Policies of Jimmy Carter,* ed. Herbert D. Rosenbaum and Alexej Ugrinsky (Westport, Conn.: Greenwood Press, 1994), pp. 33–44; Hugh Davis Graham, "The Ambiguous Legacy of American Presidential Commissions," *Public Historian* 7 (spring 1985), pp. 5–25.

59. Myers, *Within the System,* pp. 31–34.

60. Robert Ball, "Note to the File," February 17, 1982, Ball Papers.

61. See, for example, Robert Ball to Senator Daniel Patrick Moynihan, February 2, 1982, Ball Papers; Ball, "What Happened on the

National Commission on Social Security Reform," February 13, 1983, Ball Papers.

62. Robert Ball, "Notes for Lunch with Nancy Altman," April 20, 1982, Ball Papers.

63. Ball to Moynihan, Pepper, Keys, and Kirkland, April 23, 1982, Ball Papers.

64. Myers, *Within the System*, p. 40; Robert Ball, interview by Larry DeWitt (unedited transcript), interview 5, May 22, 2001, Alexandria, Va.

65. Robert Ball to Members of the National Commission on Social Security Reform, May 1, 1982, Ball Papers; Myers, *Within the System*, p. 40; Robert Ball, "Why is social security in trouble—personal-confidential," May 6, 1982, Ball Papers.

66. Robert Ball, "Alternative Actions that at some point will probably be considered by the National Commission on Social Security Reform," May 5, 1982, Ball Papers; Ball, "Informal Notes," May 12, 1982, Ball Papers.

67. I base this account of the meeting on Robert Ball, "Note for the File: Meeting with Lane Kirkland, Wednesday, June 2, 1982," June 11, 1982, Ball Papers.

68. National Commission on Social Security Reform, "Transcript of Commission Meeting," June 21, 1982, Ball Papers.

69. National Commission on Social Security Reform, "Transcript of Commission Meeting," July 19, 1982, Ball Papers.

70. Robert Ball, "Talking Notes for Discussion on Social Security Program," July 16, 1982, Ball Papers.

71. Robert Ball, "Memorandum for the Files: Meeting with Senator Russell Long, July 27, 1982, from 3:45 to 4:30 P.M.," July 29, 1982, Ball Papers.

72. I base these statements attributed to Greenspan on Robert Ball, "Confidential—for the Files: Summaries of Recent Conversations with Alan Greenspan," August 23, 1982, Ball Papers.

73. Robert Ball, "Items for Possible Changes in Social Security," July 29, 1982, Ball Papers.

74. Robert Ball to Frank Bayo, July 26, 1982, Ball Papers; Ball to Howard Young, Betty Duskin, Merton Bernstein, and Eric Kingson, August 13, 1982, Ball Papers; Ball to Robert Myers, September 7, 1982, Ball Papers.

75. National Commission on Social Security Reform, "Transcript of Commission Meeting," August 20, 1982, Ball Papers; Michael J. Boskin, *Too Many Promises: The Uncertain Future of Social Security* (Homewood, Ill.: Dow Jones-Irwin, 1986).

76. National Commission on Social Security Reform, "Transcript of Commission Meeting," August 20, 1982, Ball Papers.

77. Ball, "Summaries of Recent Conversations with Alan Greenspan," August 23, 1982.

78. Robert Ball, "Key Points That Led to a Solution," April 26, 1983, Ball Papers; Ball, "The Problem and the Solution in the Negotiation," November 3, 1983, Ball Papers. Ball wrote these and other fragmentary essays after the completion of the commission's work in preparation for writing a memoir about the commission. That memoir never got written, in part because Ball felt he could not report on his own role in the negotiations with sufficient modesty. Hence, he entrusted others to write about the experience and offered them considerable advice.

79. Robert Ball, "What Happened on the National Commission on Social Security Reform," February 13, 1983, Ball Papers; Robert W. Merry, "Social Security Panel Democrats Soften Opposition to Reducing Benefit's Growth," *Wall Street Journal,* November 15, 1982; Ball to Commission Members, November 29, 1982, Ball Papers.

80. Ball, "What Happened on the National Commission"; Light, *Artful Work,* pp. 173–17; Robert Ball, "Compromise Proposal," November 29, 1982, Ball Papers.

81. Merry, " Social Security Panel Democrats Soften Opposition"; AP wire story and other press clippings in Ball Papers.

82. Ball, interview by Larry DeWitt, interview 5, May 22, 2001, Alexandria, Va., available on the Web at http://www.ssa.gov/history/orals/ball5.html; Ball, interview by J. Halamandaris, December 1987, p. 26, SSA History Archives.

83. I base this account of the meeting on Ball, "Confidential—Meeting which never took place on December 17, 1982," December 21, 1982 Ball Papers.

84. For more on this point see Light, *Artful Work,* p. 179.

85. Ball, "Meeting which never took place."

86. Light, *Artful Work,* p. 181; Berkowitz, *America's Welfare State,* pp. 78–79.

87. Ball, DeWitt interview, May 22, 2001.

88. Robert Ball, "Compromise Proposal," January 5, 1983, Ball Papers.

89. Ball, "Compromise Proposal," January 5, 1983.

90. John Trout, "The Necessary Man," November 1992, draft chapter for a biography of Robert Ball.

91. Light, *Artful Work,* p. 105; Robert Ball, "Compromise Proposal," January 11, 1983, Ball Papers; Ball, "Miscellaneous Items in the Negotiations," June 3, 1983, Ball Papers.

92. Robert Ball, "Potential Solution," January 13, 1983, Ball Papers.

93. Ball, "Miscellaneous Items in the Negotiations"; Robert Ball, "Recommended Bi-Partisan Solution to the Social Security Problem," January 15, 1983, Ball Papers.

94. Ball, "Recommended Bi-Partisan Solution."

95. Robert Ball, "Notes on Meetings of the National Commission on Social Security Reform," November 3, 1983, Ball Papers; Light, *Artful Work,* p. 193; Trout, " Necessary Man," p. 56.

96. Light, *Artful Work,* p. 192.

97. Robert Ball, "Notes for John Trout: For beginning of biography," April 2, 1990, Ball Papers.

98. Spencer Rich, "Robert M. Ball, Democrats' Outside Insider on Social Security Issues," *Washington Post,* November 17, 1986.

99. "Transcript of phone call from Ronald Reagan," January 22, 1983, 5:30 P.M., Ball Papers; Berkowitz, *America's Welfare State,* pp. 79–80; Ball, "Key Points."

100. See Berkowitz, *America's Welfare State,* pp. 80–81.

101. Ball, "Key Points"; Trout, "Necessary Man."

102. Ball, "Key Points."

103. For more detailed background on this matter see Light, *Artful Work,* pp. 212–15, and Trout, "Necessary Man." I have relied on Ball, "Key Points." My characterization of "discontinuing" federal civil service retirement benefits needs to be modified. "Nobody proposed that," Ball writes in a typical explanation of the subtleties of the programs with which he worked. "What we did propose was an extension of Social Security to federal employment with the consequent necessity of adjustments in the civil service retirement system to make it supplementary. Nothing became 'discontinued' except the unfair situation in which civil service employees received not only a pension that was set up on the assumption it was the only pension that people were going to receive and then in addition they got Social Security under conditions that were especially favorable because they were designed to apply to low wage earners" (Ball to Berkowitz, August 15, 2002).

104. Ball, "Key Points."

105. Robert Rubin, interview by Edward Berkowitz, Fairfax, Va., August 16, 1995, HCFA Oral History Collection; also available on-line at http://www.ssa.gov/history/rubin.html.

106. Richard Neustadt and Ernest May, *Thinking in Time: The Uses of History for Decision Makers* (New York: Free Press, 1986), pp. 17–33.

107. "Remarks of the President at the Signing Ceremony for Social Security Amendments," South Grounds, April 20, 1983, White House press release; Svahn and Ross, "Social Security Amendments of 1983."

7. Closing Time

1. Julie Kosterlitz, "The Patron Saint of Social Security," *National Journal,* November 26, 1994, p. 2791.

2. Robin Toner, "A Great Defender of the Old Social Security Battles On," *New York Times,* May 3, 1999, p. A-16; Joe Volz, "He Says 'No' to Privatization: 'Mr. Social Security' Sees a Better Way," *AARP Bulletin,* July–August 1999, pp. 18–19.

3. Robert Ball to Stuart Eizenstat, January 14, 1985, Ball Papers.

4. Theodore R. Marmor, with Philip Fellman, "Entrepreneurship in Public Management: Wilbur Cohen and Robert Ball," in *Leadership and Innovation: A Biographical Perspective on Entrepreneurs in Government,* ed. Jameson W. Doig and Erwin C. Hargrove (Baltimore: Johns Hopkins University Press, 1987), p. 269.

5. Robert Ball, "Ronald Reagan and Social Security," July 31, 1984, Ball Papers; Ball to William Galston, Ted Marmor, and William Drayton, August 1, 1984, Ball Papers. Mondale scored his most telling point when he made a reference to Reagan's attitude toward Medicare in their first campaign debate.

6. Robert Ball to Nancy A. Lupo, January 11, 1985, Ball Papers; Ball, autobiographical memorandum prepared for Edward Berkowitz, SSA History Office Archives (hereafter Ball Memoir), p. 268.

7. Ball to Lupo, January 11, 1985.

8. Marmor, "Entrepreneurship in Public Management," p. 274.

9. Ball Memoir, p. 245.

10. I base much of this account of the National Academy of Social Insurance on my own observations as an academy member and as a visiting scholar at the academy in 1988.

11. See Edward D. Berkowitz, *To Improve Human Health: A History of the Institute of Medicine* (Washington, D.C.: National Academy Press, 1998) for an account of how the institute operates.

12. Robert Ball wrote a complimentary biographical sketch of Alicia Munnell in the memoir that he prepared for me and that is available in the SSA History Archives, Baltimore. The Brookings book on Social Security on which she worked is Joseph A. Pechman, Henry J. Aaron, and Michael K. Taussig, *Social Security: Perspectives for Reform* (Washington, D.C.: Brookings Institution, 1968).

13. Alicia Munnell's *The Effect of Social Security on Personal Savings* (Cambridge, Mass.: Ballinger, 1974) is based largely on her dissertation. Her Brookings book on Social Security is Alicia Munnell, *The Future of Social Security* (Washington, D.C.: Brookings Institution, 1977).

14. Ball Memoir, p. 254.

15. I base this sketch of Henry Aaron on personal observation and on a biographical sketch of Henry Aaron that Robert Ball prepared for me as background material for this book and that is available at the SSA History Archives.

16. Robert Ball to David Hamburg, August 25, 1988, Ball Papers. For

more on David Hamburg see "National Academy of Sciences Press Release," October 30, 1975, National Academy of Sciences Records, National Academy of Sciences Archives, Washington, D.C., and Berkowitz, *To Improve Human Health,* pp. 95–133.

17. Robert Ball to Dwight Bartlett, September 30, 1988, Ball Papers; Ball Memoir, p. 270.

18. Ball Memoir, p. 250; Edward Berkowitz, *Mr. Social Security: The Life of Wilbur J. Cohen* (Lawrence: University Press of Kansas), pp. 53–54.

19. Ball Memoir, p. 270; Robert Ball to John Heinz, November 5, 1986, Ball Papers.

20. Ball Memoir, pp. 271–72.

21. Ball to Hamburg, August 25, 1988.

22. Ball Memoir, p. 272.

23. To read this mission statement, readers can go to the National Academy of Social Insurance home page on the Web at http://www.nasi.org, select "About the Academy," and on that subpage select "Mission."

24. Ball Memoir, pp 274–75; A. Haeworth Robertson, *The Coming Revolution in Social Security* (Reston, Va.: Reston, 1981); Carolyn L. Weaver, *The Crisis in Social Security: Economic and Political Origins* (Durham: Duke University Press, 1982). I sat in on the discussion of Carolyn Weaver's candidacy for membership in the summer of 1988. Weaver first joined the organization and then resigned.

25. Toner, "Great Defender of the Old Social Security."

26. Ball Memoir, p. 205.

27. Robert Ball to Rufus Miles, March 3, 1987, Ball Papers; Ball to Alvin M. David, March 6, 1987, Ball Papers; Ball to Dr. Yung-Ping Chen, February 10, 1987, Ball Papers.

28. See Office of the Chief Actuary, Social Security Administration, *History of Provisions of Old-Age, Survivors, Disability, and Health Insurance, 1935–1996,* SSA publication no. 11–11515 (Washington, D.C.: Government Printing Office, 1997), pp. 20–27, available on the Web at http://www.ssa.gov/OACT/HOP/hoptoc.htm; Robert Ball, "The New Catastrophic Health Insurance Program: Notes for Harvard U.—JFK School—Seminar for Congressmen," December 6, 1988, Ball Papers.

29. Edward D. Berkowitz, *America's Welfare State: From Roosevelt to Reagan* (Baltimore: Johns Hopkins University Press, 1991), pp. 189–90; Molly Sinclair, "Coalition Backs Long-Term Care," *Washington Post,* October 6, 1987, p. A-10; "Long-Term Care: An Idea That Can Elect the Next President," pamphlet published in 1988 by the Villers Foundation.

30. Robert Ball, with Thomas Bethell, *Because We're All in This Together: The Case for a National Long Term Care Insurance Policy* (Washington, D.C.: Families USA Foundation, 1989), p. 36.

31. Ibid., pp. 70–72.

32. Ibid., pp. 76–82. On the volatility of the disability insurance program see Edward D. Berkowitz, *Disabled Policy: America's Programs for the Handicapped* (New York: Cambridge University Press, 1987), and Berkowitz and Richard Burkhauser, "A United States Perspective on Disability Programs," in *Curing the Dutch Disease: An International Perspective on Disability Policy Reform*, ed. Leo J. M. Aarts et al. (Alderstot, U.K.: Avebury Press, 1996), pp. 71–91.

33. Ball, *Because We're All in This Together*, pp. 82–84; Robert M. Ball, "Public-Private Solution to Protection against the Cost of Long-Term Care," *Journal of the American Geriatric Society* 38 (January–February 1990), pp. 156–63.

34. Ball, *Because We're All in This Together*, pp. 88–89; Berkowitz, *America's Welfare State*, pp. 83–87.

35. Ball, *Because We're All in This Together*, pp. 90–91.

36. I base this section largely on Ball's recollections. See Ball Memoir, pp. 298–303.

37. "Critical Questions for Discussion by the Advisory Council on the Financing of Health Care," in Robert Ball to Anne LaBelle, April 24, 1990, Ball Papers; "Comments on the First Part of the Advisory Council's Outline for the Final Report," in Ball to LaBelle, May 7, 1991, Ball Papers; "Continuation of Comments on the Outline of the Advisory Council Report," in Ball to LaBelle, May 22, 1991, Ball Papers; Ball, "Approach: Filling the Gaps, Buildings on What We Have," November 15, 1990, Ball Papers.

38. Robert Ball, draft of "Medicare Revisited," January 9, 1984, Ball Papers.

39. Robert Ball, "Approach: Filling the Gaps, Building on What We Have," November 15, 1990, Ball Papers; Ball, "An Affordable Health Plan For All Americans: Building on What We Have," February 21, 1991, Ball Papers.

40. Ball Memoir, pp. 302–3; Robert Ball to John Trout, February 26, 1991, Ball Papers.

41. Bob Ball to Honorable Gene Sperling, director, National Economic Council, December 10, 1987, in Robert Ball, "Issues related to the future of Social Security: A series of memoranda by Robert M. Ball," Ball Papers; Alan Greenspan, Robert Myers, and Robert Ball, "Social Security: It's Almost Secure," February 1984, Ball Papers; Ball, "Confidential Note to files—conversation with Rick Foster, Office of the Actuary, SSA," February 17, 1984, Ball Papers; statement by Robert Ball before Joint Economic Committee, Hearing on Social Security Fund Surplus, June 16, 1989, Ball Papers.

42. "Appendix I: Developments since 1983," in *Report of the 1994–1996*

Advisory Council on Social Security, vol. 1: *Findings and Recommendations* (Washington, D.C.: Government Printing Office, 1997), pp. 163–64.

43. Edward D. Berkowitz, "Social Security Celebrates an Anniversary," in *Social Security after Fifty: Successes and Failures,* ed. Edward D. Berkowitz (Westport, Conn.: Greenwood Press, 1987), pp. 12–13.

44. Ball Memoir, pp. 337–39.

45. Ibid., p. 342; Edward M. Gramlich, "The Future Outlook for Social Security," in *Social Security Reform: Links to Saving, Investment, and Growth,* ed. Steven A. Sass and Robert K. Triest (Boston: Federal Reserve Bank of Boston, 1997), pp. 187–92; "Statement by Edward M. Gramlich and Marc Twinney," in *Report of the 1994–1996 Advisory Council,* pp. 155–57.

46. Ball Memoir, pp. 344–45.

47. Spencer Rich, "Panel Suggests Bold Changes for Social Security," *Washington Post,* January 7, 1997, p. A-1.

48. *Report of the 1994–1996 Advisory Council,* p. 11.

49. "Findings, Principles, and Recommendations Regarding the Overall Social Security System," in *Report of the 1994–1996 Advisory Council,* pp. 15–21; Ball Memoir, p. 354.

50. *Report of the 1994–1996 Advisory Council,* p. 17.

51. Ball Memoir, pp. 348–49.

52. Ball's group wrote that the idea had "merit—but we also think it requires careful study, public debate, and perhaps even the convening of an expert commission to explore the pros and cons." This cautious passage reflected the ambivalence of groups such as organized labor toward the idea. *Report of the 1994–1996 Advisory Council,* p. 86.

53. Robert Ball to Paul Simon, March 14, 1984, Ball Papers.

54. Robert M. Ball, Edith U. Fierst, Gloria T. Johnson, Thomas W. Jones, George Kourpias, and Gerald M. Shea, "Social Security for the 21st Century: A Strategy to Maintain Benefits and Strengthen America's Family Protection Plan," in *Report of the 1994–1996 Advisory Council,* pp. 80, 83–84.

55. *Report of the 1994–1996 Advisory Council,* pp. 94–95.

56. Robert Ball to John Trout, December 22, 1997, Ball Papers.

57. "Proposals for Social Security: What's Wrong with Partial Privatization," in Robert Ball to Gene Sperling, October 27, 1997, Ball Papers.

58. "Partial Privatization of Social Security: Administration," in Robert Ball to Gene Sperling, November 6, 1997, Ball Papers.

59. "Restoring the Social Security Program to Long-Term Balance: What Should be Done," in Robert Ball to Gene Sperling, December 1, 1997, Ball Papers.

60. Robert Ball, "Social Security Plus," July 1998, Ball Papers.

61. Kenneth Apfel, "Creating a Solid Framework for Retirement Security," in *Social Security and Medicare: Individual versus Collective Risk and Responsibility,* ed. Sheila Burke, Eric Kingson, and Uwe Reinhardt (Washington, D.C.: National Academy of Social Insurance, 2000), pp. 144–49.

62. "The Nine Guiding Principles of Social Security" and "Supporting Social Security from General Revenues," in *Insuring the Essentials: Bob Ball on Social Security: A Selection of Articles and Essays from 1942 through 2000 by Robert M. Ball,* ed. Thomas Bethell (New York: Century Foundation Press, 2000), pp. 7, 229.

63. Robert M. Ball, "Social Security Plus," May 2001, Ball Papers.

64. Bob Ball to Larry Summers, Gene Sperling, Jack Lew, Ken Apfel, and Stu Eizenstat, "The Next Budget and Direct Social Security Investment in Equities," n.d., but 1999, Ball Papers; Ball to Edward Berkowitz, February 20, 2000, Ball Papers.

65. Robert Ball, "The Report of the Technical Advisory Panel to the Social Security Advisory Board," January 23, 2000, Ball Papers; Ball to Berkowitz, February 20, 2000.

66. "Another ad featured former Commissioner of Social Security, Robert Ball, warning about the risk of the Bush proposal. The ad tested well with focus groups; a top Gore aide called it, 'The one bomb, the one hope of the campaign'" (*Newsweek,* November 11, 2000, p. 117). I am grateful to Larry DeWitt for bringing this material to my attention.

67. "In an op-ed piece in the LA Times in July 2001 I made a very fundamental criticism of the long-range costs for Medicare and I am circulating currently a new version of Social Security Plus and am planning a new volume of Insuring the Essentials, this time Bob Ball on Medicare with Tom Bethell as editor. The very latest is an open letter to Moynihan in the Washington Post of September 8, 2001" (Robert Ball to Edward Berkowitz, September 7, 2001).

Conclusion

1. Theo Lippman Jr., "Social Security's Robert Ball, 'The Compleat Bureaucrat Bows Out,'" *Baltimore Sun,* February 5, 1973, Robert Ball files, SSA History Archives, Baltimore.

Index